D1320166

MONTRÉAL

WORLD CITIES SERIES

Edited by
Professor R.J. Johnston and Professor P.L. Knox

Published titles in the series:

Beijing	*Sit*
Birmingham	*Cherry*
Budapest	*Enyedi and Szirmai*
Buenos Aires	*Keeling*
Dublin	*MacLaran*
Glasgow	*Pacione*
Harare	*Rakodi*
Havana	*Segre, Coyula and Scarpaci*
Hong Kong	*Lo*
Lagos	*Peil*
London	*Hebbert*
Los Angeles	*Keil*
Mexico City 2nd edition	*Ward*
Montréal	***Germain and Rose***
Paris	*Noin and White*
Rome	*Agnew*
Seoul	*Kim and Choe*
Singapore	*Perry, Kong and Yeoh*
Taipei	*Selya*
Tehran	*Madanipour*
Tokyo 2nd Edition	*Cybriwsky*
Vienna	*Lichtenberger*

Forthcoming titles in the series:

Brussels	*Murphy*
Johannesburg	*Beavon*
Lisbon	*Gaspar and Williams*
New York	*Smith and Hackworth*
Ranstad	*Dielman and van Weesep*
St Petersburg	*Bater*

Other titles are in preparation

MONTRÉAL

The Quest for a Metropolis

ANNICK GERMAIN and
DAMARIS ROSE
*Institut national de la
recherche scientifique
Montréal
Canada*

JOHN WILEY & SONS, LTD
CHICHESTER • NEW YORK • WEINHEIM • BRISBANE • SINGAPORE • TORONTO

Published 2000 by John Wiley & Sons Ltd,
Baffins Lane, Chichester,
West Sussex PO19 1UD, England

National 01243 779777
International (+44) 1243 779777
e-mail (for orders and customer service enquiries): cs-books@wiley.co.uk
Visit our Home Page on http://www.wiley.co.uk or http://www.wiley.com

Other Wiley Editorial Offices

John Wiley & Sons, Inc., 605 Third Avenue,
New York, NY 10158-0012, USA

WILEY-VCH Verlag GmbH, Pappelallee 3,
D-69469 Weinheim, Germany

Jacaranda Wiley Ltd, 33 Park Road, Milton,
Queensland 4064, Australia

John Wiley & Sons (Asia) Pte Ltd, 2 Clementi Loop #02-01,
Jin Xing Distripark, Singapore 129809

John Wiley & Sons (Canada) Ltd, 22 Worcester Road,
Rexdale, Ontario M9W 1L1, Canada

Library of Congress Cataloging-in-Publication Data

Germain, Annick, 1948–
    Montréal : the quest for a metropolis / Annick Germain and Damaris Rose.
        p. cm. — (World Cities series)
    Includes bibliographical references (p.) and index.
    ISBN 0-471-94907-8
        1. Montréal (Québec)—History. 2. Montréal (Québec)—Social conditions. 3. City
planning—Québec—Montréal—History. 4. Montréal (Québec)—Economic conditions.
I. Rose Damaris. II. Title. III. Series.

F1054.5.M857 G475 2000
971.4'27—dc21   00–027093

British Library Cataloguing in Publication Data

A catalogue record for this book is available from the British Library

ISBN 0-471-94907-8

Typeset in 10/12pt Garamond by Mayhew Typesetting, Rhayader, Powys
Printed and bound in Great Britain by Biddles Ltd, Guildford and King's Lynn
This book is printed on acid-free paper responsibly manufactured from sustainable forestry,
in which at least two trees are planted for each one used for paper production.

To Cliff   To Phil and Nico

CONTENTS

PREFACE

There is a certain quality about Montréal's physical, social and cultural features that frequently prompts visitors to comment that the city has both European and North American qualities. How is it that Montréal has sustained this dual identity in the face of the homogenizing forces of Americanization and globalization? Intuitively one might think that the answer lies simply in the presence of French language and culture on a predominantly English-speaking continent. In fact, however, its urban fabric is a product of a much more complex set of historical influences and contemporary attempts to redefine its position in the world. What could be more exciting for a specialist in urban studies than the prospect of writing an entire book on such a city, especially when it is the city one has chosen to live and work in? Yet at the same time, what could be more nerve-wracking than the search for that elusive thread that, while reflecting the intrinsic duality of Montréal, would make for a coherent and stimulating reading of this city?

When first approached by the editors of the World Cities series to contribute a volume on Montréal, Damaris Rose, an urban geographer, knew instinctively that a trans-disciplinary and cross-cultural perspective was required, not only to cover adequately the range of urban issues dealt with by all volumes in this series – including built environment, regional planning, transportation, population, the economy and the social patterning of urban space – but at the same time to convey the flavours of everyday life, its qualities and its paradoxes. She was delighted when her colleague at INRS-Urbanisation, urban sociologist Annick Germain, enthusiastically agreed to co-author the book. Thus began an intense collaboration which has turned out to be an enriching experience for both of us. It has crossed the lines not only of academic discipline, but also those of linguistic and cultural reference points – with one of us being anglophone, the other francophone, our collaboration in a sense reflects the bicultural, bilingual character of Montréal. Yet we did not want to follow the all-too-frequent practice of merely juxtaposing two distinct visions – one 'French', one 'English' – of Montréal's development. As it turned out, even the challenges (and occasional frustrations!) of translating between the two languages provided us with many opportunities for stimulating debate. Our 'take' on Montréal is also undoubtedly influenced, in ways that we ourselves may not fully appreciate, by the fact of us both being European immigrants. While a mesh of personal and professional reasons led us to make our homes in this city, the appeal of its unique quality of life makes it difficult for us to imagine leaving.

We seek to offer an up-to-date portrait of urban issues in Montréal. We use recent and diversified source material including a vast array of limited-circulation research reports available only in French, many of which were produced by colleagues at our research centre (which specializes in urban studies and is a constituent of the Université du Québec), as well as our own documentary and statistical research carried out expressly for this volume. Although our book is addressed mainly to readers beyond the borders of our city and those of Québec, we also hope that local readers will be drawn to our pages and in so doing will come to see their city in a new perspective. Notably, being perhaps more comfortable with the notion of multiple identities than are many residents of Montréal and Québec, we do not feel the need to insert Montréal into a singular narrative. On the contrary, we have found ourselves fascinated by the perennial coexistence of a 'dual discourse' characterizing the divided society that is Montréal, a city whose identity and mission have long been tugged in two different directions by what is termed the 'double majority', meaning on the one hand Québec's majority francophone society and on the other Canada's predominantly anglophone society.

Following a brief introduction to the city and some of its paradoxes, Chapters 2 and 3 place its economic development and its built form in historical perspective. In Chapter 2 we examine how this city, whose origins lie in a missionary scheme of French colonists, was built up by an Anglo-Protestant bourgeoisie into a major North American pivot in the mercantile system and then into the uncontested industrial metropolis of Canada, only to find itself, by the latter part of the twentieth century, with a truncated hinterland essentially limited to the province of Québec and consequently embarked on a quest, at once pragmatic and profoundly symbolic, for a new identity. Chapter 3 shows how these successive transformations came to be inscribed in the built forms of Montréal's urban landscape, and how, under the resolute grip of a mayor with a mission to put the city back on the map, the face of the city came to embrace modernity. In Chapter 4 we examine the problems of defining where the metropolis begins and ends from the point of view of regional planning and governance; the Montréal region, like many in North America, faces problems associated with urban sprawl and municipal fragmentation, but in this case with some unique complications which impede the implementation of solutions. Chapter 5 analyses the paradoxes and contrasts of the present-day Montréal economy. Notably, the rapid transformation of the city's industrial base from labour-intensive manufacturing to high technology and knowledge-based sectors in recent years has firmly established Montréal in the new global system of cities but also poses marked challenges to Montréal's mission and identity as a French city, the metropolis of Québec. At the same time, this trend reinforces the dualization of a local labour market which still has one of the highest unemployment rates on the continent.

If Chapters 3 and 4 point to some of the weaknesses of urban planning in Montréal, there is one area in which the local state has consistently been one of the most interventionist in North America in recent decades. Chapter 6, whose focus is on demographic and socio-economic shifts in the inner city, includes a detailed analysis of the role of City of Montréal agencies in housing and neighbourhood revitalization policies and programmes aimed at repopulating the inner city. Montréal is also perhaps an exemplar of the construction of a multiethnic metropolis which is managing to take diversity in its stride. But as we show in Chapter 7, this metropolis, which wants to position itself both as the showcase of cosmopolitanism and as the guardian of the French identity of Québec, is today facing profound cultural dilemmas in consequence. Yet notwithstanding the image and the realities of a divided city there is a broad consensus about the qualities that continue to make Montréal a uniquely 'liveable' city. We argue in conclusion that the Québec 'national' question (meaning, its identity and its place vis-à-vis the Canadian federation) imparts a unique coloration to a wide range of urban issues in Montréal – even those that at first appear no different than in other North American cities. These issues, ranging from the location of immigrant settlement to urban sprawl to metropolitan governance, are caught in the perennial cross-currents of Québec nationalism and Canadian federalism. Conversely, many aspects of the national question would not exist if Montréal did not have to serve as the metropolis for the rest of Québec.

In sum, while we have deliberately only granted theory a discreet presence in these pages, they, and the multiple issues we explore in the book, are bound together by the underlying theme of what permits a city to lay claim to the title of 'metropolis'. This theme is embedded in the history of Montréal and is far from being just an economic issue. It is an intrinsically cultural and political one which shapes many of the urban issues facing Montréal in a different and unique way than in other North American cities.

This volume has been a good number of years in the making, and in this respect we owe a huge debt to the series editors, to the editors at Wiley and to our colleagues at INRS-Urbanisation for their patience, tolerance and their continuing faith in the project – as well as to those close to us who had to live with both the material clutter and the existential dilemmas it generated. We also offer our particular thanks to everyone who contributed in big or small ways to making this book what it is. The Direction scientifique of the Institut national de la recherche scientifique provided a small grant defraying some of the costs of preparing the manuscript. At

INRS-Urbanisation, we are especially grateful to: Julie Archambault and Christiane Desmarais, for cartography; Nathalie Vachon and Jaël Mongeau, for assistance with census data; Hélène Houde and Ginette Casavant, for bibliographic support; Mario Polèse; Marc Termote; Richard Shearmur, Yvon Martineau and Michel Trépanier for access to unpublished data; to Julie-Elizabeth Gagnon, for indispensable help with a variety of editorial tasks, and to Francine Bernèche, for saving us from missing critical deadlines. Clifford Hastings (Dawson College) made significant intellectual contributions to Chapter 2, helped with the revisions to Chapter 3, and made many excellent editorial suggestions; Jean-Claude Marsan (Université de Montréal), who wrote the first and the best book on Montréal's built form, gave helpful advice for Chapter 3. Evelyn Lindhorst translated early versions of parts of Chapters 2, 3 and 4, which were first drafted in French.

Many people supplied references or statistical data, among them Martin Wexler and Suzanne Chantal (Ville de Montréal, Service de l'habitation); Daniel Jost (Citizenship and Immigration Canada, Strategic Policy, Planning and Research), Douglas O'Keefe (Statistics Canada, Transportation Division), Richard Harris (McMaster University), Richard Morin (Université du Québec à Montréal), Brian Slack (Concordia University) and Patricia Lamarre (Université de Montréal). David Ley (University of British Columbia) kindly furnished the maps comprising Figure 6.19. Marc-Aurèle Marsan took some of the photos (see Photo Credits). Claude Boudreau (Archives cartographiques et architecturales, Archives nationales du Québec) found Figure 2.3 for us, while Josette Michaud and Aislin (Terry Mosher) generously allowed us to reproduce their artwork (Figures 3.16 and 7.10, respectively). We also thank the World Cities Series editors, Paul Knox and Ron Johnston, and all the past and present members of the editorial and production teams at Wiley with whom we have had the pleasure to work, namely Iain Stevenson, Tristan Palmer, Louise Portsmouth, Maggie Toy, Mandy Collison, Abigail Grater, Isabelle Strafford and Sam Clay. To anyone we may have unwittingly omitted to mention, our sincere apologies.

Finally, Damaris is deeply grateful to her partner Cliff for his feedback, companionship and unconditional support which made all the difference in the world in helping to bring this project to final fruition. Madron and Chloe, and more recently their worthy successors Sitka and Emma, furnished essential lap-warming services and, by their untimely assaults on fingers, keyboard, screen and mouse, made sure she kept her priorities straight. Annick would like to thank Philippe and Nicolas for sharing her passion for city life along so many walks through the streets and parks of Montréal, and to reassure them that in spite of seeing their mother spending so many weekends toiling away at the book, they should not be discouraged from embarking on their own writing ventures should the fancy take them – ultimately, producing this book was great fun!

LIST OF ACRONYMS

NB: The forward slash character is used to indicate acronyms and names of officially bilingual organizations. Square brackets are used to designate English translations of French-language organizations, where appropriate.

ACFAS — Association canadienne-française pour l'avancement des sciences

AMT — Agence métropolitaine de transport [Metropolitan Transit Agency]

CACUM — Conseil des arts de la communauté urbaine de Montréal [Montréal Urban Community Arts Council]

CBD — Central Business District

CCA — Centre canadien d'architecture / Canadian Centre for Architecture

CDEC — Corporation de développement économique communautaire [Community Economic Development Corporation]

Cégep — Collège d'enseignement général et professionnel

CMA — Census metropolitan area

CMHC / SCHL — Canada Mortgage and Housing Corporation / Société canadienne d'hypothèques et de logement

CN(R) — Canadian National (Railways)

CP(R) — Canadian Pacific (Railway)

CREEEM — Comité pour la relance de l'économie et de l'emploi de l'est de Montréal [Comittee for the Economic and Employment Renewal of East-end Montréal]

CREESOM — Comité pour la relance de l'économie et de l'emploi du sud-ouest de Montréal [Comittee for the Economic and Employment Renewal of South-west Montréal]

CUM [MUC] — Communauté urbaine de Montréal [Montréal Urban Community]

HLM — Habitations à loyer modique [Public (Low cost) housing]

IATA — International Air Transport Association

ICAO — International Civil Aviation Organization

INRS — Institut national de la recherche scientifique

MAIICCQ	Ministère des affaires internationales, de l'immigration et des communautés culturelles du Québec [Québec Ministry of International Affairs, Immigration and Cultural Communities]
MCCIQ	Ministère des Communautés culturelles et de l'Immigration du Québec [Québec Ministry of Cultural Communities and Immigration]
MCM / RCM	Montréal Citizens' Movement / Rassemblement des citoyennes et de citoyens de Montréal
MRC	Municipalité régionale de comté [Regional County Municipality]
NAFTA	North American Free Trade Agreement
NFB / ONF	National Film Board of Canada / Office national du film
OSM / MSO	Orchestre symphonique de Montréal / Montréal Symphony Orchestra
PIQA	Programme d'intervention dans les quartiers anciens [Program for intervention in old neighbourhoods]
SAMP	Société pour l'amélioration de Milton-Parc [Milton-Park Improvement Corporation]
SDA	Société de développement Angus [Angus Development Corporation]
SDM	Société de développement de Montréal [Montréal Development Corporation]
SHDM	Société d'habitation et de développement de Montréal [Montréal Housing and Development Corporation]
SIDAC	Société d'initiatives et de développement des artères commerciales [Corporation for Initiatives and Development of Commercial Streets]
SPUM	Société du patrimoine urbain de Montréal [Montréal Urban Heritage Corporation]
SQDM	Société québécoise de développement de la main-d'œuvre [Québec Manpower Development Corporation]
STCUM [MUCTC]	Société de transport de la communauté urbaine de Montréal [Montréal Urban Community Transit Corporation]
STL	Société de transport de Laval [Laval Transit Corporation]
STRSM	Société de transport de la Rive-Sud [South Shore Transit Corporation]
UQAM	Université du Québec à Montréal

1

INTRODUCTION

IN WHAT SENSE A WORLD CITY?

If criteria for inclusion in the present series on the world's cities were restricted to the usual economic ones – a hub of international prestige and power participating in a global network of command centres for organizing international business and financial transactions (Friedmann, 1995) – the case for including a volume on Montréal would be highly debatable. Though a sizeable city of one million in a metropolitan area of some three million inhabitants, most observers characterize the contemporary Montréal space-economy as primarily a diversified regional service and industrial centre on a par with north-eastern American cities like Boston or Baltimore. A recent ranking of the world's top equity management centres placed Montréal a modest twentieth (Lee and Schmidt-Marwede, 1993) and since the 1960s it has been Toronto (ranked tenth on the same list) that has assured Canada's presence as an international financial player.

Historically, however, Montréal could definitely lay claim to international status. Founded in 1642 as a French missionary colony, it came to great prosperity as North America's fur trading capital before expanding into a major industrial and port city. In the latter part of the nineteenth century it competed with New York for the title of principal port of the north-east. Its well-known locational advantages at the confluence of the Ottawa and St Lawrence Rivers, 1000 kilometres into the interior of the continent (Figure 2.2), contributed to its pre-eminent position in British North America, a position from which it had displaced Québec City by the 1860s. By the turn of the twentieth century Montréal's mercantile and industrial bourgeoisie, which held sway over a vast hinterland spanning most of the northern half of the continent, had amassed around 70 per cent of all Canada's wealth.

This elite, predominantly of Anglo-Scottish origin, invested some of this wealth accrued from mercantile activities into industrial development. With a variety of specialized industries linked to the city's role as transportation hub as well as labour-intensive consumer goods industries that mainly employed impoverished rural French-Canadian and Irish immigrants, Montréal became Canada's premier manufacturing centre. The anglophone elite also built themselves sumptuous residences in the 'Square Mile' district adjacent to downtown and nudging the slopes of Mount Royal, and developed an array of educational and cultural institutions, hospitals and social service agencies for the less fortunate members of their community. They indulged in aristocratic pretence, maintained strong cultural and commercial ties with European and American capitals and drew royalty, industrialists, architects and scholars of international repute into their midst. Early twentieth century Montréal, then, had all the trappings of a world city of its time. However, events at national, regional and global scales have long since eclipsed this era of bourgeois extravagance and have radically reshaped Montréal's role in the world and Canadian economy, its economic and political elites and its population composition.

The dominant narrative of Montréal's political–economic development during most of the twentieth century is a two-fold one. On the one hand, Montréal lost its traditional status as a world class metropolis essentially controlled by an Anglo-Protestant bourgeoisie. Its decline as Canada's major city and gateway to the industrial complexes and vast and resource-rich hinterland of the St Lawrence Great Lakes region set in as far back as the 1920s. While the Toronto region did not outstrip Montréal in population until the late 1970s, it overtook it as headquarters city for Canadian corporations in the 1960s – although a good number, especially in the transportation and telecommunications industries, have maintained head offices in Montréal. Were Québec to separate from Canada, however, all these head offices would have to relocate to Canada in order to maintain their federal charter.

On the other hand, the Montréal region came to attract half of the province of Québec's population and 60 per cent of its jobs, the province, unlike Ontario, having very few intermediate-sized service centres. It became a regional metropolis, the pre-eminent provider of business, communications and public services for the rest of Québec and the primary conduit for the export of goods and services from this hinterland to the rest of Canada and the rest of the world. Montréal thus took on a new strategic role: it became the primary base for the growth of a francophone middle-class and business elite, even though Québec City, some 250 km further down the St Lawrence, remained the seat of government. Starting in the 1960s, the francophone middle class was nurtured by the mushrooming of public and parapublic services, as the Québec state took over the realms of health, social welfare and education of the francophone population, formerly under control of the Catholic Church. At the same time, the state facilitated the expansion of a network of francophone-controlled businesses in various sectors of the economy and the 'francization' of management structures in corporations formerly controlled by the Anglo-Protestant elite.

The massive shift of Canadian head offices out of Montréal (mainly to Toronto) since the 1960s – which accelerated in the immediate aftermath of the election of the first *indépendantiste* Parti Québécois government in 1976 – undeniably removed a great deal of wealth and skimmed off the highest-paid classes of management who were no longer needed in Montréal. An acquaintance of one of the authors tells of how the tips at the downtown restaurant where she would sing songs on request from the well-heeled business clientèle dropped from $20 to as low as $2 in the space of a few years. Yet these changes did not destroy the allure of the central business district. Downtown's cachet was preserved, in part due to grandiose and largely successful projects such as the Métro, Place Ville-Marie, Place des Arts, Complexe Desjardins and McGill College Avenue. These schemes combined commercial, cultural and infrastructural development with the promotion of a 'liveable city' organized around both above-ground public spaces and – in deference to the rigours of winter in the snowiest major city in the world – the world's most extensive below-surface shopping and entertainment network, known as the 'underground city'. Most of the principal offices of powerful Québec-based financial corporations, together with a few international banks, regional head offices and ancillary business services, have consolidated spatially around this network.

Yet the 'regional city' identity has not sat well with the city's political leaders, who, with the backing of local business elites as well as to some extent from the federal and provincial governments, have sought out new avenues and new symbols for renewing Montréal's international presence. This was the driving force behind mega-projects such as Expo 67 and the ruinously-costly 1976 Olympics. More recently, there have been largely unproductive attempts to persuade continental European financial institutions to make Montréal their North American beachhead. More successful strategies have included lobbying to bring the headquarters of international agencies to Montréal; in terms of the number of such agencies Montréal is now second on the continent only to Washington DC, and some would like to see the city become the 'Geneva of North America'.

The rejection of a purely regional role for Montréal is partly, of course, a question of civic pride – local politicians flinch when academics or the media refer to the 'Milwaukee-ization' of Montréal (Milwaukee being the archetypal city with but a regional vocation, albeit a diversified and prosperous one). But it is also more and more a question of concern for the sustainability of the economy and the population base. The region, and especially the central municipality, were beset for most of the 1980s and 1990s by the decline of traditional industries, by persistent high unemployment, by sluggish rates of job creation and fixed capital investment. The growth of middle-class prosperity has been highly dependent on the public and parapublic sectors as well as government support of key industries. However, as Canada and its provinces have gone through a self-imposed 'structural adjustment' process in the 1990s to reduce the heavy burden of foreign debt, government cutbacks have posed a threat to this prosperity.

Like many other North American cities, Montréal has only a weak form of metropolitan government, the Montréal Urban Community. Moreover, this only includes the core city and the suburbs on the Island of Montréal, but not the rest of the metropolitan region, and consequently there is a lack of coordinating mechanisms that could orchestrate the enhancement of the economic competitiveness of the region as a whole within North America. This means that Montréal-area municipalities sometimes compete with each other for the most desirable investments. In addition, Québec's depressed peripheral regions, restive and politically powerful within the provincial government, clamour for a larger share of business and public services presently concentrated in Montréal. These developments have raised serious doubts as to whether Montréal can survive at its present size as a purely regional city for the province of Québec – or, as some hope for, eventually as the largest city in a new country of Québec – without also having a broader, international mission.

To some extent, such an international vocation, or at least a continental one, *is* developing, through the emergence of a 'new economy'. While Montréal's manufacturing sector has experienced dramatic job losses in traditional industries, restructuring has led to the establishment of specialized market niches in sectors as varied as women's fashions and aerospace. 'Knowledge-based' industries have developed rapidly since the late 1980s, relying on a pool of highly educated and highly skilled workers who are, however, not always easy to recruit locally, given the slow demographic growth of the region and the province of Québec as a whole. Assisted by government programmes and tax breaks, the Montréal region, with four large universities, has become a major continental centre for high technology and for research and development in certain fields, notably the biomedical sector.

This said, the Montréal region today is also one of significant economic dualization. A large proportion of residents have seen little benefit from the 'new economy'. Deindustrialization has taken a heavy toll on Montréal's traditional working-class neighbourhoods and poverty has become more widespread, especially within the City of Montréal. More than any other metropolitan region in Canada, Montréal suffers from the 'doughnut effect', meaning that its core municipality (the City of Montréal) has one of the highest unemployment rates and the highest percentage of poor families, while middle-class and wealthy families with children have increasingly opted for home-ownership in suburban municipalities on the North or South Shore, whose development has been effectively subsidized by provincial policies favouring suburban sprawl. Poverty rates in the inner city are augmented, moreover, by the migration of low-income youth from Québec's peripheral regions, historically dependent on primary resource extraction and processing and now on the losing end of economic restructuring and globalization. Montréal tends to be the end-point in these migrations, even if job prospects disappoint, due to the migrants' profound attachment to Québec's francophone culture as well as, in many cases, a lack of knowledge of English. The decline of traditional 'ethnic' job niches ('enclaves') combined with the sluggish rate of job creation and recessions of long duration in the past two decades have also made job market access more difficult for recent international immigrants than for their pre-decessors.

A 'LIVEABLE CITY'

Nevertheless, the 'social safety net' of the welfare state (in spite of cut-backs), the very active 'third sector' of non-profit community organizations, the relatively low cost of basic necessities (food and housing) and the absence of spatial 'ghettoization' of low-income people and minorities have combined to minimize the crime and social unrest that have stemmed from socio-economic marginalization in many other major cities around the globe. In this sense, the lack of true 'global city' status in economic terms and a *relative* lack of extremes of wealth and poverty, puts Montréal in an advantageous 'quality of life' situation as compared with, say, New York or Los Angeles, London or Paris. Both the low cost of living and the quite low rate of crimes against the person (for example, the murder rate in the Montréal Urban Community averaged 3.8 per 100 000 inhabitants between 1988 and 1997, compared to an average of 20 for the major United States cities) are among the reasons that the city sometimes scores highly in the 'quality of life' indexes put out by various organizations. For instance, in 1990 the Population Crisis Committee ranked Montréal, Seattle and Melbourne as the most liveable of the world's 100 largest cities (Sufian, 1993). Although notoriously unscientific, such indexes are increasingly popular as 'boosterist' promotional tools as cities around the continent – and around the world – increasingly compete with each other for economic investment and pools of talent (Milroy, 1998).

Montréal has an undeniably magnificent setting (Figure 1.1). It is built around the immensely popular 'Mountain', Mont-Royal, from which it takes its name – a volcanic intrusion with three summits, the highest being 233 metres in elevation (Figure 2.1) and incorporated into a rambling park of 400 acres designed by Frederick Law Olmsted in the 1870s. The city is surrounded by navigable waterways on and along which recreational opportunities abound. It was named North America's best bicycling city in 1999 by a speciality American bicycling magazine – in spite of its somewhat deserved reputation for drivers with no respect for traffic signals and pedestrians and cyclists who behave in like manner!

But the sense of 'liveability' in Montréal derives perhaps most of all from the city's unique kind of urbanity, embodying a European flavour but one that has been transplanted to a resolutely North American context where culture seems much more fluid than in the Old World. It is renowned for the civility of day-to-day social interactions – in spite of the highly segmented

FIGURE 1.1 Panorama from Mount Royal, looking south-eastwards over the downtown core. (Damaris Rose)

nature of its ethnic mosaic and the tendency of French- and English-speaking Montrealers to move in parallel social universes. These are all key attributes of Montréal life, and ones that keep many Montrealers from moving away from their city even though their economic prospects might be better elsewhere in Canada and despite the perennial rumblings of Québec's 'national question'.

Inner-city Montréal is very much a 'federation of neighbourhoods' where local commercial streets remain the hub and where daily life is lived in low-rise medium-density housing. It was through walking the streets of Montréal where he grew up that architect and urban planner Oscar Newman developed his now-renowned ideas about 'liveable housing' and 'defensible space' as key elements in the development of humane urban living environments (see Pacione, 1990). Newman readily admits that 'I got my ideas in Montreal, took 'em to the States and sold 'em as new stuff' (*Montreal Gazette*, 4 October 1996). Usually lacking backyards to relax in on warm summer evenings, inner-city Montrealers make intensive use of the front balconies and porches that are a classic feature of the vernacular architecture. In the words of one (wistful) ex-Montréal writer:

> Balconies are the punctuation in Montreal's distinct handwriting, the commas where you pause and take a breath, the parentheses that embrace gossip and small talk. Flower-trimmed or rusting, ornate or ordinary, balconies are both

soap box and sanctuary, a small personal patch where you can rant about urban life, or retreat from it. (Sher, 1991)

As in most parts of Canada, weather and climate play a significant role in the daily life of Montréal and its inhabitants. The city is in the mid-latitude humid continental climatic zone and has four distinct seasons, including cold and quite long winters and warm to hot summers. It is not for nothing that Québécois *chansonnier* Gilles Vigneault's haunting melody *Mon pays, ce n'est pas un pays, c'est l'hiver* ('My country is not a country, my country is the winter') is one of Québec's unofficial anthems. Hearing that the city has winter temperatures similar to those of Moscow (mean January temperature about −10°C) but more than twice as much snowfall (Canada, Environment Canada, 1987) might make the outside observer think the term 'liveable' city must be an oxymoron when applied to Montréal. It is true that walking along downtown Sherbrooke Street on a biting January day can be a gruelling experience, with the coldest winds being generated by 'wind tunnel' effects from high buildings – in this respect, Montréal's modernist architecture has been less sensitive to the pedestrian outdoor experience in winter than that of cities like Stockholm, for example. However, Montréal is much further south than the world's other 'Winter Cities' – it shares its 45°N latitude with Turin, Bordeaux and Portland, Oregon. Consequently its winter days are not nearly as short as those of Scandinavian cities, or those of London, England. At the winter solstice there are 8 hours and 42 minutes of daylight, and, moreover, in February – by which time the winter is starting to feel as though it has gone on for ever – the city gets 44 per cent of the possible sunshine maximum, or an average of about 5 hours per day. Sunshine, reasonable day length, and winds that are usually light to moderate (averaging 18km/hour between January and March) make out door activities like walking, jogging, tobogganing, skating or cross-country skiing attractive on all but the coldest (below −18°C) days.

The arrival of the first snow that will settle, usually in December, tends to be welcomed by the population since it brightens the streetscapes after the fall colours (spectacular in Montréal as in most of the New England and the Upper St Lawrence Valley region) have faded into drabness. Much less welcome are the periodic thaws that bring rain or freezing rain that makes the sidewalks and kerbs difficult to navigate with deep slush puddles, and worst of all, ice. Snowfall averages 243 cm over the winter, although snow cover (i.e. what remains on the ground) varies considerably over the winter, averaging about 25 cm. To cope with the amount of snow that falls, the City of Montréal has an elaborate plan of action, unrivalled anywhere else in the world, that keeps the above-ground city moving in all but the most intense snowstorms, and even then, it never completely comes to a standstill. Crews set to work to plough, grade, sand, grit and salt the streets and sidewalks as soon as 2.5 cm of snow has fallen, and once there is a significant

FIGURE 1.2 Montréal's 'armies of the night': snow removal operation in full swing. (Damaris Rose)

accumulation a massive round-the-clock snow-removal exercise gets under way with the precision of a military operation involving truck size snow-blowers and convoys of dump trucks (Figure 1.2). Clean-up begins on the major through arteries and proceeds until all the snow is removed, even on minor residential streets – moderate-to-high residential densities and the high degree of dependence on on-street parking make this imperative. With 2010 km of roads and 3300 km of sidewalks to cover, it typically takes five days to complete a snow removal operation in the City of Montréal, and the City's annual snow removal budget is generally in the $50–100 million range (André, Deslisle and Fortin, 1998).

By late March or early April Montrealers are glad to see the snow disappear, and the donning of shorts and dusting-off of bicycles are prominent early-spring rituals of the young and the physically active (although diehards and bicycle couriers will cycle even at −28°C!). Springtime brings an increase in day-to-day contacts between neighbours, notably among the older and less mobile for whom winter obviously poses major challenges. Summers are warm to hot; July averages only 1.2 days when the daily high temperature fails to exceed 20°C and 4.3 days when average maximums reach 30°C or higher. Hot spells, meaning above 30°C, generally only last a few days in the peak months of June to August. Summers are also sunny, with 60 per cent of the potential maximum hours of sunshine in July (8–9 hours), although rainfall (totalling 777mm for the year) also peaks in July and August, when there is significant thunderstorm activity. Generally, summer days are pleasant; humidity levels, however, are quite high (although not in the same league as the eastern seaboard of the United States). The 'humidex' (humidity index) rises above 30 for about half of July; and there are usually a few days when it goes above 35, beyond which point heavy physical exertion is not advisable. Doubtless this may explain in part why Quebecers have Canada's highest per capita ownership of backyard swimming pools, which can readily be seen from the air as one flies over Montréal-area suburbs. Inner-city residents have access to neighbourhood public pools and a very popular artificial beach on Île Notre-Dame, an island in the St Lawrence created for Expo 67. Fortunately, air quality is good to very good most of the time, the geographical setting and wind patterns making the temperature inversions that are favourable to smog build-up unusual occurrences.

The exuberance and desire to spend time outdoors that summer tends to bring out in Montrealers is doubtless part of the reason that 'festival culture', a growing phenomenon in many of the world's cities, has become so successful in Montréal over the past decade and a half. The city's high concentration of arts and cultural workers from both the francophone and anglophone milieux and, increasingly, from other ethnocultural communities, also provides a critical mass that has helped develop a series of major annual festivals that run consecutively from June through August, including comedy and the world's largest jazz festival, which regularly attract audiences from all over northeastern North America and even from Europe, in addition to fostering the development of a cluster of new-technology industries associated with film and video. These festivals take place in the heart of downtown, involving extensive closures of major streets to vehicular traffic. They reinforce the 'safe' ambience of the central city (crowd control and opportunistic crime pose minimal problems) and have made a major contribution to the revival of Montréal as an international tourist destination in the 1990s following a long moribund period. Over the same period, Montréal has become one of North America's major convention centres and an important international conference venue, even in the winter months.

PARADOXES OF A BICULTURAL CITY

The successful promotion of festival and convention-based tourism has undoubtedly been due in part to organizers capitalizing on the city's unique cultural cachet. It is, after all, the third largest French-speaking city in the world, after Paris and Kinshasa, and the only large French-speaking city in North America (64 per cent of the City of Montréal's and 71 per cent of the metropolitan area's population speak French as their home language), and it has a distinctive cultural life that fuses North American and European traditions. Moreover, it is one of the very few genuinely bilingual major cities in the world, with close to a million of the metropolitan area's residents claiming to be able to speak both French and English. Most of today's Montrealers share the belief that maintaining the city's predominantly French character is indeed essential for preserving francophone culture in North America. This desire to ensure the survival of the French language and Québec culture is an issue that unites most Quebecers (not only sovereignists, and not only francophones . . .), for although French is one of Canada's two official languages, francophones constitute a declining share of Canada's total population and the principle that Canada is quintessentially defined by its two 'founding nations' is increasingly contested in the rest of Canada.

This bilingual and bicultural character of Montréal has created some profound paradoxes that greatly complicate its attempt to recreate itself as an international metropolis while maintaining itself as Québec's primary city. Importantly, while Montréal is the economic 'engine' of Québec and the 'window on the world' for the overwhelmingly francophone rest of the province (where 95 per cent are French-speaking, 80 per cent of these being unilingual), many Québec nationalists view its bilingual character with great ambivalence rather than embracing this as a strategic economic advantage. Given the cultural relations of force in North America, a bilingual Montréal is often perceived as a potential threat to the French language and culture in Québec as a whole.

Consequently, some hard-line Québec sovereignists, especially those not from the Montréal region, see nothing problematic in the reduction of Montréal to regional city status, since this would reduce the need for interactions in English. However, this view seems to be losing strength; as the city enters a new millennium one can detect a maturation of political thought and a growing consensus as to the objective of 'reinternationalizing' Montréal. Today, growing numbers of Québec nationalists (and some who call themselves 'post-nationalists') simultaneously see themselves as cosmopolitan citizens of the global village and want to see Montréal re-establish itself as an international city. (Somewhat paradoxically, many francophones, sovereignists among them, do not feel their language and culture to be threatened by economic globalization, claim to have a 'continentalist' vision and espouse greater cultural and philosophical affinities with that most 'assimilationist' of nations, the United States, than to the rest of Canada (Bernier and Bédard, 1999). However, they still want the new international face of Montréal to be a resolutely French one, which means maintaining French as the only language of internal communication in the workplace and ensuring that the visible presence of English in public life be kept to a minimum, especially in the symbolically important downtown area. But whether Montréal can in fact become a member of the new league of international cities and simultaneously remain the metropolis of French

Québec is a question with no easy response. Scholars increasingly argue that establishing a role as a metropolis in this day and age has less and less to do with forging synergies with a regional hinterland and more and more to do with securing a position in 'the space of flows' between world cities. Today's Montrealers with an internationalist vision are well aware of this while not forgetting that the French character of their city remains an integral part of its *raison d'être* and that without such a character its claim to be a world-class metropolis would be a dubious one indeed.

Adding to these paradoxes, an increase in international immigration since the early 1980s has made the city increasingly multiethnic and culturally pluralistic. Such diversity, important to cultural life in some parts of the city since the turn of the century, has now come to permeate neighbourhoods, schools and workplaces, the arts and cultural fields throughout the City, the Montréal Urban Community and beyond. In this respect too, Montréal increasingly finds itself on a different wavelength from the rest of Québec, where ethnocultural homogeneity and very little immigrant settlement remain the rule. As we shall see, this 'new immigration' renders even more acute the question of how Québec can ensure the preservation of its cultural heritage, while coming to terms with the inevitability that increasing cultural diversity is changing the meaning of what it is to be a French-speaking Montrealer.

Montréal remains, then, distinctly present on the map of world cities. Much as in the case of Dublin as MacLaran portrays it in another volume in this series (MacLaran, 1993), its claim to a place on that map is today tied more to its cultural than to its economic or political dimensions – although the three are intimately entwined as Montréal occupies a strategic but ambivalent place in the forging and renewal of Québec's identity as a 'distinct society' in North America. In this introduction we have sketched out the strategic questions that form a pervasive subtext to the development and reshaping of Montréal's positioning in the North American urban-economic system, its built form, its local economy, residential patterning and mode of governance. We invite you to explore with us in the following pages these various facets of Montréal's at times elusive quest for a metropolis.

2

A METROPOLIS IN TRANSITION

If there is one thing that Montréal takes pride in today, it is being and remaining a predominantly French-speaking city in a sea of English- (and increasingly Spanish-) speaking North Americans. However, Montréal's historical trajectory has certainly not led unequivocally in this direction. France gave but lacklustre support to its colonial enterprise. The cession of New France to Britain led to a mounting use of English in Montréal's economy and society as the city became a British imperial command post and came to serve more as a metropolis for Canada as a whole than for the rest of Québec – a situation that endured until recent decades when the city's economic development became more enmeshed in the affirmation of the identity of francophone Québecois. Meanwhile, the descendants of the French settlers no longer had an affinity to France but neither did they share the respect and admiration British immigrants felt for the British Empire. Differences in perspective and territorial ambition between the elites of Canada's two 'founding nations' (an expression designating the French and English Canadians whose governments successively gained control of the territory of Québec) affected the types of undertakings the two language groups would be involved in on the new continent and would make distinctive imprints on the city's position in the broader Canadian and continental urban system as well as on its internal development. In this chapter, we explore how policies and goals implemented under the French, British and then Canadian national regimes reinforced and abetted Montréal's transcontinental orientation up to the time when its Canadian hegemonic position was secured at the turn of the twentieth century. We then indicate how, beginning in the early decades of the century, the national and continental hinterland began to slip from Montréal's grasp and how the city began to focus on assuming a more ambiguous role, that of metropole for French Québec. Contemporary economic restructuring warrants a more detailed study, and so is accorded its own chapter, Chapter 5.

THE 'ISLAND AMIDST RAPIDS' AND THE MYSTERY OF HOCHELAGA

When in 1535 Jacques Cartier stepped on to what was to become known as the Island of Montréal, he was merely following in the footsteps of the Native Americans who had been living in this part of the continent for more than six thousand years. Progressive phases of native occupation and cultural development succeeded the retreat of the Champlain Sea – a saltwater consequence of the retreat of the last continental ice sheet – from the present-day St Lawrence and lower Ottawa valleys. Shifts in climate conditions led to successive changes in vegetation culminating in the establishment of a mixed deciduous–coniferous forest overlaying predominantly clay soils. At the time of Cartier's arrival the area was peopled by the Iroquois of the St Lawrence valley who hunted, fished and, much like their neighbours to the south, cultivated a variety of crops, including corn, squash, beans, sunflowers and tobacco.

The Island of Montréal is in fact the central and largest land body in an archipelago at the confluence of the St Lawrence and Ottawa Rivers that also includes Île Jésus to the north (the present-day suburb of Laval) and a multitude of smaller islands, some of which are still uninhabited today. Historian Jean-Claude Robert (1994) compares the island's shape to that of a boomerang, 58 kilometres long and 18 kilometres wide, that has landed some 1500 kilometres upriver from the Atlantic. Cartier was met by some 1500 Iroquois living in a stockaded village called Hochelaga located somewhere on the Island. Where exactly remains a mystery, primarily because Cartier failed to provide detailed accounts of his landing. Moreover, the village and its inhabitants had disappeared by the time Samuel de Champlain reached the island in 1603. All that remained were clearings of formerly cultivated fields. What had happened in the meantime is left to conjecture. Had illness inadvertently transmitted by Cartier and his men decimated the Iroquois? Had they been displaced by rivalries among Native peoples (Hurons, Stadaconians, Algonquins, and the like)? Was this warfare aggravated by the arrival of Europeans? Or was their disappearance simply part of one of the periodic cycles of cultivators? Modern historians continue to debate its precise location. But the site of this former Native village is definitely not today's Hochelaga district in the south-east of the city. Indeed, it is not even clear whether this name referred to the village alone or to the entire archipelago.

At the centre of the Island of Montréal is what Montrealers call 'the Mountain', actually a mere bump at most 234 metres high although very steep on its east and north-east sides (Figure 2.1); it is one of a few volcanic intrusions that dot the broad and fertile plain that was once the Champlain sea. Mount Royal was named by Jacques Cartier, who climbed its slopes during one of his visits. Along with the river, Mount Royal is still a vital part of Montréal's identity, just as is Arthur's Seat, a similar geological formation enthroned in the heart of Edinburgh in Scotland. In fact Montréal's 'Mountain' pleasantly includes three rounded summits providing vistas on to different parts of the island (Figure 1.1; Figure 3.25). The celebrated Native village of Hochelaga may well have been situated on one of the slopes of Mount Royal, or indeed right in the middle of the three summits.

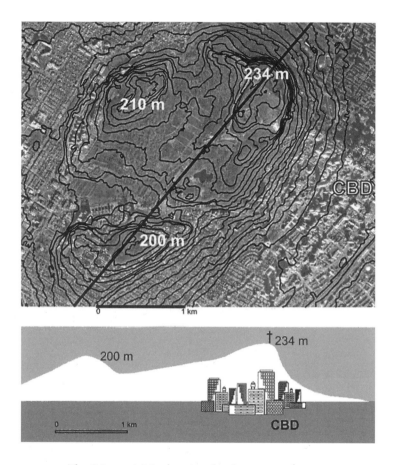

FIGURE 2.1 The 'Mountain' in the city: the three summits

The uncertainty surrounding the village's location and history may not be as anecdotal a matter as it seems, given the importance Native issues have recently assumed.

What we do know is that the Iroquois called the island *Totiake*, which means 'island amidst rapids'. The largest of these rapids, off the south-central portion of the island and made especially turbulent by the strong currents around Montréal, became known as the Lachine Rapids. These rapids were to play a crucial role in the city's history since they marked the head of navigation for small ships heading up the broad St Lawrence River, the first link in an inland chain of waterways serving as the major artery leading into the North American continent from the Atlantic Ocean to the Great Lakes, where the river has its source some 3000 kilometres upstream. The terrain close to the rapids was remarkably flat, however, making it relatively easy to create a bypass route. In addition, just upstream from the

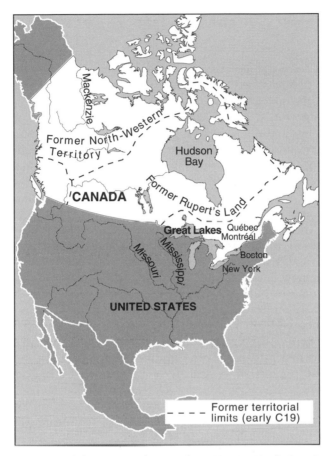

Former territorial
limits (early C19)

F I G U R E 2.2 Montréal's strategic historical position in North America

rapids, the river begins to widen before opening up into Lake St Louis
whereas just downstream the Île Sainte-Hélène and a few other islands
afforded some protection from currents and, in conjunction with Mount
Royal, lessened the effects of the prevailing westerly winds, thereby making
trips to the south mainland shore less treacherous.

The Island of Montréal had thus long been an important point of reference
for Native peoples. For these migratory people, safe waterways were a key
means of travel, and in this respect Montréal represented an extraordinary
crossroads. Much like the Iroquois, the French recognized the geographic
significance of the south-central portion of the Island. In the eighteenth and
nineteenth centuries the St Lawrence up to the Island of Montréal provided
the single most important northern waterborne access to the Mississippi,
Missouri and Mackenzie river basins, the latter reaching far into the most
northerly extremes of the continent (Figure 2.2).

A FRENCH CITY IN NORTH AMERICA: FROM RELIGION TO TRADE[1]

Unlike most colonial enterprises in North America, Montréal did not begin as a colony destined for European settlement or as an economic venture. Throughout the sixteenth century, French explorers in quest of gold and precious stones found little to attract them to Canada, which Voltaire dismissed as 'a few acres of snow'. This attitude lasted at least until the end of the century, when they began to take an interest in the fur trade. It was at this point that Québec City was founded in 1608 by Samuel de Champlain, who established the new colony's civil and military administration there. As a result of the desire of France's Cardinal Richelieu to combine trade and evangelization in a true colony, Jesuits were dispatched to the region in the mid-1630s. Three decades later they had set up villages for converted Iroquois, two of which are still important Montréal-area Native reserves: Kahnawake and Kanesatake. Récollets and Sulpicians soon joined the Jesuits in the new land.

The founding of Montréal, initially called Ville-Marie, was inspired by such missionary projects. At that time, in reaction to the doctrines of Martin Luther, France and all its territories were swept by renewed Christian fervour. Converting the 'savages' and recreating a true Christian community were notions that galvanized not only the French elite but more modest sectors of the population as well. Jérôme Le Royer de la Dauversière, a visionary from rural France, undertook to raise funds to purchase the Island of Montréal and finance an expedition of believers led by Paul de Chomedey, sieur de Maisonneuve, a retired officer, and Jeanne Mance, who dreamed of founding a hospital in New France. In 1642, an organization calling itself *les Messieurs et Dames de la Société de Notre-Dame de Montréal pour la conversion des sauvages de la Nouvelle-France* founded Ville-Marie. Forty or so *Montréalistes* settled, with rather meagre provisions, around Place Royale at Pointe-à-Callière (see Chapter 3).

These pious individuals, however qualified they may have been in preaching, were less skilled in agricultural techniques, and the tiny settlement grew very slowly. The harshness of the climate compared to that of France was a further setback, along with the fact that the Natives they had come to convert proved more than a little resistant to such overtures.

Meanwhile, the financial situation of the Société de Notre-Dame went from bad to worse, and in 1663 the group disbanded. The seigneurie of the Island of Montréal then came under the control of the Seminary of Saint-Sulpice. The colony itself was placed directly under the authority of the King of France, Louis XIV, and so New France was from then on administered like a French province. Henceforth, Ville-Marie, under its new name of Montréal, was less involved in missionary endeavours as it increasingly targeted commercial goals.

In addition, the small colony soon found itself embroiled in the Iroquois wars. These conflicts were linked to the westward expansion of the fur trade that made the Ville-Marie site the 'vanguard position in the struggle for empire in America' between the British and the Iroquois who were in alliance, and the French, Huron and Ottawa (among others) (Roberts, 1969: 67). The protracted warfare led to a militarily weakened Iroquoian confederacy which finally agreed to a durable peace between themselves, the French and some thirty other native nations, during a large meeting convened in Montréal in 1701. The final document was called 'the Great Peace of Montréal' (Linteau, 1992: 36). In this document the Iroquois agreed to remain neutral in all conflicts between the French and the English. In 1997, the city honoured the then-presiding Iroquoian leader, Kondiaronk, who brokered the peace accord, by naming the belvedere and chalet on Mount Royal, overlooking downtown, after him.

Apart from the growth associated with the increased presence of the military command during these years, the fur trade offered little impetus to urbanization, and the itinerant lifestyle of the inland fur traders hardly encouraged settlement. So Montréal remained a small town of dirty, congested streets, with a social structure resembling that of French towns of that time, without the aristocracy. (In the next chapter we will examine what remains today in the built form from the French period.) Military personnel, clergy and seigneurs then reigned as masters over a local populace of craftspeople, domestics and shopkeepers. However, as a fur trading centre, Montréal's commercial role continued to expand due to its geographically and economically significant location, at a time when waterways were crucial. Every spring, the canoes left the island near Lachine, using the routes established by Native traders. By around 1700, inland fur traders were criss-crossing the continent, from Hudson Bay to the Gulf of Mexico, and as far west as the Mississippi basin. Montréal was thus at the heart of a vast territory as the principal transhipment centre and *entrepôt*. And yet, when it was captured by British troops in 1760, it was still a small French town of some 5000 inhabitants, much smaller than the main centres in the continent's English colonies. There were at least twice as many people in Boston, New York or Philadelphia; New France had a total population of only 65 000 when the other colonies had reached a figure of 1.5 million.

Although Montréal was well positioned to grow into a larger urban centre under the French regime, its growth was truncated by French colonial policy. True to its mercantile nature, colonization and economic growth stagnated as the economy remained strictly controlled by the French government. The peasant farmers (*habitants*) produced little of value for France, and that which they did produce for the local economy was taxed by the owner of their lands (Deschênes, 1988). Little money circulated in this sphere of the economy. The fur trade, Montréal's lifeline, was by the

1700s very heavily regulated in favour of the established merchants, with licensing arrangements preventing freer trade from developing in and around Montréal. As the French market for furs became glutted and prices fell, orders were sent to Québec to close down many inland posts to reduce the flow of furs, consequently curbing any potential growth for Montréal. Unlike the English colonies to the south which had a more diversified economic base, Montréal's dependence on the economic fortunes of a single commodity as well as the vestiges of an old feudal system of land tenure dampened its economic potential up to the time of the Seven Years War of 1755 to 1762 in Europe, at which point in time France lost control of its New World colonies to Britain.

The negotiations leading up to the Treaty of Paris in 1763 are testimony to how French mercantile policy viewed the value of its colonial possessions. As a defeated country which deemed that the only acceptable peace treaty would be one in which some of its colonial possessions were returned, France quickly ceded New France (Canada) to the English under the agreement that French fishermen retained the 'immemorial right' to fish in the waters off Newfoundland. Only the merchants of Bordeaux, who already had a vested interest in New France, lobbied to retain it (Frégault, 1969: 320–325). In addition to these fishing rights Britain ceded back to France the Islands of Guadeloupe and Martinique and the associated lucrative sugar trade. New France, including its most westerly urban centre, Montréal, was thus incorporated into the British Empire.

France, then, saw colonial possessions purely as sources for raw materials extraction, with no true view to colonization nor seeing colonists as consumers of French wares. Salted cod and sugar were staples everyone consumed back in France; fur, on the other hand, was a luxury item that was increasingly expensive to extract, and so seen as expendable. Unfortunately, so too were the colonists, seen as rather redundant to France's new position in global affairs. Britain, on the other hand, was embarking on a new phase of colonial expansion; it not only saw colonies as producers of raw materials, but also saw colonists and indigenous peoples as consumers of their manufactured goods. British North America, including the newly acquired French colonists, was seen to fit in well with this new colonial policy. Commercial interests within the American colonies favoured the retention of the territory of New France because they believed this would help them control trade as these colonies expanded westwards, while Britain wanted to see northward and westward extension of the fur trade without the added expense of defending it against the French (Naylor, 1987: 122). Montréal was destined to grow in economic power, ultimately into Britain's primary city on the North American continent.

THE RISE OF A MONTRÉAL EMPIRE

A city under Anglo-Saxon influence

When New France became part of the British Empire, it became known as Canada. (With Confederation in 1867, Lower Canada would become the Province of Québec, and Upper Canada the Province of Ontario.) The new colonial administrators initially excluded Catholics from senior administrative posts, though they ensured that the religion, the clergy, the civil code, the language and French educational institutions would be respected, much to the chagrin of the leadership of the thirteen American colonies. Indeed, this decision by the British Colonial Office appears to be one of many unsatisfactory policies that culminated in the American War of Independence in 1776.

Some of the colony's French elite voluntarily returned to their homeland, selling their seigneurial land to others, including recently arrived and influential British subjects. But most of the population stayed in the new Lower Canada, which was increasingly marked by the coexistence of two different cultures: the Catholic and Protestant religions, French civil law and English common law, the seigneurial regime and the system of free and common socage. Local governors often had to persuade London to adapt colonial policy to the needs of a French and Catholic society in order to ensure their compliance and support.

The Conquest fostered the emergence of new economic actors of British nationality who soon overshadowed the French-Canadian merchants. The fur trade quickly fell under the control of English-speaking interests, as did a great portion of the import and export trade whose locus was now Britain. The anglophones who successively arrived in Montréal, however, were a far from homogeneous group. Alongside the English, and a few Americans, were Catholic and Protestant Irish and especially Scots. It was notably the Scottish merchants who were to play a leading role in the city's economic growth. They were involved in the carrying trade and in the trading of textiles. Moreover, Scotland at that time was experiencing rapid industrial and commercial development, and Scottish businessmen were seeking new commercial territories. It was a segment of this business class that lobbied London not to cede the colony to France (MacMillan, 1972).

The new arrivals, with their vigorous entrepreneurial spirit, gradually forged what could be termed a Montréal empire, an empire that would dominate the Canadian scene until the early twentieth century. Economic factors driven by international politics were the agents of change that transformed Montréal over the next one hundred years into a growing metropolis and Canada's primary city. Merchants from Britain and the USA used Montréal as a vehicle to expand their markets and hinterland, and to diversify the types of products traded. Some of these merchant capitalists, and many of their representatives, moved to Montréal and were counted among its growing and very influential bourgeois class. During this period, two significant focal points in the building of this empire can be identified: the first centres on Montréal's role in the new mercantilism of Britain, whereas the second centres on the industrialization of the city and its geographic, social and political position in enhancing trade between the Americans and the British, and in the extraction of resources from the Québec hinterland.

Montréal under British mercantile control

The end of the Seven Years War marked the pre-eminent position Britain had taken in the expanding world economy. Apart from its inability to hold on to its colonies to the south of Canada, Britain had created a network of international trade second to none. Its colonial possessions were fed by its manufactured goods, financed by its banking interests, and they returned to Britain compliance and the desired raw commodities that fuelled its industrial and commercial base. Selected colonies also quickly came to serve as repositories for Britain's unemployed and disenfranchised rural population. Canada proved to be able to offer Britain, at the appropriate time, furs, lumber, fish, and cultivatable land: a commodity to be manufactured for export, a commodity for the replenishment and expansion of its sailing fleets, a commodity to feed the masses, and a resource for the settlement of potential consumers of British wares. After the 1783 Peace of Paris, which recognized the newly independent United States of America, Montréal proved to be the best positioned urban centre to coordinate the commerce of the interior of British North America.

The first set of merchant traders was the Scottish-dominated fur traders who supplanted the French in expanding the trade and looked north to the Arctic and west to the Pacific for untapped sources. The more powerful traders joined forces and launched powerful companies, such as the XY and Northwest Companies. The wealthiest traders, dubbed the Fur Barons, became a veritable establishment, operating in private clubs, sitting in the legislative assembly and acquiring the old *seigneuries* from the French regime. These newly bourgeois traders soon started behaving like an urban patriciate, as they came to identify their interests with those of the city that served as their base for a commercial system built on import-export and a vast transportation network. The development of a genuine metropolis and of a continent-wide commercial empire seemed to go hand in hand.

While the fur trade expanded and then consolidated the square timber trade was developing west along the Ottawa River. Merchants in both Montréal and Québec City negotiated contracts between the newly established logging barons and British purchasers. Massive log rafts passed by way of Montréal to Québec City for shipment by boat to British ports. The ships returning to Canada brought with them boatloads of new immigrants; many were dispossessed Scottish clan folk forced to the new land due to the enclosures of their ancestral lands, while many others were Irish, who due to hard economic times or periodic famines, made their way via Montréal to Canada and the USA. Montréal merchants added to their wealth by provisioning these people with tools, providing them with inland water and coach passage, and selling them uncleared township lots.

Although there was a good critical mass of immigrants settling as agri-culturalists west of Montréal, once they were settled it was not clear that Montréal was the best channel through which to move their produce. Indeed, fierce competition from the ice-free port of New York in the import-export sector, especially in the wake of the opening of the Erie Canal route, prompted important Montréal merchants to undertake major infrastructure projects to control exports of wheat from Upper Canada to England and the provisioning of Upper Canada with British as opposed to American imple-ments. To this end the Lachine Canal was built in 1825 to bypass the Lachine Rapids. Today, the Canal is the site of important industrial, recreational and tourism redevelopment projects (see Chapters 5 and 6).

Building a system of canals required access to a capital market as well as government involvement to secure such major infrastructure investments. By 1817, Montréal businessmen had already begun to set up financial institutions with the founding of the Bank of Montréal, the country's first bank.

In response to intense lobbying by the city's merchant class, Lower Canada's legislature, while refusing to subsidize navigation improvements along the St Lawrence, did authorize the creation of an independent Ports Commission in 1830 to supervise dredging and improve port facilities, which were to play a decisive part in Montréal's economy in the second half of the nineteenth century, consolidating its position in east–west trade and providing a stimulus to the growth of diverse manufacturing industries (Brouillette, 1943). The development of steam navigation gave a further boost to Montréal as a port since it enabled ships to travel counter-current without being towed. The Lachine Canal was also deepened and widened several times. In the late nineteenth century the Canadian federal govern-ment took over the port's accumulated debt and the Public Works ministry embarked on further modernization with a view to having Montréal capture the Western Canadian wheat trade. By the end of the century, Montréal would be ranked as the second largest port in the north-east, after New York. Grain and livestock were the major exports in the now bustling Port of Montréal.

Economic growth was one thing, political growth quite another. It was not until 1832 that an act to incorporate the City of Montréal was passed. Although the merchants were continually expanding their trade, little attention had been directed to the proper management of the city. The system of municipal government struggled to maintain itself for the next seven years before it took hold permanently in 1843 (Leacock, 1942: 148). For the first forty years of the nineteenth century activities within the borders of Montréal were directed by the government in Québec City. Municipal politics were non-existent and inconsequential to the development of the city as an important mercantile centre. Improvements to the urban fabric were the product of private ventures into such matters as street lighting and water supply.

More serious for the colonial administrations of British North America was the fact that local governments could not secure loans on the British market. Many important francophones and some anglophones were growing increasingly impatient with the prevailing atmosphere of the 'old regime', combining feudal tenure with a strongly authoritarian Catholic Church, the power of London-appointed magistrates, and influential anglophone merchants who ultimately controlled the legislative assembly and hence the laws supporting their economic endeavours. Multiple issues overlapped in these political conflicts, including an opposition between social control and control over the economy. Social control was in the hands of local forces marked by a strong French-Canadian presence, while the economy was controlled by anglophone merchants with the backing of the British Empire. Discontentment led to an unsuccessful rebellion in 1837. These limiting conditions on the internal development of not only Montréal, but also the rest of both Lower and Upper Canada, were remedied with the establishment of responsible government by an act of Parliament in London in 1840. Lower Canada (now southern Québec) and Upper Canada (now southern Ontario) were united, with Montréal acting as the new union's capital from 1844 to 1849.

The 1840 union of the two Canadas was intended to strengthen a state structure oriented toward economic development, by, to some extent, marginalizing French Canadians: Upper and Lower Canada were given equal representation even though Lower Canada had a larger population, and for a number of years English was designated as the official language. Although it was advocated by many of French Canada's elite, some scholars argue that Confederation (in 1867) became another means toward the same ends. What Confederation did do was to distribute the accumulated debt over a larger population thereby enabling the federal government to secure more loans for infrastructural development. Québec henceforth formed part of a much larger whole that initially included Ontario, three Atlantic provinces (New Brunswick, Prince Edward Island and Nova Scotia), and later came to embrace an immense northern region including the Northwest Territories and Rupert's Land (Figure 2.2), the western Prairie provinces (Manitoba, Saskatchewan and Alberta), and British Columbia on the shores of the Pacific. As its motto noted, the country was to extend from sea to sea.

Although responsible government served its purpose of quelling discontentment the policy was but a preliminary step to reducing British responsibility over its British North American colonies which were seen as expensive to maintain. The 1840s were recession years. Britain's growing industrialization induced it to adopt a free-trade policy, so that Montréal lost its preferential tariffs with the 'home country' and its special relationship with London in its role as a gateway into North America. The economic and political situation of the time would again force Montréal's bourgeoisie to reorient their business strategies, not without difficulty. Trade with the United States became more of a priority though Britain remained the dominant export destination. Most imports passed through Montréal, and Québec City had to forever relinquish its earlier dominance especially as the square timber trade was supplanted by the sawn lumber industry. But by 1849 Montréal was losing river traffic to American railway competition as a serious side effect of the repealing of the British 'Corn Laws' in 1845 as Britain flirted with free trade (Naylor, 1987: 286–290). 'Western wheat and timber went via New York and Philadelphia, and Montréal was left staring at idle mills and an empty river' (Cooper, 1942: 73). Montréal's business leaders then rechannelled their efforts toward developing rail networks so as to remain competitive with New York City as a year round transhipment centre. The first section was built in 1853, linking Montréal to Portland, Maine, a port able to operate year-round and thus compensate for the constraints of the Canadian winter. The Grand Trunk Company also completed a line between Ontario and Québec. In 1859 at Montréal, where its main shops were located, the company completed construction of the Victoria Bridge, the first to span the St Lawrence. The bridge was the subject of considerable discussion at that time. Its record-breaking length, one and a half miles long set on piers capable of resisting the damaging effects of heavy ice formation, was considered an engineering feat, so much so that it was considered one of the eight wonders of the modern world.

Later, other railway lines would unite the new territories brought together by the 1867 Confederation of the new Canadian nation; one line – the Intercolonial – would link Québec, New Brunswick and Nova Scotia, while another – the Canadian Pacific (CPR) – would extend across the entire western section of the country, right to Vancouver.

These massive undertakings were largely the work of Montréal businessmen who succeeded in securing substantial involvement by the federal government who sought out British finance capital and, on occasion, American capital, backed by the Canadian taxpayer. Not so curiously, most of these railroad charters were secured by businessmen who were themselves elected members of parliament, and who had voted themselves various other charters in the past (Myers, 1975: 157). Consequently, the interlinkages between railroad magnates, Canadian banking and insurance institutions, and private corporations were pronounced. The rail links provided access to the new protected markets created with the launching of the Canadian nation. They ensured an east–west trading axis through Canadian territory, guaranteeing economic spin-offs for the Province of Ontario and continued profits for Montréal merchants by curtailing the north–south flow of trade from the north-west through Pembina and then to St Paul. Moreover, such colonial developments benefited not only the British railroad industry, which supplied the steel and the technological expertise, but also British financiers who put up much of the capital (Barratt Brown, 1974). The greatest prize was the winning of the charter for the Canadian Pacific Railway by a group of Montréal investors headed by George Stephen of the Bank of Montréal and involving Donald Smith, later to become governor of the Hudson's Bay Company, among others. Montréal had clearly become the transportation hub of Canada and wealth continued to accumulate in the city well into the first quarter of the twentieth century.

But if the adventures of trans-oceanic trade and rail transport were both the symbol and instrument of the power of the Montréal bourgeoisie, they were also a reminder of the growing gulf between Montréal and the rest of the province to which it remained tied politically. With the ongoing efforts to link Montréal to the rest of the continent, Québec's internal rail network was entirely centred around Montréal, virtually ignoring interregional connections, with the exception of the burgeoning agricultural area of the Eastern Townships. For Montréal's status as a metropolis had never rested with its regional linkages with the rest of Québec. Almost immediately in its existence it had assumed a role of administering and spearheading economic expansion continent wide. Regional ties would develop only to the extent that resources, including people, could be channelled through Montréal. But while Montréal was building a commercial empire that began at Québec's borders, growth in the province's rural economy was sluggish. Québec's territory is certainly vast, but its land is not uniformly hospitable. The ecumene would appear limited, first by the fact that many of the most fertile areas are found in the flatlands around Montréal, and second by the fact that the seigneurial system kept the rural population along the St Lawrence River, thus restricting access to farmland. Rural areas were unable to retain their fast-growing populations and the late nineteenth century saw a massive exodus of these rural populations toward Montréal – whose population tripled from 1861 to 1901 – and New England – where nearly a million expatriate French–Canadians eventually settled.

This situation led to a macrocephalic urban structure for Québec, with only a small number of moderate-sized cities and a substantial demographic and economic gap between Montréal and the province's other cities. By 1901 there were only ten municipalities with over 5000 inhabitants in all of Québec, whereas Ontario already had 30. In 1881, 48 per cent of Québec's population was concentrated in the Montréal area, while only 18.4 per cent of Ontario residents were in the Toronto area.

The city thus became much more removed from the more inwardly focused rural parishes of the rest of Québec. Because of its multiethnic character, and a clearly international orientation, in the eyes of some French Canadian nationalists it was as though in attempting to conquer the West, Montréal had turned its back on the rest of the province, when, in fact, its corporatist mission was all along greater than that of a regional societal identity. It is precisely this influential role and this distinctiveness that underlie the strained relationships that continue to exist between Montréal and the rest of the province. Quebecers from outside Montréal have always found very little reflection of themselves in their metropolis.

Canada's cradle of industry and seat of power

The second focus of Montréal's growth as a city of international stature was the development of its industrial base and its continued role as merchant trader with a renewed emphasis, after about 1880, on the exploitation of the Québec hinterland. The impetus for both these developments lay in Montréal's role as a transhipment centre and as the pre-eminent financial power base of Canada.

Early in the eighteenth century wealth was created through the carrying trade. Artisanal production of industrial goods was present to some degree, but most of the manufactured items sold and used in Canada were imported as were the skilled masons and engineers, the latter being the employees of the British military. Most of these people were brought over to construct the first canal system. The canal system helped to generate an extensive water-borne transportation industry both above and below the rapids, centred on Montréal. Local merchants set up foundries, boat building yards and con-structed their own inland steam boats and barges. Sir Hugh Allan, founder of the Montréal Steamship Company (also known as the Allan Line) had begun as a contractor and shipbuilder and by the 1860s expanded his empire to include a transatlantic steamship line, telegraph, coal, iron, cotton manufacturing, sewing machine, rolling mills, car and elevator companies (Myers, 1975: 224).

Montréal became a true industrial centre by the 1840s, the expansion of the port of Montréal proving a key to its development. The port also influenced the location of manufacturing industries within the city, not only maritime industries such as shipbuilding, but also industries that needed to locate close to raw materials easiest to transport by water and those that could harness the water-power furnished by the Lachine Canal locks. By the 1850s the Canal district and adjoining zones in the city's south-west were home to a growing number of large, relatively mechanized factories which put Montréal on the road to becoming Canada's most important and biggest industrial centre, a status it held by 1870. This area was to become the foremost industrial district in all of Canada by the early twentieth century, employing about one-quarter of Montréal's industrial working-class in sectors ranging from the original 'transhipment industries' of flour-milling and sugar refining to paint manufacture to textiles to specialized metal works (Brouillette, 1943; Nader, 1976: 128). The city produced a vast array of manufactured goods, but Montréal's industrial landscape primarily featured consumer goods (food, clothing and footwear) and heavy equipment for the rail and maritime transportation industries.

The railway networks that were developed from the mid-nineteenth to early twentieth century, making Montréal Canada's foremost railway terminus, were also crucial to the growth of manufacturing since they enabled the importation of raw materials and the distribution of finished goods (Delage, 1943; Linteau, 1992: 143–145). They forged through or looped around the city's oldest neighbourhoods and enabled the development of linear manufacturing zones, numbers of which persist today, as well as new industrial suburbs. At the turn of the twentieth century the most heavily capitalized industries were located at the edge of the urban core close to one of the major rail lines (Lewis, 1985). The Lachine Canal district's importance was consolidated with the opening of the Victoria Bridge in 1860, which linked Montréal with the American railroad network. The railways themselves also generated industrial production and ancillary services – one of Montréal's two major poles of manufacturing employment was in heavy industries directly and indirectly associated with the production of rolling stock (Linteau, 1992: 148–149). In Pointe St-Charles, close to the Lachine Canal, the Grand Trunk (later Canadian National) rail yards, completed in 1854, provided thousands of jobs, many of them well-paid, that were a major source of employment for immigrants from the British Isles recruited for their specialized skills, and were pivotal to the development of the working-class suburbs of south-west Montréal (Hoskins, 1986; Reynolds, 1935), as was the case with the Canadian Pacific's Angus Shops in the East End some fifty years later.

Much as in other major metropolises founded on mercantilism – such as London and New York – labour-intensive consumer goods industries (clothing, shoes, tobacco, candy-making and the like) also formed a major component of Montréal's economy from the mid-nineteenth century onwards, attracted by its abundant supply of cheap labour (French-speaking rural–urban migrants, Irish immigrants and, later, other immigrant labourers). The city soon became the dominant Canadian centre for labour-intensive goods. Foremost among these was the apparel industry, protected against imports by tariffs (Nader, 1976: 128–129), and comprising clothing of all kinds – including as a major component, of course, furs – as well as footwear and textiles. Initially this industry, traditionally a low-wage sector located in small workshops and factories in inner city neighbourhoods, employed mainly French-Canadians (Bradbury, 1993: 32), but with the waves of Jewish and other European immigration that began in the 1880s the garment industry became increasingly associated, in terms of both entrepreneurs and workers, with the city's 'immigrant corridor' along St Lawrence Boulevard, whereas textiles and shoes tended to locate in new industrial suburbs like Maisonneuve (Linteau, 1992: 149, 325–326; Steedman, 1986). By the 1930s Montréal's garment industry held a dominant place in Canada especially in the women's fashion clothing sector (Linteau, 1992: 300).

In the last third of the century, light industry benefited from the protective tariffs ushered in by Canada's new National Policy. The new nation had in part resulted from a desire by the 'Fathers of Confederation' to create a domestic market to offset the difficulties encountered by an economy until then focused on exports, and to counterbalance pressures exerted by the American economy, especially in Ontario. The founding of the Canadian nation also provided the latter with the means to support the great adventure of rail. The National Policy of 1879 provided the income to help pay for such industrial expansion. One economic historian argues that the heavy tariffs placed on imported goods were established at the behest of the commercial elite of Montréal. The policy effectively re-established Montréal as the pivot of British and American trade (Naylor, 1987: 443). It benefited not only the Montréal carrying trade, but also the sugar refineries, and the cotton and woollen textiles sector by closing off the importation of American finished goods. The tariff also led to American companies setting up branch plants in Montréal and elsewhere in order to get around the prohibitive rates and gain access to the British market and also to the bountiful supply of natural resources essential to their own industrial expansion: pulp wood and then paper, lumber, and then by the 1930s magnesite, copper, and asbestos. The influx of American capital and the employment of Canadian agents were viewed as positive developments, given that more money circulated through Montréal (as well as Toronto) and new and important contacts were made with American industrialists who would use the merchant services of the Montréal elite. Montréal's elitist Hunt Club, which indulged in unabashed aristocratic pretence and which played host to the Prince of Wales and the Governor General of Canada in the 1920s, had developed a reputation of style and grandeur among the business elite of the USA and was clearly a social club of stature where influential guests from both sides of the Atlantic could meet and mingle (Westley, 1990: 154). Joint American and Canadian efforts were made to develop areas of Québec as expensive private clubs. In addition to elitist activities, American culture penetrated the Montréal market through cinema, night club acts, music, and popular food products like Coca-Cola and Chiclets gum, through branch plant operations located in Montréal (Linteau, 1992). Apart from the the industrial development associated with the war effort of 1914 to 1917 which obviously saw military goods shipped to Britain, the National Policy 'prompted a profound restructuring of the flow of Canadian industrial activity into a continental nexus at the expense of an imperial one' (Naylor, 1987: 444).

Another distinctive feature of the economy in the late nineteenth century was its rapid transition from competitive capitalism to powerful monopolies, a phenomenon happening continent wide. The textile industry offers an especially striking example of this trend. Ten years after its remarkable growth, spurred by the National Policy, this sector became the target of massive concentration, resulting in the 1905 formation of a trust that brought the country's major industries under the control of Montréal financiers. As we have mentioned in the case of Sir Hugh Allan, the Montréal elite were consolidating their empires themselves. The turn of the century also saw increasing horizontal integration as Montréal businessmen moved to diversify their investments. A prime example is Herbert Holt, an Irish engineer who began his career in the rail sector with Canadian Pacific who, by the eve of the First World War, held 24 administrative posts including six chairmanships in important companies in the electrical, financial, iron and steel, textile, pulp and paper, and flour industries. He was also a very active land speculator, involved in the development of what was (and remains) one of the area's wealthiest municipalities, Hampstead. Within the railroad sector, the CPR remained a powerhouse while its competitors were consolidated, by federal law, into the Canadian National Railway (CNR). To place the financial and industrial strength of the Montréal elite into context, some two thirds of Canada's wealth at the turn of the twentieth century was owned by the male heads of the households who lived within the area bounded by present-day La Gauchetière Boulevard to the south, Guy Street and Côte-des-Neiges Road to the west, Bleury Street and Park Avenue to the east, and Pine Avenue to the north. This area was once known as the Square Mile (dubbed 'Golden Square Mile' by some scholars), and had many stately mansions (only a few of which have survived to the present day). Most of them were of Scottish Protestant background, and they all aspired towards an English aristocratic lifestyle. Many had received knighthoods and were entitled to use the prefix, 'Sir'; a select few others were offered lordships, such as the wealthiest of them all, Donald Smith, Lord Strathcona. These examples effectively illustrate the powerful commercial, financial and industrial integration of this Montréal empire that stretched right across the country and which had interests and powerful links to the United States and Britain.

THE SEEDS OF DECLINE OF A CONTINENTAL METROPOLIS

In the decade from 1900 to 1910 Montréal grew from 13th to 10th ranked city in North America in population size. A measure of its importance as an industrial and transhipment centre was its standing as the third largest city in North America's industrial heartland – the Great Lakes/St Lawrence region –

after Chicago and Cleveland (Harris, 1996). Yet, by the end of the 1920s Montréal's status within Canada was being irrevocably transformed by the international and local events we have outlined here. The decline of the British Empire, its resources consumed by the First World War, the rise of the American 'empire', and the inability of the Montréal elite and their heirs to reposition themselves and their empires would have a significant impact on the shift of the Canadian economy's centre of gravity and thus on Montréal's position in Canada's urban hierarchy. Much has been written about when this process really began, at what point Toronto truly overtook Montréal, and what the time lag was between the objective reality and social perceptions of this reality. For a long time, each city clearly had its own strengths in certain areas. But whereas in the minds of the Québec public, Montréal retained its undisputed role as Canada's metropolis up to the 1950s, a number of scholarly studies trace the decline of Montréal's metropolitan status as far back as the early twentieth century – or even the mid-nineteenth century when legislation first made it possible for Toronto traders to ship goods in and out of the port of New York in bond using the Mohawk–Hudson route, breaking Montréal's hegemony over the Upper Canada hinterland (Kerr, 1968).

It is true that in the early twentieth century the natural resource sector was showing unprecedented growth. In Québec, hydroelectricity, pulp and paper, and mining were among the most capital-intensive of these primary-sector industries. There was a massive influx of American capital in the mining sector, and the provincial government also welcomed several US controlled pulp and paper industry giants. But American investments were especially substantial in Ontario, closer to the Great Lakes Industrial heartland. This development, a clear by-product of the National Policy that Montréal business interests had wanted so much, would gradually shift the centre of gravity of the Canadian economy towards Toronto. By 1913, 21 per cent of American-controlled corporations in Canadian urban areas were concentrated in Toronto, compared to only 12 per cent in Montréal. In 1931, 66 per cent of American-controlled corporations in Canada were located in Ontario, compared to only 16 per cent in Québec (Roby, 1976), in spite of the latter's cheaper labour – a fact which one scholarly study conducted at the time attributed to the American companies' desire to locate in an English-speaking atmosphere (cited in Delage, 1943). Montréal had in fact begun to lose ground to Toronto as a manufacturing city by the late nineteenth century. One telling indicator was the lead taken by Toronto in 1911 in the number of head offices of Canadian manufacturing, whole-saling and retail businesses (McCann and Smith, 1991); moreover, the value of manufacturing shipments from Toronto had virtually caught up with Montréal by this time (Delage, 1943).

For the first two decades of the twentieth century Montréal as a port (Figure 2.3) owed much of its prosperity to the development of the

FIGURE 2.3 The port and the downtown, 1926; rue de la Commune in foreground. Reproduced by permission from Archives nationales du Québec (591/13, NC 94-1-3)

Canadian West. But, after completion of the transcontinental railway lines the western Canadian trade was increasingly being captured by Vancouver, and to a lesser extent Prince Rupert. By the late 1930s, Montréal had lost a great deal of ground to Vancouver as a grain port, with the opening of the Panama Canal and lower ocean freight rates. Further competition from the new grain port of Churchill, Manitoba (on Hudson Bay), from the eastern ports of St John, Halifax, New York and other American ports and even from Québec ports on the Lower St Lawrence, led the Port of Montréal to specialize increasingly in imported goods such as coal, oil, sugar, iron and steel; and by the time of the outbreak of the Second World War New York had overtaken Montréal as the continent's largest transhipment port (Brouillette, 1943; Nader, 1976: 130).

As Gad and Holdsworth (quoted in Harris, 1996: 23) note, Montréal's decline as a financial centre relative to Toronto also set in around this time:

> By 1911 Toronto already had more people employed in 'finance' than Montréal; by 1924 a larger volume of bank cheques was cleared in Toronto than Montréal; in 1932 the volume of transactions on the Toronto stock market exceeded that on the Montréal market; during the 1950s Toronto took the leading role in insurance.

Some scholars see this decline as having been triggered by the failure of Montréal's business elite, mired in a traditionalist and risk-averse attitude (Westley, 1990), to take an interest in capturing a potential new hinterland back in the 1920s when gold was discovered in the Rouyn–Noranda–Val d'Or region several hundred kilometres north-west of Montréal. The Board of Directors of the Canadian Pacific Railway refused to finance a railway line linking this region directly to the metropolis, nor would the Montréal Board of Trade support the project; consequently the Québec government refused to subsidize construction of the line. This enabled Toronto interests to step into the breach by getting a spur to the Rouyn region built from the new line of the Toronto and Northern Ontario Railway which passed close by on the Ontario side; this line, initially built so as to open up the Clay Belt for agriculture, stimulated the hard-rock mining industry in north-east Ontario (Kerr, 1965). With the help of US financiers, the Toronto Stock Exchange gained pre-eminence in the area (Kerr, 1968; Westley, 1990). In 1931 Great Britain came off the gold standard; this encouraged the expansion of medium-grade gold mines and Toronto financiers provided much greater impetus than their Montréal counterparts to launching these enterprises (Favreau and Charbonneau, 1943). The booming mining sector greatly helped the Toronto Stock Exchange to surpass that of Montréal thus assuring the latter's trajectory of decline as a financial centre and also helping to focus manufacturing growth in southern Ontario.

Thus, once a vital gateway city linking Britain and its colonies, Montréal gradually lost its predominance as a financial and industrial centre, supplanted by the Great Lakes region, largely under the impetus of the American economy. Besides being nearer to US markets, Toronto was closer to Canada's western provinces, now enjoying significant growth as the Atlantic provinces stagnated. Toronto also had a more prosperous hinterland to help sustain its growth, whereas Montréal, rightly or wrongly, was said to have ignored and even hampered regional development. Nor did large-scale natural resource harvesting, supported by the Québec government, encourage the expansion of a still-embryonic domestic market. By 1950, Montréal had slipped to twelfth place overall in the North American population stakes and fourth in the Great Lakes region, where the economic locus had clearly shifted to the US 'automotive belt' centred on Detroit, which also gave a great boost to the Toronto area, by this time rapidly gaining on Montréal in population (Harris, 1996).

Moreover, because of the classist, status conscious and fixatedly anglophile orientation of the Anglo-Scottish elite, other cultural groups were treated with disdain, along with the English-speaking working class. Consequently, some potentially creative industrialists had difficulty expanding their operations and contributing to a global economic outlook rather than having to operate only at a local or regional level. Under these circumstances, though most wanted to profit from British imperial connections, an entire generation of regional francophone entrepreneurs was hindered by problems of undercapitalization, and so were placed at an economic disadvantage even during times of growth: historian Ronald Rudin has clearly shown how, especially during the nineteenth century, the availability of credit depended on informal ties in a network entirely dominated by anglophone Montréal financiers (Rudin, 1988). French Canadians were therefore forced to develop their own financial networks, which included, from the 1880s onward, a few local banks, the Caisses populaires Desjardins – today the largest cooperative financial institution in the country – and the French-speaking equivalent of the English Board of Trade, the Chambre de commerce.

In sum, whichever interpretations of the gradual 'de-metropolization' of Montréal in favour of the 'Queen City' Toronto we choose to emphasize, it is clear that the First World War marked the end of a time when Montréal's empire had reached its height. From then on, the city underwent a long series of secular economic crises up until the Second World War, and a period of gradual social fragmentation, after which it emerged transformed, like a chrysalis, from its status as Canada's metropolis to a more ambiguous role as Québec's largest city and 'window on the world'. During this time, a number of major social trends were gradually reshaping Montréal.

A society in crisis

As more and more factories studded the industrial landscape, a growing mass of workers was making its presence felt not only in the unions but in the political sphere as well. Mainly comprised of rural French-Canadian and Irish immigrants, this new working class was concentrated in neighbourhoods close to the downtown core where living conditions were often deplorable. At the turn of the century, among other sorry records, Montréal still had one of the highest infant mortality rates among major cities in Canada and the United States, more that twice that of New York, for example (Copp, 1974: 26). At the same time, the city's Anglo-Protestant bourgeoisie, which had for a time led a number of reform movements, gradually retreated from the Montréal scene, unable to deal with the francophone masses under the leadership of the all-powerful Catholic Church, who were increasingly populating the city's working-class districts. Little by little this anglophone bourgeoisie withdrew to wealthier neighbourhoods in the central and western parts of the island (Westley, 1990), leaving, nevertheless, as its legacy an influential network of private, cultural, educational, charitable and civic organizations.

Other social groups were also appearing, including a growing number of white-collar workers – both francophone and anglophone – in an economy now featuring a large service sector. This group gradually moved to the suburbs. The period prior to the First World War also witnessed the rise of a

French-Canadian *moyenne bourgeoisie*, mainly concentrated in the liberal professions and, occasionally, in the business sector. In mid nineteenth century, many of these francophone bourgeoisie owned residences in the St Jacques ward and in the vicinity of Viger Square. But after the Great Fire of 1852, which destroyed a large portion of the ward's buildings, and especially following the establishment of the Université de Montréal in what was to become the Quartier Latin (Latin Quarter), the francophone bourgeoisie began its relocation process. They progressively moved north along St Denis, St Hubert and adjacent streets and established new quarters around St Louis Square (Figure 3.14) and in the new residential developments facing the Hôtel Dieu hospital.

As in many other North American cities, these growing divisions in Montréal's social fabric were for a time polarized, at the level of municipal politics, by conflicts between 'bossism' and 'reformism'. Movements to reform municipal politics, often headed by an alliance of urban elites and middle classes, thus confronted populist currents led by a mayor, called a 'boss' (Anderson, 1972; Banfield and Wilson, 1963; Callow, 1976; Hays, 1974; Miller, 1973). These regimes were rooted in an urban populace with undeniable social and political influence, despite their still having been denied the right to vote. In contrast to the patronage of the 'bosses', the urban elites sought to overhaul municipal administrations and run them like businesses while the bosses claimed to speak for the growing numbers of working (and often immigrant) classes, who tended to identify with politicians of more modest backgrounds, with their often demagogic and even charismatic political styles.

Rivalries between bossism and reformism took on a special meaning in Montréal, in that they underscored tensions between ethno-linguistic groups, which resulted in a number of celebrated successes for bossism (Gauvin, 1978; Germain, 1983). This period was in fact marked by a succession of populist mayors, several of whom surpassed all previous records of political longevity. We shall see in Chapter 3 how the reformists left few permanent traces, especially in urban planning or in the modernizing of municipal institutions. And, in Montréal as in other cities, the Depression of the 1930s would severely test these institutions, which had until then played a leading role in cities' economic and social development. It is important to remember that up to the 1920s, social policy issues were mainly handled at the local level, including education, health, aid for the poor, etc. But municipalities soon faced budget deficits due to the severity of the economic crisis, leaving the way open for higher levels of government to step in. In Canada, municipal difficulties allowed the federal and provincial governments to expand their areas of jurisdiction. The Second World War represented another opportunity for central governments to increase their power and legitimacy, thus further undermining the authority of local administrations.

In Québec, the state would become even more important, given its crucial role in the Quiet Revolution, a broad movement of national self-affirmation during the 1960s and 1970s that was based on creating a strong provincial state to spearhead a pervasive modernization of Québec society. Sweeping reforms, which included nationalizing hydroelectricity, democratizing education, reorganizing the health care system, setting up health insurance, and launching financial institutions and planning and development agencies, would also help to move the political agenda to the provincial level. Although Montréal was the scene of major political events such as the 1970 October Crisis when acts by radical *indépendantistes* culminated in the kidnapping and assassination of a government minister and the ensuing implementation of the War Measures Act, all the key issues underlying the future of Québec society would in fact crystallize at the level of provincial politics. This shifting of the nexus of political and economic power away from the Montréal business elite would have a decisive impact on Montréal and significantly alter its urban landscape.

We now turn our attention to the historical 'sedimentation' process through which Montréal's built form acquired its specific character. This next chapter will analyse the city's urbanistic context, characterized by a type of 'planning by non-planning' which allowed the blending in of the city's architectural legacy with major contributions dating from the modern era.

ENDNOTE

[1] Clifford Hastings contributed significantly to the research and writing of this section and the next (The rise of a Montréal empire).

3

MONTRÉAL'S BUILT FORM: FRENCH HERITAGE, VICTORIAN LEGACY AND MODERNIST AMBITIONS

Montréal, New York, Berlin, Paris, to name but a few, all became pre-eminent metropolitan centres within their respective countries by the beginning of the twentieth century, when the 'metropolitan era' was proclaimed to have arrived. Each became a metropolis of a hinterland, be that hinterland defined in terms of consumers, or producers, or both, who depend on the control and influence of the metropolis's brokers and institutions, both private and public. These cities' greatness is unquestionably rooted in what Peter Hall (1986: 135) has called 'the original *raison d'être* of the metropolis: government, trade and conspicuous consumption'. Yet, for as much as they are similar in their function as metropolises within the urban system, each has not ended up as just another 'primary city'. Each city has its character, each has a distinctive texture. Although each metropolis experiences and responds to dominant, more universal issues of urban development, they have turned out to be remarkably varied in their composition and popular appearance.

Much of this variation is rooted in the manner in which various 'urban regimes' operated within the metropolitan centre at various times in its historical development and how current urban regimes try to preserve, modify, or give different meaning to the existing urban fabric. The concept of urban regime refers to a political accommodation that reconciles the popular control of government and private-sector interests. Stone and Sanders (1987) distinguish between the *corporate regime*, dominated by the private sector, the *progressive regime*, primarily influenced by middle- and lower-class neighbourhood groups, and the *caretaker regime*, a coalition of small businesses and property owners. How did municipal governments organize themselves to deal with these stakeholders in these various regimes? The answer is not entirely clear. For instance, in North America, urban planning became professionalized during the early years of the twentieth century, as it came to target both public health and civic beautification objectives. Yet urban planning was hardly at the forefront of Montréal's municipal politics during this time – nearly a century would pass before the city adopted its first master plan. Although it is true that the First World War and the economic depression between the wars seriously hampered any attempts in this direction, an approach to planning was nevertheless germinating, albeit one where urban planning as a professional domain would play a secondary role. This did not necessarily mean that Montréal's urban development was characterized by total anarchy or that the city was the capital of laissez-faire in which urban planning would gain no foothold whatsoever, but it raises the question of the role played by the private sector in the development of the city.

Development of the metropolis was largely shaped by the successive types of urban regimes that dominated the polity of the city over its evolution and how popular governments participated in and responded to pressures from the private sector and other key actors in the local civil society. Montréal has experimented with several of these regimes. Each has left its legacy, which contemporary urban planning must work with and around. For each definable period these regimes had generated an urban culture that was indissociable from an image these regimes had of the city itself, and from the city's relationship to the metropolitan region. These images had and continue to have concrete and tangible qualities that are reflected in the built environment and consciously help distinguish Montréal from other metropolises. According to historian Anthony Sutcliffe (1981), this is why architecture and urban planning are so crucial in the development of the metropolis. The urban environment – what is built, what is preserved and what is destroyed – is a cultural representation of the various urban regimes at work at various times in the city's history.

So it is from the perspective of a dialogue between the sometimes lofty goals and products of past regimes and the present stakeholders of Montréal that we intend to examine the three main periods of architecture and urban planning, from the city's founding to the 1980s: the French period, the Victorian era and the modern age, including some explorations into post-modernism. The first two have given Montrealers what we today call their heritage. This was followed by a period of economic crises and experimentation which paved the way for modernism and the rise of the corporate city. The latter saw its efflorescence in Montréal under the reign of a visionary and authoritarian mayor whose grandiose plans would bring both himself and the city to international attention.

THE LEGACY OF FRENCH COLONIAL SETTLEMENT
PLANNING AND VICTORIAN BOURGEOIS PRETENCE

The French heritage

Montréal's architectural legacy from the days of New France is scant. Although there are reminders of the first villages founded at the far ends of the island and the forts that protected them, few traces of this history can be found within the boundaries of the City of Montréal itself. Even in the historic district of Old Montréal only a handful of structures date back to the first half of the eighteenth century or earlier. Much like other towns of that era, Montréal was a victim of fires, as recently as the mid-nineteenth century, that periodically ravaged large areas of the town, destroying much of the city's built heritage except where stone had replaced wood exteriors as a building material. The major legacy that has been handed down from the French regime to the contemporary urban form of Montréal is the urban morphology itself, as Jean-Claude Marsan (1981) has clearly shown. This morphology has two components, one being the street plan for the clustered habitat of Ville-Marie, and the other the scattered settlement pattern of the 'côte' system adopted for the interior of the island; this will be described first.

At first glance, with its grid pattern of streets, Montréal resembles most North American cities. But closer examination reveals a fairly irregular orthogonal grid that follows certain geographical features of the land. Under the French regime, agricultural land was divided into long, narrow lots, roughly 2 arpents wide by 20 arpents deep and perpendicular to the waterways (especially the St Lawrence River), in order to allow easy access to water and water transportation (an arpent is approximately ⅚ of an acre). This type of land occupation, called the *côte* system, clearly distinguishes the orthogonal rural landscapes of Québec from the territorial units of the United States and that of other parts of Canada which were based on the quadrilinear township system. (It should be noted that the *côtes* are not synonymous with slopes although the French word is the same.)

A similar system of rural planning was applied to the colonization of the Island of Montréal; this system was originally set apart from the clustered dwelling model forming the nucleus of strategically located villages dotting the perimeter of the island, Ville-Marie being the largest. The *côte* system of development on the island was identical to that of other colonization areas in New France, but was quickly applied to the subdividing of land away from shorelines (Marsan, 1981). Much like the subdivision process that occurs today at the urban/rural fringe, surveyed lands in the interior of the island were separated by non-surveyed lands, resulting in the formation of distinct strip developments, or colonization districts. These districts were also referred to as *côtes*, following the appellation of the major connecting roads. To these roads were attached (typically at right angles) more minor roads. As the population of the Island of Montréal grew over the next 250 years, the long lot fields were easily subdivided into orderly urban development grids with each of the districts gradually filling in the then unsurveyed lands. In this way a reasonably seamless road network was created for the island with clearly identifiable major and minor, commercial and residential roads. Most of the major roads that traversed these districts still survive today (Côte-Sainte-Catherine, Côte-de-Liesse, Côte-Vertu, Côte-Saint-Antoine roads, etc.) and have become major traffic arteries, Côte-des-

Neiges (Figure 3.1) being one of the oldest (Marsan, 1981). These *côtes* represented significant territorial units for their inhabitants, creating a village-like atmosphere for each of these districts that, in many respects, continues today in many of Montréal's city neighbourhoods (see Chapter 6).

Although the street grid was not the focus of systematic planning efforts like those influencing the development of Manhattan, San Francisco, Washington DC, or even Latin American cities such as Puebla or Mexico City, it is noteworthy that the original clustered settlement of Montréal (Ville-Marie) was also the object of a development plan (long before such a term existed) charting the layout of the city's first streets. This plan dates back to 1672 and was laid out by Dollier de Casson, *seigneur* of the island of Montréal and superior of the Saint-Sulpice Seminary. One of the first of its kind in North America, the plan was not very elaborate, although it did follow the classical concept of an orderly spatial disposition, highlighting certain emblematic sites such as Place du Marché, Notre-Dame Church, Hôtel-Dieu, and the Seminary (Marsan, 1981). The settlement measured roughly one mile from east to west, by one quarter of a mile inland from the shoreline, and was separated into an upper town centred on rue Notre-Dame, and lower town encompassing rue Saint-Paul and the area south to the river's edge (Nader, 1976). Infill streets loosely followed the grid pattern laid out by de Casson and were by 1688 regulated at a standard width of 30 feet. In the course of its development, up to the time of the British conquest some 90 years later, the town of some 4000 inhabitants had taken on the morphological characteristics of what Marsan (1981) identifies as those of European towns of the Middle Ages: fortified for defence, a central market place for commerce and social interaction, and religious buildings including a significant parish church. The latter two features helped to create designated spaces and poles of development that served to distinguish different land-uses.

The only 'historical monuments' remaining from this period are, essentially, the Old Seminary of Saint-Sulpice (1682–1685); Notre-Dame Basilica (first built from 1672 to 1682 and subsequently rebuilt after 1824 in a neo-Gothic style by New York architect James O'Donnell – it was at the time one of the largest churches in North America) (Figure 3.2); Château Ramezay (built in 1705 and rebuilt in 1755), a Breton-style urban residence on Notre-Dame Street across from City Hall (Figure 3.3); and a few homes in outlying districts.

Most of these 'monuments' are actually quite modest. During the French regime, Montréal was only a frontier town, especially in comparison with Québec City, the centre of religious and administrative power, and thus more opulent in appearance – although opulence is a strictly relative term in the context of New France. But nostalgia for the city's past often overshadows its historical reality. Today, when the quest for a collective identity is a central issue in contemporary Québec society, any reminder of New

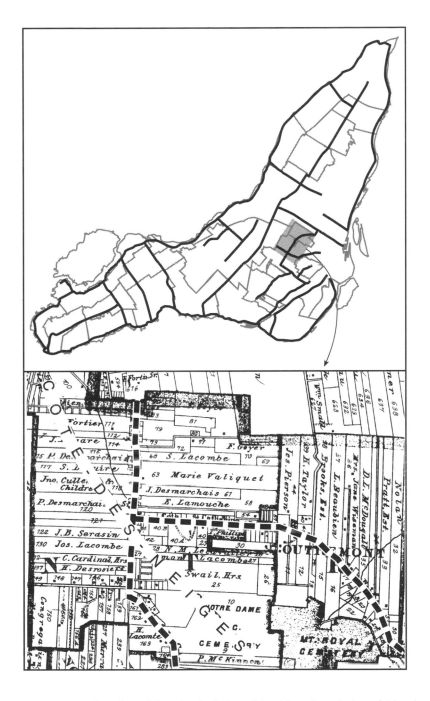

FIGURE 3.1 The *côtes* of the Island of Montréal, with cadastral plan of Côte-des-Neiges, 1879

F I G U R E 3.2   Notre-Dame Basilica, showing Place d'Armes, a typical British square, 1876. Reproduced by permission from McCord Museum of Canadian History

France is invested with a strong symbolic mission. Many Montrealers feel that the Old Town's French heritage ought to serve as the sole reference point for redevelopment in this historic district, despite the fact that most of its buildings date from the nineteenth century – after the colony had passed into British hands.

This helps explain the radical divergences of opinion that emerged from the 1978 public hearings on redevelopment of the Old Port, adjacent to the historic district of Old Montréal. Some groups proposed commercial developments similar to the public markets designed by the Rouse Corporation in US cities like Boston or Baltimore (Hall, 1988), while others sought to recreate urban forms reminiscent of the French regime. The latter could have been achieved by eliminating all traces of port activities associated with the nineteenth century, so that de la Commune Street would front directly on the St Lawrence River, as it did in the eighteenth century.

In the end, unlike waterfront revitalization schemes in Toronto or Québec City, the concept of a public promenade area won out over commercial activity or private development (Marsan, 1991). The old sheds perpendicular

FIGURE 3.3 The Château Ramezay, rebuilt in 1755, one of the few remaining legacies of the French colonial settlement period. Reproduced by permission from Archives of the Ville de Montréal

to the waterfront were transformed into entertainment facilities, yet ships would continue to dock along the piers, as a marina has recently been added to this development. The Old Port has become Montréal's most popular leisure area and tourist attraction, judging by the crowds who stroll, cycle or roller-blade along the promenade during the summer months (Figure 3.4). In the winter, a skating rink facing Bonsecours Market also attracts large numbers of citizens and visitors, despite often bitterly cold weather (Figure 3.5). With the redevelopment of the Old Port, carried out by the federal government under the leadership of architect and city planner Aurèle Cardinal, Montréal's oldest city district has once again become one of the city's most popular social gathering places.

Finally, archaeologists were also involved in this renewed interest in Montréal's French heritage. The opening in 1992 of the archaeological crypt recovered from under the Place Royale at the Pointe-à-Callière Museum of Archaeology and History helped to promote public fascination with urban archaeology. The museum has developed a number of animation activities to spark the interest of Montrealers and tourists alike for an important slice of the city's past. But the museum's daring architecture, the work of architect Dan Hanganu, generated some controversy: in order to reconstruct the crypt, it was necessary to significantly alter Place Royale, the site of the city's foundation. To allow visitors to look down at the remains from above

FIGURE 3.4 Summertime, Old Port and rue de la Commune, Old Montréal.
Reproduced by permission from Jean-Claude Marsan

FIGURE 3.5 Skating at the Old Port, showing part of downtown skyline.
(Damaris Rose)

FIGURE 3.6 Montréal Harbour, Royal Insurance Company Building, 1870. The building was destroyed in 1947 and would be replaced by the Éperon. Reproduced by permission from McCord Museum of Canadian History

rather than from the side it was necessary to raise up a part of the old Place Royale and to build a granite platform on the top (Marsan, 1994). The new building itself - the Éperon (meaning a ship's prow) (Figure 3.6) – built on the site of the first fort of Ville-Marie is a 'flat-iron' design reproducing the form of the historic Royal Insurance Building (built in the mid-1800s and destroyed by fire in the 1940s) that once stood nearby, but with a contemporary architectural style (Figure 3.7). Most recently, efforts have been undertaken to expose portions of the remaining perimeter walls of the old city.

A multifaceted British heritage

Most of what makes up Old Montréal today was built in the nineteenth century, after the British conquest. It bears witness not so much to the medieval forms of a French colony as to the legacy of an Anglo-Saxon industrial city. But the change of imperial governance in 1763 did not have an immediate impact on the urban landscape, as urban growth began to accelerate only in the following century. Transformations in Montréal's

FIGURE 3.7 Éperon Building of Pointe-à-Callières, Montréal Museum of
Archaeology and History, on rue de la Commune. Reproduced by
permission from Marc-Aurèle Marsan

urban form in the first half of the nineteenth century did not stem from
decisions by a municipal agency, but rather from the ideas and the actions
of a powerful merchant class involved in urban development (from land
speculation to architecture) and in economic development projects.

In the early years of the century, three volunteer commissioners (two
anglophone merchants and one francophone notary) were mandated by
the Parliament of Lower Canada to draw up a plan for the demolition of
the city's fortifications and providing for a number of improvements to the
existing town. Redeveloping important public spaces associated with the
French period, such as Place d'Armes, Place du Marché-Neuf (now Place
Jacques-Cartier), the Champ-de-Mars esplanade (completely redesigned for
the city's 350th anniversary in 1992), the Hay Market (now Victoria Square),
and a waterfront esplanade (today, de la Commune Street), was a significant part of the revitalization of the old town. Improvements also involved
the creation of a number of British-inspired public squares (Lambert and
Stewart, 1992). It was expected that the dismantling of the fortifications
would stimulate the growth of the *faubourgs* beyond the walls, as had
happened in a number of European walled towns.

This phase of redevelopment of the old town included the construction
of Bonsecours Market (Figure 3.8). This impressive building embodied
the integration of economic, sociocultural and political activities as was

FIGURE 3.8 Bonsecours Market and its Dome, between the Old Port and the downtown core. Reproduced by permission from Marc-Aurèle Marsan

characteristic of such public structures of the nineteenth century. Begun in 1844 and completed in 1847, the building would, for a short time, serve as Town Hall and Parliament in addition to hosting market activities and cultural events. It is probably one of the most well known and most emblematic of Montréal's historic buildings. This 150-metre-long neoclassical structure, crowned with an impressive dome, faces the city's Old Port. Set on the eastern edge of de la Commune Street, it forms an attractive counterpart to the Pointe-à-Callière Museum at the western end of this street marked by some architecturally refined and distinguished commercial greystone buildings facing the river. The Market's conversion into an administrative building for the City of Montréal in the 1960s kept it more or less out of the public eye for a time. In 1996, however, the City and its partners planned to restore the structure to its original triple vocation: a market, a civic space housing a city information centre and a conference hall, as well as a cultural exhibition site for historic and contemporary crafts and design, including products featuring new technologies.

Bonsecours Market was built during an era marked by the flight of the city's anglophone elite to newly developing residential neighbourhoods on the slopes and at the foot of the mountain, where they sought refuge from the dual threat of fire and disease. The area originally served for the country residences of Montréal's established merchant class. Influential merchants – of Scottish, American, English and, more rarely, French origin – first settled on the mountain's southern flank in the Square Mile district (see Chapter 2). It was here that James McGill, after making his fortune in the fur trade, bequeathed land and money for what would become in 1821 McGill University, an institution that soon gained the international reputation it has maintained ever since. Today, surrounded by urban development, it sits in the heart of the city's downtown core, where land value is the highest. The university now enjoys the advantage of an exceptional and central location, and graces the downtown area with the benefits of its attractive open spaces and a view of the mountain (see cover photo).

A Victorian suburb predating the office towers dominating the area today was constructed south of McGill University. It was in fact planned as a New Town, designed to attract well-to-do residents; it featured an orderly layout of stylish row housing with panoramic views and, for those who could afford them, opulent bourgeois mansions. The district's typically ostentatious architecture reflected the tastes of an elite entirely focused on the British Empire. The development plans for this New Town thus resembled residential ensembles typical of Edinburgh's Georgian period, including, for example, a number of terraces, i.e. homogeneous groups of attached houses with a uniform façade. This model was especially likely to please the many Scots among Montréal's bourgeoisie. Unfortunately, almost nothing remains today of this gracious urban housing so prevalent in cities such as Bath, London and Edinburgh. But several architectural features of this type of housing were integrated into subsequent residential forms: row housing, flat roofs, elegant cornices, stone porticos, etc. (Hanna, 1980).

In addition to the terraces stood the stately mansions of Montréal's industrial and financial elite. Graced by attractive gardens and substantial conservatories, these mansions showcased the wealth and pretence of their owners. Many of these buildings have since been demolished in the face of pressure for high density redevelopment, but many still remain with some now used as consulates, condominiums and corporate offices while others bequeathed to McGill University (and so far preserved) serve as faculty, hospital and administrative buildings. The Mount Stephen Club on Drummond Street, once the home of industrialist and financier George

FIGURE 3.9 The Scottish influence: middle-class housing in Shaughnessy Village. Reproduced by permission from Marc-Aurèle Marsan

Stephen, continues to attract members of the Montréal business community and attests to the pretentions and conservatism of Montréal's nineteenth-century Anglo-Scottish bourgeoisie. When it was constructed in 1884 the mansion had an estimated value of $600 000 (Mackay, 1987). Styles such as Second Empire, Renaissance Revival, Queen Anne, neo-Tudor (Rémillard and Merrett, 1990) were in evidence in the construction of these mansions found mostly along and above Sherbrooke Street.

Middle-class homes were also subject to Victorian inspiration, with design features becoming increasingly elaborate. The middle-class neighbourhoods of the Saint Louis district east of McGill University, and the Shaughnessy Village just west of the Square Mile district and south of St Catherine Street remain today as fine examples of this legacy (Figures 3.9 and 3.10). The 1880s also saw a trend toward extremely ornate 'gingerbread' houses (balconies with spindle balusters turned on a lathe, tin cornices, plaster capitals, columns of various styles, multicoloured stained-glass windows, etc.), which supported a large craft industry. Around 1900, there were more than 250 local firms specializing in this type of woodwork (Leduc and Marchand, 1992) (Figure 3.11).

In the course of these fifty years, Montréal increasingly asserted its position as Canada's metropolis, and its institutional architecture took on a correspondingly grand scale. Examples include the expansive greystone structure built to house the powerful Canadian Pacific Railway and to which

FIGURE 3.10 Late Victorian middle-class housing in Shaugnessy Village. (Damaris Rose)

FIGURE 3.11 Typical ornate woodwork of a 'gingerbread' house. Reproduced by permission from Marc-Aurèle Marsan

is connected Windsor Station (now used for West Island suburban commuters) and the Windsor Hotel building at Dominion Square (now Dorchester Square). Some buildings incorporated stylistic influences from Roman classicism, as exemplified by the Bank of Montréal Building, while others drew on Medieval Gothic forms, as in the case of Notre-Dame Basilica, St Patrick's Cathedral and the Anglican Christ Church Cathedral. Indeed, one of the Square Mile's wealthiest residents, Sir Hugh Allan (whose expansive residence now houses the Allan Memorial Psychiatric Institute), would play a major role in the relocation of Montréal's commercial downtown in the last quarter of the nineteenth century. In the mid-1870s, he built Cathedral Block (which no longer exists today), the first commercial establishment to mark the new downtown in what was until then a purely residential area of the city. The commercial activity promoted by this development initiative led to the rise of St Catherine Street in the 1880s as the new downtown pole with architecturally significant retail buildings being constructed, examples of which are the Ogilvy Building, the Morgan building (presently owned by The Hudson's Bay Company), and the Birks building, the latter two being located at Phillips Square. Today, St Catherine Street remains a vibrant retail district and still boasts Montréal's largest department stores, now linked by Les Promenades de la Cathédrale, built under a shopping centre near the small Christ Church Cathedral (Figures 3.12 and 3.13).

The early proponents of Québec's heritage preservation movement refused to admire these fragments of the Victorian city: '. . . [such structures] irritate the eye with their pretentiousness and mar the landscape with their ugliness', declared art historian Gérard Morisset in 1941 – such an ardent nationalist that he believed that only French-Canadian architectural forms should be preserved. Be that as it may, these Victorian forms have left us the legacy of an urban landscape characterized by the picturesque in both architectural styles and in the design of green spaces. Although Montréal was not yet involved in urban planning as such in the second half of the nineteenth century, considerable activity was devoted to the design of approximately twenty urban parks and squares. Unlike the classicism and grandeur of cobblestone and terracotta *places* and plazas in France and Italy, these British-inspired squares were meant to be intimate green oases in the midst of residential neighbourhoods. Initially reserved for the use of local residents, these squares are today open to all. With their romantic design, the comfort they afford passers-by, and the trees that represent their dominant feature, such squares have significantly helped in humanizing the cityscape (Figure 3.14).

Besides the squares and rows of trees lining the streets, celebrating the presence of nature in the city, the Victorian period also witnessed the development of large parks within Montréal's urban fabric. The most notable of these parks, Mount Royal Park, was preceded by the landscaping

FIGURE 3.12   Excavations for the Promenades de la Cathédrale underground shopping concourse, 1987; the cathedral is being supported on new concrete pillars to correct a subsidence problem. (Damaris Rose)

FIGURE 3.13   St Catherine Street between Eaton and The Bay department stores, showing entrance to Les Promenades de la Cathédrale (part of the Maison des Coopérants complex and linked into the 'underground city' network). (Damaris Rose)

FIGURE 3.14   Square ('Carré') St-Louis, a meeting place and green oasis from the
bustle of nearby thoroughfares. (Damaris Rose)

of two very large mountainside cemeteries, which now help to extend its
green spaces. The park has become an important city landmark, owing in
part to the qualities of the site itself, but also to the talent of landscape
architect Frederick Law Olmsted who 'saw in Montréal's topography an
opportunity to enhance the feature that most defined the city: "Its scenery . . .
is but relatively mountainous. Yet, whatever special adaptation it has to
your purpose lies in that 'relative' quality. It would be wasteful to make
anything else than a mountain of it"' (Demchinsky, 1999, quoting Olmsted).
The designer of New York's Central Park and other parks and green spaces
in many large American cities was hired in 1873 to lay out this 180-hectare
park, the land itself being acquired at the astronomical cost of one million
dollars when Montréal had a population of only 100 000 inhabitants – truly
indicative of the grand vision for Canada's metropolis that was held by the
city's elite. Yet the project was a source of controversy in the contemporary
French press because it was, rightly or not, associated with the anglophone
community, since the site abutted several primarily anglophone neighbourhoods. (Ironically, the idea for such a park initially arose after a francophone landowner named Lamothe felled a number of trees on his hillside
property.)
  Similar criticism resurfaced in 1990 during the public hearings for the
conservation and redevelopment of the park, which some people perceived
as not accessible enough for the francophone community in the eastern part

of the city. Since then, the city has increased the number of pedestrian paths leading up the east flank of the mountain, thereby making the mountain top and its lookouts more accessible. In reality, there would seem to be more cause for concern about overuse than underuse of the park (for example, issues have arisen relating to the use of mountain bikes and high-speed cycling), and about actual and potential encroachments along the parkland slopes of the mountain by nearby institutions (universities and hospitals) for the purposes of their expansion projects. In fact, it was the construction of a six lane avenue, a multi-artery interchange and a university sports complex in the 1950s and 1960s that made the mountain virtually inaccessible from the south-east. The division of the mountain between three municipalities – Montréal, Outremont, and Westmount – does not help conservation efforts, despite special regulations adopted for historic sites into which the park falls.

In fact, if there is one Montréal landmark that attracts people of all ages and all social and cultural backgrounds, it is indeed Mount Royal Park. Olmsted would surely have been happy to see the success the park has achieved as a gathering place, deserving maybe of the same lyrical comments he made about parks in New York and Brooklyn. To him, these were

> the only places in those associated cities where . . . you will find . . . all classes largely represented, with a common purpose, not at all intellectual, competitive with none, disposing to jealousy and spiritual or intellectual pride toward none, each individual adding by his mere presence to the pleasure of all others, all helping to the greater happiness of each. (Olmsted, 1987 [1870]: 241)

For instance, by the early twentieth century the park had become a favourite recreational spot for, among others, working-class Jewish Montrealers from the 'immigrant corridor' lying just below the Mountain's eastern flank – a linguistically mixed neighbourhood epitomized in stories like Ted Allan's 'Lies My Father Told Me' and illustrated in paintings by Louis Muhlstock (Trépanier, 1987). Today the Mountain is a favourite destination for outings by immigrants and ethnic minority families while its popularity among residents of the predominantly francophone Plateau Mont-Royal district continues unabated.

In addition to Mount Royal Park, two other extensive pockets of land were preserved during this period. The eastern part of Montréal gained an urban park with the development of Lafontaine Park in the Romantic style in 1891 by a French horticulturist, Louis-Frangois Chollet (de Laplante, 1990) on land acquired from the federal government. Finally, but no less impressive, as early as 1875 Île Sainte-Hélène in the midst of the St Lawrence River, opposite Old Montréal, had already become a park designed to serve the recreational needs of the *masses populaires* (popular classes).

The industrial heritage and the city's working-class districts

As the 'Golden Square Mile' expanded along the southern flank of Mount Royal, another side of Victorian Montréal was rapidly developing below the mountain. It comprised the working-class districts described in *The City Below the Hill*, one of the first sociological studies on working-class conditions in Montréal (Ames, 1972 [1897]). Its author, Herbert Brown Ames, a shoe manufacturer, was a social reformer concerned, like others of his kind in the late nineteenth century, about the ravages of industrialization on the urban situation of the masses.

The city's landscape was rapidly transforming as factories proliferated, and landless rural French-Canadians and Irish immigrants – especially after the famines of the 1840s – started streaming into Montréal. One cluster of working-class districts developed around the Lachine Canal in the southwest, another extended along the port area to the East, and a third followed the clothing industry north-west from the downtown core. Roman Catholic working-class life in these districts was controlled by the Church and organized into social units based on the parish, which perpetuated a lifestyle similar to that of a rural village as the *côte* system was intended (Ferretti, 1990). These working-class districts lived in the shadow of the Church, whose grandeur often seemed inversely proportional to the poverty of its faithful (Figure 3.15). Superimposed on these parishes were religious and social institutions for non-Catholic residents.

A great variety of churches now dotted the territory of Montréal, frequently described as the city of a hundred spires. If Catholic churches dominated the eastern part of the city, the diversity of the shrines in western Montréal reflected the cultural characteristics of the local population. For example, Pointe St-Charles, a working-class district south of the Lachine Canal, was sprinkled with Protestant sanctuaries (including Presbyterian, Methodist, Anglican, Baptist and Congregationalist churches). In nearby Saint-Gabriel district, two impressive Catholic churches stood side by side on the same block: one for the French-Canadian community and another for the Irish.

This being said, aside from the influences of particular socio-linguistic distribution of Montréal's population, the urban development that accompanied industrialization assumed broadly the same forms in Montréal as in most western countries (Bellavance, 1993). As elsewhere, the industrial city was organized around the growth of industrial sectors, the development of communication and transportation networks, and residential differentiation along social class lines. If Montréal produced distinctive urban forms, it was more in the area of popular domestic architecture. Indeed, over the years, a relatively unique Montréal style of housing gradually emerged.

FIGURE 0.15   Imposing Catholic parish church in Hochelaga, a working-class
neighbourhood in the east end. (Damaris Rose)

This original housing form was shaped by a variety of architectural
influences combined with the needs and constraints of the local environment, together with the internal dynamics of the building industry.
Montréal was a city of tenants, and became increasingly so in the late
nineteenth century. Whereas 32 per cent of Montrealers were homeowners
in 1847, this figure fell to 15 per cent in 1881 as a result of rural and
international migration (Choko and Harris, 1989). A major fire in 1852 and
a wave of intense land speculation hastened the demise of the small,
sloping-roofed, rural-inspired single-family home. These were replaced
with row housing incorporating two or three apartments (known as flats)
one on top of the other. This was the type of housing that came to be
known as 'plexes and which came to dominate the city's residential landscape (see Table 6.1).

    As the rectangular city blocks were created and subdivided into build-
able lots (in widths of twenty or twenty-five feet) these 'plexes – at times
mixed in with single family row houses – were constructed as demand for
housing was generated. This very widespread form of housing in Montréal
reflected both the needs and the housing budget of a clientele with often
modest income, and a supply dominated by small scale local entrepreneurs
with limited capital. The latter were able to build only a few houses at a
time, or at best one row, generally on deep lots serviced by a back alley,
locally known as a laneway. Réjean Legault (1989) has shown, moreover,

that the triplex model developed gradually, obviously influenced by cost constraints, but also evolved into different variants including models targeting the burgeoning lower middle-classes with styles imitating the housing of the anglophone bourgeoisie. Row housing of this nature, usually no more than three storeys high, produced a moderate density urban fabric; in this context, residual spaces such as backyards, sheds, garages and back lanes took on a strategic utilitarian and social function. Originally designed to facilitate various services, in many neighbourhoods the laneway became a preferred site of sociability for children and adults alike, and even a symbolic place that stimulated the imagination of residents . . . and artists, who have celebrated Montréal's laneways in literature and painting (Figure 3.16).

The exact design of 'plexes' varied, depending mainly on the number of units per building (Figures 3.17 and 3.18; see also Figures 6.2 and 6.7). A building with two units, one on top of the other, sharing the same cadastral number but with different civic addresses, is called a duplex. If there are three such units, this is a triplex, whereas a building constructed of two three-storey units sharing the same cadastral number is referred to as a six-plex (the only visual distinction between these two lies in the architectural style and construction material common to the units). Some 'plexes had internal staircases leading up to the second and third floor flats while the great majority had outside staircases servicing the second floor and inside ones for the third floor. The outside staircases were made of cast iron rails and wooden steps and stringer that could be curved or linear. It is these outside staircases and their variety of forms that remains as one of Montréal's most visually distinctive and, some will say, most endearing mass archi-tectural features. The ceiling height, the degree of detail in the finishing of the plasterwork, the presence of bay windows, and the quality of the construction materials (the modest red brick versions contrasting with more elegant greystone types) all indicate the income levels of the target tenant clientele.

According to Hanna (1992), these duplexes and triplexes exemplify an 'architecture of exchange' wherein the collective building know-how of three groups having the most influence on the housing stock – the French, Scots and English – was gradually combined. Italian immigrants would later produce their own version of the famous 'plex now characteristic of certain suburbs, adding to an already wide variety of types. But in the minds of many Montrealers, the most typical housing style is the triplex, dating from the late 1880s to the 1930s, comprising three to six flats with outside staircases, each usually bearing its own street number. This type of housing still provokes a variety of reactions. On the one hand, it is criticized because of the limited amount of sunlight afforded by its length-wise layout, as well as its impractical and often unsafe exterior staircases, especially in winter (in the 1940s, the City of Montréal prohibited exterior

FIGURE 3.16 A typical laneway pastime (Reproduced by kind permission of Josette Michaud)

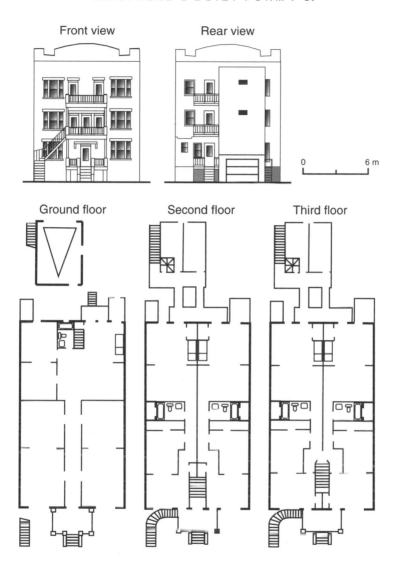

Front view   Rear view

Ground floor   Second floor   Third floor

0   6 m

FIGURE 3.17 Floor plan of typical 'multiplex' flats. Reproduced by permission of Jean-Claude Marsan

front staircases for new constructions but they have been permitted again since 1994). On the other hand, the style was developed in response to tenants' modest incomes at that time, and when the owner lived on the first floor, which was often the case, the buildings were well kept. (We return to the current role of 'plexes in recent urban revitalization, in Chapter 6.)

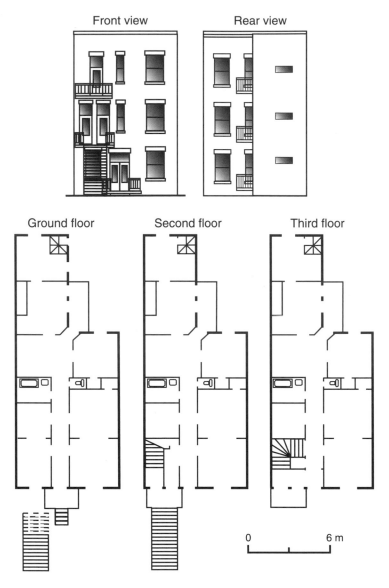

Ground floor   Second floor   Third floor

0   6 m

FIGURE 3.18   Floor plan of typical 'triplex' flats. Reproduced by permission of Jean-Claude Marsan

MODERNITY REVISITED

Despite the fact that Montréal's typical popular housing did not reach the density of nineteenth-century lower-class housing in cities such as Paris, London and Manhattan, health conditions in Montréal's working-class districts were particularly distressing (as we saw in Chapter 2). The extreme social disparities that typified the Victorian era were flagrant and had a dramatic impact on Montréal's urban landscape, as in other metropolitan centres suffering from poorly planned and poorly administered urban growth. Modernism was a response to a disorganized city and to impoverishment. The movement was varied in its goals, with different representations of modernism dealing with the re-ordering of the built environment. Urban poverty and squalid living conditions tended to be regarded as something of the poor's own creation and were therefore frequently dealt with in a brusque manner through slum clearance and relocation schemes. Until the 1940s in Montréal many of the ideas of social reform were adopted from other areas of the western world, from France, Britain and the United States. They were promoted mostly by the agents of urban regimes involving private sector conceptions of planning and beautification mostly in the suburbs. The first half of the twentieth century was marked by proto-modernist planning with a strong design focus led by reformers: garden-city and City Beautiful projects directed toward the skilled worker and the middle and upper classes. Another set of projects, this time cooperative ones, tended to reflect some of the original social spirit that guided Ebenezer Howard (1946 [1898]).

New designs for suburbs

In the deplorable environment of late Victorian Montréal, and for various reasons, conditions were especially difficult for the French-Canadian working class (Sweeny, 1982). However, so-called working-class districts in late nineteenth-century Montréal were often fairly socially – as well as linguistically and culturally – mixed, especially in the southwestern part of the city. The homes of the local elite were often quite close to those of modest white-collar workers and not far from working-class housing. The presence of factories also gave these districts a diversified urban fabric. Today some of these factories, especially in the Lachine Canal district, have been converted to residential, cultural or mixed use (Lessard, 1997).

In the late nineteenth century, some members of Montréal's elite – like their counterparts in many other industrial cities of the time – began to exhibit concern with the distressing conditions in the city's working-class districts. Public health movements were launched, rallying not only the Anglo-Protestant establishment but also a few members of the French-Canadian elite. The latter included doctors, who would play a leading role in this arena. Public health agencies were set up, municipal by-laws were adopted (although rarely enforced where they were seen to impede business), and charitable associations were formed. Although these initiatives produced relatively few results, they did trigger a movement that eventually led to the development of professional urban planning in Montréal, as elsewhere in North America. Moreover, the public health movement pre-figured an overall vision of urban development that encompassed environmental aspects, resource management and control over development (Wolfe, 1994). The Conservation Commission set up by the federal government in 1909 in fact advocated ideas that closely matched the concerns of today's environmental planners. The journal published by the commission was entitled *Town Planning and the Conservation of Life*. In 1914 the federal government hired Thomas Adams, the former town manager of the garden city of Letchworth in England, to promote urban planning in every Canadian province. Consequently, most provinces ended up adopting legislation before 1920 largely or partially inspired by the British Town Planning Act. Québec, however, would take another half century before adopting its own urban planning legislation.

Housing conditions were a major concern for proponents of the public health movement, but only from a health perspective. No one seemed willing to intervene in an area that was perceived as falling exclusively within the realm of private sector development. This liberal view was further shared by the Catholic Church, which, as we have already noted, was a major agent of social control in working-class districts. In fact, after 1910, reformers focused less on housing for the most underprivileged and more on homes for the skilled working class, the new lower middle class and the established middle class. In the euphoria that characterized the turn of the century, the reformers were less motivated by social compassion than by the City Beautiful movement and the garden-city concept. So when a typhoid epidemic broke out in 1909, compromising the already poor quality of Montréal's drinking water, the municipal administration, then in reformist hands, decide to improve the water supply system. A number of urban planning improvements were quickly grafted on to this infrastructure project to effectively clean some slums of the 'indolent' poor through the opening of a large boulevard spanning the city from east to west, and to construct a series of new public buildings in the tradition of the City Beautiful movement (a city hall, a courthouse and a museum of fine arts, as well as an underground tramway and a cluster of garden cities along the aqueduct canal). This extract from a 1911 speech by pro-reformist mayor Dr J. J. Guérin describes the projects his administration was preparing to implement and vividly illustrates this change of attitude:

> It must be understood that these new Garden City Dwellings are not intended to replace the slums and disease-infected districts which the new east and west boulevards will wipe out. . . . The idea of the Garden City is more to provide a comfortable and pretty home for the mechanic and the clerk than to make things easy for those who choose to disregard all the natural and physical laws in existence, maintaining a hand-to-mouth existence by day, and retiring to their dark, noisesome rooms at night huddled together, six, eight and ten in a room. (*The Montreal Herald*, 23 December 1911)

To effectively carry out these projects designed to turn Montréal into a prestigious metropolis, several reformist groups called for the institution of a Metropolitan Parks Commission, like the one created in Boston in the 1880s. A planning committee was set up and subsequently hired Frederick Law Olmsted's son to outline an approach. In 1909 Québec's association of architects drafted a master plan inspired by Daniel Burnham's now famous Chicago plan. But when the matter of financing came up, representatives of island municipalities quickly put the projects on the back burner (Germain, 1985). The few development projects that were launched at that time were located not in the City of Montréal itself but in neighbouring municipalities such as Westmount, Outremont, Hampstead, Town of Mount Royal and Maisonneuve (Collin, 1984; Linteau, 1982; Wolfe, 1998). Urban planning in Montréal thus began in the suburbs.

The plans for Hampstead were in the tradition of the numerous garden-city initiatives spawned in the early twentieth century. But unlike many of these projects, which never developed beyond the planning stage, this garden suburb west of the central city became a reality and remains one of the wealthiest municipalities in the Greater Montréal area. The impetus for this project came from Herbert Holt, the Irish engineer who began as a contractor for the Canadian Pacific Railway Company and became a leading Montréal financier by the turn of the century. In 1911 he commissioned a plan for a garden city destined for the upper middle class. This plan, devised by the American Leonard E. Schlemm, included a series of curved and dead-end streets in the manner of British garden cities. In Montréal, the garden-city concept was clearly reduced to emphasize only its urban design aspect, whereas in the mind of the concept's originator, Ebenezer Howard, the garden city was first and foremost a socio-economic organizational model for the cities of the future.

Urban design also became a growing trend in the eastern part of the city, in Maisonneuve. This newly created municipality was experiencing rampant growth due to the port's development. It became a major industrial suburb, attracting downtown businesses in search of inexpensive land on which to mechanize their operations. It was proudly presented as the Pittsburgh of Canada. When Maisonneuve was founded in 1883, it had a mere 350 inhabitants. Thirty years later, its population had grown to nearly 20 000, thanks to the dynamic efforts of the city's developers, most of whom were French Canadian. The French-Canadian bourgeoisie that had begun to emerge at the turn of the century was becoming an important force in Maisonneuve. They were involved in industrial and real estate development, and had ambitious plans for their municipality (Linteau, 1985). Inspired by the City Beautiful movement that was sweeping across the US, they dotted the city with grand civic monuments in the Beaux-Arts style (Figure 6.14), facing impressive boulevards (Morgan and Pie IX). But although their attempts to populate the city were successful and met the needs of local manufacturers by providing them with a readily available workforce, their policy of grandeur proved too costly for the municipality. Crippled by debt, it was annexed to the City of Montréal in 1918.

Another early twentieth century urban development project was linked to a more successful initiative. The idea for the Town of Mount Royal originated with a project to dig a tunnel under Mount Royal to bring Canadian Northern Railway Company lines (today Canadian National or CN) into downtown Montréal, on the site where one of the first real skyscrapers of the modern city, Place Ville-Marie, would be built 50 years later. At the same time, a new model city was planned for the other side of the mountain, with the profits from this new development to be used to pay for the costs of digging the tunnel. In 1912 the property was acquired by the Canadian National Railway (CNR) and was first subdivided using an orthogonal plan, with diagonal streets to facilitate access to the train station at the centre. The developers then asked Frederick Todd, a landscape architect and a disciple of Olmsted, to improve on the plan by using ideas from the City Beautiful movement, with the main purpose being to give the new city the appearance of a wealthy suburb. Today's Town of Mount Royal is still a well-off municipality with quiet residential neighbourhoods effectively protected by the labyrinth of streets that make up its urban design. It stands in sharp contrast to the high density low income neighbourhood of Park Extension, immediately adjacent on the east side, and built on a traditional grid plan. Nevertheless, residents from these two communities rub shoulders at the large shopping centre on Town of Mount Royal's eastern edge. Quite unlike the 'gated communities' found in many of today's North American cities, the fence and hedge separating the two districts have a number of pedestrian access points – the Town is certainly not a 'Fortress City' (Christopherson, 1994). The Town also has an industrial area which provides the municipality with sizeable tax revenues, thus helping to lower property taxes for homeowners.

The years prior to the First World War were thus marked by the growth of urban planning in Montréal's suburbs and a series of similar projects in the central city that were never completed. As in most large cities across Canada however, this growth trend was halted by the First World War. Subsequent economic crises continued to curb growth impulses, so that urban planning was virtually put on hold until the end of the Second World War. But in the worst years of the Depression, as elsewhere in North America, major public works were launched to help Montréal's unemployed: these included Central Station, Beaver Lake and the chalet on Mount Royal as well as the main Botanical Garden pavilion, not to mention a number of decorative and practical structures installed in city parks (including public urinals called 'camiliennes' in honour of the mayor Camilien Houde who launched these public works) (de Laplante, 1990). The First World War nonetheless seemed to mark the end of a period when an influential business class single-

handedly controlled urban development. But the public sector was as yet
unprepared to assume leadership in this area. Several decades would pass
before all the conditions were in place for modern urban planning to
develop.

Between two eras: residential planning and social corporatism

For urban planning to develop, a certain number of conditions have to come
together: the necessary political will, a professional class, a public administration uncorrupted by patronage, and a spirit of reform in civil society
(Spragge, 1975; Wolfe, 1989). These conditions were clearly not in place in
Montréal immediately following the First World War. Municipal power had
been severely eroded by the financial problems that paralysed the city.
Montréal was now heavily in debt due to its annexation of financially insol-
vent municipalities. The situation was aggravated by the serious economic
crises that further rocked its financial base. In 1918 the provincial government placed Montréal under trusteeship for the first time in its history,
further undermining local political power. This was the era of bossism in
Montréal, when patronage enabled charismatic and populist mayors to
repeatedly return to power. But these celebrated figures in the history of
Montréal, especially Médéric Martin and Camilien Houde, were in reality
mayors who ruled but did not govern; their power was rather limited at a
time when municipalities were staggering under the burden of their ever-
growing social responsibilities, coupled with intense economic hardship.
Several decades would come between the Victorian period, typified by the
triumph of local power and liberalism, and the era of the modern welfare
state.

However, contrary to the generally accepted notion that the apparatus of
the nation-state of Québec developed in the early 1960s, the modernization
process actually began in the 1940s and 1950s, mainly prompted by changes
in civil society – as we shall illustrate below. But first, it is interesting to note
that an urban regime marked by a form of social corporatism had already
emerged in the 1930s, inspired by the social doctrine of the Catholic Church
in response to the triple 'menace' of unbridled capitalism, communism and
the growth of socialism. In 1940, a reform of the City of Montréal charter
ushered in a new form of representation of municipal interests. The city
council now included a category of councillors who were not elected but
instead appointed by eleven associations representing the interests of the
business, labour, and higher education sectors, as well as those of reformers
and homeowners. Each association named three councillors to this new
'Class C'. There were also 33 'Class A' councillors elected by homeowners
and 33 'Class B' councillors jointly elected by homeowners and tenants.
Together they formed a 'democracy tempered by corporate representation'

in the words of T.D. Bouchard, the municipal affairs minister who had launched the scheme when the city was, for the second time, placed under trusteeship (Collin and Germain, 1986). Such corporatism sought, in part, to limit the influence of bossism and to restore the influence of wealthier interest groups, yet also expressed the vitality of civil society at that time.

After the Depression and the Second World War, Montréal faced a severe housing shortage and serious deterioration was detected in several areas of the city that were being designated as slums. A variety of groups and institutions – from the business sector, union members and organizations, Catholic circles, etc. – increasingly rallied around the housing issue. In 1952, an umbrella organization, the Comité des cinquante-cinq associations, was formed to lobby the municipal administration in order to eliminate the slums and to build low-rent housing. Together with the federal government, which had recently introduced laws and financial incentives to spur the redevelopment of Canada's downtown cores, these groups agreed to set up an urban renewal program, which would begin with the project known today as Les Habitations Jeanne-Mance. This project, built between 1959 and 1961, would be the first of the city's low-rent housing complexes and, in the same way as Le Corbusier's *Cité radieuse*, would include 800 housing units in five 12- to 14-floor towers and several rows of low-rise apartments (Bacher, 1993; Choko et al., 1987).

But another development experiment had already marked the Montréal landscape in the early 1940s: the Cité-jardin du Tricentenaire, commemorating the three hundredth anniversary of the foundation of Montréal. In a city where tenants comprised 88.5 per cent of the population, a lawyer and a Jesuit priest developed a project for a model city of homes to be owned by the working class, based on French-Canadian values (largely shaped by the Catholic Church) and inspired by English and American garden cities (Choko, 1989). It is interesting to note the active role played by groups associated with the Catholic Church in promoting the single-family home as the only suitable form of housing for Christian families. Centred on issues of morality (a restoration of family values), economics (an emphasis on the cooperative model) and urban planning (a pattern of dead-end streets, a network of green spaces, etc.), the Cité-jardin du Tricentenaire was only partially completed. Today, this group of 167 homes still constitutes a sought-after residential sector near the Olympic Stadium. But it also served as a pilot project for programmes launched by the federal government, which supported the project and subsequently introduced housing policies that would have a major impact on future urban development.

The federal government, through its housing agency, the Canada Mortgage and Housing Corporation, would help revive the housing market, which had collapsed during the Second World War when all building materials were requisitioned for the war effort. This revival would include subsidizing the construction of single-family homes and 'walk-ups' in the suburbs (Bacher, 1993). This type of housing consisted of modest apartment buildings with 6 to 20 units each on three or four floors without an elevator. Walk-ups were built in large numbers after 1950 in Montréal and its suburbs. This model would predominate in new housing construction until the late 1960s (Divay and Gaudreau, 1984), partly in response to the severe housing shortage which raged after the Second World War, and especially to accommodate the growing number of smaller households with few or no children. Furthermore, many households could not afford to own their own home (see Chapter 6).

Consequently, the suburbs spreading around Montréal did not simply consist of single-family housing, and the proportion of tenants remained higher than in other Canadian cities (see Table 6.2). Apartment buildings were in fact a common feature in Montréal and the surrounding suburbs after 1920. But at that time, they were built to address the needs of young, middle-class singles and couples. Again in this case, the early prototypes for this model were designed for the bourgeoisie. The city's first apartment-hotel, the Sherbrooke, dates back to 1889. Located on the prestigious street of the same name, it offered quality accommodation and a range of services (a restaurant, laundry, etc.) in the North American tradition. Over the following decades, this type of building, usually no more than 15 storeys high, proliferated throughout Montréal and its wealthier suburbs, initially attracting English Canadians and Eastern European immigrants, and later, middle-class French-Canadian households. These buildings accounted for nearly half of all housing units built in Montréal from 1921 to 1951 (Choko, 1994). In recent years many have been targeted for conversion to condominiums – an issue we will discuss in Chapter 6.

Another project, this time a housing cooperative, begun in 1956, presaged a much larger cooperative housing movement that was to emerge in the 1970s and 1980s under a federally funded programme. The Saint-Léonard-de-Port-Maurice project, which built 655 single-family homes in a suburb north-east of central Montréal without any government funding, succeeded in establishing a network of cooperative services (building materials and hardware store, restaurant, grocery, distribution of heating oil, Caisse populaire (credit union), etc.) to meet the day-to-day needs of its members (Collin, 1998a). Based on solidarity and community building principles, the co-op soon extended its services to the entire population of Saint-Léonard, namely through involvement in local politics and the founding of a local newspaper centred on the needs of the local community as a whole. However, in spite of community development success stories such as this one, the co-op movement in the 1970s and 1980s was oriented more toward building management than to housing construction (see Chapter 6).

Projects such as these demonstrate the vitality of civil society in Montréal in the 1940s and 1950s, although this period is generally described as one of 'darkness', when Québec supposedly remained a traditional, conservative society dominated by the Church and controlled by foreign capital. But modernity did not suddenly burst upon Québec in the early 1960s. As we have seen, it was germinating well before then, although political events in part catalysed this transition: for example, the election of the Liberals in Québec helped to launch the Quiet Revolution (an expression first used by a Toronto journalist) in the 1960s. Another catalysing event was the 1956 election of Jean Drapeau, a reformer who would soon turn into a famous city boss.

A BOSS AND HIS VISIONS OF A CORPORATE CITY

The mature modern period of urban architecture and development in Montréal corresponds to some extent to the rise of the corporate city and of a 'growth machine', but with twists and turns unique to the Montréal situation, as we shall see. Both concepts relate to a shift away from undertaking urban land development in a highly speculative unorganized urban land market to operating in a more orderly and orchestrated environment (Roweis, 1981; Roweis and Scott, 1978). For Molotch (1976), post-Second World War American redevelopment and inner city revitalization campaigns led to alliances of developers, investors, planning professionals and municipal and federal politicians. These alliances operated as 'urban growth machines' that coordinated, among other things, land clearances and consolidation, downtown development planning and private and public sector financing for large scale projects. This was the 'corporate city' *par excellence* (Gordon, 1978; Reid, 1991).

The scale of the urban development projects during this time had become so large that forming coalitions of interest groups was the only way to ensure their successful completion. But rationalizing urban space for production, circulation and consumption for a newly emerging reconfigured corporate society is highly problematic and expensive, requiring the costly destruction and reconstruction of the city's physical infrastructure (Roweis and Scott, 1978; Harvey, 1990: 232). However, such projects have the added advantage of putting the city on the international map, primarily through the construction of striking modern architectural structures, mass transit systems and the hosting of international events. These vehicles for urban redevelopment increase the city's attractiveness to national and international investors and travellers. In Montréal's case, the need to develop a large tract of centrally located publicly held land and the election of a widely trusted and visionary mayor with broad-based support over a period of more than 25 years enabled the Montréal variant of the corporate city to unfold, along with its international reputation. This mayor was Jean Drapeau.

Mayor Drapeau would oversee the transformation of Montréal's downtown core from the mid-1950s right through to the mid-1980s, almost without interruption: during this time, except for the years between 1957 and 1960, he was repeatedly re-elected with overwhelming majorities. A visionary yet authoritative figure, he played a key role in the city's development, which benefited from his determination to promote major projects. Underlying his every action was the vision of Montréal as a world-renowned modern metropolis. He thus welcomed foreign expertise and capital in order to transform the city's downtown into an avant-garde central business district, while orchestrating a major overhaul of the city's traffic networks (pedestrian, motor vehicle and mass transit) and firmly directing projects designed to attract international tourism to Montréal. Corporations profited from their consequent ability to reduce their risk exposure but Drapeau's, at times, extremely liberal and, at times, strongly interventionist policies, while meeting with considerable success at some levels, were also resounding failures at others. For instance, the mayor, an ardent nationalist, was unable to implement a viable economic pole for the francophone business class in the eastern downtown area.

Yet in his quest for a modern city, he ignored an entire segment of Montréal's social reality. Although the 1960s were still marked by euphoric growth, the downturn that began in the 1970s further deteriorated living conditions for the poor and brought to light the important drawbacks and sociocultural shortcomings associated with this growth-at-all-costs policy. Finally, one of his last grandiose projects, the 1976 Olympic games is still being paid off by Montréal taxpayers; and this for an event he said would be self-financing! Although the corporate city is premised on capitalist ventures in an organized market environment, and this being achieved through growth machine coalitions, Mayor Drapeau, as well as some private developers and most definitely public agencies, soon realized that time and space were not totally organizable and that growth machine coalitions could dissolve in midstream development. By the end of the 1970s, the slowing of growth and mounting opposition, especially by middle-class groups, obliged him to modify his vision of urban development, to reform his political machine and modernize the municipal administration, clearing the way for the transition from a corporate to a more progressive urban regime.

Modernization of the downtown core

In the 1950s, Montréal's downtown was still fairly modest with its business and financial district still mostly situated along and near to St James Street, and its skyscrapers typically overlooking Victorian squares. But after a 20-year metamorphosis, the downtown core would resemble the central business district of other North American cities. However, unlike so many of its American counterparts, but like a number of other Canadian cities (Goldberg and Mercer, 1986), Montréal's downtown also remained a lively, densely populated area (Figure 4.5) – and a veritable neighbourhood. Nevertheless, this dual nature, emphasized in the urban master plan the city adopted in 1992 (Ville de Montréal, 1993), was not planned as a coordinated effort. The same is true of the immense 'underground city' that is one of present-day Montréal's most distinctive features – to which we will return shortly. Drapeau was not a good planner, and much was left to the private sector. Nevertheless, under his rule, Montréal was transformed into a major modern city. It now boasted a remarkable Métro system; 'superblocks' (the new 'places' of the modern city) proliferated, and, as we shall see, experiments were launched with three-dimensional development, where open spaces and public areas are seen as structural elements of the urban form.

The new 'places' of international architecture   Until the 1950s, Montréal's skyscrapers remained fairly conservative in design. A municipal by-law had limited their height to ten floors until 1927 (see Figure 2.3), after which a number of high-quality – although not very innovative – structures appeared, including the Art-Deco-influenced Aldred Building (1929) near Notre-Dame Church, the Beaux-Arts-style Royal Bank Building (1927–28), and the Sun Life Building completed in 1933 (at the time the tallest building in the British Empire, Figure 3.19). It was only in the late 1950s that a truly international style of architecture emerged. It was then that international design, international finance and international developers were called in by local corporate interests to begin the era of construction of modern architectural forms in Montréal.

The first and most important project in the development of Montréal's contemporary downtown core was the construction of Place Ville-Marie, completed in 1962, on the site of a former Renaissance Revival home surrounded by an English garden. This cruciform complex, similar in shape to Pittsburgh's Gateway Center (built by the same developer, Webb and Knapp), would revolutionize urban design in Canada due to its multilevel structure, with each level devoted to a particular type of traffic (pedestrian, motor vehicle, rail). Moreover, different types of activities (office, retail, transport) were integrated within a superblock that replaced the traditional street grid. The building of this huge complex was made possible in part by the fact that a large central property (three blocks adding up to nine hectares) belonged to a single owner, the Canadian National Railway (CNR), a crown corporation. As we mentioned earlier, the Canadian Northern Railway Company, which was developing the new Town of Mount Royal on the other side of the mountain, had purchased the downtown property in order to build a train station in the heart of Montréal, which it intended to link to its new residential development by digging a tunnel through the mountain. In the late 1920s, a plan – similar to the 1950s concept inspired by New York's Rockefeller Center – had already recommended adding office buildings and space for retail businesses to the train station. The Depression interrupted the project, although the train station was completed in 1938. Later on, the Queen Elizabeth Hotel was built over the station, but the rest of

FIGURE 3.19   Place Ville-Marie and the Sun Life Building in the late 1960s, viewed from above; McTavish reservoir and part of McGill University in foreground. Reproduced by permission from the Archives of the Ville de Montréal

the site remained for many years a gaping hole. In 1955, representatives of the CNR asked the American developer William Zeckendorf to develop this portion of the site. He met with four local backers of the project, one the head of the CNR, two others from the private sector and, the fourth being Jean Drapeau, the new mayor of Montréal, whom he characterized as a 'political Hercules' (Zeckendorf, 1970: 167). Financing came from New York and London as well from Canadian sources, and resulted in the creation of the real estate giant, Trizec Corporation. Preparations began by involving the now-famous architect, Ieoh Ming Pei, and Webb and Knapp's own town planner to prepare a development plan for the complex.

The multifunctional complex designed by Pei in association with Montréal architects Affleck, Desbarats, Dimakopoulos and Lebensold, includes office space (3530 square metres per floor in a tower rising to 42 floors), a shopping gallery of some 150 shops, parking levels and the CN tracks, as well as an outdoor public plaza, which is unfortunately often windswept and thus rather uninviting (Marsan, 1981). This combination of office space and shopping galleries would be featured in most of the major projects that followed not only in Montréal but in other Canadian cities. Place Ville-Marie (Figure 3.19), until recently Montréal's highest building, would also help turn the newly inaugurated Dorchester Boulevard since renamed Boulevard René-Lévesque into a central artery for the city's new downtown. But most of all, the construction of Place Ville-Marie was to become the key element in the development of the biggest underground city in the world, as we will see later on. All in all, not only did it initiate Montréal's participation in modern architecture's quest for the heavens at a time when Montréal was still nominally perceived as the metropolis of Canada, but it was also instrumental in the exploration of a third urban dimension, the underground, for urban development purposes. The building remains to this day a major landmark in the Montréal landscape.

Throughout the 1960s, other well-known architects also worked with local firms to develop the new central business district. The modernist-influenced American firm Skidmore, Owings and Merrill advised architects Greenspoon, Freedlander and Dunne in their design for the Canadian Industries Limited Building (now called the Royal Trust Building), completed in 1959. The Stock Exchange Tower (1963–66), praised by architectural critics for its elegance, was designed by the Italian architect Moretti and the engineer Nervi. This project was undertaken by the (Italian) Società Immobiliare with Belgian financing and was projected to include three towers. The project had to be scaled back to one tower when the developer was not able to sign up enough long-term tenants. Zeckendorf (1970) argues that the project was too costly and the location inappropriate. Rather than building in the new uptown district near to Peel Street or University Avenue and Dorchester Boulevard they chose to develop land situated down the hill at the perimeter of the old financial district. It would take another 30 years before most of the original property was developed. On the western edge of downtown, two significant development projects were undertaken next to the Montréal Forum sporting and entertainment building, Plaza Alexis Nehon and Westmount Square. The internationally renowned Mies Van der Rohe drafted the plans for Westmount Square in the purest tradition of the international style. In the late 1980s, renovation of the underground shopping gallery in this complex prompted groups interested in the city's heritage to heatedly debate the need to preserve . . . modern architecture. Twenty years later, the city would gain other skyscrapers of considerable architectural merit, not the least of which is one of the most recent, the IBM-Marathon Building completed in 1993, designed by well-known American architects Kohn, Pederson and Fox, in collaboration with the local firm Larose, Petrucci et Associés.

Local architects also helped to modernize the downtown core. Place Bonaventure, built in 1966–67 near Place Ville-Marie, employed the same design principles of a multifunctional complex linked to a hotel and various types of circulation networks. Shortly after, Complexe Desjardins – whose development represents a particular and symbolic case, to which we return later in this chapter – followed in the same tradition, but also represented a

FIGURE 3.20 Complexe Desjardins: the interior concourse is being used for an exhibition. (Damaris Rose)

further contribution to Montréal's inventory of urban forms. Its 'basilaire' (an open central area surrounded by a multilevel shopping promenade) broke with the tradition of earlier superblocks, cut off from their external environments. Here, large glass surfaces provided a visual link from the interior to some of the building's surroundings. And the enormous atrium soon became a lively indoor public gathering place featuring significant cultural events as well as semi-commercial exhibits (Figure 3.20), so successful that it signalled the rediscovery of the importance of public spaces, even enclosed ones, for urban sociability. The Maison des Coopérants, built in 1988 in a neo-Gothic style, included an outdoor public garden in the form of a cloister, as well as linking to the previously mentioned Les Promenades de la Cathédrale shopping concourse, while the 1000 de la Gauchetière Building included an indoor garden and skating rink.

Overall, these superblocks embody the triumph of filled spaces over open spaces, to use Camillo Sitte's expression (Sitte, 1979). But in the 1980s, there was a renewed emphasis on city streets as structural spaces. The battle over McGill College Avenue became a turning point in this respect, especially since it coincided with a new, postmodernist shift in Montréal architecture. The forms of the 1980s would be marked by the rediscovery of the merits of integrating architecture into its environment, an environment that modernism in part chose to ignore, and by the harmonious combination of new forms and new uses for heritage buildings. This rediscovery is part

FIGURE 3.21 McGill-College Avenue, looking from Place Ville-Marie towards McGill University, at dusk showing winter illuminations. (Damaris Rose)

of the defining features of what is called post-modernism in architecture and urban planning (Beauregard, 1989; Dear, 1986; Harvey, 1990; Rossi, 1981). The Maison Alcan is probably one of the first and best examples of a well-designed postmodernist building. Architect Ray Affleck, who had previously designed a number of successful modernist structures, together with architects Peter Rose, Peter Lanken and Julia Gersovitch, paved the way for an important new direction in Montréal's architectural landscape: the Alcan building, carefully aligned with other structures on Sherbrooke Street, is a combination of heritage buildings (four Victorian homes and the former Berkeley Hotel), two new wings (which, appropriately enough for the headquarters of a major aluminium producer, feature aluminium cladding!), and several public spaces (an atrium, a piazza and pedestrian walkways). This remarkable ensemble contrasts sharply with the often uninspired architectural forms postmodernism would take elsewhere in the downtown core, particularly along McGill College Avenue (Figure 3.21). But the re-development of this street in the heart of the business district merits closer examination, since it typified the urban planning controversies that flared up during Drapeau's administration. But to do so, we must go back to the beginnings of the Place Ville-Marie project.

The original 1920s plan had already conceived of a grand perspective linking the CN station to the elegant forms of the McGill University campus, set against the greenery of the mountain. After the Second World War, the idea re-emerged of a vista over a site still then dominated by the trenches dug for the rail tracks running under the mountain. This concept of a Montréal-style 'Champs Élysées' warranted the widening of McGill College Avenue and later, the careful arrangement of the office towers and shopping centres along the avenue in order to preserve the view. But in 1984, Mayor Drapeau gave his support to a project to build a large commercial and cultural complex (including a hall for the Montréal Symphony Orchestra) on the northwestern corner of St Catherine Street and McGill College Avenue, a complex that would link up with the then Simpson department store on St Catherine Street. If carried out, this project would, however, have obstructed the view of the mountain for this part of the downtown area. Yielding to the fierce criticism raised by the issue, the developer agreed to organize public hearings on the urban design of the complex, the result of which was a recommendation to preserve the view and to develop the avenue accordingly. The project for the complex was abandoned, as were many other subsequent projects subjected to public hearings. So the avenue and its eye-catching view survived, although the examples of postmodern architecture standing on either side of the vista scarcely live up to the grandeur of the Champs Élysées!

Accommodating mobility: Montréal's Métro system Encouraging the spatial mobility of individuals is one of the leitmotifs of modern urban planning. To this end, the modern city has produced new types of specialized places and thus new types of urban behaviour. The transformation of Montréal's urban fabric throughout the 1950s and 1960s effectively illustrates these processes, especially in regard to differences between above-ground and underground uses. The large complexes and buildings that have profoundly altered the city's skyline are in fact part of a new circulation network, which has been completely reorganized by the separation of the various types of traffic. However, this new network does not integrate too well with the traditional system of multifunctional streets, which for a time appeared to be seriously threatened. Again, although Montréal's traditional urban fabric has not been spared by the ravages wreaked by modernism, damage has apparently been limited. But this owes not so much to careful planning as to 'planning by nonplanning'. The preservation of Old Montréal is a convincing example of this.

In many North American cities, one of the first examples of the spoils of modernism was the construction of costly and spatially divisive above-ground expressways to re-route traffic away from the downtown area. Some cities are now remedying the resulting situation by demolishing these expressways. Boston, for example, is currently attempting to make up for the unfortunate mistake of building an expressway separating the down-town area from the waterfront. Montréal almost made the same mistake when it was faced with the need to reorganize its downtown core by improving traffic flow, building high-rise office towers and strengthening the commercial centre.

Old Montréal lies between the new downtown and the waterfront. The area had been more or less isolated by the shift of economic activity towards the north-west, as we will see, and, because it was generally overlooked by developers, it had not been significantly altered. It would appear that Old Montréal was largely saved by the relocation of the downtown business district, though other factors played an important role as well. One plan for Old Montréal, prepared by Jacques Gréber in 1953, called for the preservation of certain buildings – and an expressway along de la Commune Street that would run right in front of Bonsecours Market. In 1958 another plan reiterated the idea of an elevated, eight-lane expressway. It was the Port of Montréal authorities who most strongly opposed this plan in 1960, fearing the impact the expressway would have on port activities. A comprehensive traffic study (which also looked at the feasibility of a subway system) was later supported, funded by several large corporations. The first recommendation made by this study was to rehabilitate Old Montréal. The study also recommended using the natural terrace located further to the west as the site for the proposed expressway and also building an underground autoroute through the downtown area. The plan thus respected the original morphology of the city, and Old Montréal was to be spared as a historic district (it being so declared in 1964). The below-ground expressway was built, although taking a slightly different route from that first proposed; however, it was never fully covered over, which created dead spaces between Old Montréal and downtown. Thus, resolving one problem contributed to the creation of another. The Cité internationale Project (see Chapter 5) is striving to bridge this gap in the urban fabric.

The main element in the reorganization of downtown traffic flow, however, was not the construction of expressways, but the realization of an old dream: to build a Métro system. By 1951 the City of Montréal's population had reached the one million mark (see Figure 6.1), so it was now large enough to justify the construction of a subway system. Mayor Drapeau, who for a long time felt that the notion of rapid mass transit was outdated, was eventually convinced of the major impact this kind of infrastructure would have on making Montréal a modern metropolis. In 1960 and without any outside help, he embarked on this metropolitan-scale project (the provincial government would only begin to contribute to the investment costs after 1973): unlike most systems, it would be completely underground and would use the French technology of Métro cars on rubber tyres, and the city planning department recommended giving each of the 22 stations a distinctive character by having each designed by a different architect. The proposed routes for the two main lines had also been the object of discussion for some time. An east–west line would connect the main landmarks of the downtown area, but the Métro would run under secondary streets to facilitate its integration into the urban fabric and also allow for enough working room during its construction and, subsequently, to enable bus lines to connect with the stations without worsening traffic problems on main arteries (Marsan, 1981). The same principle was used for the U-shaped line linking the city's north and south sectors. A third line connected the central city to the South Shore via a tunnel under the St Lawrence River, with a stop on the islands which were to host the 1967 World's Fair. (The fair would in fact accelerate the construction of the Métro.) Later on, a fourth east–west line servicing the north-west side of the mountain ensured complete coverage of the central Montréal area.

The route chosen for the Métro was for a time criticized because it essentially focused on providing access to downtown businesses, i.e. it was using public money to provide the latter with customers rather than facilitating access to the city's disadvantaged, working-class districts (Limonchik, 1982). In any case, the construction of the Métro system clearly stimulated vigorous development in the downtown area. Yet it could have had a greater impact had it been integrated into an urban planning strategy in concentration with the private sector, and aimed at increasing the density of the areas surrounding the Métro stations for residential or commercial functions. The original hub station Berri-UQAM, where the three lines intersect, is located east of the Central Business District, partly because of Mayor Drapeau's efforts to spur the development of this section of downtown. More closely associated with the francophone community, this area could have attracted more interest than it actually did. But in those years, economic power was still largely in the hands of the anglophone community, leaving little opportunity for private investment in terms of actual urban development in the eastern part of the city. As it turned out, development around the hub station began with the construction of the main campus of the Université du Québec à Montréal with the Métro nested in its midst. This development may soon be followed by another major public investment, La Grande Bibliothèque du Québec (Mega-Library) which will combine provincial and municipal collections.

The technology chosen for the Métro has proven quite effective. The cars are fairly short, making it easier for passengers to enter and exit. The use of rubber tyres means that the trains are very quiet and can brake more quickly, although it prohibits any above-ground extension of the system. The Bombardier corporation, which built the trains, later exported this technology throughout the world. But the most remarkable aspect of the Métro is undoubtedly the architectural variety and quality of the stations. Each one is different, designed to suit the destination it embodies, and represents a veritable work of architecture (Figure 3.22), further embellished by a series of public artworks. Recent renovations have tried to capture the evolution of these neighbourhoods served by certain stations – for instance, the inclusion

FIGURE 3.22 Inside the McGill Métro station – Montréal's busiest. (Damaris Rose)

of rainbow murals in the station serving the 'Gay Village'. Durable, multi-coloured ceramics enliven the atmosphere of numerous stations. After the opening of the Snowdon/Saint-Michel line, which finally provided a direct link to the Université de Montréal, the stations serving this and the three other universities were renamed in honour of these important Montréal institutions. Since it was first built, the system has grown significantly: it currently includes multiple hubs and 65 stations spread out over 65 kilometres. On an architectural and urban planning level, the success of Montréal's Métro is undeniable, both above and below ground.

The underground city The Métro's success did not stop there: its construction led to the development of another network, that of the indoor or underground city. Another case of unplanned development, as Charney observes in an article evocatively entitled 'The Montrealness of Montreal':

> The innovation of pedestrian networks in the 60s was less a case of a deliberate plan than of the deliberate use of existing opportunities: the open space of an excavation created by a train tunnel, as the site of Place Ville-Marie and the slope of the land falling away from the building's podium as a continuous lower-level precinct protected from the harsh winter climate of the city. (Charney, 1980: 300)

This underground pedestrian network (Figure 3.23) connecting the main commercial complexes in the downtown area was originally a by-product

Sherbrooke Street

Peel   McGill   Place des Arts

Saint-Laurent   Berri-UQAM

Sainte-Catherine Street

René-Lévesque Blvd

Bonaventure   Square Victoria   Place d'Armes   Champ-de-Mars

Old Montréal

1 - Cours Mont-Royal (MC*)
2 - Place Montréal Trust (SC*)
3 - Eaton Centre (SC*)
4 - Promenades de la Cathédrale (SC*)
5 - Place Ville-Marie (MC*)
6 - Central Station
7 - Place Bonaventure (MC*)
8 - 1000 de Lagauchetière (OT*)
9 - Windsor Station

10 - Molson Centre (Sports Stadium)
11 - Complexe Desjardins (MC*)
12 - Complexe Guy-Favreau (OT*)
13 - Convention Centre
14 - World Trade Centre
15 - Stock Exchange

  * SC : Shopping Centre
    OT : Office Tower
    MC : Mixed-use Complex

● Metro Station
— Underground Pedestrian Links
■ Other Buildings

0   500 m

FIGURE 3.23   Montréal's Underground City: schematic map showing main links

of Place Ville-Marie which had been linked to the train station by a pedestrian passageway lined with boutiques. The expansion of this network was subsequently spurred by the Métro's development as, at that time, the municipal administration encouraged real estate developers to connect their buildings with Métro stations, while ensuring that Métro exits also connected with public areas via public rights-of-way through these buildings.

In the 1980s, the growing number of large shopping developments such as Place Montréal Trust, Les Promenades de la Cathédrale and the Eaton Centre, influenced by the design of suburban shopping centres but linked to one another via this network, resulted in the creation of an immense, multipolar, indoor shopping complex connected to the Métro stations at either end. The interconnection of several buildings in local networks around Métro stations, and the subsequent inter-linking of these networks, led to the emergence of the underground city as an urban unit spanning much of the downtown core. Given the complexity and the extent of this network, and because it refers as much to facilities above as below ground level, the term 'underground city' as adopted in common language falls a bit short in expressing the importance of these installations (Brown, 1992).

Nevertheless, it has been preferred by authors over more appropriate terms, such as 'indoor' or 'interior city', perhaps because of the futuristic image associated with 'underground'.

In the scope and connectivity of its network, Montréal has moved ahead of other cities where moderately-sized indoor developments, presently dispersed across the city map, have of late spread their interconnecting tentacles. Montréal's indoor network is currently the largest in the world: extending for 31 kilometres, it links the main downtown commercial establishments, hotels, office buildings, cultural and sports facilities and the three downtown universities. In 1991, it was estimated to serve 80 per cent of the office buildings and 35 per cent of the stores in the downtown area (Besner, 1991). While it is renowned for providing a comfortable and secure environment for its users, a sense of aesthetics and spatial orientation is often lacking in these indoor spaces, at times designed primarily to meet the needs of retail commerce (for example, non-contiguous escalators forcing maximum pedestrian exposure to shopping galleries on each level of Place Montréal Trust on McGill College Avenue). But this has not stopped the network from becoming a major tourist attraction.

In its morphological features, the underground city is revolutionizing the design of multilevel public spaces. Against the ordered vision of neatly separated traffic flows, the built reality of Montréal's downtown introduces an unconventional model of urban interconnection (Christozov, 1995). The theoretical assignment of the surface-and-above to the city's people and of the sub-surface to the city's infrastructure succumbed to a massive infiltration of civic uses, and hence of people, into the underground, although the obstacles posed by major conduits sometimes led to tortuous diversions of pedestrian tunnels. From down there, through corridors and passageways, the public invades the interior of privately owned buildings whose common areas accordingly expand; these grow from isolated civic addresses to embody elements of a comprehensive city unit, but one in which pedestrians could become a captive market (Hopkins, 1996). Montréal's indoor urban realm raises important questions about the frontier between private and public space, far beyond the usual blueprint theories concerning the merchandising of public space at the expense of its democratic use (Carr et al., 1992).

The first public discussion to specifically focus on the nature, uses and impact of the underground city was held on the occasion of the drafting of the city's first master plan in the early 1990s, some 30 years after the opening of the first underground passageways. Should expansion of the network be curtailed or encouraged? Two main areas of concern were raised, the first regarding the network's impact on the vitality of outdoor public spaces, and the second regarding the competition between suburban shopping centres and the downtown shopping area. A few years earlier, a number of city planners had criticized this indoor network which they saw as an unnatural way for people to escape the vicissitudes of winter. There was frequent reference to Stockholm (a city with an average annual temperature similar to Montréal's but winters not nearly as cold), where the harsh climate had apparently failed to dampen the city's lively outdoor street life. Others, such as the architects and urban planners of the Livable Winter Cities Association, advocated designs and techniques to adapt urban forms to cold climates, while avoiding excessive protection against winter weather (Pressman, 1985). Several Canadian cities have come up with various strategies to increase indoor pedestrian traffic, ranging from enclosed aerial walkways some 15 metres above street level (skywalks) to underground networks and malls, including atriums and galleria (Gappert, 1987). Over time, planners have learned to work with these indoor networks, which have in some cases proven to be relatively 'human' places, even encouraging new forms of public sociability.

In Montréal, Complexe Desjardin's huge 'agora', (which recently opened its facades to St Catherine Street), surrounded by multilevel shopping and service galleries, played an important role in shaping a new attitude towards indoor spaces. Their truly public nature had always been somewhat ambiguous, given their regulation and surveillance by private property-owners (Brown, 1992), but they were now seen as livable, friendly environments, in fact well before postmodern critics denounced the privatization/commercialization of the public domain in the 'Corporate City' (Sorkin, 1992). We have seen how the intermingling of the public and private domains in the underground city has yielded new dynamics in the definition of spaces, and ultimately an expansion and differentiation of the public realm. Surprisingly, the vitality of the outdoor network of streets does not seem to have greatly suffered from the proliferation of climate-controlled indoor networks, to the point where some observers now speak of complementarity rather than competition between the two types of spaces (Brown, 1992). But the vitality of these two types of networks is in turn largely due to the renewed interest in public sociability in downtown Montréal, where outdoor cafés and restaurants are increasingly spilling over on to public sidewalks, not to mention the growing popularity of many public places such as parks and squares. It is also owing to the persistent social diversity of downtown, which remains a non-exclusive space very different from the segregrative urban fabric of many cities (Caldeira, 1996).

The other theme in the debate on the underground city concerned the danger of a serious commercial decline in the downtown area, triggered by the profusion of suburban shopping malls. Between the late 1980s and mid-1990s, retail business downtown was indeed showing signs of drying up, especially along St Catherine Street, giving rise to the looming threat of an increasingly deserted downtown core, as seen in many American inner cities. In a society in transition (a growing number of women in the workforce, rising consumerism, changing lifestyles, etc.), would the indoor network hasten such a decline, or on the contrary increasingly counteract competition from the suburbs?

As it turned out, the late 1990s witnessed a major revival of St Catherine Street, supported by a recovering economy, infrastructure improvements and the increasing 'savvy' of local merchants in providing different and more specialized kinds of stores than the chains that dominate the underground shopping galleries. The second scenario seems to be closer to reality at present, although it is obviously difficult to pinpoint such a trend with any certainty. In any case, downtown Montréal remains an inviting destination for shoppers and strollers (Figure 3.13).

Development of the downtown core: urban planning and linguistic issues

Signs of another facet of the Quiet Revolution – the emancipation of French Québec, in its quest to regain control over its economy by developing a state apparatus – could also be found in the transformations occurring in Montréal's urban landscape. After the building of Place Ville-Marie, the development of the central business district remained largely under the influence of the anglophone business elite. Or, at least, that is how the situation was perceived by francophones who, it is important to note, for many years represented a minority in the municipal administration and in professional domains such as architecture and urban planning. Increasing the influence of the francophone elite in the downtown area had been one of Mayor Drapeau's objectives since the mid-1950s. This aspect of the 'national question' is important in order to fully understand the gradual relocation of the downtown core from the beginning of the century, and that ultimately led to the fragmented layout of today's downtown.

The epicentre of Montréal's downtown area is McGill College Avenue (see Figures 3.21 and 3.23). This modern centre is some 2 km away from the city's initial downtown around St James Street in Old Montréal. In 1909, when the Province of Québec's Association of Architects prepared its first plan for the city core, the boulevards designed to satisfy the aims of civic beautification were centred around Victoria Square, outside the historic district (Germain, 1985: 112). The establishment of the first department stores along St Catherine Street – Morgan's and Ogilvy's in the 1890s, Eaton's in 1927 and Simpson's (replacing Murphy's) in 1929 – where several high-status retail businesses were already located (including Birks and Goodwin's, the latter refurbished to accommodate Eaton's), hastened the advance of the downtown sector towards the north. In the past few years, the municipal administration has attempted to re-establish a certain continuity between Old Montréal and the central business district, especially with its project for 'La Cité internationale', an area specifically aimed at attracting headquarters of large international organizations (see

FIGURE 3.24   Old and new façades in Old Montréal: The World Trade Centre
and the Intercontinental Hotel (left). Reproduced by permission
from Marc-Aurèle Marsan

Chapter 5). The World Trade Centre (Figure 3.24), built in 1987–91 on the
edge of Old Montréal, was designed to provide, in one integrated site,
all the infrastructures required by such organizations, including the prestigious Inter-Continental Hotel (Figure 3.24). The architects (from ARCOP,
Provencher, Roy and Gersovitch) have combined the conservation and
restoration of heritage buildings with the construction of new structures, to
form a 130 000 square metre multifunctional complex, integrating the
historic ruelle des Fortifications as a pedestrian thoroughfare (Marsan, 1991:
422–423).

The downtown area had also begun to extend eastwards. While
anglophone-controlled retail businesses had located in the west, francophones would develop theirs further east, around the main commercial
artery of St Catherine Street, with the Dupuis Frères (1880) department store
at the corner of St Hubert Street exemplifying this trend. During the lengthy
reign of Mayor Drapeau, a number of projects would be put forward,
without success, to develop a francophone pole in the downtown area east
of St Lawrence Boulevard, extending from Place des Arts (built in 1963). The
need for this kind of development clearly became a concern from the 1950s
onwards, but also raised the issue of the city's overall development, as
we will see. In briefly turning back to this period, we will also discuss how
some of the ideas later associated with the Quiet Revolution were already
emerging.

During the 1950s, at the time when the first urban renewal project, later called Les Habitations Jeanne-Mance, was launched, a historic debate would bring to light the contrasting visions of development for the downtown sector. The National Housing Act encouraged the elimination of slum areas and the building of low-cost housing on such sites. The Act would later be amended to permit other uses for these areas, providing for the construction of Complexe Desjardins. But during the 1950s, the housing crisis was so severe that the construction of low-cost housing became a crucial concern. Proponents of liberalism in the housing sector would, however, find a valuable ally in the city's new mayor, Jean Drapeau. He felt that the downtown core was not an appropriate place for housing, especially for the large families common in French Canada at that time. He advocated a residential development further away from the city centre, the Domaine Saint-Sulpice. Besides, he had other ambitions for central Montréal, especially for this specific part of the downtown area. The building of Place des Arts was already planned for a location near the Dozois site (named for the municipal affairs minister at that time, who favoured the low-rent housing project), and a site was also being sought for the projected Radio-Canada complex. Mayor Drapeau envisioned a 'Cité des Ondes' (a centre for radio and other telecommunications) that would foster the development of a mainly francophone pole in the eastern downtown area. The building of public housing on the Dozois site, he feared, would erect a concrete barrier between the city's east and west, and ultimately isolate the francophone sector.

In 1957 a journalist summarized the issues underlying this project as follows:

> Regrettably, no decision has yet been made as to the approach Montréal should take to development. If the city had a master urban plan, we would know if we are heading toward a gradual strengthening of the business and administrative centre and the displacement of residential neighbourhoods toward outlying areas and the suburbs, or if Montréal is destined to become a city divided into districts, each of which would be largely self-sufficient, with its own secondary centre for business, services, administration, etc. Drapeau's plan would seem to correspond to the first kind of development, whereas Mr Dozois' project is better fitted to the second means of promoting the city's growth. (Conrad Langlois, *La Patrie*, October 20, 1957, our translation)

The Habitations Jeanne-Mance project was ultimately built, as Drapeau lost the battle over the Dozois plan.

This development would however represent the first and last large-scale, low-rent housing project to be built in the downtown area. Subsequent development of this area was mainly promoted by institutions, including the most important project, the building of the campus of the Université du Québec à Montréal, Québec's first French public university, begun in 1979.

The campus counterbalanced the strong pole of attraction represented by McGill University in the heart of downtown. A second anglophone university, Sir George Williams (later to be renamed Concordia University), had also located in the city's downtown area, several decades after McGill's founding. It is interesting to note that Montréal's largest university, the Université de Montréal, initially located near Old Montréal, moved to Côte-des-Neiges in the late 1920s, around the time of the construction of St Joseph's Oratory. Côte-des-Neiges, then a quasi-rural village originally conceived as a *côte* development, is today one of the many neighbourhood centres that are turning the Montréal area into an increasingly multipolar region. Will Dozois's vision ultimately triumph over that of Drapeau? Possibly, but it still remains unclear?

The building of Complexe Desjardins, across from Place des Arts, from 1971 to 1976, to which we referred earlier, took on a special, symbolic importance. Financed by the Mouvement Desjardins, one of the financial institutions that best exemplified French Canadians' successful penetration into their province's economic sphere, the location of the complex had in part been chosen to offset the attraction exerted by the western pole of downtown, and its association with the anglophone community (although Complexe Desjardins is in fact situated west of the symbolic linguistic dividing line, St Lawrence Boulevard).

If Mayor Drapeau did not succeed in reversing the tendency of the downtown business and financial pole to develop primarily in the west, his predictions for the 'Cité des Ondes' project proved relatively accurate. In recent years, the south-east sector of downtown has become the site of a remarkable concentration of major radio and television broadcasting organizations (Radio-Canada, Télé-Québec, Télé-Métropole), and a cluster of smaller, associated communications enterprises.

Expo 67 and the Olympic Games: bread or circuses?

Mayor Drapeau clearly devoted a great deal of energy to two mega-projects inspired by the same strategy, namely to attract a large international tourism clientele to Montréal with important events such as the World's Fair and the Olympic Games. The 1967 Man and His World exhibition represented a turning point in the city's history: during the six-month-long event, some 50 million visitors flocked to Montréal, some of whom would stay on to swell the ranks of the city's growing immigrant population. For Montrealers, Expo '67 also meant a new openness to the world, sustained by feelings of hope and confidence in the future prompted by the wave of modernization sweeping through the city and Québec society as a whole during the 1960s. The plan of the exhibition site testifies to the audacity of its designers: it was spectacularly located on a group of islands in the middle of the St Lawrence River – some of which, like Île Sainte-Hélène, had been enlarged and others, like Île Notre-Dame, artificially created – linked by a rail transport system. Drapeau also saw this as an opportunity to demolish one of its poorest neighbourhoods, Goose Village – situated near to Victoria Bridge – by constructing parking facilities, the main entrance to the exhibition, a broadcast centre and a stadium.

Jointly funded by the three levels of government and co-organized by the federal government and local experts, the exhibition paid its way and proved a memorable success. Several major projects were accelerated for Expo, including the construction of the Métro (one line, involving a tunnel under the river, was specifically designed to provide access to the Expo site) and certain sections of the Bonaventure autoroute (expressway). For years after the exhibition, there was controversy over how to best recycle the site. But its recreational potential gradually became evident, once most of the exhibition pavilions had been demolished. In recent years the site has been redeveloped to include the Parc des Îles, a Formula One race track, a remarkably successful casino on Île Notre-Dame, a public beach, and so on.

The success of the second event was more problematic. Although there was little criticism of the development of the islands for Expo '67, the plans for the Olympic Park generated considerable opposition. The mayor was convinced that great cities need great monuments which would help the citizens to forget their daily misery: 'The ugliness of slums in which people live doesn't matter if we can make them stand wide-eyed in admiration of works of art they don't understand' (Jean Drapeau, cited in Auf der Maur 1976, p. 96).

Obsessed with the idea of giving his city a symbolic monument on the scale of the Eiffel Tower, Mayor Drapeau pushed ahead with a daring architectural concept for the Olympic Stadium, a design that has never proved entirely feasible and that Montrealers are still paying for today. The stadium, with its giant tower attached to a retractable roof (like an umbrella, to use the architect's image), has been a source of controversy for the past 20 years. The design, produced by French architect, Roger Taillibert, was based on technology that had not been tested in the Montréal climate (Marsan, 1994). The retractable roof has repeatedly failed to work properly, and the material it is made of is unsuited to bear the weight of the snow that accumulates on top of it. The problem of the roof is still unresolved, and continues to be an inordinate drain on public funds. This stadium, the costliest ever built, nonetheless remains an elegant and highly visible eastern Montréal landmark (Figure 3.25). Nearby residents have become quite attached to their stadium, despite the ongoing burden it represents for Montréal taxpayers. The Olympic Village also provoked extensive controversy, with its two pyramids of 500 housing units each built on undeveloped green spaces. Located in an area where residents had long been lobbying the city for parks and public housing, it was destined to attract criticism, which did little, however, to deter the mayor.

FIGURE 3.25   Olympic Stadium ('The Big O') from east side of Mount Royal, showing the Plateau Mont-Royal and (middle-distance) the former CPR Angus Shops under redevelopment. (Damaris Rose)

Whereas in 1967 the hosting of the World's Fair marked the culmination of a period of euphoric growth and modernization as Montréal joined the ranks of the world's major cities, the Olympic Games coincided with a time when growth was being questioned and large projects were being assessed in light of the public's overall well-being. The coalition between developers, government and organized labour crumbled when mismanagement, greed, self-interest and accusations of corruption jeopardized the Games as a whole. People were no longer willing to accept fencing around deteriorated areas to keep them from being seen by tourists. The lack of political openness at city hall also fuelled the flames of discontent. The motto the mayor used to counter journalists' questions, to the effect that good deeds make little noise and noise does little good, clearly proved inappropriate when the economic situation transformed the urban development agenda, and citizens' movements, which had remained fairly quiescent since the late 1950s, became increasingly vociferous in their opposition to major development projects.

PRESERVING A CITY OF NEIGHBOURHOODS

Heritage and housing were among the crucial issues opposing developers – whether from the public or the private sector – and citizens. The Quiet

Revolution had produced a new generation of educated, middle-class individuals who took a renewed interest in their city and embraced a number of urban causes (Germain, 1988). They were increasingly involved with the *classes populaires* in urban struggles that would highlight the existence of that 'Other Montréal', hidden from the view of tourists (Hamel, 1995). During the 1970s, a series of controversies gradually forged a new conception of urban planning, quite different from the modernist approach (Germain and Guay, 1985).

These issues came together in one of the first of such controversies, revolving around the Milton-Parc project. It has also remained one of the most important, given the scope of the project (one of the largest cooperative urban renewal projects in North America), the scale of the confrontations, and the extent of the project's impact on planning practices (Helman, 1987). In the late 1950s, a real estate company called Concordia Estates (headed by two former communist activists!) began purchasing land near the downtown area for the purpose of building what they envisioned as no less than a new type of city. Highly permissive zoning by-laws allowed them to draft an ambitious plan for 16 50-floor buildings incorporating housing, a hotel, recreational facilities and retail businesses on a site near McGill University bounded by Pine Avenue and Sainte-Famille, Milton and Hutchison streets, an area which then included six blocks of Victorian homes. The area, once home to well-to-do professionals and merchants, had lost its tranquillity since the building of the Pine-Park interchange as a rapid access route to the downtown area. This neighbourhood soon attracted students who came to live in the now-subdivided former upper-middle-class homes. It was also home to low-income residents, immigrants and elderly people.

In the late 1960s, these socially and linguistically diverse groups joined together to demand improvements to their housing and to oppose the redevelopment of the neighbourhood. In the light of some of their arguments, City of Montréal officials initially refused to allow the developers to proceed. The senior architect, also swayed by the residents' wishes, resigned from the project. But this failed to stop the development, which called for the demolition of 255 homes under the pretext of slum clearance, although these were in fact far from being slum dwellings. The citizens, with the support of local conservationist architects with good connections, formed an association in order to obtain special government grants to cooperatively purchase and renovate a certain number of these homes. By 1972, the homes had not yet been demolished, but after being left to deteriorate did increasingly begin to resemble slums. Confrontation surfaced anew, and as the economic situation also deteriorated, Concordia Estates went bankrupt. Only a third of the area was ultimately demolished. Though the original development plan was scuttled not all renewal in the area was stopped. A greatly scaled-down La Cité complex, comprising three

FIGURE 3.26 Milton-Parc, scene of a celebrated struggle that saved these late 19th century homes from high-rise redevelopment. Towering behind is the La Cité complex. (Damaris Rose)

towers including a hotel, 1350 apartments, an office building and an underground shopping promenade, was constructed.

It was only in the late 1970s, after intervention on the part of some influential individuals, that the Société du patrimoine urbain de Montréal (SPUM, a heritage preservation group) was created and commissioned to renovate the remaining homes (some 600 residential units), integrating them into cooperative and non-profit housing associations, assisted by substantial government subsidies (Figure 3.26). The Canada Mortgage and Housing Corporation acquired the homes in 1979, and subsequently ceded them to the Société pour l'amélioration de Milton-Parc (SAMP), a non-profit neighbourhood association affiliated with SPUM. More than half of the residents returned to live in the renovated housing. A number of rooming houses were preserved as well. Existing local businesses were also integrated into the co-ops via a non-profit corporation.

This collective effort to save a neighbourhood gradually evolved into a veritable model of heritage preservation. Several now well-established conservationist architects started out in the Groupe de ressources techniques de Milton-Parc (this strategy of a 'technical resource group' would subsequently be used in many other neighbourhoods). In the wake of the Milton-Parc saga, the Heritage Montréal foundation was set up in 1975, and continues to play an important political and educational role today in preserving the city's built heritage and assessing the impact of development projects.

What is also very interesting in the La Cité complex today is the 'appropriation' of the shopping promenade by low-to-modest-income locals. It provides an excellent indoor environment for the elderly, for socializing, playing chess, etc. Some of these low-income people are co-op residents. Furthermore, some of the housing units in the private rental high-rises are now rented out to physically disabled people who now have easy access to the shopping centre. In a nice ironic twist, because the La Cité complex has never been very profitable, much of its semi-public space has ended up being rented for low-margin and non-profit uses, increasing its benefits to the local community – even the cinema is now run as a repertory, with very inexpensive admission.

During these same years, other battles were waged on the heritage front, often involving the same actors. The Green Space Association was launched in 1971 as a result of a controversy over a project to build 5000 residential units on a Sherbrooke Street property owned by the Sulpicians. The property was afforded partial protection by zoning by-laws, which did not, however, stop the construction of luxury apartments in an adjacent wooded area about 20 years later. But the most galvanizing event in the history of urban heritage preservation issues was undoubtedly the 1973 demolition of the Van Horne Mansion on Sherbrooke Street, the former home of a major figure in the building of the railways across Canada and thus in the building of the country. The universally decried destruction of this Victorian mansion, one of the few remaining structures from the days of the Golden Square Mile, led to the creation of Save Montréal, a volunteer group that was a precursor to Heritage Montréal.

Heritage Montréal was originally set up and presided over by architect Phyllis Lambert, a leading light in Montréal's heritage preservation movement, who also later founded the Canadian Centre for Architecture, which rapidly acquired a worldwide reputation. The CCA building's harmonious composition integrates the original Victorian mansion that houses it and contemporary architecture (Figure 3.27). The garden facing the building features interesting pieces of public art, constructed forms inspired by typical elements drawn from Montréal's architectural and industrial heritage. All in all, the CCA links past and present, art, architecture and landscape, and celebrates the fusion of place and culture in the urban fabric.

In the early 1970s, extension of the east–west Ville-Marie expressway resulted in the demolition of housing in Montréal's east end, a process that had already begun with the 700 housing units torn down for the building of the Radio-Canada building (Figure 6.4) and its parking areas (Morin, 1987). Such damage to the urban and social fabric of neighbourhoods around the downtown core was done in the name of a series of projects to modernize and revitalize the central city, projects that would eventually lead to other

FIGURE 3.27 Canadian Centre for Architecture, combining the old Shaughnessy House and the new building designed by architect Peter Rose. Reproduced by permission from Alain Laforest

uses for areas once slated for housing. We have already mentioned some of these, including Complexe Desjardins. Other renewal projects, which would prove equally devastating, were aimed at remodelling certain neighbourhoods. The Little Burgundy project was probably the most spectacular instance of this kind of public intervention, although perhaps the least representative of projects targeting Montréal neighbourhoods. Indeed, rarely was the inner city the focus of a public project with such a massive and severe impact, not only on the urban fabric of the neighbourhood but on its social dynamics as well. Although it is important to keep in mind the exceptional nature of this project, it is interesting to note that it triggered broad-based social movements against modern urban planning policies that sacrificed neighbourhood life to the imperatives of a redeployment of urban activities . . . and urban populations.

Unlike the Dozois project, which was based on completely tearing down existing structures, the urban renewal plan for Little Burgundy, an area south-west of the downtown core, included restoring a number of homes as well as demolishing a large portion of the existing housing stock. The area featured a number of charming houses built in the nineteenth century for lower-middle-class people who had moved away from nearby working-class districts to settle in the area. A large number of working-class residents also moved into the neighbourhood, which maintained a population of over 20 000 until the early 1950s, when the area began to depreciate. Demographic decline, deterioration of the built environment and the neighbourhood's increasing impoverishment were some of the concerns that led to the urban renewal plan of 1965.

Although the 1264 dwellings demolished were replaced by 1441 low-rent (public) housing units, the neighbourhood underwent further population loss as household size decreased. By 1973, only 7000 residents remained, and low-rent housing accounted for 40 per cent of the housing stock in the area, a situation which was extremely unusual for Montréal (Little Burgundy's low-rent housing represented a tenth of all such housing in the entire City of Montréal). Wage-earners, already in decline in the area, increasingly began to leave the neighbourhood when in the early 1980s the provincial government decided to eliminate the ceiling it had set on rental increases for public housing. From then on, these increases were tied to increases in household income (with rents fixed at no more than 25 per cent of household income). The result was the departure for other neighbourhoods of the 'working poor' with low earnings once their income began to increase, since the Little Burgundy rents were no longer competitive. The municipal housing bureau brought in to Little Burgundy new tenants from those already on waiting lists for low-rent housing in other areas, including a large number of anglophone Blacks. Conditions favouring a dynamic of ghettoization began to set in. The social climate of the area seriously deteriorated in the late 1980s, prior to the emergence of new dynamics (Germain, 1995), which we will discuss in Chapters 6 and 7.

Despite its good intentions, this urban renewal operation, conducted in a highly technocratic, top-down manner seriously disrupted the local community. Later public planning and development initiatives would be more modest in scope and more sensitive to the need for integration into the existing urban fabric. However, it was only in the mid-1980s that urban planning began to feature some degree of participatory democracy. For this to happen, the city clearly had to await the election of a new mayor.

Overall, urban renewal undoubtedly wreaked less devastation in central Montréal than in many other North American cities, paradoxically due to the belatedness of the City of Montréal's forays into such ventures. In fact, there was a simultaneous focus on rehabilitating older housing, rather than razing it to the ground. But although Montréal adopted regulations for this purpose as early as the mid-1960s, effective restoration practices were only developed much later on (see Chapter 6).

Mayor Drapeau was emphatically opposed to the idea of urban planning, and would often cite the merits of the lack of zoning in Houston, Texas.

While he was in power, developers had the upper hand. But it would be incorrect to say that Drapeau's was a liberal administration. Drapeau primarily concentrated on large projects – even mega-projects – and the Métro is surely one of his finest achievements. However, for many years, he ignored the rampant deterioration afflicting many of the city's neighbourhoods. As we will see in Chapter 6, it was only in the late 1970s that, fearing the demographic decline of the city, he began to recognize the potential of older neighbourhoods for repopulating the inner city.

4

THE SHIFTING BOUNDARIES OF THE METROPOLIS: THE STRUGGLE TO GOVERN A MOVING TARGET

After a century of urban development, the once moderate-sized city of Montréal would become a city-region. This expansion of Montréal's ecumene propelled political leaders into an unending race to adapt political boundaries to the needs of metropolitan government. Even today, the debate on the political/administrative boundaries and status of the metropolitan region is far from over. Should Montréal give in to the tendency toward municipal fragmentation seen in many sprawling American cities, or institute a European-style metropolitan government to limit urban development (Collin et al., 1996)? Montréal has continued to waver between the two philosophies, unlike Toronto for example, which in 1953 adopted a relatively strong metropolitan structure. But Montréal's situation differs from Toronto's in a number of ways, owing in part to its linguistic duality and in part to its situation as an island. Today, however, both cities face comparably difficult challenges in governing their metropolitan regions.

The city's growth took different forms at various stages of its development. Three main periods have marked the changing geography and shifting political/administrative boundaries of the Montréal metropolitan region. First, its territory was restructured through numerous annexations; then it began to expand ever outwards under the impetus of what appeared to be insatiable growth; and finally, the metropolis now seems to be dissolving into a large region with multiple urban centres.

A TERRITORY EXTENDING BEYOND THE LIMITS OF URBAN DEVELOPMENT

A diversity of suburbs

By the end of the eighteenth century, Montréal possessed an extensive territory that it would take almost a century to populate. By the middle of the next century, alongside the city's *intra muros* urbanization (Montréal's fortifications were in fact destroyed in the early nineteenth century, and the *faubourgs* that developed outside the walls were already incorporated into the municipality's political territory), the first real suburbs began to appear.

These began as enclaves for the well-to-do. As elsewhere in North America, the bourgeoisie, seeking to avoid the physical and social disturbances of the central city, were the first to flee toward areas where they could preserve their quality of life (Collin, 1984). The slopes of one of the three summits of Mount Royal proved an ideal location, at first for summer homes, which were later transformed into luxurious main residences, Westmount being the perfect example of this process (Wolfe, 1998) (Figure 4.1). Today, urban development has caught up with many of these wealthy neighbourhoods, which represent privileged enclaves in the urban fabric, thus diversifying its social mix. Mount Royal's proximity to downtown has in a sense curbed the tendency for the well-off classes to flee the urban core (see Figure 6.23).

Other suburbs grew up close to the city limits, under the leadership of developers – often French Canadians – whose policy of boosterism matched that practised in other Canadian cities (Stelter and Artibise, 1977). Landowners, local elected officials and managers of public utilities (water, gas, electricity and tramway companies) worked together to attract businesses seeking advantageous conditions and the open spaces they needed for the mechanization of their operations. Later on, the extension of the tramway system would facilitate the development of more remote areas, in the same speculative approach. But this urban development was not continuous, as small cores of growth appeared at intervals along the tramway lines (Dansereau and Foggin, 1976; Hanna, 1998). Consequently, some of these suburbs resulted not so much from industrial decentralization – which was the case for the municipality of Maisonneuve – as from increasing residential mobility on the part of workers. For example, Verdun, to the southwest of Montréal, would experience remarkable growth: by the early 1930s, with 60 000 inhabitants, it ranked as Canada's 14th largest municipality. Like the *faubourgs*, these new cities were centred around an institutional core similar to that found in rural areas, with the parish constituting the heart. Rural immigrants in the city thus encountered familiar social structures on the local level (Ferretti, 1990).

In short, the late nineteenth and early twentieth centuries were a period of rampant urban development, combining rural and international immigration, a deconcentration of factories, an exodus towards more protected living environments, and a growing appetite for space on the part of the many companies that constituted the then-prevalent and prosperous 'economy of urbanization'. As a result, the metropolitan area experienced a surge of demographic and territorial growth. Yet, if its territory extended beyond the limits of urbanized areas, the latter were still of fairly high density, due in part to the belated development of mass transit. The proximity of housing, services and work was a necessity for most Montrealers until the beginning of the twentieth century. The many new districts around the downtown core were thus functionally mixed, as well as fairly socially mixed. The working classes and the elite lived close to one another in

FIGURE 4.1 Victorian bourgeois prestige in Westmount. Reproduced by permission from Marc-Aurèle Marsan

neighbourhoods that were to remain, however, quite far apart in terms of social distance.

Costly annexations

Beginning in the 1880s, Montréal's political territory also grew substantially. Boosterism was proving expensive, as developers' ambitions, encouraged by widespread patronage, often stretched municipal budgets beyond reasonable limits. Some municipalities opted for annexation to Montréal if the latter agreed to pay for certain infrastructures or absorb their debts. During the 1880s, Montréal's territory was extended in this way with the annexation of the municipalities of Hochelaga, Saint-Jean-Baptiste and Saint-Gabriel.

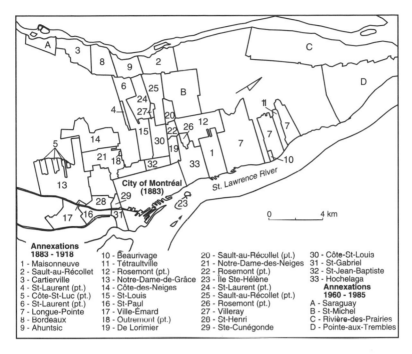

Annexations
1883 - 1918
1 - Maisonneuve
2 - Sault-au-Récollet
3 - Cartierville
4 - St-Laurent (pt.)
5 - Côte-St-Luc (pt.)
6 - St-Laurent (pt.)
7 - Longue-Pointe
8 - Bordeaux
9 - Ahuntsic

10 - Beaurivage
11 - Tétraultville
12 - Rosemont (pt.)
13 - Notre-Dame-de-Grâce
14 - Côte-des-Neiges
15 - St-Louis
16 - St-Paul
17 - Ville-Émard
18 - Outremont (pt.)
19 - De Lorimier

20 - Sault-au-Récollet (pt.)
21 - Notre-Dame-des-Neiges
22 - Rosemont (pt.)
23 - Île Ste-Hélène
24 - St-Laurent (pt.)
25 - Sault-au-Récollet (pt.)
26 - Rosemont (pt.)
27 - Villeray
28 - St-Henri
29 - Ste-Cunégonde

30 - Côte-St-Louis
31 - St-Gabriel
32 - St-Jean-Baptiste
33 - Hochelaga
Annexations
1960 - 1985
A - Saraguay
B - St-Michel
C - Rivière-des-Prairies
D - Pointe-aux-Trembles

FIGURE 4.2 Annexations to the City of Montréal, 1888–present

But this was only the beginning of a 30-year trend that would radically transform the political/administrative boundaries of the metropolis. In 1881 Montréal had a population of 140 747. Forty years later the population had risen to 618 506, and Figure 4.2 clearly shows how the city's territory had swelled considerably through a series of annexations (Linteau, 1992).

But annexations during the first decade of the twentieth century proved enormously costly for the City of Montréal, which had to absorb the huge debts amassed by overly 'enterprising' municipal teams. The 1918 annexation of the municipality of Maisonneuve, extolled by its promoters as the 'Pittsburgh of Canada,' set a new record for indebtedness (Linteau, 1985). This trend of annexations, common in many North American cities, had a major political impact on the Montréal metropolitan area. It increased the political power of Montréal's mayors who, besides representing a larger territory, often had ties with the developers who were building the new suburbs. By 1918 the City of Montréal had become a heavyweight political entity: its budget was nearly as large as that of the entire province. But this situation would rapidly change. Montréal's poor financial situation soon prompted the provincial government to curtail the powers of local officials, and the city was placed under trusteeship a number of times beginning in 1918, when the provincial government created the Municipal Affairs department to control municipal indebtedness. (Over several decades, the power of municipal institutions would be gradually eroded, in the face of an emerging welfare state (Collin, 1997)). In 1921, the City of Montréal failed in a bid to annex all island municipalities. The propertied classes, a minority in the central city, had retreated to the suburbs where they refused to relinquish the tools that enabled them to safeguard their privileges. Political autonomy was one of these and, as we have seen, urban planning was another. To avoid annexation by Montréal, the wealthy suburbs adjacent to the central city agreed to allow the provincial government to set up a metropolitan commission for the Island of Montréal, a body empowered to authorize loans secured by municipalities (except Montréal) and absorb the debts of bankrupt or struggling municipalities such as Pointe-aux-Trembles, Saint-Michel and Montréal-Nord (Linteau, 1992).

Annexations had another important political effect on the metropolis: an ethno-linguistic one. With a few exceptions, most of the annexed municipalities had a large francophone majority, so that each annexation brought in not only more francophone voters, but also two or three francophone city councillors. The linguistic balance that had prevailed during part of the nineteenth century was thus called into question. No longer would anglophone and francophone mayors successively alternate, and the city council minutes, recorded in English until 1883, would henceforth be bilingual.

Last but not least, this territorial expansion was accompanied by a social and cultural fragmentation of the metropolis. Montréal was in fact unable to incorporate certain municipalities near the city centre which still represent distinct social enclaves, especially in the case of wealthier municipalities such as Westmount, Outremont, Hampstead and Town of Mount Royal. Nor did it integrate all the West Island suburbs mostly populated through the exodus of the city's anglophone middle class, including Baie d'Urfé, Beaconsfield, Pointe-Claire and Roxboro (Figure 4.3.). By the end of the First World War, the political geography of the Island of Montréal was marked by numerous social and linguistic divisions. In 1921, while francophones were a minority on the island outside the City of Montréal, anglophones amounted to only a quarter of the population of the city *per se* (Sancton, 1985). Ethno-linguistic divisions often seemed to overlap with social divisions in the urban environment. But closer analysis of the population makeup in various neighbourhoods reveals a far greater mix (see Chapter 7).

It was as far back as 1910 that the idea had first emerged of coordinating municipal administration not through annexation, but by setting up a metropolitan government. The concept was put forth by G.A. Nantel (1910) in a short essay entitled *La métropole de demain* (The Metropolis of Tomorrow), in which he also stressed the virtues of urban planning that such a modern government would foster (Germain, 1985). But as we saw in Chapter 3, the movement to promote urban planning was forestalled in its early stages.

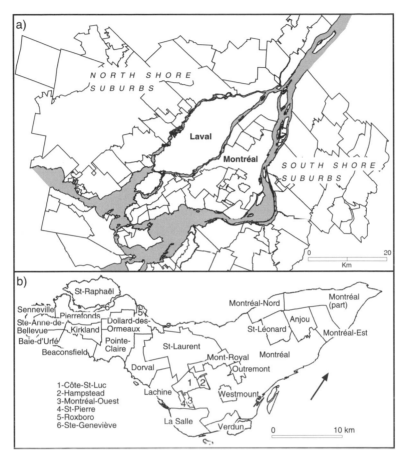

FIGURE 4.3 (a) The Montréal Census Metropolitan Area, showing municipal boundaries; (b) The municipalities of the Montréal Urban Community (Montréal Island)

URBAN SPRAWL: UNCONTROLLED METROPOLITAN GROWTH

After 1945, the pace of urban development quickened. Although in part driven by strong population growth characterizing the 1950s and 1960s, the situation would rapidly change in the following decades. By the early 1970s, the economic decline of the metropolis and a slackening of population growth had already set in. No one seemed to notice this, however, and notions of regional planning continued to lag behind the times.

Due to the phenomenal postwar growth of North American suburbs, a new urban model appeared. To paraphrase urbanist Hans Blumenfeld

(1967), the city was transformed into a metropolis by dissolving into a far larger whole. As he stated: 'It is, indeed, neither city nor country. No longer can it be identified from the outside by its silhouette, clearly set off from the surrounding fields' (Ville de Montréal, Service d'urbanisme, 1968, 3). Montréal was no exception to the rule, although it had, in terms of urban sprawl, as much in common with European cities as it had with its North American counterparts.

By the time of the 1951 census, the City of Montréal's population topped the one million mark. But Montréal then still claimed 45 per cent of the metropolitan area's total population; by 1961 it accounted for barely 22 per cent (see Figure 6.1). Suburbs were growing up haphazardly, encouraged by the construction of a tunnel and of a series of bridges (currently totalling 14) all around the island, giving the metropolis a star-shaped structure: one branch toward Repentigny in the northeast, another southeastwards to Beloeil and Saint-Hyacinthe, one westward to Dorion, another northwest to Sainte-Thérèse (Marsan, 1991; Wilson, Poussart and Lelièvre, 1999).

Dormitory suburbs generally sprang up around existing village cores, quickly transforming the character of the local landscape with a proliferation of bland-looking bungalows, based on the American model. The first suburban shopping centre appeared in 1952 in Ville Saint-Laurent. Fifteen years later, there were as many as 40 in the metropolitan area. This large-scale dispersion of the population to outlying areas obviously triggered a substantial decrease in overall residential density. The average residential density gradient (calculated in terms of the distance from the downtown core) plummeted from 1.33 in 1941 to 0.30 in 1976. But residential density was even lower in Toronto (0.19) and Vancouver (0.23) around the same time (Ville de Montréal, 1993).

The relatively unrestrained growth of these suburbs clearly spawned considerable urban sprawl. Ironically, government policies tended to encourage rather than impede the latter. From 1958 to 1976, the provincial government blithely constructed 400 kilometres of expressways on and around the island (Figure 4.4); it assumed the land servicing costs for properties slated for private sector development (unlike Ontario); and implemented a series of measures that ultimately reduced the costs of housing in peripheral areas. The federal government also contributed to this urban exodus by offering guaranteed, low-rate mortgages for new homes, most of which were in the suburbs (Charbonneau et al., 1994). The scenario is a classic one: widespread automobile use, unrestrained construction of a subsidized autoroute (expressway) network and a marked improvement in living standards, in part owing to postwar economic restructuring, collectively fuelled an unprecedented development of urban fringes, thus weakening their central cities. Montréal was however a relatively compact agglomeration when compared with US cities (Bussière and Dallaire, 1994a; Goldberg and Mercer, 1986) (Figures 4.5 and 4.6).

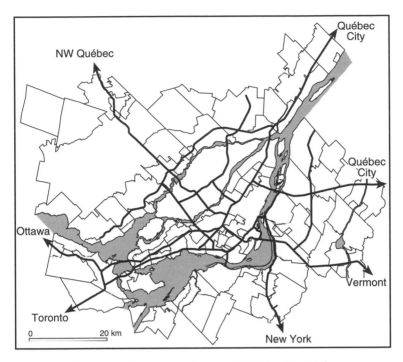

FIGURE 4.4 Autoroute (expressway) network in the Montréal area

At the time, the potential for growth seemed unlimited. On the political level, the Quiet Revolution expressed French Canadians' determination to catch up economically and reaffirm control over the province's development, as they sought to become 'masters in their own home'. But this determination did not seem to include control over land use planning in the Montréal metropolitan area. Urban planning at that time was more interested in projecting future growth than in controlling it. For example, in 1965 the government authorized the merger of the 14 municipalities on Île Jésus, the second largest island in the Montréal archipelago. By also incorporating two smaller islands, nearby Île Laval and Laval-sur-le-Lac, the new municipality of Laval became Québec's second largest city in terms of population size (see Figure 4.3). Its first urban development plan forecast lightning-speed growth: one million inhabitants by the year 2000. Today this city, with a population of 314 398, has emerged as a leading *ville-campagne* (both 'city and country'), proud of its agricultural vitality (Archambault and Godbout, 1988; Beaudet, 1998). The City of Montréal also anticipated massive growth for the metropolitan region. A 1967 strategic plan called 'Horizon 2000' projected a metropolitan region of seven million people by that magic date (Ville de Montréal, 1967). Today, however, as we enter the new millennium, the metropolitan area has only about 3.3 million inhabitants.

FIGURE 4.5 High-density residential zones like this one, in the downtown west near Concordia University, were typical products of urban renewal in Canadian cities in the 1960s and early 1970s. (Damaris Rose)

FIGURE 4.6 Typical inner-suburban low-rise apartment buildings, 1960s. (Damaris Rose)

By the 1970s urban growth was no longer as directly associated with population growth (Divay and Gaudreau, 1984). The urban exodus was sustained in part by the breaking-up of larger households that accompanied the emergence of the nuclear family as a central sociological unit. Once known for their extremely large families, French Canadians saw their birth rate drop to a record low within a few decades. Urban development was also sparked by a major wave of land and real estate speculation. In short, the metropolitan area was anticipating continued growth even as it hovered on the verge of relative stagnation.

One island, one city, one municipality?

Jean Drapeau re-entered city hall as Montréal's mayor in the early 1960s after a short period in office in the 1950s, and would remain the city's chief executive for the next 25 years. His ambitions spanned not just Montréal, but the entire island. Without waiting for the approval of the provincial government or of any of the other island municipalities, he began the construction of the Métro (subway) and launched the above-mentioned 'Horizon 2000' regional development plan. He also advocated the annexation of all of the remaining municipalities of the island under the slogan '*One island, one city*'. Aside from Montréal itself, the island formed a veritable mosaic of small cities, often interspersed within the administrative boundaries of the City of Montréal. The journalist Lysiane Gagnon uses the image of a Swiss cheese city filled with holes, the holes being the enclaves formed by wealthy cities such as Outremont, Westmount, Mount Royal and Hampstead (Gagnon, 1999). But after incorporating Rivière des-Prairies, Saraguay and Saint-Michel, Drapeau encountered fierce resistance from municipalities who wanted to preserve their local autonomy to maintain their social standing, as in 1921. Moreover, many of them had English-speaking majorities. Drapeau envisioned Montréal as a great, cosmopolitan, world metropolis in which English Montrealers would be proud to share (Sancton, 1985). But he had underestimated the social and linguistic divisions that underlay local autonomy, as well as the distrust the City of Montréal continued to elicit from suburban municipalities and the provincial government. Comprising one sixth of the province's population, the central municipality had a potentially substantial political importance, especially under the rule of the charismatic Jean Drapeau, the mayor being elected by more people than the Premier of Québec. However, the provincial government, long dominated by rural interests, was little attuned to the need for a metropolitan policy. So municipal fragmentation prevailed, although, unlike American cities, municipalities had a limited realm of action since the provincial government controlled key areas, most notably education, thus avoiding the problem of major inequalities in the quality of services between municipalities.

The Montréal area clearly lacked the necessary conditions for increased regional planning. Toronto, on the other hand, had set up its metropolitan council (Metro Toronto) back in 1953 and put forth a fairly integrated vision of regional development, centred in particular on the promotion of mass transit (extension of the subway and development of a solid network of suburban trains). Urban sprawl had long been an important concern, as Toronto authorities sought to maintain the density of the urban core and to guide suburban development (Frisken, 1994). There was no such strategy in Québec, and no special emphasis on any given mode of transport. More-over, unlike Ontario, developers did not have to assume the costs of new subdivision infrastructures; this opened up the market to small developers, and hardly encouraged compact urban growth (Bacher, 1993).

But Montréal could not continue assuming regional public infrastructure costs on its own. The rising costs of mass transit (since the advent of the Métro) and of the police department were especially worrisome. It seemed inevitable that a cost-sharing system would have to be put into place to ensure the fair distribution of the financial burden created by these services among the island's municipalities. A 1969 police strike hastened the matter: that same year, the provincial government created a metropolitan structure for the Montréal area, the Montréal Urban Community (MUC), and similar bodies in the Québec City and Hull-Aylmer-Gatineau regions. The MUC integrated the 29 municipalities on the Island of Montréal (as well as Île-Bizard and the tiny rural retreat of Île-Dorval) into a federation with far fewer powers than Metro Toronto (Trepanier, 1993). The latter had juris-diction over a number of social spheres, such as education and local welfare. Its structure was also less fragmented in that it included only six municipalities after 1967, representing a total population of 2.3 million in 1991, compared to the MUC's population of only 1 775 871. (In 1997, the Ontario government forced the merger of these six municipalities into a single mega-city.) Moreover, the MUC had been set up when most of the development was occurring off the Island of Montréal, unlike the situation when Metro Toronto was formed approximately 15 years earlier. Since the 1966 census, the total population on the Island of Montréal had been growing very slowly and gradually began to decline after 1971, whereas the population of the outer suburbs increased significantly until in 1991 it represented 43.2 per cent of the population of the entire census metro-politan area (CMA) (Figure 6.1).

The MUC's mission did not seem to be the supervision of urban growth, although it was required to lay out a development plan. (It was only 15 years later that such a plan was in fact adopted, and it seemed to focus primarily on taking stock of existing development rather than orienting new development.) As Marie-Odile Trépanier (1993: 72) has noted: 'Institutional arrangements for the MUC combined recognition of the principle of local autonomy with the imperative of developing important regional services.'

The police department and mass transit were to be the main spheres overseen by the MUC, in addition to property assessment, traffic regulations, construction standards, air pollution and public health. The MUC municipalities were unable to agree on water supply or waste disposal strategies. Nevertheless, there was less difficulty reaching a consensus over the management of parks and open spaces; in 1986 the MUC would take advantage of the dynamism of Montréal's new municipal administration to create seven regional parks (Ducas, 1987).

Thus, the structure of the MUC was one of compromise with regard to the ambitious plans of Mayor Drapeau, who had to agree to share the management of important services with other island mayors. He did succeed in having all of Montréal's city councillors represented on the MUC council, thus acquiring 66.2 per cent of the seats, whereas the other municipalities were represented by their mayor alone. However, a double majority system gave the suburbs the right to veto measures they unanimously opposed. Moreover, the Conference of Suburban Mayors was set up in 1975 as a forum in which to air the views of each municipality.

Montréal's urban sprawl problem in comparative perspective

When we compare urban sprawl in the Montréal area from 1960 to 1980 to the situation in other cities, we arrive at a rather mixed assessment. There is a clear trend toward dispersion of urban development towards the periphery and a blurring of the boundaries between urban and rural. Yet in many ways, the urban form of the Montréal area (although less compact) more closely resembles European cities than North American cities. Comparisons are always tricky because of the difficulty of defining equivalent territorial and statistical units. But Montréal's particularities are distinct enough to say that they do not simply stem from measurement problems.

Three of these particularities are especially striking. First, the growth of Montréal's suburbs was not entirely separate from earlier development. The urban exodus to the island's periphery, and to the north and south shores off the island, was centred around existing village cores, which city planners have paid more attention to since the renewal of interest in communities focused around a downtown core. Longueuil, Saint-Lambert, Boucherville, Laprairie, Pont-Viau and Chomedey are good examples of this continuity of urban form. Also, as Marsan (1994) points out, the area's new expressways initially followed the routes of the old *chemins du Roy* (King's ways) dating back to the French regime.

Second, even though the city's postwar residential developments are generally of far lower density than developments having occurred in the past three centuries of the city's history, Montréal's suburbs are clearly much higher density than those in American cities: high-rises are not unusual, albeit less frequent than in Toronto (Figure 4.5). The urban fabric of Montréal's suburbs is more diversified, including for example a significant proportion of duplexes and small buildings with six to 20 rental units on three or four levels without an elevator, commonly (and appropriately) termed 'walk-ups' (Figures 4.6 and 6.10). This feature of residential development throughout the entire metropolitan area brings us to another of Montréal's distinctive characteristics.

The growth of typical low-rise residential suburbs in the Montréal area was probably checked by what we may describe as a merely moderate increase in living standards after the Second World War. In Québec, as elsewhere, conditions obviously improved during the three decades of postwar growth. But many Montrealers did not have the means to join the middle-class suburban exodus or to own single-family homes. Widespread automobile use came fairly late to Montréal. Yves Bussière (1989) notes that in 1950, there were only 11 cars for every 100 Montrealers. Even today, the level of car ownership is lower than in most North American cities, including Toronto, which nonetheless has an efficient mass transit system to serve outlying areas. It is even below levels in European cities such as Brussels or Paris, two cities with very different public transit systems, the system in Paris being far more developed (Bussière and Dallaire, 1994b).

But the dynamics of urban sprawl are also linked to those regulating the city's urban core. Although the population levels of central Montréal began to spiral downwards in the 1960s as people moved out to the suburbs, and although Montréal's urban exodus of the 1960s and 1970s seemed beyond the metropolis's control due to inadequate political institutions and insufficient political will, this decline was less dramatic than in some American inner cities. The fact is that the central and downtown areas of Montréal remain relatively attractive places in which to live and work, an aspect we will return to in Chapter 6. Nevertheless, the long-term consequences of urban sprawl are becoming an increasingly important concern.

FROM METROPOLIS TO CITY-REGION

From urban sprawl to disparities between urban cores and peripheries

Urban sprawl ceases to be an indicator of growth and becomes a regional problem when it wastes resources and depletes the urban core. In the 1970s the problem of urban sprawl in the Montréal area emerged as an important issue. In the wake of the Quiet Revolution, the Québec government began to set up regional planning and development agencies. The Montréal branch of the Office de planification et de développement du Québec published a series of studies that helped sensitize people to regional problems, even if the Office itself ultimately did very little planning. And urban growth in the 1970s was taking a different form from development in previous decades. It was, first of all, increasingly spread out. From 1971 to 1981 a growing ring of ever-more-distant suburbs attracted 62 per cent of the metropolitan area's new households (Fauteux, 1986). These new developments were costly to the community since they generally occurred in unserviced areas and often gobbled up prime Québec farmland.

After the election of the Parti Québécois in 1976, a series of measures were introduced to limit this costly sprawl. A 1977 moratorium on autoroute construction was the first step. Then, with the 1978 agricultural zoning act, the provincial government attempted to control and limit the development of non-agricultural activities within a certain area. This emphatic green-belt initiative was also motivated by the Parti Québécois' objective of agricultural self-sufficiency. The government simultaneously tabled the Preferable Development Option for the Montréal region. This new policy was to encourage government departments to concentrate their activities within a designated urban area so as to strengthen the existing urban fabric. But paradoxically, since the mid-1980s, the government has fragmented the metropolitan area by dividing it up among five of the provinces 16 administrative regions, Laval, Laurentides, Montérégie, Lanaudière, and Montréal, the Montréal administrative region corresponding exactly to the territory of the Montréal Urban Community (Collin, 1998).

From 1981 to 1986, urban sprawl appeared to slow down. Was this due to the provincial government's policies or to the severe economic recession that gripped the Montréal area from 1982 to 1984, combined with slower population growth after 1970? It is difficult to say. A number of observers have noted that the government's much-vaunted Preferable Development Option, reaffirmed in 1984, does not seem to have curbed development in unserviced areas (Charbonneau et al., 1994). Besides, every year seemed to produce further exemptions from government regulations, so that very little remained from the initial policy In any case, this slackening of growth proved temporary, as urban sprawl soon quickened its pace, and now occurred in a leapfrog pattern, with the new suburbs not necessarily representing a continuation of earlier ones.

Moreover, with slower population growth, urban sprawl assumed a new, interconnected forum. Growth in the periphery was henceforth at the expense of the urban core. This triggered considerable discussion on the extent and impact of the deconcentration of certain employment sectors and on the 'doughnut effect', that typically North American phenomenon of an impoverished inner city surrounded by middle-class suburbs. Moreover, these suburbs were attracting families with children, leaving the inner city with a population pyramid very different from the rest of the region (Figure 4.7).

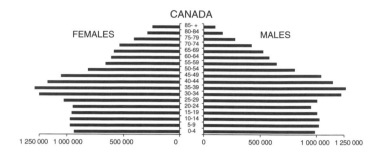

CANADA

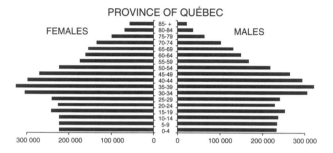

PROVINCE OF QUÉBEC

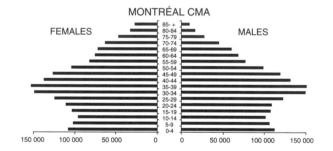

MONTRÉAL CMA

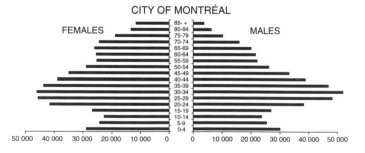

CITY OF MONTRÉAL

FIGURE 4.7 Population pyramids: Canada, Québec, Montréal Census
Metropolitan Area, and City of Montréal, 1996

Developmental disparities fuelled municipal representatives' mutual distrust and ultimately isolated the central city, with its repeated denunciations of fiscal inequity. As most municipal revenues derived from property tax revenues, Montréal felt that the suburbs were not paying their fair share of the costs of certain regional infrastructures, especially cultural facilities, primarily concentrated in the downtown area (Beaudoin and Collin, 1997). The suburbs, whether part of the MUC or not, in turn refused to link their destiny to Montréal's, a city they considered poorly managed. Such a context was hardly conducive to planning, other than by intervention from higher levels of government. But the central city had little representation in the provincial government, and senior civil servants in the small provincial capital of Québec City, inclined to view Montréal's development as antithetical to regional development, felt that the Québec state must primarily support the latter. The 1980s and 1990s would thus represent a time of hesitation, indecision, and abortive reform.

Blueprints for inertia

The adoption of the Land Use Planning and Development Act in 1979 established Regional County Municipalities (known by their French acronym, MRC) across the province, with the mandate to prepare development plans for their respective territories. In the Montréal area, 13 MRCs were thus set up in addition to the existing MUC, a body evidently in need of reform given the growth of the off-island suburbs on the one hand, and the weakness of the MUC's administrative structure, dominated by local officials and limited in its powers, on the other. In 1982, after much hesitation, the government finally enacted a reform of the MUC, recognizing the new balance of power between the central municipality and the island suburbs while leaving the actual working out of this compromise in the hands of local authorities (Trépanier, 1993). To foster a renewed sense of regional awareness, the MUC was equipped with five permanent commissions, co-chaired, on an equal basis, by Montréal and suburban elected officials who were also represented on the MUC's executive committee. Moreover, a new sphere was added to the MUC's responsibilities: support for culture and the arts. The MUC's long-awaited development plan was finally delivered in 1985, in compliance with the recently adopted Bill 125.

The plan cautiously recommended a structure that was in fact already in evidence, i.e. supplementing the existing downtown core with the established sub-centres of Anjou, Pointe-Claire and Saint-Laurent. Ten years earlier, a preliminary version of the plan had anticipated two of the three satellite centres, around two suburban shopping centres: Fairview Shopping Centre in the west, and Galeries d'Anjou in the east. The planners felt that this proposal would reduce pressures on the downtown core and help to guide suburban development and expansion of the public transit network, even though the two satellite poles were not central to the network. As Andrew Sancton (1983) notes, the preliminary scheme could have sparked an interesting public discussion on the future of the metropolitan region (whether to concentrate development in the centre or encourage a 'multipolar' structure), and on the desired vocation of area suburbs (whether they should be planned for households with cars or centred around shopping centres served by public transit). But nothing of the sort occurred, as suburban mayors opposed the proposal which they saw as overly favourable to the central city, and a timid MUC was reluctant to press these issues.

The case of mass transit   The whole issue of mass transit clearly illustrates the impasses that have resulted from continual squabbles among the various local authorities and between the latter and the provincial government. Unlike Toronto, the Montréal metropolitan region has never been able to successfully integrate the development of transportation and land use planning (Frisken, 1994). As in many other North American cities, mass transit was initially developed by the private sector, as were most public utilities, except water. In 1951 the provincial government forced the City of Montréal to purchase the Compagnie des Tramways de Montréal, and the new Commission des Transports de Montréal subsequently replaced the tramways with a fleet of buses to serve the city and 15 of its suburbs. But from 1950 to 1971, at the height of the suburbs' growth, mass transit was funded on a purely local, largely self-financed, basis (Lamonde, 1990). It was also at this time that the provincial government began to massively subsidize autoroute construction and that the City of Montréal started the construction of a series of expressways, often cutting through older residential sections of the urban fabric. In the 1960s the mayor of Montréal unilaterally launched the construction of a subway system which, as we have seen in Chapter 3, he envisioned as far more than a municipal infrastructure. He foresaw an island-wide, integrated transportation network, and even planned to incorporate the financially-threatened suburban commuter rail lines into his projected multimodal (Métro, bus, train) system. His ambitions aroused the suspicion of the West Island suburbs, who wanted to handle their own area transportation. However, no one, whether Montréal's mayor, the other mayors or the provincial government, had considered the idea of a hierarchy in transportation modes. In other words, no special priority was accorded to mass transit.

It is thus not surprising that the number of people using the network soon began to plummet, adding to its initial deficits. In the early 1970s, the provincial government decided to help finance mass transit by paying a portion of the cost for new bus acquisitions and for the Métro's debt servicing (Lamonde, 1990). However, unlike the situation in Toronto, the government refused to contribute to operating expenses (Frisken, 1994). A few years later, it also assumed the cost of infrastructures for Métro extensions and for the network of suburban trains, of which two of the three lines were then run by the Compagnie des transports de la Communauté urbaine de Montréal (currently the Société de transport . . . or STCUM, known in English as the Montréal Urban Community Transit Corporation, or MUCTC). But the former became the focus of growing controversy, first between the MUC and the provincial government, which favoured a less costly, above-ground light rail system, which it also wanted to see extended northward rather than eastward, in keeping with its vision of a regional rapid transit system. The Québec government's 1979 integrated transportation plan represented a major policy shift: after mammoth investment in the autoroute network, the state had turned to the planning of regional, Montréal-area public transport, but with an equally authoritarian and centralist stance. A power struggle ensued, with local officials and the MUC clearly unhappy about this interference from the government, even though the latter had now become a major sponsor (assuming 45 per cent of total transit costs by 1983) (Roy, 1984).

Controversies also raged among Montréal-area municipalities. In the mid-1980s, mass transit was handled by the STCUM, the Société de transport de Laval (STL) (Laval Transit Corporation), the Société de transport de la Rive-Sud de Montréal (STRSM) (South Shore Transit Corporation), and some 20 other smaller operators. The first three corporations (and the local officials who headed them) were unable to agree on cost-sharing: MUC authorities criticized Laval and South Shore officials for refusing to share in the STCUM's operating costs even though residents in their areas used the STCUM network, and the suburbs were unwilling to help pay for a transit system they had no say in planning. Moreover, MUC officials were themselves unable to agree on Métro extension projects, which some saw as encouraging the urban exodus at the expense of the city core, while others were concerned about the costs of new Métro stations or felt that the routes chosen ignored the needs of people in their districts, etc. The conflicts that traditionally opposed the central city and the suburbs, and the Island of Montréal and the North and South Shores, were thus intensified in the sphere of mass transit.

In 1989 the Québec government finally succeeded in setting up the Conseil métropolitain de transport en commun (Metropolitan Public Transportation Council) which brought the MUC, South Shore and North Shore transit corporations together. But the following year, the economic recession prompted the government to announce a partial reduction of funding for mass transit. The municipal fiscal reform adopted in 1991, the so-called 'Ryan Reform', in fact allotted municipalities a greater share of the burden of public financing. This was a terrible blow to the MUC and to the City of Montréal in particular, especially with regard to funding for mass transit, only partially compensated by a tax on car registration fees in the

Montréal area to subsidize public transit. This cutback in government funding inevitably resulted in fare hikes for users and decreases in the contributions of island municipalities, which could also mean a serious drop in user numbers, and, consequently, a growing deficit. Since an ageing population would obviously lead to a decline in the clientele for public transit services, the future of mass transit did not seem very bright. (More recent forecasts suggest a rapid growth in automobile use in the next decade as more households set up residence in the suburbs and purchase a second car (Bussière et al., 1998)). In 1992, the government agreed to start working on a development strategy for the Greater Montréal region, aimed at revitalizing the local economy and rethinking the region's metropolitan organization. The Task Force on Greater Montréal would subsequently produce a report known by the name of its chairman, Claude Pichette (Trépanier, 1998). This report was destined, as the expression goes, to gather dust on the shelf. But the discussion it stimulated clearly highlighted the growing political and economic influence of the larger suburbs and of their newly emerging lifestyles.

A city-region or a region of cities?

Urbanization continues to produce new forms (Stanback, 1991). In recent years, American researchers have noted the development of 'edge cities' spawned by the decentralization of employment in the advanced tertiary sector (Garreau, 1991). These new suburban forms may significantly alter metropolitan dynamics, especially the relations between urban cores and their peripheries. In Chapter 5, we will examine more closely the new geography of employment in the Montréal area. Here we simply wish to point out the changes occurring in many suburban landscapes and the impacts of these changes on relations between the different geo-administrative entities in the Montréal area.

The urban fabric of large North and South Shore suburbs such as Laval and Longueuil has become increasingly diversified. These cities, outside the MUC territory and thus not contributing to tax-base sharing, currently represent important labour markets. In recent years, they have developed cultural and recreational activities of often major scope, and have begun to create their own downtown cores around existing shopping centres or existing village cores. In short, they are increasingly less inclined to see themselves as suburbs of Montréal. Studies on travel within the census metropolitan area emphasize the extent of the ongoing changes: the volume of travel between suburbs, whether for work, recreation, shopping, etc., has risen significantly. In 1987, 55 per cent of daily trips within the metropolitan region were from one suburb to another, whereas in 1974 the same percentage of trips had been directed toward Montréal, clearly indicating the decline of the central city as a main point of attraction (Collin and Mongeau,

1992). In other words, the suburbs are less 'dependent' on Montréal than ever before. The city's actual downtown core, however, remains a preferred destination, especially for students. For the moment, it does not seem to have lost its power of attraction.

In addition, some suburbs also enjoy considerable political weight in the provincial government, thanks to the influence of their elected provincial representatives or their mayors. Although in principle municipal political parties have no ties with provincial or federal parties, certain political affiliations do come into play. While Montréal's mayors have always kept their distance from provincial politics, suburban mayors have often been more willing to make their political affinities known.

Consequently, it was only with the setting up of the provincial government's Task Force on Greater Montréal in 1992 that the positions of all sides were clearly heard, especially as concerns the implementation of new regional structures. Indeed, presentations during the public hearings that preceded the tabling of the Pichette Report underscored the extent of fragmentation in the metropolitan region and the suburban municipalities' lack of solidarity with the weakened central city. On the Island of Montréal, after debating the idea of dividing the metropolitan area into a sort of federation, the municipalities outside Montréal arrived at a consensus on the idea of a regional agency, while refusing to pay for the consequences of the City of Montréal's policies. On the South Shore, it appeared difficult to reconcile the annexationist aims of the mayor of Longueuil, who wanted to increase his municipality's power *vis-à-vis* the MUC and Laval (also created from a merger of municipalities, as we have seen) on the one hand, and internal differences between other South Shore municipalities, opposed to any merger or to the formation of an urban community for their sub-region, on the other hand (Collin, 1998). To the north, Laval and other municipalities denounced what they saw as unwarranted fears about urban sprawl and the resultant impoverishment of the central city, but were willing to accept, if necessary, a council of Greater Montréal mayors responsible for preparing a common strategy on the region's future.

The Pichette Report put forth the notion of a city-region as a basic concept (Trépanier, 1998). The report, made public in December 1993, noted that the area was made up of a number of cities which interacted to form a unique entity. The notion of a metropolis no longer adequately described this reality in that it suggested a central point of reference for an entire urban region. Moreover, in line with its regional policy of the 1980s, the provincial government had already split Greater Montréal into five administrative regions, four of which were under the control of suburban authorities, as we have already mentioned. It was suggested that this city-region might be headed by a regional agency for what could be termed the Montréal metropolitan region, since its area of jurisdiction would correspond to the census metropolitan area. Its responsibilities would include the following spheres: land use planning and development, economic development, the environment, culture and the arts, transportation and public security. The Pichette Report also recommended abolishing the Regional County Municipalities, and establishing inter-municipal service agencies of which the MUC would be one.

But there has never been consensus over what the region of Montréal really is, namely in regards to the delimitation of its boundaries. A currently used expression, the Montréal Metropolitan Area, actually refers to a statistical unit used by Statistics Canada, whose delimitations change with every census (it was made up of 102 municipalities in 1991, whereas this number increased to 110 with the publication of the data from the 1996 census). Another statistical unit frequently referred to is the Greater Montréal area, which comprises the MUC and 12 MRCs and includes 136 municipalities (Collin, 1998). But, fundamentally, the report's recommendations for profound institutional reform made its successful implementation unlikely and it is not surprising that it was shelved, at least for a time.

More than ever, since the 1995 referendum on Québec sovereignty, the Montréal region has become a politically explosive area where structural reform appears unavoidable, yet impossible. In the mid-1990s the Québec government created a ministry responsible for the Greater Montréal region (with yet another territorial delimitation), which has nevertheless remained on the sidelines. However, the government and local authorities did enter into a power struggle over who would chair the new Agence métropolitaine de transport (Metropolitan Transit Agency), set up in 1995: local officials named the mayor of Montréal-Nord, who chaired the STCUM, as their preferred candidate, a choice opposed by the minister responsible for the Montréal region due to the potential conflict of interest. In December 1996, the minister also tabled a bill aimed at setting up a Commission de développement de la Métropole (Metropolitan Development Commission). Two thirds of this commission would be made up of local elected officials, predominantly from outside the MUC, and the remaining third of its members would be appointed by the minister from among business, community and union leaders and decision-makers in the transportation, tourism, environment and cultural sectors. The commission would be purely advisory in function, its main mandate being to plan strategic orientations in the spheres of economic development, land use planning, transportation and waste management, after considering government strategies targeting these areas (Ducas and Trépanier, 1998).

In other words, although convinced of the need for serious metropolitan planning, the provincial government had again postponed the implementation of a real metropolitan-scale structure. The Québec government appears to be in no rush to authorize the creation of a regional body representing 3.3 million inhabitants, namely almost half the population of the province – a body that would thus wield considerable political clout . . . . In Québec, this political problem is more acute than would be the case in other Canadian provinces because the metropolis is not the capital of the province (as is the case for Toronto) and because of the extreme political divergences between the core of the Montréal region and the rest of the province, which constantly leads Québec City to try to control the reins at every turn. Moreover, the commission's proposed make-up left little room either for the views of business and community leaders, often the most ardent defenders of a metropolitan vision, or for representation from local authorities on the island, who form a majority of those opposed to the current government's separatist objectives. The proposed metropolitan development commission was, as expected, rejected by the suburbs. Since then, the government has set up a commission on local public finance, whose recommendations were made public in a document entitled Pact 2000 (Québec, Commission nationale sur les finances et la fiscalité locales, 1999).

This report reviews the range of possibilities in terms of politico-administrative reform, from total or partial mergers of the island's munici-palities to the creation of a supra-municipal regional entity resembling the Metropolitan Development Commission in its scope of action, with at-large elections of members. The Bédard Report, named after the commission's chair, once again raised a whole pot-pourri of various issues and matters at stake for the metropolitan region, further contributing to the divergence of opinions. These issues included: the fiscal pact promised by the govern-ment to the City of Montréal to compensate for costs associated with its function as the core city (concentration of poverty, cultural facilities, integ-ration of immigrants, etc.); local government finance and issues associated with decentralization; the conditions required for the integrated manage-ment of the metropolitan territory (especially in terms of urban sprawl); the demographic evolution of the Island of Montréal's French-speaking popu-lation; the dialogue needed between the region's economic actors in the context of a globalizing economy; and the future of Québec with respect to the Canadian federation. These many issues call for action, but also for political circumspection . . . . The Montréal region entered the new millennium amid a new round of controversy around the merger issue, beginning with the report's recommendation of creating either three or five cities in the western, central and eastern parts of the island instead of the present 29[1]. Montréal's current mayor is promoting the 'One island, one city' idea first put forward by Mayor Drapeau, as a way of sharing the tax burden more fairly, since there would still be major disparities between the three or five cities proposed. This idea is also supported by those who criticize the fact that the autonomy of the enclaves of Outremont, Westmount, Hampstead and Town of Mount Royal means that the '(City of) Montréal's political culture is hugely handicapped by the absence of a large, solid, educated middle class . . . (and) has been easy prey for all sorts of demagogues and ideologues, with the result that it's been badly run for years' (Gagnon, 1999). But the 'One island, one city' scenario, while being taken seriously, has not been endorsed by the provincial government: it immediately expressed its preoccupation with the demo-linguistic consequences of this kind of amalgamation which would lead to a reduced francophone majority in the proposed new single city on the island compared with that of the present City of Montréal.

Meanwhile, population projections appear to show a slowing down of urban sprawl under the pressures of demographic decline, the increasingly precarious nature of employment and the ageing of the region's population, factors which also contribute to suburbanites wanting to get closer to major social service points and economic centres (*La Presse*, 1999) as well as asking for more decentralized medical services. But the problems created by inefficient suburban development may prove difficult to remedy. The Montréal region has undergone some major transformations in the course of the last 30 years (Grégoire *et al.*, 1999), which public authorities have been powerless to control. It is perhaps only under the threat of crises that a comprehensive, regional, sector-by-sector approach has a chance of taking hold. In this respect recent developments in the public transit field may give some cause to end this chapter on a more optimistic note.

A NEW WAY OF GOVERNING?

By the late 1990s traffic congestion on the bridges linking the Island of Montréal to its suburbs, as well as on certain arteries in the vicinity of Dorval international airport, was becoming more and more severe (for instance, commuter trips from the South Shore regularly taking 90 minutes each way, about double the average of a few years earlier). It was becoming increasingly evident that an integrated regional perspective was needed. The provincial government committed itself in 1998 to extending the métro system further into the north-east of the Island and across the Rivière-des-Prairies to Laval, although at the time of writing the exact routes, and the division of responsibilities and costs for these projects are still matters of considerable controversy – especially when the province proposed that the MUC be responsible for all the costs of operating into Laval.

Meanwhile, the new Agence métropolitaine de transport has begun to improve several aspects of the regional transit system, including the establishment of new commuter rail routes utilizing existing Canadian Pacific and Canadian National railway tracks, services for which 40 per cent of the financing comes (albeit sometimes reluctantly) from the municipalities whose residents benefit from the system. Motorists throughout the Montréal region also contribute to public transit financing through a tax on motor vehicle registration permits and through a special levy on motor fuel. While there is still a long way to go, the financing of public transit is thus now more equitable than it was prior to the establishment of the AMT, in that the tax burden is now shared by off-island municipalities rather than entirely falling on MUC residents. There is also more comprehensive region-wide management of services including adapted transit for those with special mobility needs (Agence métropolitaine de transport, 1999). Other projects, including a light rail system, are still on the drawing board, and the AMT still has to negotiate the various dossiers with 102 municipalities, five administrative regions, 12 MRCs, the MUC, three sub-regional public transit corporations, 17 municipal transit agencies and 13 adapted transportation services . . . . Should an integrated metropolitan government system ever see the light of day, the AMT would doubtless play a key strategic role. For the time being, it appears to operate quite efficiently without having created yet another large bureaucratic structure (it only has about 20 employees). On the negative side, however, it has been accused of autocratic behaviour, notably in ignoring the wishes of some municipalities and the concerns of residents as regards automobile commuter traffic management on certain neighbourhood streets that are designated provincial traffic arteries and therefore come under the AMT's aegis. All in all, the Montréal regional government situation remains a far cry from the 'mega-city' recently created in the Toronto region, although this option – or another form of strong metropolitan government – could be legislated at a moment's notice on the whim of the provincial government.

ENDNOTE

[1] At time of press, two MUC municipalities (Lachine and Ville-St-Pierre) had just decided voluntarily to merge, reducing the MUC total to 28. Whether this marks the beginning of a trend remains to be seen.

5

MONTRÉAL'S ECONOMY: DECLINE, CONVERSION – POLARIZATION?

If, for Mayor Drapeau, netting Expo 67 World's Fair was a 'prize catch' and if many city-watchers saw the most successful World's Fair of the twentieth century as a crowning moment, the apogee of Montréal as an international city, a longer historical perspective and the benefit of hindsight reveal the naïveté of this viewpoint. In fact, at least since the 1920s a set of intertwined economic, geographical and political changes had been set in motion which chipped away directly at Montréal's supremacy on the Canadian economic scene as a financial power centre, communications hub and manufacturing powerhouse; a fact gradually revealed by the shift of financial transactions and corporate headquarters to Toronto and of shipping tonnage to west coast ports. Indirectly, these changes were also beginning to erode its status as a metropolis of international calibre in spite of the establishment of several important international organizations in Montréal in the aftermath of the Second World War. Yet from the post-war years until the mid-1970s, the city administration operated under the view that the city 'should lose its status as an industrial city in order to join the club of tertiary cities and be classified among world cities', and even considered studies of the inherent weaknesses of the Montréal economy to be 'subversive' (Léveillée and Whelan, 1990: 158)!

The political transformations in Québec – first, the 'Quiet Revolution' and then the rise of the independence movement – that were to accelerate the pace of the 'decline of the Montréal empire' (the metaphor is that of Coffey and Polèse, 1993) in the 1970s had been well under way since the beginning of the 1960s. While Montréal's civic boosters were preoccupied with modernizing the city's infrastructure and carving out a symbolic place in the world's civic league, a very different vision of the city was being forged by nationalists in Québec City, in Outremont – an enclave municipality (Figure 4.3) home to a huge proportion of Montréal's *indépendantiste* intelligentsia – and in francophone working-class neighbourhoods a few short Métro stops from the Expo site on Île-Sainte-Hélène. Essential to the nationalist project was the transformation of Montréal into the economic capital of the hoped-for new country, or, at least, in the milder versions of nationalism, harnessing the city to the goal of becoming *maîtres chez nous*. This entailed a number of transformations, both material and symbolic, which have been ably documented elsewhere (Levine, 1990, Chs 7 and 8; Linteau et al., 1991, Ch. 38; McRoberts, 1988, Chs 5 and 12; Vaillancourt, 1993). In essence, these involved: first, building and strengthening both public and private financial institutions whose primary concern was the management and circulation of capital for use in Québec's economic development; second, developing business services that would help manufacturing enterprises throughout the province to forge strong links to export markets; third, ensuring francophone dominance of management boards of major Québec-registered companies; fourth, making French the language of internal business and communication with customers in all but the smallest businesses; and fifth, erasing from downtown Montréal the visual trappings of a bilingualism historically associated with anglophone dominance.

The new corporate management class – often dubbed 'Québec, Inc.' because of its nurturing by a host of government policies – was largely headquartered in a new late-modernist 'landscape of power' (see Zukin, 1992) constructed in the eastern part of downtown (see Chapter 3). Here, it could further its business interests through locally-based networks while maintaining hotlines to Québec City. It is not by chance that the Montréal office of the Québec Premier is housed in a penthouse suite at the top of the Hydro-Québec building, the headquarters of the mammoth Québec-government controlled electric utility and the first building (early 1960s) to anchor this new landscape. As Coffey and Polèse (1993: 433) point out, these types of 'networks of complicity' between business and the state have helped other North American cities, such as Pittsburgh, make a successful economic turnaround. In addition, enlarging the provincial government presence in Montréal (even though most ministries remained in Québec City), as well as promoting state-subsidized cultural industries and providing funds for a massive expansion of the city's health care and higher education institutions, were means of enabling unilingual French-speakers to obtain good jobs without having to learn English. In this way, the state fostered the growth of the francophone middle class, and helped it diversify its employment options from the traditional liberal professions into a wide range of sectors of the economy (Levine, 1990, Ch. 7; Vaillancourt, 1993).

To recycle an oft-used cliché, there is no such thing as an innocent reading of the transformation of Montréal's economy since the 1960s. None would dispute that in the three decades since Expo 67 Montréal was definitively eclipsed as Canada's major metropolis and lost at least some of its visibility on the international scene. Yet while these developments are matters of profound regret for those who identify themselves as both Montrealers and Canadians, many Québec nationalists have an entirely different perspective. What appears for the former as the growing provincialism of the city (see e.g. Côté, 1996; Décarie, 1996) is, on the contrary, a matter of considerable pride for the latter (see e.g. Linteau, 1989, 1992) inasmuch as it amounts to a 'reconquest of Montréal' (Levine, 1990). For those committed to the independence of Québec, Montréal's successful harnessing to this project necessitates eclipsing its pan-Canadian vision and reining-in its bilingual tendencies. Consequently, throughout the 1970s and 1980s, Québec nationalists of all hues were relatively unconcerned, or at least ambivalent, about the international standing of Montréal, as long as key agencies in the city (staffed by bilingual people experienced in continental and international networking) could act as 'brokers' between francophone producers of goods and know-how and their markets outside Québec. Only in the 1990s, amidst growing doubts that Montréal can survive at its present size with a purely Québec-centred vocation (be this within or outside the Canadian federation), has the city seen a clearly emerging if fragile consensus – among both federalist and sovereigntist sympathizers in its local political and business elite – around the need to stimulate the economy through various strategies that would 'reinternationalize' Montréal. It is far from evident, however, that political leaders in Québec City embrace this viewpoint. In this chapter's account of the reshaping of the Montréal economy we make no attempt to harmonize these dual, and at times discordant perspectives, for to do so would be to underplay the tensions, both creative and destructive, that are central to understanding the city's current metropolitan dilemma.

FROM NATIONAL COMMAND CENTRE TO REGIONAL CITY: THE TRUNCATION OF MONTRÉAL'S HINTERLAND

The erosion of Montréal as pan-Canadian financial and corporate command centre

We have already discussed (in Chapter 2) the centrality of the metropolis-hinterland model in explaining Montréal's historical development and subsequent decline as a national and international city. A crucial dimension of metropolitanism in the Canadian context, as the influential historian Maurice Careless (1954, 1979, 1989) argued, is the exercise of economic power from major urban centres where companies make investment decisions that significantly affect regional or national development. This is why the ability of cities to attract or keep head offices, especially those of major financial institutions, as well as data on financial transactions, figure so significantly in the debate about their metropolitan status. This is also why, for most of the twentith century, analysts of Montréal's economy have had a seeming obsession with looking over their shoulders at Toronto (located some 550 km to the south-west; see Figure 5.1) and why we retain some elements of comparison with Toronto in the present chapter; for after all, as Kerr (1968: 540) pointed out, 'very few if any of the primates of the last century have lost their status in the twentieth', making Montréal an unusual case.

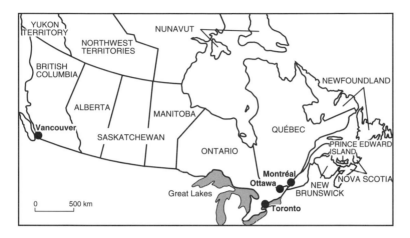

FIGURE 5.1 Canada: provincial and territorial boundaries, showing the four largest metropolitan areas

According to 1998 data ranking Canadian companies by revenue (*Financial Post*, 1998), six of the top 10 financial institutions were headquartered in Montréal compared to four in Toronto. However, since in the case of Canada's two largest banks most of the head-office personnel and the decision-making power have been transferred gradually to Toronto since the late 1970s, in effective terms all of the top five financial institutions are Toronto-based.[1] In addition, since office space is also often taken as an indicator of a city's importance as a corporate control centre, it is telling that in total, Toronto has 123 million sq. ft of office space to Montréal's 65 million and that between 1990 and mid-1996, a period when economic recession was followed by recovery in most of Canada, Toronto filled 6 million sq. ft of new office space, Vancouver 3 million. Calgary 2 million, but Montréal less than 500 000 (Levitt, 1996: 9).

We showed in Chapter 2 that Montréal's decline as a pan-Canadian financial centre relative to Toronto began in the early twentieth century. By the late 1980s the shift was virtually complete; in 1989 firms based in Toronto controlled 48 per cent of the assets of the Canadian financial system, compared to 28 per cent in the Montréal case (Semple, 1996). However, Montréal's decline as a national centre of finance and high-level corporate management has not been a linear one over the course of the century. Employment in the financial, insurance and real estate sectors suffered an accelerated decline relative to that of Toronto between the early 1970s and mid-1980s (Figure 5.2; see also Polèse, 1990; Coffey and Polèse, 1993). The departure of Sun Life Insurance, staged in a highly theatrical manner to underline the opposition of its management to the Québec independence movement and the quantitative importance of the capital outflow involved (Levine, 1990: 172–173), had great symbolic weight since

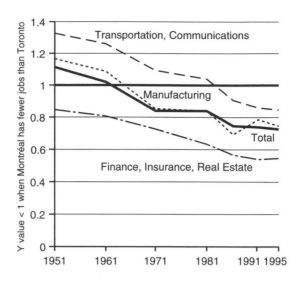

FIGURE 5.2 Employment in key sectors: Montréal's importance relative to Toronto, 1951–1995. Sources: Statistics Canada, Historical Labour Force Statistics, 1991. cat 71–201, 1997, cat. 71–201XPB; Statistics Canada, Canadian Economic Observer, Historical Statistical Supplement, 1992/93. cat. 11–210

its headquarters had once been the tallest building in the British Empire (Figure 3.19), but it was only the tip of the iceberg. Between 1978 and 1981 alone about 30 major companies in a wide variety of economic sectors moved their head offices out of Montréal, in most cases shifting to Toronto (Levine, 1990: 41–43). Subsequent new arrivals and the occasional reverse migration have never been sufficient to counter such losses.

The erosion of Montréal's position in the chain of command of the Canadian economy was undoubtedly much accelerated by the rise of Québec nationalism and especially by the 1976 election of the first Parti Québécois government which ushered in new language laws and gener-ated great uncertainty over the political future since its avowed aim was to take Québec out of the Canadian confederation. Head-office moves out of Montréal took place not only because of fears as to the value of investments in an independent Québec, nor only for cultural reasons linked to the preferences of anglophone managers and professionals, although the latter were undoubtedly important (Rudin, 1985: 214–217). Pragmatic assess-ments of comparative advantage were also made: for firms that would not 'normally' need to operate wholly or partly in French, the laws promoting French as the language of business and restricting access to English schools reduced the comparative advantage of Montréal *vis-à-vis* Toronto as regards the ability to attract key workers and the costs of business communication (Polèse, 1990; Levine, 1990: 172).

As Table 5.1 shows, by 1991 both the finance, insurance and real estate group and that of business services employed a smaller share of Montréal's service workers than those of Toronto, or even Vancouver in the case of the FIRE group. Detailed occupational data from the 1996 census underline the supremacy of Toronto in terms of the numbers of high-level managerial and professional positions in the financial sector (Statistics Canada, 1998a). Among those in senior management occupations in general, Torontonians earn on average almost 40 per cent more than Montrealers – a telling indicator of the relative importance of the two cities in high-level corporate decision-making. As we shall see in Chapter 6, this truncation of the supply of wealthy 'urban professionals' resulting from the change in Montréal's position in the urban hierarchy has had significant implications for the nature of and forms taken by inner-city revitalization processes, as compared with cities with the stature of national or global command centre.

Nevertheless, it would be erroneous to conclude that Montréal's national role in finance has been completely eclipsed. Although unable to compete in general terms with Toronto or major world centres, its core of expertise makes it able to support important niche markets that involve specialized financial instruments or partial deregulation. In 1999, as part of a major reorganization of stock exchange trading in Canada, the Montréal exchange ceded its remaining 10 per cent share of the nation's stock trading to Toronto and Vancouver but became the sole Canadian centre for trading in the growing 'derivatives' sector (stock options and futures contracts). Moreover, Montréal is the power base of the extremely powerful Québec-controlled Desjardins-Laurentienne financial and insurance conglomerate as well as of the government-controlled Caisse de dépôt et placement du Québec, the investment arm of one of the largest pension funds in North America, respectively ranked sixth and eighth by the *Financial Post* (1998; see Levine, 1990, Ch. 7). In fact, by the mid-1980s 10 of the 50 largest financial institutions in Canada were francophone (mainly Québec) firms (McRoberts, 1988: 428). The city has also been able to exploit its French character and cosmopolitan image to attract the North American head offices of several major continental European banks.

The movement of major corporate head offices to Toronto has tended to draw ancillary business and professional services with it. For example, the Canadian Bond Rating Service, founded in Montréal in 1972 and typical of the growing knowledge-based sector of the economy, shifted its base to Toronto in 1997 in order to maintain essential face-to-face contacts with its clients and with the investment community, although it had been thought for a time that new communications technologies would permit the agency to remain Montréal-based (*Globe and Mail*, 8 March 1997). Hence the relative stagnation of Montréal's business services sector – which researchers view as the 'dynamo' of the tertiary sector because of these services potential for rapid growth and their tendency to export their expertise beyond

TABLE 5.1 Labour force in service industries, by sector, 1991, and evolution, Montréal, Toronto and Vancouver CMAs, 1986–1991

	1991			Growth, 1986–1991		
	Montréal	Toronto	Vancouver	Montréal	Toronto	Vancouver
Total, service industries	1 221 905	1 650 865	698 710	14%	19%	21%
PUBLIC AND PARAPUBLIC SERVICES	29%	25%	25%	13%	25%	24%
Government service industries	7%	7%	6%	11%	28%	14%
Educational service industries	9%	8%	8%	8%	24%	32%
Health and social service industries	13%	10%	11%	17%	24%	26%
Business service industries	10%	13%	10%	34%	39%	40%
Finance, insurance and real estate	9%	12%	10%	16%	21%	24%
Communications and other utilities	5%	5%	5%	18%	17%	20%
Transportation and storage	6%	5%	7%	-4%	6%	4%
Wholesale trade industries	7%	7%	8%	7%	-7%	27%
Retail trade industries	17%	17%	16%	10%	17%	19%
Accommodation, food and beverage	8%	7%	10%	16%	7%	13%
Other service industries	9%	10%	10%	18%	23%	16%

Source: Statistics Canada, Census of 1986, Summary Tabulations, all CMAs, Table LF86B05; Census of 1991, C91, Profile Series B, CMAs and CAs (electronic product).

the metropolitan area. Although, according to one estimate, these types of services accounted for well over a fifth of tertiary sector job growth between 1971 and 1991 their performance was weaker than in Toronto and Vancouver, and that of the financial services component was particularly lacklustre (Coffey, 1998). Nonetheless, Canada's two largest engineering consulting firms, giants on the international scene, are francophone companies controlled from Montréal (McRoberts, 1988: 428; Barlow and Slack, 1985).

The loss of financial sector head offices was all the more painful given a parallel trend that was occurring over broadly the same period, namely the gravitational shift of manufacturing head offices away from Montréal towards North America's industrial heartland; for as Canada's branch plant economy developed in the 1960s and 1970s new headquarters tended to gravitate to Toronto. In 1989, corporations headquartered in Toronto were responsible for 49 per cent of manufacturing revenues compared to only 20 per cent for those based in Montréal (Semple, 1996). In 1998, of the seven US-controlled companies that were ranked in the top 50 in the *Financial Post* 500, not one had its Canadian headquarters in Montréal while four of them were in Toronto. Nevertheless, the headquarters of key players in some resource-based sectors remained in Montréal: in particular, Montréal remains the administrative centre of Canada's diversified pulp and paper industry. The industry, which has undergone massive restructuring in recent years, was for decades Canada's most important export earner, and even today is second only to telecommunications equipment in this respect. Québec's vast forest resource hinterland, abundant hydro-electric resources, accessibility to US markets and sources of recyclable paper, as well as its specialized labour pools, continue to favour the province as a location for major mills and Montréal as the location of the country's largest cluster of head offices, R&D activities and an annual industry convention giving rise to a City-designated 'Pulp and Paper Week'. Not even a recent wave of consolidations in this industry has unseated Montréal in this respect. In 1997 the formation of Canada's largest player in this sector, through the merger of two companies, one based in Toronto, the other in Montréal (though controlled by American interests since a previous merger in the 1980s) led to a toss-up between Toronto and Montréal as to the location of the merged head office. After an intense period of negotiations during which the symbolic importance to Montréal of not losing yet another head office in a key strategic sector became abundantly clear, it was in Montréal that head office functions were preserved, because of its geographical centrality for the pulp-and-paper sector including the greatest pool of expertise on the continent, and because of its bilingual workforce as well as lower head-office operating costs than in Toronto.[2]

In the early 1980s Montréal was still indubitably the rail transportation hub of the country – a fact reflected in Figure 5.2 which shows that for the transportation and communications sector as a whole, Toronto did not overtake Montréal in terms of employment numbers until after 1981. The Canadian National Railway (a crown corporation) controlled most of its 'empire' from its Montréal headquarters as well as still employing some 5000 workers in its Montréal railway shops. In 1996 the CN was still extremely important on a continental scale (the sixth largest railroad in North America) but by this time the corporation had been privatized, there had been major layoffs throughout the job hierarchy and its anchorage in Montréal was becoming looser. In contrast, Canadian Pacific Railways has long been part of a much more diversified conglomerate whose historic ties to Montréal, dating back to 1883, had weakened considerably in recent decades as it took on an increasingly Western Canadian focus. These shifts are related to continental-scale restructuring of the industry in the context of deregulation and the North American Free Trade Agreement rather than to political considerations. Nonetheless, the pivotal importance of this company in securing Montréal's historic dominance made the 1995–1998 head office moves of both the CPR and the main holding company to Calgary a loss of enormous importance to many Montrealers as 'the last surviving symbol of Montréal's days of reaching out, from Atlantic to Pacific and across both oceans to the world' (Décarie, 1996: 45).

Throughout the 1970s and 1980s Montréal's decline as a pan-Canadian head office centre was partially mitigated by the presence of federally chartered and regulated corporations, some government-owned crown corporations and other public companies, including several in the com-munications and transportation sectors (Rose and Villeneuve, 1993; Lamonde, 1994). The federal requirement for full bilingualism in these cases clearly favoured a Montréal location and in some cases (like Air Canada) the corporation's charter specified that the head office be in Montréal. On the other hand, these corporations' charters also require that the head offices be in Canada, meaning that should Québec leave Canada, the departure of these major employers and office-space tenants would be automatic. Montréal has also maintained its control on the headquarters of print and telecommunications media serving a francophone market (Polèse, 1988).

An advanced tertiary centre for a redefined hinterland

It has been argued, especially by Polèse (1990), that while Montréal has lost its traditional 'empire', namely its Canada-wide hinterland, as regards most branches of the advanced tertiary sector, its economy has in a significant sense been 'saved' by the Québec nationalist project. With the growth of the francophone business class, the city was able to consolidate its hold on the head offices of financial institutions servicing the province, and on ancillary business services, while Anglo-Canadian or American companies wishing to do business in Québec needed to have major regional offices in Montréal in order to provide service in French.

The public and parapublic sectors In addition, Montréal's economy was given an enormous boost from the 1960s through to the early 1990s by the mushrooming of provincial and municipal government employment and higher education and health services, which form part of the parapublic sector (Lamonde, 1994). These, as we have already explained, were an integral part of the Québec government's strategy of fostering the growth of a strong state and a powerful and diversified francophone middle-class. A network of public community colleges (known by their French acronym, *Cégep*) was set up, which all students must attend after high school to obtain technical qualifications or be eligible for university. The number of universities grew from three to four and the existing ones experienced major expansion (Linteau, 1992: 521–523). Today Montréal consistently draws more federal university research funds than any other Canadian city and McGill alone, for example, generates some 23 000 jobs and brings in some $350 million annually from outside the province. The hospital sector was also expanded with strengthened research links to the universities. Some of the effects of this strategy can be seen in Table 5.1 which indicates the greater importance of employment in educational, health and social service industries in Montréal compared to Toronto and Vancouver; 1996 occupational data confirm this portrait.

Moreover, within Québec, there is a strong centralization of the province's major medical and higher education institutions in the Montréal area. The hospital sector alone is the largest single source of jobs located within the City of Montréal; it employed some 90 000 workers in the mid-1990s, many of them inner-city residents. However, since educational, health and social services are highly dependent on funding from the provincial government, a city that is strong in these sectors is also very vulnerable to the effects of cutbacks, which have been implemented on a massive scale in the late 1990s. Especially hard-hit have been jobs in the hospital sector where several large institutions have closed or merged as part of major restructuring operations aimed at cost rationalization and modernization of facilities and organizations.

Employment in government services (i.e. the public sector) also forms a significant component of Montréal's tertiary sector. This sector is also strongly concentrated in the downtown area and over the past decade and a half has, like that of health and education, provided an important stabilizing element for the inner-city economy, since it includes a strong component of managerial and professional employment as well as generating thousands of reasonably paid unionized technical, blue- and 'pink'-collar positions at a time when corporate restructuring in the private sector has been eliminating these types of jobs. While the strength of the professional component in the public and parapublic sectors has significantly shaped the social character of inner-city revitalization, as we shall see in Chapter 6, the strength of these sectors as a whole has helped stave off the much-commented phenomenon of the 'declining' or 'missing middle class' observed in much of North America in the 1980s and 1980s (Rose and Villeneuve, 1993). Moreover, it has been shown that major centres of high-level government activities attract private sector business services generating significant multiplier effects (Lamonde, 1994).

However, the public sector's growth, like that in the parapublic sector, slowed in the late 1980s (Table 5.1); and in the 1990s employment levels have been reduced in all three tiers of government. An additional factor of concern to Montréal is the policy of the current Parti Québécois government (elected in 1994 and re-elected in 1998) to consolidate the provincial civil service in the capital city, Québec City. Only about one-fifth of provincial government jobs and an even smaller share of high-level managerial and professional positions were located in the Montréal Urban Community in the early 1990s (Lamonde, 1994) and the implementation of the 'national capital' policy is further eroding Montréal's position. In respect to state-sector employment then, Montréal's relationship with its regional hinterland remains a shaky and unreliable one, arguably a legacy of the historical tenuousness of the city's relationship with the rest of Québec (which we discussed in Chapter 2).

Arts and cultural industries   Montréal's position as metropolis of French Québec has also been pivotal in persuading governments (provincial and federal) to help maintain the vitality of its artistic and cultural industries – especially given the fragility of such industries in the province and indeed in Canada as a whole in the face of the homogenizing influences of American-dominated mass media and the erosion of national protection for cultural industries under new international trading agreements. It is not surprising that the city's unique cultural-linguistic make-up has generated a large and diversified cultural-artistic sector. The variability of definitions and the dearth of statistics make any estimate risky, but it probably employed around 26 000 people in the early 1990s (Latouche, 1994a). Between 1971 and 1991 census data show that Montréal had a larger percentage of its workforce in the arts and cultural industries than in any other Canadian metropolitan area although 1996 occupational data suggest that Toronto may now have caught up.

Certain parts of this sector have lost ground over the 1990s as government cutbacks have greatly shrunk major institutions such as Radio-Canada/ Canadian Broadcasting Corporation, Télé-Québec and the National Film Board of Canada/Office national du film (Trottier, 1998). One major Québec writer and film-maker saw sombre symbolic implications in the NFB's 1995 decision to move all its English-language production facilities to Toronto

(Godbout, 1995). Other segments of the industry are growing, however, notably in the digital video and multimedia field, to which we return later, but also in film production – here we are referring not only to local film-makers but to Montréal's growing importance as a *scène* for American and European films and television series, a sector that injected $1.2 billion into the local economy in 1997 and has become a major source of revenue for the City of Montréal. Aggressive promotion of Montréal's streetscapes, some of which can double for European cities, while others apparently evoke the quintessential eastern North American city, as well as low production costs and a pool of technical expertise, has had much to do with this development. Local film-makers hope that it will help build the local industry as well through synergistic effects and encouraging investments.

The 'edge city' phenomenon: a threat to Montréal as tertiary centre? North American cities in the 1990s have seen increasing research interest in and policy concern over the phenomenon dubbed 'edge cities' by journalist-turned-urban essayist Joel Garreau (1991). Over and above the well-established trend of decentralization of consumer services jobs and 'back offices' to suburban areas, the 'edge city' concept evokes the idea of the ever more autonomous suburban community, where a well-educated workforce and high quality infrastructure attract high-level tertiary activities such as major corporate offices and ancillary business services (as well as, frequently, high-technology 'parks'). Eventually, these communities may come to compete with the traditional central business district of the core city of the metropolitan area as a nexus for the face-to-face contacts still needed for key business transactions. To the extent that the economies of older central cities are dependent on the local multiplier effects of downtown corporate nexuses, the edge city represents a worrisome dynamic, especially in the absence of fiscal mechanisms for tax-base sharing across the entire metropolitan area.

As yet though, there is little evidence of a strong edge-city phenomenon taking hold in the Montréal region. The absence of a regional government policy of promoting outer-suburban office complexes, the relatively afford-able price of downtown commercial real-estate in Montréal's slow growth economy, and the continued attractiveness of the downtown core and adjacent residential districts to key 'knowledge workers' (see Chapter 6) may all have been offsetting factors (Coffey, Drolet and Polèse, 1996). The absence of consistently reliable time-series data at a fine spatial scale pre-vents exact measurement of locational shifts in financial and other producer services, but although the 1980s saw a rapid expansion of business and producer services in Laval and some of the outer suburbs on the North and South shore, the downtown core and adjacent neighbourhoods like the gentrifying Plateau Mont-Royal seem to have held their own. Services located in the downtown core continue to have the biggest gross sales and, as well as catering to downtown clients, service businesses in the rest of the province. Other parts of the old urban core seem, however, to be losing out in relative or even absolute terms in this process of bipolarization of growth in high-level services between the CBD and the outer suburbs (Coffey, 1998). Nevertheless, the 'edge city' question is by no means foreclosed in the Montréal case, especially as regards the high technology sector, which we will come to later in this chapter.

Beyond regionalism – a centre for international organizations?

Since the late 1980s, advocates of a renewed international presence for Montréal have increased their focus on expanding its role as a home to the headquarters of international organizations. While the strictly economic multiplier effects of such bodies are relatively modest, they are important for a city's participation in global networks of cities because of their high knowledge content: they draw key workers well-placed on international circuits of innovation and know-how and generate numerous symposia and conventions. The less-tangible overall prestige and promotional aspects are also not to be discounted: as Latouche observes, '[these] international organizations bear witness to the openness and cosmopolitan character of Montréal society' (1994b: v; our translation).

Reflecting the contrasting perspectives on Montréal's vocation alluded to early on in this chapter, the federal and muncipal governments have been much more active and more enthusiastic in this regard than the provincial government, although all three levels of government have contributed funding to a private non-profit agency mandated to lure more international agencies to the city (Latouche, 1994b).

Although this feature of the city's economy is not well-known to outsiders, with close to 50 such agencies Montréal is presently second only to Washington, DC on this indicator of internationalism. Not surprisingly, this number includes a variety of scientific and cultural agencies devoted to promoting international links between the countries of *La Francophonie*, but other types of activities are also represented. Several specialized international scientific associations are Montréal-based. The Secretariat for the Americas of the World Tourism Organization is also headquartered in Montréal. In quantitative terms, it is the aviation sector that is most important. In the immediate aftermath of the Second World War, Montréal's status as aviation centre led to a major specialized United Nations agency, the International Civil Aviation Organization (ICAO) being established in the city (Roberts, 1969: 367). The International Air Transport Association (IATA), a voluntary grouping of the world's airlines, followed suit and is still based in Montréal (although head office functions are shared with Geneva) and today several other private international aviation-related organizations are also Montréal-based, in part due to various fiscal incentives usually only offered to governmental agencies (Latouche, 1994b). In the mid-1990s ICAO's continued presence was assured with the construction of a new world headquarters close to the Palais des congrès (convention centre) and the World Trade Centre, located in the sector of lower downtown where a non-profit corporation set up by the Québec government and its pension-fund investing arm, the Caisse de Dépôt et Placement, hopes to create an integrated *Cité Internationale* district linked into the 'underground city'. A greatly expanded convention centre forms an integral part of this plan.

Lobbying efforts have concentrated on drawing new environmental agencies to Montréal, not without success, as witnessed by the arrival of the Multilateral Fund for the Implementation of the Montréal Protocol (to protect the earth's ozone layer) in 1987, the North American Commission for Environmental Cooperation (a NAFTA agency) in 1994, and the United Nations Environmental Secretariat in 1996. The last-named is doubtless the most significant as the choice resulted from a vote of government delegates from around the world in a tight contest between Geneva, Madrid and Nairobi; Montréal's low cost of living relative to quality of life may have been a significant factor. While it may be far too fanciful to imagine, as do some 'boosters', Montréal as the Geneva of North America, it would certainly seem that with two of the United Nations' five official languages, an increasingly multicultural workforce and a reputation for 'liveability' Montréal can reasonably expect a gradual increase in its role as a centre for international organizations, especially if the *Cité Internationale* project is successful.

INDUSTRIAL RESTRUCTURING AND CONVERSION

The recurrent debate about the significance of trends in advanced tertiary employment for Montréal's position in the international, national and regional urban hierarchies has at times tended to obscure a crucial aspect of the economy of the City, the Island and the metropolitan region – manufacturing. It is obviously the case that the secular trend of growth in tertiary (services) sector employment relative to jobs in manufacturing has greatly reshaped the Montréal region over the past two decades or so: by 1991 some three-quarters of CMA employment was in services (Coffey and Drolet, 1994), a trend broadly similar to that seen in other major Canadian centres – and indeed in large metropolitan cities throughout the developed world. Nevertheless, more than one outside observer has expressed surprise at the continued importance of some of Montréal's traditional industries, in both the manufacturing and the transportation sectors, especially in view of the erosion of its historical locational advantages as a water and rail transhipment hub with the construction of the St Lawrence Seaway in 1959. In fact, growth trends since the mid-1980s in some branches of the manufacturing sector can be seen to be providing a counterweight to the undermining of Montréal's status as a North American metropolis, in the sense that their production is increasingly oriented, not towards the rest of the province of Québec, but to the rest of Canada, the United States and beyond.

Still a port city, after all these years . . .

As we saw in Chapter 2, Montréal's historical *raison d'être* was its strategic location as a transhipment point at the head of navigation of the St Lawrence, a locational advantage which would lead to the city becoming a major continental hub for both maritime and railway traffic by the late nineteenth and early twentieth century, but that in subsequent decades the port progressively lost ground to the West Coast and to New York (Laserre, 1972, 1980). The opening of the St Lawrence Seaway in 1959, which had been opposed by Port of Montréal interests, inspired further pessimism as to the Port's future. Montréal's transhipment traffic in bulk cargo subsequently stagnated while that which bypassed Montréal's port facilities by using the Seaway grew by leaps and bounds (Nader, 1976: 134–135). Overall, Montréal has lost out significantly in terms of tonnage and number of ships using the port, due to shifts in trade flows from the Atlantic to the Pacific as well as to its having insufficient draught for bulk cargoes (Slack, 1996). Today the last of the huge grain silos looms empty at the entrance to the Lachine Canal, preserved as a heritage structure – to the chagrin of residents of a new condominium whose view out into the St Lawrence it helps block – and awaiting an imaginative conversion project, perhaps into a cultural/arts complex as is being done with a similar structure in Toronto.

Nevertheless, a specialized nexus of expertise and port-related services as well as improvements in ice-breaker technology have continued to make Montréal attractive for general cargo. With the closure of the Lachine Canal, commercial port facilities were shifted from the old urban core and consolidated in a 17 km long complex in the east end of the city. In the mid-1980s, Montréal was still the largest general merchandise port in Eastern Canada and was experiencing a rapid growth in containerized shipments, over half of which entered and left the port by rail (Comité pour la relance de l'économie et l'emploi de l'est de Montréal (CREEEM), 1986: 71), using the excellent railway connections that already existed. It was well-suited to take advantage of the new 'piggy-back' technologies to regain importance as a transhipment centre (water, rail, road) for containers. By the late 1980s Montréal had become Canada's leading port for containers leaving Canada by water, having captured a large share of the midwestern and northeastern US traffic to the point where the latter slightly exceeded Canadian cargo (McCalla, 1994: 33; Port de Montréal, 1997). Since then, Montréal has managed to show stronger and more consistent growth than competing East Coast ports by positioning itself as the 'express lane' from Europe to the industrial belt of Southern Ontario and the US Midwest. International container cargo increased by 60 per cent compared to 34 per cent for the next fastest in growth, New York (O'Keefe, 1996). In fact, by 1996 Montréal had overtaken New York as the leading port in eastern North America for containers in the North Atlantic market. The Port is also benefiting from increased trade with the Mediterranean and south-east Asia via the Suez Canal. Within the local economy its role is considerable, with some 14 000 direct and indirect jobs attributable to the port.

. . . and still a manufacturing stronghold

In spite of the gravitational shift to Southern Ontario that began in the early twentieth century (see Chapter 2), traditional manufacturing remained strong in Montréal, perhaps due to the city's accumulated expertise in particular specialized sectors and to the control of key industries by powerful monopolies keen to safeguard their interests in the city (Delage, 1943). Back in 1938, just before the outbreak of the Second World War, manufacturing industries in the core municipalities of the Montréal region (then 12 in number, including the South Shore city of Longueuil) furnished employment to 113 553 people, which amounted to 17.7 per cent of all manufacturing jobs in Canada and 53 per cent of the provincial total (Delage, 1943: Table 1); the latter proportion has remained at about 50 per cent to the present day (Table 5.2), but the Canadian share had slipped to 14.4 per cent by 1981 and by the mid-1960s Toronto had overtaken Montréal in terms of the absolute number of manufacturing jobs (Manzagol, 1972: see Figure 5.1). After a decade of massive restructuring, however, employment declined from the 1981 total of some 305 000 to about 296 000 by 1990 – with job losses being particularly severe in the clothing, petroleum refining and petrochemical sectors – but the relative position of the Montréal region *vis-à-vis* the rest of Québec and Canada as a whole was virtually unchanged (Lamonde and Martineau, 1992: Tables 2.6, 2.7). While many job losses were due to *in situ* rationalization of facilities, in other cases plants moved to other regions of Canada (mainly Ontario) in order to simultaneously both modernize and gain a more central location with respect to the North American market.

Manufacturing nonetheless still employed 20.7 per cent of the Montréal region's workforce in 1990, a higher share than in Toronto or any of the major northeastern and mid-western cities of the United States (apart from Cleveland and Detroit) (Lamonde and Martineau, 1992: 85, Table 2.8).[3] In fact when the performance of the Montréal region's manufacturing sector from the early 1970s to the early 1990s is compared with that of comparable American cities it becomes quite clear that the general trend has been one of 'conversion' rather than 'deindustrialization' (Lamonde and Martineau, 1992). The 1980s in fact saw considerable diversification of the manu-facturing base of the region. Looking at employment change can give us a

TABLE 5.2 Manufacturing employment in the Montréal CMA, 1981–1991

	Number		Per cent	
	1981	1991	1981	1991
Clothing, leather and related products	64 803	43 733	20.2	14.1
Textiles	15 679	13 377	4.9	4.3
Food, beverage, tobacco	35 727	32 600	11.1	10.5
Wood products, furniture	16 821	18 111	5.2	5.8
Printing, publishing, paper	31 061	35 459	9.7	11.4
Chemical, petrochemicals, rubber products	30 970	30 799	9.7	9.9
Non-metallic mineral products	8 491	8 908	2.6	2.9
Primary and fabricated metal products (except machinery and transportation equipment)	37 082	37 084	11.6	12.0
Transportation equipment	23 825	28 060	7.4	9.0
Industrial and commercial machinery (including computer equipment)	20 182	21 540	6.3	6.9
Other electrical and electronic equipment and components; measuring instruments	27 977	32 940	8.7	10.6
Miscellaneous manufacturing industries	8 271	7 701	2.6	2.5
Total	320 889	310 312	100	100

Source: INRS-Urbanisation, manufacturing industry data base.

rough indication of this process (data on value-added or value of shipments have unfortunately been unavailable at a detailed spatial scale since 1986).[4] Notably, the traditional labour-intensive sectors of clothing, leather and related products lost some 20 000 jobs and their share of manufacturing fell from 20 per cent to 14 per cent between 1981 and 1991. Meanwhile, electrical and electronics industries, transportation equipment and printing and publishing increased significantly in absolute and relative terms (Table 5.2; see also Martineau and Rioux, 1994).

Moreover, in spite of the secular trend for suburbanization of manu-facturing industry in search of sites appropriate to modern production techniques and shipping modes – a process which in the Montréal case got under way in the 1950s and accelerated in the 1980s (Manzagol, 1998) – manufacturing remains highly concentrated on the Island of Montréal (Montréal Urban Community). Despite a 7 percentage point drop from a decade earlier, three-quarters of the CMA's total manufacturing jobs were located there in 1991 (Martineau and Rioux, 1994: 18 and Table A-13). The trend toward conversion to a more diversified and higher technology base is also evident at this scale, particularly in Ville St-Laurent and several West Island municipalities which have gained jobs, most notably in the electronics and pharmaceutical industries, as have the off-island suburbs which have seen increases in a variety of heavy and light industries. The same cannot be said, however, for the City of Montréal itself, or for the East Island municipalities of the MUC, where not only have absolute job losses been major (some 35 000 in the City of Montréal) but where diversification is still very limited – almost 40 per cent of the City's manufacturing jobs remained in clothing and textiles (mainly the former) as of 1991 (Martineau and Rioux, 1994: Table 5), whereas for Canada as a whole the clothing industry only accounted for about 5 per cent of total manufacturing employment in 1995 (Canada, Industry Canada, 1998). Since space does not permit us to detail trends in all manufacturing sectors, we now focus selectively on two of its contrasting poles – the Montréal region's burgeoning 'high technology' sectors, concentrated in the West Island and increasingly in outer suburbs, and the struggling clothing industry, overwhelmingly concentrated in the City of Montréal.

The emergence of high technology and research and development clusters

While the symbolic and material dimensions of Montréal's loss of Canadian head offices were continuing to capture the headlines during the 1980s and early 1990s, major developments were simultaneously taking place in some of its traditional manufacturing sectors that would, by the mid-1990s, firmly place the Montréal region on the map as a 'high technology' centre (Shearmur, 1997 and 1999). Not only did this mean that reports of the Montréal economy's imminent death – widely circulated in the rest of Canada – were greatly exaggerated but it also signalled the beginnings of a re-internationalizing of Montréal that would both capitalize on the city's bicultural characteristics and at the same time create new dilemmas for those intent on establishing its identity as a French rather than a bilingual city.

The industries generally considered to form the core of the Montréal region's high technology sector – although there is admittedly no unequivocal definition of what this term includes (Bataïni and Coffey, 1998; Boisvert, 1992) – are telecommunications equipment, aeronautics, biopharmaceuticals, and, to a lesser extent, certain types of specialized software and computer graphics hardware. As is typically the case in the old slow-growing eastern North American cities (Boisvert, 1992), the first three of these developed out of some of the city's traditional industrial strengths but have restructured their production so as to capture specialized export markets. In order to reduce the costs of research and commercialization and establish a competitive advantage in both research and development and production, there is an increasing tendency for strategic alliances between firms and between industry and universities. Considerable government aid (especially from the province) is provided to these endeavours through tax

TABLE 5.3 Importance of research and development-intensive manufacturing in Montréal and the rest of Québec, 1995

	Greater Montréal	Rest of Québec	Montréal's share of provincial total
Total manufacturing	244 818	254 244	49%
Intensity in research and development:			
High	16%	2%	89%
Medium-high	13%	7%	63%
Medium-low	19%	23%	45%
Low	52%	68%	42%

Source: Calculated from Québec, Ministère de l'Industrie. . . (1996), Table 22, Table E (based on a special tabulation).

Note: The classification is that of the OECD, based on mean R&D expenses relative to sales of the different industrial groups in the main OECD countries. The definition of Greater Montréal used here includes a slightly larger area than the Montréal CMA.

breaks for R&D, loans and other incentives such as a publicly funded venture capital corporation which assists new high technology industries (Niosi, 1995; Trépanier et al., 1994). One of the main reasons they are nurtured by government is that these high technology industries are strongly oriented towards international exports: 1990 data for those located on the Island of Montréal indicate, for example, that 65 per cent of production is shipped outside Canada in the case of transportation equipment, and 38 per cent for electrical/electronics, versus only 13.5 per cent for the average of all manufacturing industries (Société québécoise de développement de la main-d'oeuvre de Montréal [SQDMM], 1995, Annexe 13).

As Table 5.3 shows dramatically, the greater its orientation towards research and development – a key dimension of high-technology and knowledge-based industries – the more likely it is that a manufacturing-sector job will be located in the Montréal area rather than elsewhere in the province of Québec. This reflects a much broader trend, to which we shall return later, for knowledge-based activities around the globe to be organized into a network of major urban centres or city-regions between which key workers circulate as 'transmigrants'; this growing transnationalism (Glick-Schiller et al., 1995) is giving serious cause to rethink the very notion that a 'metropolis' can only exist in the presence of a 'hinterland'. The overwhelming metropolitan concentration of R&D also further underlines the gulf between Montréal and the rest of Québec, whose depressed peripheral regions, restive and politically influential, have long insisted that the economic problems of Montréal should not be given priority by the provincial government.

A 1995 study of North American metropolitan regions of over 2 million inhabitants, conducted by Price Waterhouse, ranked Montréal ninth for the number of high technology firms with over 100 employees. Although only fifteenth in population, Montréal was the top-ranking in the ratio of number of high technology jobs per capita in the information technology, aerospace and biopharmaceutical fields. In terms of absolute numbers of jobs in the field, it ranked fifth in aerospace, sixth in biopharmaceuticals and tenth in information technology. However, only 10 per cent of the *Fortune* magazine 50 top-ranked high technology companies were present in Montréal, indicating that the region's strengths are still to a large extent in smaller and medium-sized businesses. At the Canadian scale, it is the Ottawa region (with a population of just over one million) that has the highest number of high technology jobs per capita, but a comparison of occupational data from the 1996 census between the Montréal and Toronto CMAs indicates that Montréal has, for example, a higher percentage of physical science and life sciences professionals, aerospace engineers and technicians and, moreover, that these occupations have grown much faster in Montréal than in Toronto since 1990 (authors' calculations). A 1998 study by the KPMG group found that Canada's business costs were the lowest of any G7 country in pharmaceuticals, telecommunications equipment, electronics and advanced software; Montréal thus clearly makes a major contribution to Canada's international competitiveness in the 'new economy'.

This restructuring of high technology industries has also often entailed a series of locational shifts – from inner-city zones such as the Lachine Canal district to older industrial suburbs and then to newer suburban locations in Ville St-Laurent, the West Island and the South Shore (Chevalier, 1993; Comité pour la relance de l'économie et de l'emploi du sud-ouest de Montréal [CREESOM], 1989a: 184). Suburban municipalities have long played an active role in this process through the development of industrial parks (Manzagol, 1998). The growth of the major industrial suburb of Ville St-Laurent – strategically located close to expressways and Dorval airport – owes its initial impetus to the establishment of munitions and aeronautics firms, Canadair in particular, during the Second World War (Manzagol, 1972). More recently, West Island municipalities have promoted industrial condominiums suitable for small firms in the microelectronics sector, although the City of Montréal has nonetheless managed to 'capture' almost half of Québec's electronics firms within its own boundaries (Trépanier et al., 1994). A newer trend, perhaps presaging the beginnings of an 'edge city' after all, is represented by an ambitious science and technology park set up by the City of Laval. It is designed so as to facilitate inter-firm networking between firms specializing in one of four different high technology fields, and its biotechnology sector includes a centre designed to assist 'incubator businesses'; this is supported by a para-state agency and a major research institute located in the park (Manzagol and Sénécal, 1998). In particular, growth in the R&D-intensive biopharmaceutical sector is increasingly taking place in this research park as well as in new outer suburban research parks

on the South Shore, to which some firms are relocating from MUC municipalities – a disquieting trend from the Island municipalities' point of view in
the current fiscal context in which (as we discussed in Chapter 4) tax-base
sharing does not extend to off-Island municipalities.

Aeronautics and aerospace   Building on the Montréal region's traditional
strengths in transportation equipment engineering, the aeronautics sector,
first established in the inter-war period, developed rapidly during and after
the Second World War. Major players included Canadian-owned firms such
as Canadair (later merged with the hugely successful Québec-owned
transportation equipment corporation Bombardier, whose largest division
is now aerospace) and CAE Electronics, as well as Canadian divisions of
American corporations, most notably Pratt and Whitney Canada (Boisvert,
1992). Some of these firms established themselves right away in suburban
locations, while others moved from the inner city, as in the case of an RCA
electronics plant in the Lachine Canal district that metamorphosed into
Spar Aerospace in Ste-Anne-de-Bellevue on the West Island.

   Since most of the production had been geared to defence contracts
(Manzagol, 1972), the winding-down of the Cold War meant this sector had
to restructure radically and seek out new market niches around the world. It
also needed to form strategic alliances to share the high costs of innovation
and has increasingly moved in this direction (Trépanier et al., 1994). Products include specialized aircraft lines, components and ancillary equipment such as flight simulators and navigation systems. As elsewere in the
world, there is still strong government financial support for this industry:
Canadian military purchases have been replaced by loans, loan guarantees
and grants for R&D to consolidate and enhance a company's expertise in a
particular niche market, and to foster the commercialization of new products for export to the United States, France and elsewhere in the world.
Canada now ranks as the sixth most important nation globally in the aeronautics and aerospace fields, with over two-thirds of production being for
the export market; more than half of this production and three-quarters of
the R&D are located in the Montréal region and the two 'home-grown'
companies are world leaders in their field despite fierce competition. With
some 35 000 direct jobs and $5 billion in shipments in 1996 – representing
an expansion of over 10 per cent since the early 1990s – this sector is a
pillar in the provincial government's strategic clustering policy of industrial/
regional development (Québec, Ministère de l'Industrie du Commerce, de
la Science, et de la Technologie, 1996b).

Telecommunications equipment   Telecommunications equipment, another
key sector in Montréal's emerging high technology nexus, is also an old-
established one. The Northern Electric & Manufacturing Co. was split off
from Bell Telephone in the 1890s and the industry experienced spectacular

growth with the spread of the telephone in the first half of the twentieth century (Boisvert, 1992); in the 1920s, its manufacturing plant in Pointe St-Charles was reputedly the largest brick building in the British Empire. Nortel Networks (as it is now called) moved its national headquarters from Montréal to the Toronto area during the post-1976 'exodus', but major production activities are located both in Ottawa and Montréal, with R&D in both places (Chevalier, 1993). Its Montréal telecommunications-transmission equipment complex – which in 1997 was producing the systems used by more than half of the Internet traffic in North America – is now at the core of a major telecommunications nexus with a number of companies together employing some 7000 people in total, mostly in Ville St-Laurent. Fibreoptics and various types of wireless telephone systems, for both of which there is a surge in demand worldwide, are among the market niches successfully exploited. Major expansions of Nortel's production facilities in the late 1990s, creating hundreds of new jobs for engineers and computer scientists, targeted the existing complex, rather than locating elsewhere. This strategy was influenced by the attractiveness of the 'people-base', Montréal's strong network of universities, and the cluster of related firms in the area. European firms cite similar reasons for establishing new R&D facilities in the area, as well as welcoming the chance to establish a beachhead to the US market and the added bonus of substantial provincial tax credits. This industry also has significant multiplier effects for local software and micro-electronics firms with the flexibility to adjust production lines frequently to meet its needs for very short production runs (Québec, Ministère de l'Industrie du Commerce, de la Science, et de la Technologie, 1996b). Furthermore, the strength of the telecommunications cluster, along with the region's bilingual workforce, is making Montréal an attractive location for the burgeoning national, continental and international 'call centre' business which has a great deal of job creation potential for semi-skilled workers.

Pharmaceuticals and biotechnology Today another horizontally and vertically integrated industrial cluster of major significance to the restructuring of Montréal's economy in the 1990s, the pharmaceutical industry has been an important player since the beginning of the twentieth century, attracting both local and foreign investment capital. Indigenous firms were increasingly taken over by or merged with American and foreign multinationals, creating a branch-plant structure (Manzagol, 1972). Unlike the trend in numbers of other economic sectors, Québec's share of Canadian pharmaceutical jobs grew considerably relative to that of Ontario after the Second World War, and although it has somewhat fewer total jobs than Ontario Québec has surpassed Ontario in value added per production worker.

Although a number of major drug company multinationals moved their Canadian head offices out of Québec between 1976 and 1983 (Canada, 1985), the Québec sovereignty movement seemed to have no negative effect on the research and development component of this industry. There has in fact been significant creation of professional and technical jobs in the R&D sector, and the Québec affiliates of several of the multinationals have achieved a very high profile within the corporations for the quality of their research activities (Bataïni, Martineau and Trépanier, 1997). This has been accompanied, however, by simultaneous losses in lower-paying manufacturing jobs as the multinationals have restructured and consolidated their production facilities, some of which have been relocated to other parts of Canada and to the United States (Trépanier et al., 1994). The Montréal industry has developed a strong focus on clinical research, a rapidly growing field on a world scale. Clinical trials are conducted in-house or, increasingly, contracted-out to private pharmaceutical services laboratories as well as to universities. Hand-in-hand with drug-testing are small flexible firms that can make drugs in small quantities, much as in the case of telecommunications equipment mentioned above.

Montréal's success in developing this clustering of R&D-oriented biopharmaceutical companies is often attributed to the generous federal and provincial tax breaks available for R&D that, as the companies often acknowledge, help make the province of Québec one of the world's best environments for pharmaceutical research and development. Competitive land costs and the overall 'liveability' of the Montréal area also play a role (*Montreal Gazette*, 7 Nov. 1996). Two other factors seem to be primordial, however. First, Canadian federal law and Québec government policies support the brand-name drug industries over their competitors, the manufacturers of 'generic' drugs. The pharmaceutical companies claim that their investment in primary R&D is contingent on the profits generated by their maintaining patent protection for their products for an extended period of time so as to delay the introduction of generic versions of these products. Accordingly, in 1987 and 1992, Canadian law extended such patent protection; it now covers 20 years, more or less in line with measures in force in the other countries where these firms tend to locate; moreover, regulations unique to Québec further enhance this protection. Between 1988 and 1994 well over 1000 direct and indirect jobs were created in the R&D sector of this industry in the Montréal area (Bataïni, Martineau and Trépanier, 1997).

Secondly, Montréal is the primary health and life-sciences research centre in Canada. The city has a large and closely integrated complex of university hospitals and specialized research centres, some of which are among the world leaders in several fields of clinical research and practice. A 1990 estimate put the number of Montréal-based researchers in the overall biopharmaceuticals field at well over 2000 not counting graduate students and post-doctoral fellows (Trépanier et al., 1994). McGill University's McIntyre Medical Building, jocularly known as the 'beer can' and omnipresent in vistas from the top of Mount Royal (Figure 1.1), houses the country's most extensive medical library collection. This research network's capacity to produce leading-edge specialists is enhanced by the unique access to both French- and English-language international networks of medical expertise. Moreover, industry–university links are characterized by close cooperation. These factors create an ideal milieu for recruitment of new talent as well as for clinical testing of the drug companies' new products. In turn, research clinicians generally reinvest the honorariums they obtain for carrying out these contracts into fundamental research activities. Industry–university links do not necessarily form part of a *local* cluster of synergistic networks, however, since the universities tend to obtain their grants and contracts via international-level contacts with the parent companies rather than with their Québec affiliates. The industry's contribution to Montréal's economy is thus not so much one of generating manufacturing production in this sector as in reinforcing some of the key strengths of its universities (Bataïni, Martineau and Trépanier, 1997).

The pharmaceuticals sector has generated important spinoffs into the burgeoning realm of biotechnology, in which Canada is now strongly represented on a world scale relative to its population size. This field involves numerous small local firms and university hospital labs active in fundamental research, developing a variety of innovative products and increasingly establishing strategic links with biotechnology complexes in other regions, such as the Boston area. By the late 1990s Montréal was home to 40 per cent of Canadian biotechnology companies, including 66 per cent of those at the start-up stage, and was the tenth most important centre in North America for this field. Some of these innovative enterprises are indigenous, while others are drawn to the Montréal region. Factors attracting them include the presence of a cluster of multinationals, some of whom will nurture them financially, and to whom they hope eventually to licence their products, and the availability of financial support from venture capital funds – a sector in which Québec leads the rest of Canada due to the collaboration of state agencies, private financial institutions and labour union investment arms – which can assist them until they can commercialize their production and know-how. A non-profit centre helps 'incubate' innovative small firms in the field by providing services to them in a cost-effective manner. Once again, however, it is the strength of life-sciences research in Montréal's universities and affiliated hospitals that has led to the rapid growth of the biotechnology industry cluster.

Nonetheless, Montréal's future as a leader in the biopharmaceuticals field is not entirely assured. The second half of the 1990s saw drastic government budget slashing in the health and higher education fields, threatening not only the quantity and quality of front-line services in the hospitals and clinicians' working conditions, but also the universities' abilities to maintain a research infrastructure of international calibre. Particularly in the more footloose anglophone milieux centred on the McGill University hospitals, vigorous efforts are being made to recruit and retain international-calibre talent to ensure that the Montréal life-sciences research complex carries its world-class status into the new century.

Microelectronics   With an estimated 12 000 jobs in 1992, Montréal's micro-electronics industry has about 70 per cent of provincial employment in the field, but is not as well-developed as that of Toronto or Ottawa (Trépanier et al., 1994). Toronto, for instance, had close to twice the number of computer engineers, systems analysts and computer programmers as Montréal in 1995, according to the 1996 census. The Montréal industry includes relatively standardized but high-quality production facilities for semiconductors and other components, mainly involving firms that subcontract for larger corporations and who are drawn by the relatively low costs of skilled labour as well as by low-cost land and utilities. The availability of universities for developing and testing circuitry is also a drawing card (Trépanier and Bataïni, 1993). Expansion of more specialized R&D and production has been hampered by an inadequate supply of graduates and college-trained technicians in electronics engineering and related fields; this is a Canada-wide problem but is more acute in Québec in spite of recent improvements. Nevertheless, Montréal firms have successfully developed certain market niches in hardware and software. The most important of these are high-performance graphics boards and digital video (to which we return below), in which there is now an established cluster of international-calibre firms.

One of the difficulties with a sector whose local prosperity is based on small innovative flexible firms exploiting specialized market niches is that they may not be able to remain in town if they need to pursue strategic alliances with larger firms that are located elsewhere. As we have seen, this issue does not arise in the case of the integrated biopharmaceuticals complex or for microelectronic firms associated with the telecommunications sector, but it has arisen for some innovative software developers – one local firm, for example, had to shift most of its operations to the high tech centre of Austin, Texas in order to pursue its strategic alliances with major US customers (*Montreal Gazette*, 28 Oct. 1995).

Key workers, global networks – reinternationalizing the local economy? Access to specialized labour is a crucial locational factor for the high technology fields we have referred to here as well as for other knowledge-intensive fields (Boisvert, 1992). As can be seen from Table 5.4, the Montréal region's labour force has become considerably 'upgraded' over the past two decades. However, slow demographic growth in the Province of Québec (as evidenced by the population pyramids shown in Figure 4.7) as well as severe cuts to university funding in the late 1990s have posed a challenge for a city trying to renew its economy based on a youthful and highly skilled workforce. It is difficult to recruit sufficient key workers from within the

TABLE 5.4 Occupational structure, Montréal Census Metropolitan Area (1981 boundaries), 1971, 1981 and 1991

Occupational category	1971	1981	1991
Managers	3.5%	5.9%	7.5%
Professionals	12.7%	12.6%	15.1%
Supervisors	9.9%	8.8%	8.4%
Upper-level white-collar/technical	18.9%	20.7%	21.2%
Lower-level white-collar/sales/service workers	29.2%	28.5%	28.7%
Skilled blue-collar production workers	12.4%	10.9%	9.7%
Semi- and unskilled blue-collar production workers	13.4%	12.6%	9.4%
Total	953 375	1 348 055	1 509 140

Source: Statistics Canada, Censuses of Population, special compilations for D. Rose and P. Villeneuve

Note: Those whose occupations were not stated in the census questionnaire have been excluded from the totals on which the percentages are calculated.

province; higher education institutions are unable to keep pace with the demand for information technology specialists, according to a study by a non-profit organization set up to develop the region's high tech community. Montréal's high technology and research-oriented enterprises now find themselves, moreover, competing in a labour market global in scope where the largest corporations regularly 'head-hunt' in cities around the world.

The world's major urban centres are today the crossroads for such strategic workers, including immigrants and key personnel on shorter-term sojourns. These key workers are less and less likely to remain with the same employer, let alone in the same city, for most of their working lives. Indeed, to continue to be a centre of innovation, the contemporary metropolis increasingly depends on information flows and therefore on being on national and international circuits of talent (Castells, 1989); as Hall (1986: 141) observes, 'the great city has remained vigorous in part because of the entrepreneurial traditions that have come from the injection of new blood'. 'Quality of life' considerations are thus becoming increasingly important in the recruitment of dynamic businesses and key workers – which is largely what explains the popularity of 'urban liveability' indicators. In this respect, some see a silver lining in Montréal's protracted economic slump; in the mid-1990s the Montréal Urban Community was promoting its low housing costs and the relatively uncongested expressways on the Island (compared with other large cities in this part of North America) as lures to potential investors, and pointing out the appeal of growing businesses to cities that have not exhausted their 'growth potential' (Communauté urbaine de Montréal, 1995). By late 1997, office vacancy rates had been reduced considerably – a turnaround not only attributable to a gradually improving economy but also to the fact that Montréal's office rental rates are a bargain in the North American market.

Montréal's unique cultural-linguistic situation can be either an asset in a global economy or a liability in a borderless labour market. On the asset side, francophone talent may be less inclined than anglophone talent to be 'drained' away from Montréal to English-speaking cities. Also, it can be argued that Montréal has the potential to become a Mecca for businesses seeking mobile and cosmopolitan key workers for an internationally oriented economy, because of its exceptionally high rate of bilingualism, its increasingly multiethnic school population and growing numbers of young people whose first or home language is neither French nor English and who tend to be trilingual by the time they have finished their schooling – indeed, Montréal is probably the most trilingual city in North America (Jedwab, 1996). As one local business leader in the mercantile banking field opined: 'The assessment that Montréal should be the Geneva of the twenty-first century is based on cultural reality, geographical reality and historical reality' (Culver, 1996). In this respect a single anecdotal example is revealing: Montréal has spawned a firm that has become one of the world's two largest companies involved in the development of multilingual Internet software; its mix of cultures and the atmosphere of acceptance of diversity apparently made it easy to recruit a staff speaking a total of 16 languages, 'an important asset for a company that's out to make the global village a reality' – its main competitor is located in another bilingual, multicultural city, Jerusalem (*Montreal Gazette*, 28 Oct. 1996).

On the negative side, Québec's language policies have indubitably contributed to the difficulties many high technology companies have experienced in recruiting international talent in spite of Montréal's atttractiveness in terms of many quality of life factors and its low housing costs (Levitt, 1996). For example, a major graphics board firm opted to hedge its bets by dividing an expansion plan between Montréal and Florida over concerns that political uncertainty in Québec threatened its chances of recruiting a full complement of talent to its ranks – an identical strategy to that adopted by Pratt and Whitney in the aeronautics sector for the same reason.

This dilemma is not one that can be resolved simply. As we mentioned in Chapter 1, the Québec state and Montréal municipal and business leaders continue to have difficulty dealing with the implications of Montréal being the place that is not only the dynamo of French Québec but also the gateway where French Québec meets the rest of the world – not only a utilitarian gateway for exporting Québec products but an interactive connection into the 'space of flows'. Promoters of economic development in Montréal must juggle with the paradox of 'selling' its bilingual character to potential foreign investors while not wanting to enshrine this fact in government policy, since the official line is that any measures seen as institutionalizing bilingualism would jeopardize the cultural survival of Québec. More pragmatically, it has been argued that were Montréal to distance itself from the language of the province's majority, it would be stripped of its position as regional metropolis for the Québec hinterland (Polèse, 1996) and thus suffer further job losses, especially in the government, parapublic and cultural sectors which, as we have mentioned, have been an important anchor over a couple of economically and politically turbulent decades.

In partial recognition of the difficulties arising from the fact that internationally oriented Montréal companies have to manage 'a complex linguistic interface' between a local society functioning mainly in French and a world-wide milieu where English is the language of business (Levitt, 1996: 3) successive provincial governments have – very discreetly – made some compromises on the question of schooling, which is a pivotal dimension in quality of life considerations for high technology workers, according to a study by the Conference Board of Canada (cited in *Montreal Gazette*, 13 Sept. 1997). R&D based businesses were exempted from the requirement to conduct all internal operations in French and the children of key employees temporarily assigned to Québec were allowed to attend English-language schools for a period that was initially restricted to six years. In 1997, at a major 'economic summit' a committee of business leaders, while expressing solidarity with the social goal of maintaining French as the primary language of Québec society, forcefully argued that these provisions were still not enough to enable them to recruit the desired talent. Consequently, the Parti Québécois government lifted the time limitation on English schooling for children of foreign workers on employment contracts in Québec as long as these contracts were defined as 'temporary', as well as easing restrictions on employment for their spouses.

We have seen that trends in a number of key industries, as well as – more tentatively – the growing presence of international organizations, give indications that Montréal is beginning to outgrow its traditional dependence on a 'hinterland' and to take steps toward claiming a place in global networks of city-regions. Indeed, these networks seem to eclipse the very model of 'metropolis–hinterland' relationships, however important these relationships may have been in shaping the city's historical trajectories of development and decline. Moreover, various economic studies indicate that economic ties (in both directions) between the metropolitan area and the rest of the province have weakened in recent years. Export-oriented enterprises in the regions have become less dependent on Montréal-based services as intermediaries, while between 1974 and 1990 the share of manufacturing shipments exported outside of the province increased much faster among metropolitan Montréal companies than for those in the rest of the province. At the same time, inter-business linkages have strengthened between different parts of the metropolitan area, notwithstanding the continued intermunicipal fragmentation and rivalries we referred to in Chapter 4, thus bringing the 'city-region' concept closer to reality (Bélanger and Léveillée, 1996). The political implications of these trends for the relationship between Montréal and the rest of Québec are wide-open to speculation.

Industrial decline and its consequences in the inner city

Coping with economic globalization: the case of the clothing industry Far removed from the circuits of high-powered international labour markets are Montréal's traditional labour intensive industries, which are still crucial to the regional economy. High tech sectors in fact employ only about 3 per cent of the Montréal labour force whereas 'traditional' low value-added industries provide work for close to four times that number, according to 1996 census data (Shearmur, 1999). We referred in Chapter 2 to the historical centrality of the garment trade. It has remained the largest single component of the region's manufacturing employment structure right up to the present day. Montréal is the hub of the Canadian clothing industry with some 40 per cent of Canadian jobs in 1996 (Shearmur, 1999). It continues to benefit from a pool of specialized labour – from designers to pattern-makers to sewers. Census data indicate that in 1995, there were 25 670 people working as machine operators or related workers in fabric, fur and leather products in the Montréal region compared to only 14 840 in Toronto. Nevertheless, this industry has undergone major Canada-wide restructuring since the early 1970s, as domestic production struggled to compete with imports in a globalizing market (Cannon, 1996). In Montréal this has entailed drastic job losses that began in the 1980s (Table 5.2), especially in the low-wage parts of the industry. The machine operator category referred to above shrank by about 5 per cent between 1990 and 1995. However, an exact picture of job change is difficult to glean from the statistics, because one of the strategies to which major manufacturers resorted in an effort to cut costs in the face of increased foreign competition was to subcontract to small operators who employ home-workers – mostly immigrant women (see Labelle et al., 1987) – for some stages of the production process (Lipsig-Mummé, 1983; Tufts, 1998).

Skilled jobs within the industry have fared somewhat better although new technologies have reduced their numbers as well. It is evident that only by becoming a high value-added sector where producers can rapidly adapt to changing demand can Montréal's clothing industry compete with cheap-labour countries (Cannon, 1996). Thus, the industry is being refocused on 'fashion' rather than 'garments', especially as regards women's clothing. Its capital-intensity is increasing, and with some government assistance, parts of the industry have shifted away from production into marketing and design, as well as into the importation and distribution business. Over 80 per cent of Montréal shipments are destined for the internal Canadian market but with the Free Trade Agreement, the United States is becoming an important target market (Québec, Ministère de l'Industrie, 1996b), a key challenge being to establish a place in the US distribution network (Shearmur, 1999). Clothing exports are almost exclusively destined for the US, mainly to the New York and New England regions. The low value of the

Canadian dollar in the late 1990s (in the 64–68 cent range compared to the US dollar) has increased the attractiveness of Canadian clothing exports to US buyers (Shearmur, 1999).

The success of this strategy is as yet far from evident, however. Canada-wide trends covering the period 1990–1996 for those parts of the clothing industry in which Montréal specializes paint a disturbing portrait of continuing dramatic job losses and lack of increase in productivity (Canada, Industry Canada, 1998), and in the Montréal clothing industry employment declined by a further 11 per cent from 1991 levels, although there were signs of improvement by the late 1990s (Shearmur, 1999). These trends are not necessarily attributable to the North American Free Trade Agreement since in a number of sub-sectors of the clothing industry job losses were relatively worse in the United States than in Canada, but are undoubtedly linked to wider processes of economic globalization and trade deregulation (see Ville de Montréal, 1995: 101). The only sector where recent employment trends are strongly positive is that of sports clothing, a growing market in which Montréal's clothing industry participates (but which it shares with other parts of Canada to a much greater extent than women's fashions). Even in this sector, government grants and municipal tax breaks are sometimes used as incentives to job-creating investments in high-unemployment areas.

Restructuring and relocation are, of course, linked processes, as Massey (1982) demonstrated. The general trend in Montréal's garment industry has been for plants producing non-speciality and long-production-run items to decentralize to suburbs, or very commonly to small towns elsewhere in the province (Manzagol, 1983; Colgan, 1985), while 'flexible' factories producing short-production-run fashion items remain concentrated relatively close to the downtown core, to facilitate negotiations with and deliveries to brokers and sales outlets. Nevertheless, some less specialized production has remained in the inner city due to 'industrial inertia' – in this case being able to maintain cheap premises and have easy access to a largely female and heavily immigrant workforce dependent on public transportation (Steed, 1976a, 1976b; Chicoine and Rose, 1989). Over time, with the exception of the fur industry which remains concentrated in a tiny pocket of old medium-rise buildings in the downtown core, the industry's centre of gravity has shifted several kilometres north-west from its historical hearth, but it remains predominantly in the city of Montréal. The clothing industry remains a pillar of the inner-city economy, albeit now a somewhat shaky one.

Inner-city deindustrialization In general then, the mushrooming of certain high technology sectors and the successful restructuring of some of the region's traditional industries have substantially maintained Montréal's strength as a major manufacturing centre in North America. However,

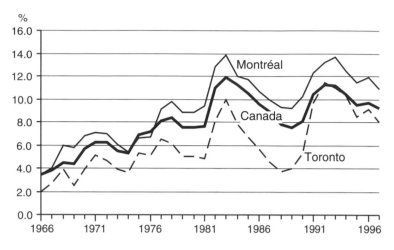

FIGURE 5.3 Unemployment rates: Montréal, Toronto and Canada as a whole, 1966–1995

while 'conversion' rather than 'deindustrialization' may be the appropriate epithet to characterize the *overall* tendency in the manufacturing sector (Lamonde and Polèse, 1984; Lamonde and Martineau, 1992), through most of the 1990s this conversion did little to diminish the region's long-standing high levels of unemployment (which are compared to those of Toronto and Canada as a whole in the time-series data in Figure 5.3).[5]

Between 1971 and 1991 Montréal ranked eighteenth among the 25 Canadian CMAs for employment growth. Its unemployment rate dipped below 10 per cent only once between 1982 and 1997 and reached 13 to 14 per cent in the recessions of the early 1980s and early 1990s, and continued to post the highest unemployment rates of any major metropolitan area in Canada or the United States. Moreover, the first half of the 1990s saw a considerable increase in the duration of spells of unemployment, especially for older workers, even after the onset of recovery from the early 1990s recession (Société québécoise de développement de la main-d'oeuvre de Montréal [SQDMM], 1995: 11). The weakness of major segments of the manufacturing sector is a substantial contributor to high unemployment (Chorney, 1990); thus, workers laid-off from manufacturing jobs consistently face greater difficulties than other workers in obtaining another job (SQDMM, 1995: 27). Unemployment rates are doubtless also swelled by the the fact that the city remains the main pole of attraction for migrants from peripheral regions of Québec hard hit by the decline of natural resource based industries (Conseil des Affaires sociales, 1989; Beaudin, 1987).

The depth of the unemployment problem varies considerably by region within the CMA, however (Séguin, 1998). According to 1991 census data, unemployment rates were lower than the Canadian average (10.2 per cent) among residents of the South Shore suburbs (apart from the old industrial centre of Longueuil), North Shore suburbs, Laval and the West Island. They were much higher in the City of Montréal (14.6 per cent) and most of the other municipalities of the old urban core (see Mongeau, 1994, Table 2.5; SQDMM, 1995, Annexe 2). Even within the City of Montréal, however, there are great variations (see Morin, 1997, Map 1). These variations reflect a growing socio-economic polarization between municipalities and neighbourhoods with high concentrations of university-educated people working in high-technology or advanced tertiary sector jobs and those containing high proportions of people marginalized by economic restructuring – a point we return to in Chapter 6.

Particularly on the Island of Montréal, plant closures have been a major contributing factor to structural unemployment. To take just one example, in the south-west part of the city, around the old industrial core of the Lachine Canal, over 20 000 manufacturing jobs disappeared from the late 1960s to the late 1980s, largely attributable to the closure of the canal (partial closure in 1965 and definitive closure in 1970) and the obsolescence of the old industrial buildings and the surrounding infrastructure. Many of the job losses were due to actual plant closures or drastic downsizing – deindustrialization in the true sense. In other cases, the plants moved to suburban locations in the Montréal region and simultaneously restructured, changing their production processes and their product lines – as was the case for several major firms in the electrical and pharmaceutical sectors (CREESOM, 1989a: 183–196).

A number of daunting challenges confront residents of Montréal's deindustrialized inner city districts like Rosemont, Hochelaga-Maisonneuve, Centre-sud and Pointe St-Charles, many thousands of whom have been displaced from their jobs in the traditional manufacturing and ancillary industries that anchored their neighbourhoods for up to a century (Morin, 1983, 1987; CREEEM, 1987; L'Actualité, 1995) or who are trying to enter the labour market for the first time. The same is true of neighbourhoods at the north east end of the island whose residents were heavily dependent on jobs in petrochemicals. This sector, focused on refining with relatively little diversification into related petrochemical industries (Manzagol, 1972), was gutted during the 1980s as the major oil companies rationalized their facilities due to declining demand as customers switched to gas or electricity, as well as to corporate consolidation and changes to a federal policy that had previously protected Montréal as a producer for Eastern Canadian markets (Montreal Gazette, 1 Nov. 1992). These districts contain numerous census tracts with over 20 per cent unemployment. In some sectors a third of more of residents have completed less than nine years of schooling. This puts them in a very weak labour market position in terms of human capital, for in Canada, as in most Western countries since the early 1980s, there has been a growth in 'credentialism', meaning increasingly stringent educational and training requirements for access to the labour market, and a concomitant decline in labour market possibilities for those with little formal education (Bowlby, Lévesque and Sunter, 1997; Frank, 1996). Moreover, with increasing suburbanization of the population, the city core has fewer and fewer of the type of consumer-service sector jobs that still require relatively little in the way of education and training; and – in an example of what urban geographers have characterized the 'spatial mismatch' (Kain, 1992) – the unemployed cannot necessarily afford to travel to the burgeoning suburbs to take on such jobs (widely-dubbed 'McJobs' in North American parlance), which are typically part-time and paid at minimum wage (*Montreal Gazette*, 28 Sept. 1996). In sum, notwithstanding the diversity of the Montréal region's economy, thousands of workers or potential workers are excluded from it.

Moreover, although there was a modest net increase of 120 000 jobs (all economic sectors combined) on the Island of Montréal between 1987 and 1996, the lion's share of new jobs went to suburban residents. By 1996 off-Island commuters, some 400 000 of them, comprised over one-third of those employed on the Island. The number of Island residents who held paid jobs actually fell by 83 000 to 788 000 between 1987 and 1994 (SQDMM, 1995: x), a trend largely reflecting unemployment, exclusion from the labour force and the ageing of the population.

Reindustrializing the inner-city: local development initiatives As in a number of American cities, non-profit community organizations have sprung up since the mid-1980s in the Montréal neighbourhoods worst hit by deindustrialization, with the goal of creating or maintaining durable employment opportunities for local residents (Bouchard and Chagnon, 1998). By the mid-1990s there were seven of these Corporations de développement économique communautaire (CDEC), each one covering one of the city's *arrondissements* (major planning districts), and in receipt of funding from the municipal, provincial and federal governments. Although the CDECs' resources are limited and their territorial base covers players with disparate needs and interests, research comparing businesses that do operate in concert with the CDECs and those who do not indicates that the former are indeed more committed to the local area, more likely to hire local residents and to provide them with job training (Lemelin and Morin, 1991; Morin, 1997).

On the whole, the emphasis of CDECs has been on small and medium-sized businesses, in both manufacturing and services, including artisanal enterprises and those at the 'incubator' stage. Occasionally, however, they have helped to broker deals between unions, large employers and various levels of government so as to preserve jobs with major employers – as in the case of the Canadian National Railway (formerly Grand Trunk) locomotive maintenance works in the Pointe St-Charles district of south-west

Montréal, recently taken over by a French multinational, where 1100 direct jobs and several thousand spin-off jobs were at stake (*Montreal Gazette*, 27 Jan. 1996). In another instance, the CDEC operating in the Rosemont district was heavily involved in setting up a local development corporation, the *Société de Développement Angus* (SDA) for an innovative project in the former Angus Shops of the Canadian Pacific Railway (Klein and Waaub, 1995; Société de Développement Angus, 1997). This huge railway equipment construction and repair works was founded in 1904 and provided well-paid employment to 7000 workers in its heyday, spawning the new residential suburb of Rosemont (Linteau, 1982: 148; Reynolds, 1935). But as Canadian Pacific (CP) shifted its centre of gravity to Western Canada, the Shops were wound down in stages between the late 1970s and early 1990s. The eastern part of this huge site was bought by a paramunicipal housing corporation and is now a new residential neighbourhood of mixed housing types and income groups (see Chapter 6).

When CP closed the remainder of the Shops in 1992 a broad consensus emerged around the need to give priority to locally based industrial development, with the outcome that while CP has developed part of the site for market-rate housing and some large retail stores, the SDA has acquired the rest (2.4 million sq. ft) for an industrial park specializing in environmental technology industries, some of which are being housed in an 'industrial mall' inside the old locomotive sheds. Financing was arranged through a consortium of local businesses, venture capitalists, banks, *caisses populaires* (credit unions) and the province's electricity utility, Hydro-Québec. The project is ambitious, seeking to create 1500–2000 jobs by exploiting a niche little developed in Québec (though tried in other deindustrialized cities such as Chattanooga, Tennessee), but with the potential to create highly skilled employment and create training and job opportunities for undereducated and unemployed local youth – one of the first projects to get off the ground, for example, was a factory-*cum*-technical school recycling obsolete microcomputers and training people in different aspects of recycling technologies. The SDA and its community and government partners hope, moreover, that the 'environment technopole' will have spin-offs for other parts of the East Island of Montréal badly hit by the closure of most of its oil refineries. In addition, this project, because of its specialized nature, may avoid one of the traps that territorially based community economic development corporations often face, namely competing with their sister organizations for a very limited pool of business willing to locate in the inner city (see Morin, 1997). It is too early to assess the likely success of this venture, but it will have to overcome the fact of the environmental technology sector being less well-focused and 'networked' than Montréal's established high technology industries, especially given that science and technology parks usually do better when they specialize in a region's established strengths (Klein et al., 1998; Amirahmadi and Saff, 1993).

A much-lauded characteristic of Montréal's local economic development movement has been its capacity to develop workable partnerships between community groups representing local residents, businesses, unions and different levels of government, enabling the formation of fairly effective lobbying committees for the economic renewal of particularly depressed areas (Labelle et al., 1998). Nonetheless, the political will of a key player in such partnerships – the provincial government – may have been tempered by its continuing commitment to foster the growth of outer suburban industrial parks. Moreover, the community economic development movement itself has not escaped criticism, notably over the fact that it has been – understandably – dominated by concerns to revive the economies of traditional working-class neighbourhoods where the male working class has taken a big hit from deindustrialization. Consequently, relatively little consideration has been given to other groups hit by declining job opportunities in their 'traditional' sectors of employment – immigrant women in the clothing industry, for example. A variety of small community organizations targeting immigrants and minorities, as well as Community Loan Circles to assist very small business start-ups, have begun to address such concerns at a micro-scale, aiming to give priority to the capital needs of some of society's most excluded members (Mendell and Evoy, 1993; McMurtry, 1993). More recently, and with some government support, certain CDECs have established projects aimed at creating jobs through the provision of services for local needy groups, such as the immobile elderly; such strategies fall within the concept of the 'social economy' first developed in France (Laville, 1994). While '[t]he community sector has been active in developing new approaches and in building networks of social solidarity' (Lustiger-Thaler and Shragge,1998: 237), partnership models have not been without their costs, as greater stability in funding has often been achieved at the expense of decreased scope and autonomy for the organizations involved, and there is a strong risk of developing a 'subcontracting' relationship with the state in which the community organizations essentially recruit cheap labour.

Resulting in part from pressures from community development groups, the City of Montréal has, since the late 1970s, played quite a proactive role in conserving industry in some inner city districts, through a range of initiatives administered by its paramunicipal organizations, including the preparation of 10 industrial parks, a variety of loan guarantees and other forms of assistance to private industry (Ville de Montréal, 1992: 49). This represented a considerable change from the cavalier and neglectful perspective that had previously characterized the municipal administration (Léveillée and Whelan, 1990). For instance, in the Rouen sector of the Hochelaga-Maisonneuve *arrondissement*, a municipal industrial renewal programme set up in the 1980s included a land-banking scheme to combine small parcels of land into larger tracts suitable for constructing the type of one- or two-storey buildings needed by most present-day industries – a technique oft-recommended to counter inner-city deindustrialization (see Kotval, Moriarty and Mullin, 1993); the programme has helped maintain 2500 jobs in a mixture of light and heavy industries (Sénécal, 1995). In other instances, doubts have been raised as to whether municipal assistance was being appropriately targeted rather than seemingly entailing largesse to large breweries and tobacco manufacturers – not by any stretch of the imagination among the most fragile of local industries (Morin, 1983) – a concern that is partially addressed by the establishment of municipal partnerships with the CDECs. Moreover, the success of municipal initiatives has been muted by the difficulty of offering serviced land at prices competitive with those of the suburbs and in obtaining funds for the decontamination of 'brownfield' sites.

Commonly though, efforts to maintain or bring in new industry in old industrial neighbourhoods meet with only lukewarm support, and sometimes outright local opposition, especially when the available industrial sites or buildings are densely interspersed with residential development, raising the spectre of pollution and declining property values. In the Maisonneuve neighbourhood, located between the former Olympic Stadium complex and the St Lawrence, the community economic development corporation's efforts to revive small- and medium-sized industry in the former 'Promoters' City' (see Chapter 2) have been largely stymied by such concerns. Although the district can hardly be said to be gentrifying – it remains one of the city's poorest – well-organized groups, seeking to transform the graceful legacy of wide boulevards and heritage buildings of this planned industrial suburb of the late nineteenth century into a verdant postmodern recreational and tourist district, were able to block a new garment factory that planned to locate adjacent to the recently renovated municipal public market (Sénécal, 1995).

It has been the case of the Lachine Canal, however, that has generated the most high-profile debate about the role of industry in Montréal's inner city, entailing conflicts of vision between industry and housing, rich and poor and over the value of heritage preservation (Germain, 1990; London, 1997). Here, the major actors have been: Parks Canada, the federal government department charged with preserving the heritage form of the oldest industrial district in Canada and making it an accessible recreational corridor, linked in with the MUC's *Réseau vert* (Green Network) project; the City of Montréal, ever-concerned about its tax base; developers interested in converting old industrial buildings into lofts and condominiums and community organizations in the adjacent deindustrialized Pointe St-Charles neighbourhood, concerned to limit the spread of gentrification and above all to create new industrial jobs. To a large extent, it has been cultural-recreational and heritage concerns that have won the day. The elegant Belding-Corticelli building, which once housed a large cotton textile factory located right on the canal, was converted into an imposing fashionable condominium project

FIGURE 5.4 Belding-Corticelli building, on the Lachine Canal: this former silk
factory was converted into fashionable condominiums. Reproduced
by permission from Jean-Claude Marsan

in the early 1990s (Figure 5.4); on the north side of the canal, the former
Stelco building has also been converted to residential use (Figure 6.6); and
on the south side the former Sherwin-Williams paint factory complex has
been renovated for social housing for low-income families and people with
disabilities (funded under a joint provincial-municipal programme) as well
as for some private market loft-style condominiums. The Redpath Sugar
Refinery, the oldest remaining industrial complex in Canada, is part of the
Lachine Canal National Historic Site, but is in an advanced state of
decrepitude; here too, the City of Montréal, at the time of writing, wants to
see the site renovated for a condominium development.

Inner-city industry: towards flexible futures? Nevertheless, much of the
canal district zoning remains industrial – due in part, to successful lobbying by community development groups – and a few new factories have
located in old buildings, including a high-fashion clothing firm. Provision for
dozens of small businesses has been made in the former Northern Electric
building. Many of these businesses – whose landlord is a City of Montréal
paramunicipal corporation charging modest rents – provide specialized

services or products to large corporate offices in the CBD (printing, for example – which, as we mentioned earlier, is one of the very industrial sectors doing well in the City of Montréal). Others are artisanal manufacturers or 'incubator' enterprises in various high technology fields. Since such uses are widely considered to be compatible with adjoining residential areas, support for them by community organizations (CREESOM, 1989b: 54) seems to represent a strategic compromise with the forces of gentrification.

Finally, recent developments in a mixed land-use zone to the south of the CBD may presage the economy of the future for the inner city of a metropolis trying to reconcile culture and productive high technology industry as motors of development. The sector known as the Faubourg-des-Récollets has been almost entirely abandoned by its traditional industries and warehouses, and until recently was favoured by few except for a number of artists. Much of the land was owned by a paramunicipal corporation which had abandoned an earlier plan for high-rise residential developments due to the slumping economy of the early 1990s, while new enterprises seeking to locate there have had difficulty getting private-sector financing, seemingly due to the 'red-lining' of the area by banks who considered it too risky a location. However, it has an interesting location at the mouth of the Lachine Canal, although not yet well-linked to the revitalized parts of the canal zone. It is just west of Old Montréal and the Old Port, into which millions of federal dollars have been injected to create an all-year-round recreational and tourist development, with great success.

During the 1990s – assisted by provincial tax provisions for venture capital – the City of Montréal has seen a mushrooming of the multimedia field, estimated in the late 1990s to number some 200 firms with 2500 employees. It has spawned two of the world's leading firms in digital editing and software for the film industry allowing special effects creators to layer images seamlessly on top of one another (including the company that 'sank the Titanic' in the 1998 movie version and won a science and engineering award in the 1999 Academy Awards). Increasingly, such firms are gravitating from their original locations (in one case, a former garment factory in the Mile End district) to renovated heritage industrial buildings in this zone (*Montreal Gazette*, 19 July 1997, 14 Nov. 1997). In its recruitment advertisements, one of the firms promotes the area's industrial heritage and its bohemian ambience as well as its recreational potential as vital assets to help promote would-be employees' creative instincts, along with unlimited cappuccino and fresh fruit on the job! This spatial consolidation of multimedia firms is being encouraged by the provincial government which in 1998 designated the area as the *Cité du Multimédia* and offered generous tax credits to moves that create jobs in this zone (or relocate them from elsewhere), the rationale for such expenditures being that this is one of the few types of high technology industry that prefers to locate in the inner city. The aim is to create a synergistic nexus, corresponding to what Castells

(1989: 89) refers to as an 'innovative industrial milieu [which in terms of its locational requirements] is closer to the situation of writers and artists, or stock exchange traders in New York, or to film and television producers . . . in Los Angeles, than to the concentration of textile or steel mills in the early industrial cities'. A paramunicipal corporation, the real-estate investment arm of the Caisse de Dépôt and a trade-union based job creation fund are all involved in this scheme, which is already generating many hundreds of jobs. In addition, a Multimedia Academy set up in the area by a public–private consortium will offer specialized training in this field, in the hope of cementing Québec's strategic market position in this field. However, the success of several of these firms has attracted foreign takeovers, making their future place in Montréal less assured.

This type of endeavour stands in contrast to earlier failed municipal attempts to lure the more standard types of high technology industry to a bland corner of Pointe St-Charles, where after a decade of trying to create a Technoparc, the city opted to lease much of the site for a golf course. Some observers see these kinds of knowledge- and creativity-based industries, entailing little fixed capital investment, as highly suited to a city where uncertainty about political futures never runs far below the surface (see e.g. Polèse, 1996). Part of the Technoparc site has now been taken up by Canada's largest film studio, capitalizing on the city's growing popularity as a site for film shoots, mentioned earlier in this chapter.

A NEW SPOTLIGHT ON THE INTERNATIONAL STAGE: TOURISM, FESTIVAL AND SPECTACLE

Finally, no survey of Montréal's economy, even the necessarily partial one presented here, would be complete without reference to the tourist industry – on a world scale the fastest-growing industry, with Canada being the tenth most visited country and the ninth in terms of revenues amassed from tourism (Samson, 1994). Since the late 1980s, and even more so since Montréal's 350th anniversary celebrations in 1992 – when hundreds of millions of dollars were invested by all three levels of government in touristic-cultural attractions of international calibre, such as the Biodôme (in the former Olympic Vélodrome), the Old Port, the archaeological museum at Pointe-à-Callière in Old Montréal (see Figure 3.5), among others – the city has experienced a major revival not only as a domestic but also as an international destination both for vacationing tourists and for conferences and conventions.

This renewal of tourism is important symbolically as well as materially to a city trying to recreate and redefine its metropolitan stature, because the post-Expo 67 and post-Olympics years were a long moribund period for this sector. For much of the 1970s and 1980s Montréal suffered from a nebulous image – promoted in terms of a subtle cultural ambience and architectural features that the typical short-stay visitor could not easily discover. Despite being the locus of some 40 per cent of tourist spending in the province, the Québec Tourism Ministry seemed – repeating the classic pattern of Québec–Montréal relations which we discussed in Chapter 4 – to treat Montréal as just another administrative region among many others (Samson, 1994: 28–29). The industry was also dogged by the reputation the city acquired in the 1970s for political instability and hostility to non-francophones. Moreover, its public relations and technical competence were marred by cultural insularity and rank amateurishness. In particular, the failure to employ translators with English as mother-tongue led to promotional literature ranging from the mildly embarrassing to spectacular gaffes such as the posting of highway signs all over the northeastern United States – a region whose residents are not known for their fondness for winter – that tried to promote half-price hotel discounts with the logo 'Montréal: minus 50'!

The situation began to improve in the late 1980s with the emergence of a regional consensus that tourism could and ought to be a major motor of the new Montréal economy. A revamped *Office des congrès et du tourisme du Grand Montréal* has worked with public and private sector partners to channel government assistance (which comes from both the provincial and federal levels) to more appropriate forms of tourism promotion and to obtain new sources of funding, such as a hotel occupancy tax, for new investments and promotional budgets (Samson, 1994). By the early to mid-1990s these efforts were meeting with considerable success, especially in the northeastern US market (*Montreal Gazette*, 17 Oct. 1996, 7 June 1997). A 1992 study found that tourism created 28 300 direct jobs and injected some $1.2 billion into the local economy through direct spending, with 8.5 million visitors, of whom almost 40 per cent were from outside Canada. Two-thirds of the foreign visitors were American, and, moreover, a university survey on tourist satisfaction found that overall it was the American visitors who expressed the highest levels of satisfaction, notably as regards restaurants, shopping, general ambience, French culture and 'safe city' qualities (Samson, 1994: 2; Lagacé, 1993). Activities for children were also ranked very highly, doubtless reflecting the fact that since its revamping in 1992 the Old Port has become the city's most visited attraction, drawing 7.7 million person-visitors in 1998 (Dufresne et al., 1999). This facility appeals not only to tourists (about 900 000 of the person-visits are from outside Québec) but also enhances the liveability of the city for resident families who flock to it summer and winter (Figures 3.4, 3.5).

Underutilized land adjacent to the Old Port is slated (at the time of writing, 1999) to become a high tech indoor theme park of 1.8 million sq. ft, developed by one of Canada's largest development corporations with start-up assistance from an investment arm of the provincial government. Finally, since 1994 the provincial government has operated a casino on part of the former Expo 67 site. Notwithstanding concerns about the 'non-productive' nature of this kind of revenue-generating activity, not to mention the social problems it may contribute to (Swift, 1995), the Montréal casino has been successful beyond all expectations, creating some 1750 unionized jobs. In its first year of operation it drew 25 per cent of its clientele from outside the region including 100 000 attracted from outside the province, injecting $87 million into the local economy (*Globe and Mail*, 9 Jan. 1995), and these numbers have increased in subsequent years.

Over the same period, active promotion, especially by a non-profit public–private agency, Montréal International (headquartered in the city and also, significantly, in Washington DC), has also enabled Montréal to gain importance as a conference and convention venue, to the point where in 1995 it was third within North America and thirteenth in the world in terms of numbers of attendees at international conventions (or national ones with international participation). As mentioned earlier in the context of the Cité Internationale project, plans are underway to enhance the city's competitiveness in this arena by expanding the Palais de Congrès – and in the process recreating a physical connection between downtown and Old Montréal sundered a few decades ago by the construction of a trench for the Ville-Marie expressway. This expansion would also involve indoor links to nearby hotels so as to save international conventioneers from the vagaries of the Montréal winter.

Perhaps the most unique aspect of tourism in contemporary Montréal, however, is that the city's unique cultural *métissage* (to which we return in Chapter 7) and reputation for 'liveability' have led to a growing reputation, not only within eastern North America but also internationally, as the 'city of festivals'. In addition to annual events such as the Formula 1 Grand Prix, the International Fireworks Competition and the Tour de l'Île (a bicycle tour that now attracts 40 000 participants, a good number of them international), summer in the city is dominated by a series of cultural festivals that run one after the other – the Francofolies, the *Just for Laughs/Juste pour Rire* comedy festival, and, biggest of all, the 10-day-long Jazz Festival, now the biggest such event in the world. Studies of the economic impact of these festivals indicate that they generate some $140 million in direct spending and generate over $50 million in tax revenues while their multiplier effects include significant job creation for professionals and technicians in the arts and cultural fields; yet only about 10 per cent of their funding comes from government grants, the lion's share being from corporate sponsorships and admission to paid shows.

A 1995 survey found that one out of seven festival attendees were tourists almost half of whom (three-quarters in the case of the Jazz Festival) came to town specifically for the festival (Archambault et al., 1996). These events thus combine a minority of tourists with a majority of locals for whom the festivals are a major rite of the city's short but generally hot and humid summer, especially the Jazz Festival since it is the first one (beginning at the

FIGURE 5.5 A steamy July afternoon at the Montréal International Jazz Festival, Place-des-Arts and St Catherine Street. (Damaris Rose)

end of June). The unique aspect of the Montréal festivals, compared to those in other North American cities, stems from the fact that so much of their activities revolve around free events that take place on normally busy downtown city streets closed off for the occasion (Figure 5.5). The Jazz Festival promoters argue, with justification, that it is a major continental booster of the city's image and important symbol of its quality of life for visitors and locals alike. International visitors are particularly taken with the ambience of tens of thousands of people at any one time, of all ages and cultures, milling around in a few city blocks until midnight in a completely safe environment with very low-key security.

The 'liveability' dimension of Montréal has recently created another target for tourist promotions. Doubtless encouraged by the trendy American *UTNE Reader*'s high ranking of a few Montréal neighbourhoods in 1998, especially the Plateau Mont-Royal, the Québec government is planning to assist local non-profit organizations in promoting tourist attractions rooted in local cultures. One proposal includes a guided tour of the settings of playwright and novelist Michel Tremblay's works, including vignettes of productions staged – quintessentially – from the balconies that epitomize the life of the neighbourhood (Figures 6.7 and 7.10).

As a number of urban researchers and commentators have argued, there is a darker side to an inner-city economy increasingly focused on festival and spectacle. For the Expo 67 World's Fair the park on Île Sainte Hélène was closed to those who could not afford the admission fee to the Expo grounds because, as city officials argued, the existence of a free public park would 'detract from the unity of the fair'; when the park was finally reopened in 1970 an imposing fence topped with barbed wire separated it from the Expo grounds (Puxley, 1971: 51–52). In today's festival city, much has changed in that free outdoor events add to the cachet, yet some see shades of 'bread and circuses' in the 'feel-good' image they promote in places where poverty and marginal forms of employment are the lot of many. Representatives of low-income neighbourhoods close to the proposed Technoparc have questioned the quality of the jobs created by the private sector entertainment industry, not to mention the potential for 'Disneyfication' of a part of Montréal that is central to the city's industrial heritage (*Montreal Gazette*, 15 April 1999).

Arguably more troubling is the social 'sanitization' of the local environment in which municipalities engage, displacing marginalized groups from their everyday spaces in order to promote a perceptibly clean and safe atmosphere for the tourism and recreation of spectacle. Although not taking such extreme forms as in some American cities (see e.g. Ruddick, 1996), this has happened in Montréal with the City and institutions such as the Université du Québec à Montréal working at sprucing up the seedier margins of the festival district. Young punks and runaways, some from the Montréal area, others from Québec's peripheral regions or Canada's Maritime Provinces, fleeing severe family problems, poverty or both and facing minimal prospects in the formal economy, have been gravitating to this downtown fringe zone for a number of years. Here, becoming part of a community of street kids, they have found a place to call home and to survive by an array of more or less illicit means, but these latest attempts at urban renewal and civic beautification are eliminating the spaces they claim as their own (Parazelli, 1997). In similar vein, the City of Montréal cracked down on 'squeegee kids' in the summer of 1998, their presence seen as incompatible with the ludic images of festival and tourism promoted both internationally and to potential middle-class residents by the boosters of the 'new Montréal'. How best to harness the economic potential of festival and spectacle without contributing to new forms of social polarization and spatial exclusion is a new challenge that will have to be faced. As we shall see in the next chapter, the question 'a liveable city for whom?' is never far below the surface in debates about the principles and the practice of revitalizing Montréal's inner-city neighbourhoods.

ENDNOTES

[1] Technically, a head office only has to consist of a chairperson and a company secretary, so this indicator of a city's status can be misleading as we shall see below with respect to the banking sector.

[2] From here on, much of the material covered in this chapter has been obtained by the authors through extensive searches of the local business press, complemented with company information. So as not to overburden the text, most of these references have been eliminated.

[3] These data are based on Statistics Canada's estimates of manufacturing employment and on the 1981 definition of the Census Metropolitan Area. A data base maintained by INRS-Urbanisation obtains somewhat higher totals (310 889 in 1981 and 310 312 in 1991) due to better coverage of small production units and to the use of the 1991 CMA boundaries, which cover a larger territory (see Martineau and Rioux, 1994). The latter data base was used to compile Table 5.2.

[4] Manufacturing activity in the Montréal Urban Community alone contributes well over one-third of the value-added and value of manufacturing shipments in Québec, according to the most recent (1995) estimates available (Institut de la Statistique du Québec, 1999a: Table 12).

[5] When examining Figure 5.3 it should be borne in mind that Canada as a whole has had persistently high unemployment rates relative to the other G7 countries. Canada's economic growth strategy has long been based on the export of raw and semifinished materials, to a much greater extent than most highly industrialized countries. It is often argued that this strategy continues to hinder diversification and modernization of manufacturing industries and investment in specialized high technology sectors (see e.g. Cohen, 1991). The economy of the country as a whole, and especially that of the provinces most dependent on resource-exporting, is thus highly vulnerable to worldwide economic downturns. Even in central Canada (Ontario and Québec), where the economic base is more diversified, manufacturing in traditional sectors was hit hard from the late 1980s to mid-1990s by recession, by the closure of branch plants of American-owned corporations, and by the internationalization of production in low-skilled sectors.

6

REPOPULATING THE INNER CITY

As we saw in the last chapter, trying to reinvent the inner city as an appealing 'niche' for certain tertiarized 'industries of the future', relying on a highly qualified workforce, represents one important strategy for improving the economic fortunes of the old core city in a sprawling metropolitan region. Another, and entirely complementary, strategy that a municipality can adopt is to try to reverse the decades-long trend of population decline and promote a social as well as economic revitalization of its neighbourhoods (Esser and Hirsch, 1994). One could hardly find a more classic case in point than that of the City of Montréal, located in a metropolitan area with relatively little tax base sharing, yet dependent on property taxes for some 80 per cent of its revenues – especially since the decline of traditional heavy industry has led the City to count increasingly on the residential sector as a source of the property tax. In this context, housing became firmly incorporated into the City's economic development strategy. Moreover, a declining population meant less political power for the City relative to suburban municipalities.

As we saw at the end of Chapter 3, by the late 1970s the tide in urban policy had firmly turned away from mega-projects and towards making neighbourhoods once again appealing places to live. However, the nature of the housing stock in the city's neighbourhoods – the vast majority of dwellings being in multiple unit buildings (Table 6.1) in rental tenure (Table 6.2) – offered very little scope for the growing numbers of young people who were upwardly mobile compared with their parents' generation to fulfil their housing aspirations by becoming home-owners as they grew up and moved into the family-formation stage. Opportunities for home-ownership were much more readily available in the suburbs; and, as can be seen from Table 6.2, while the suburbs increasingly came to resemble the rest of Canada's urban areas with regards to housing tenure, the proportion of tenants diminished but little in the City until the early 1980s. Although there was unused land in the city, market forces alone could not be counted on to build houses on it, given the state of the economy and the lower cost of building in the suburbs. The City therefore needed to find ways of intervening in the housing market to increase home-ownership on its territory – this being a much more lucrative source of property tax revenues than the rental stock. At the same time, in view of the considerable age of the rental housing stock, the low incomes and consequent affordability problems faced

TABLE 6.1 Residential building types in the City of
Montréal, 1988

Single-family house	32%
Duplex (two superimposed units)	36%
Triplex (three superimposed units)	17%
Multiplexes/apartment buildings 4–11 units	11%
Apartment buildings 12 or more units	3%
Total number of residential buildings	128 654

Source: Ville de Montréal (1989: 18)

TABLE 6.2 A city of tenants: percentage of private
households in rented dwellings, City of
Montréal, rest of Montréal Census Metropolitan
Area and rest of urban Canada, 1961–1996

	City of Montréal	Rest of Montréal CMA	Rest of urban Canada*
1961	79.8%	48.8%	35.3%
1966	81.9%	49.0%	38.3%
1971	80.8%	49.3%	41.8%
1976	80.5%	47.2%	40.9%
1981	78.0%	45.3%	41.2%
1986	74.5%	42.6%	41.0%
1991	73.6%	41.3%	41.0%
1996	72.9%	40.1%	n.a.

Source: Statistics Canada, Censuses of Population, various years
(authors' calculations).

* Urban regions of Canada excluding the Montréal CMA.

by a large proportion of Montréal's renters, ways also had to be found of
protecting tenants and improving their housing conditions.

Consequently, from the late 1970s and throughout the 1980s and 1990s the
City of Montréal developed and has maintained a panoply of proactive
housing and neighbourhood policies, whose coherence through three
successive municipal administrations – the latter years of the Civic Party
regime, the reformist Montréal Citizens' Movement (in power 1986–1994)
and the current more hybrid administration of Mayor Pierre Bourque (Vision
Montréal party) – is quite remarkable. Most – although, importantly, not all
– of the efforts have been focused on promoting middle-class resettlement
in inner city areas that had lost population and industry. These measures
were and continue to be justified with reference to a discourse of urban
decline (see Beauregard, 1994) summed up in a neat spatial metaphor: the
City of Montréal is constantly referred to as the 'hole in the doughnut' of the
metropolitan area (see e.g. Aubin, 1995). City/metropolitan comparisons do

provide some support for this metaphor: for example, as regards family incomes and male wages the City was in an inferior position in 1971 compared to the metropolitan area as a whole, with the situation worsening by 1981; the City of Toronto, in contrast, saw its relative position improve over this period almost to the metropolitan average (Dansereau, 1988). Those higher income families who were inclined to live in the urban core tended to be 'siphoned' off to the enclave municipalities of Westmount and Outremont (see Beaudet, Beauregard and Wolfe, 1998) where they did not, of course, contribute to the city's property tax base.

To place this labelling of municipal action as 'interventionist' in context, we should very briefly explain the politico-legal framework of responsibilities for housing policy in the Canadian context (for details, see Carter and McAfee, 1990; Wolfe, 1998). Housing is a grey area in the Canadian constitution but is generally deemed to be mainly a provincial responsibility (Pomeroy, 1995). The federal government has nevertheless played an important role for much of the twentieth century in mortgage markets, urban renewal and renovation programmes, and programme development and subsidies for social housing. Muncipalities are, legally, creatures of the provinces and it is the latter that determine the broad parameters of municipal action in housing; in Québec, generally speaking, beyond the standard regulatory measures and a relatively small required contribution to low-rental public housing, municipalities decide for themselves on the level and type of involvement.

In a typology of municipal intervention in housing policy developed by Carter and McAfee (1990) for the Canadian context, three models are proposed, which can be seen as 'ideal types' located at different points along a continuum. First is the 'reactor' model, in which the municipality will not develop its own housing programmes but neither will it block residential developments as long as they conform to regulations and, in the case of social housing, do not provoke the NIMBY ('not in my back yard') syndrome among substantial proportions of the citizenry. On the whole, suburban and middle-class municipalities are likely to conform to the first model. Second is the 'facilitator' model, in which the municipality may, for instance, make land available on advantageous terms or alter zoning regulations so as to encourage affordable housing. Third is the 'comprehensive developer' model, which involves: making maximum use of programmes offered by higher levels of government and negotiating to have them adapted to particular local needs; complementing these programmes and trying to replace them when they are cut back; and establishing original development strategies for market or non-profit housing.

Large urban core municipalities with substantial low-income populations and a pressing need to revitalize their economies are more likely to follow the second and sometimes move into the third model. This is especially likely under the impetus of a 'reformist' administration, which, drawing its support both from the 'new urban middle class' and from community activist groups in poor neighbourhoods, establishes a 'progressive' urban regime (Stone and Sanders, 1987; see also Ley, 1994) whose vision includes quality residential opportunities for diverse income groups. Housing and neighbourhood policy under the Montréal Citizens' Movement administration (1986–1994), at least for its first few years in office, is a classic case in point (Whelan, 1991). In the 1990s the federal government has withdrawn almost completely from the affordable housing arena while provincial governments have begun to decentralize or 'download' responsibilities for affordable housing to the municipal level. As a result, large urban municipalities are increasingly finding themselves needing to take on a 'comprehensive developer' role although without sufficient resources to do so; consequently, forming partnerships with for-profit and non-profit private sector organizations is increasingly becoming the order of the day. As we shall see, the City of Montréal's housing and neighbourhood initiatives since the late 1970s place it firmly within the 'comprehensive developer' category and have earned it the justifiable reputation of the most interventionist municipality in Canada as regards the housing sphere (Gaudreau, 1992; Hulchanski et al., 1990).

This chapter focuses on the issue of repopulating and revitalizing the city, and in particular on municipal interventions in housing and neighbourhoods. We discuss supply-side initiatives to promote new residential construction coupled with demand-side incentives to home-ownership, as well as tenure conversions from rental to owner-occupancy in the existing multiple-unit stock. We also examine assistance for renovation and maintenance of older housing, measures to support affordable rental housing, and, crucially, measures aimed at revitalizing local neighbourhood infrastructure so as to increase the attractiveness of inner city living. We then take stock of the demographic and socio-economic situation of residents in inner-city Montréal in the late 1990s, after close to two decades of interventionist municipal action in the realm of housing and neighbourhoods, and in the light of the restructuring of the city's economy: we review population and household structures and labour force characteristics of inner city residents, housing tenure patterns, the extent of 'social upgrading' and the character of 'gentrification' of inner city neighbourhoods. Finally, we consider what all of these changes mean for the question of social diversity within the inner city and how they have reshaped the patterning of the urban poverty that remains a structuring feature of Montréal's socio-spatial landscape.

REPOPULATING THE CITY: TWO DECADES OF MUNICIPAL INTERVENTIONISM

In the aftermath of the 1976 Olympics, concerns about population decline, middle-class flight and neighbourhood decay began to crystallize into new municipal strategies. The neglect of the physical fabric of many of the City's neighbourhoods by an administration still bent on mega-projects was creating such serious degradation in some areas of the inner city as to seriously embarrass an administration conscious of its dependence on tourists and concerned with its international image. As in other older North American cities, the residential construction industry was losing interest in the City of Montréal and undermaintenance by landlords, arson for insurance purposes and 'red-lining' of certain districts by mortgage-lending institutions was also taking its toll on the inner city (Krohn et al., 1977; Wolfe et al., 1980), as were the processes of deindustrialization we referred to in the previous chapter. Moreover, neighbourhood commercial streets were losing out to suburban shopping centres and merchants' associations – traditionally a bastion of support for Drapeau's Civic Party – became increasingly vocal in their attacks on the administration's failure to support their neighbourhoods (Léveillée, 1988; Morin, 1985). At the same time, the reformist opposition party at City Hall, the Montréal Citizens' Movement, was also galvanizing support from community organizations for a neighbourhood-oriented vision of urban development (Schecter, 1982). Consequently, beginning in 1978, the municipal administration – which was by now being run less by the ageing Drapeau and more by the head of the Executive Committee, Yvon Lamarre – embarked on a number of policy measures both to increase new housing construction and to revitalize old neighbourhoods. This policy shift was consolidated in the early 1980s, for when the 1981 population census data were released, they showed that the number of inhabitants of the City of Montréal had dropped below the threshold of one million attained thirty years earlier (Figure 6.1a). In the face of this blow to the city's image and prestige, the Drapeau administration annexed the suburban municipality of Pointe-aux-Trembles, located at the north-east end of the island (see Figure 4.2), to the City of Montréal in 1982; this had the symbolic merit of reinflating the population to over the million mark again but also the practical value of making available a large area of land for new residential development.

While the population trends were discouraging for the City of Montréal, the demographic situation was (and remains) less bleak than in comparable American cities, in that the number of *households* continued to increase (Figure 6.1b). A decline in numbers of households inevitably brings on a drop in the purchasing power of residents and abandonment of parts of the housing stock (Goldberg and Mercer, 1986: 154–157; Mercer, 1992), contributing to a cycle of deterioration that is difficult to reverse. In Montréal, as in other Canadian central cities, it is the broader societal trend for growth in small, non-family household types, more inclined to concentrate in the inner city in spite of the demographic diversification of suburbs in recent decades (Evenden and Walker, 1993), that is mainly responsible for the increase in numbers of households in core municipalities of metropolitan

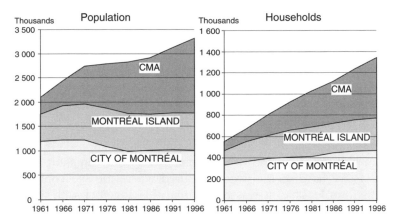

FIGURE 6.1 (a) Population change, City of Montréal, Island of Montréal (Urban Community) and Census Metropolitan Area, 1961–1996 (limits are those of the respective census years. (b) Change in number of households, City of Montréal, Island of Montréal (Urban Community) and Census Metropolitan Area, 1961–1996 (limits are those of the respective census years)

regions (Le Bourdais and Beaudry, 1988; Mongeau, 1994). The fact that household numbers have been at least stable in most inner-city districts of Montréal has no doubt increased the potential for success of policy measures designed to promote neighbourhood revitalization. As we shall see, municipal policies promoting home ownership in the inner-city have increasingly shifted away from targeting 'traditional' family households and towards targeting 'non-traditional' households more likely to embrace inner-city 'lifestyles'. At the same time, over much of the recent past, although much less so today, considerable resources have been available for non-profit groups to recycle or renovate old buildings for low-cost housing, much of it for small families and non-family units including one-person households.

Promoting home-ownership through new construction: supply- and demand-side measures

Between 1979 and 1988 some 40 per cent of all new housing construction in the City of Montréal was directly attributable to a programme called *Opération 20 000 logements*, implemented by the Housing Division of a newly formed para-municipal body, the Commission d'initiative et de développement économique de Montréal, an economic development agency whose goals included improving public–private sector linkages (and which also included divisions covering Industry, Commerce, Tourism, Cinema, Transportation, Communications and Civic Beautification) (Hamel,

1989). The goal was to create 20 000 new dwellings (increased in 1982 from an initial target of 10 000) by the City selling off most of its accumulated bank of vacant land to developers on advantageous terms. Much of this land consisted of never-developed tracts in peripheral parts of the city, especially in the districts of Rivière-des-Prairies and the recently annexed Pointe-aux-Trembles at the northeastern tip of the island, but the land bank also included substantial tracts in inner-city working-class neighbourhoods such as St-Henri, razed during the earlier phase of urban renewal.

Under this programme, designs had to fulfil criteria imposed by the City. Suburban-style developments of single-family housing – in short supply in the city, as we have seen – were favoured where the site configuration made this form feasible. It was hoped that this, together with the added 'carrot' of easy accessibility to jobs in the downtown core, would draw young families who would otherwise buy homes in suburban municipalities (Léonard and Léveillée, 1986). Higher-density although still quintessentially suburban townhouses were even built in the heart of old working-class neighbourhoods like Little Burgundy and Pointe St-Charles, generating resentment on the part of old-time residents and community groups towards these 'isolated encampments' of the new middle class who took their consumer and entertainment dollars elsewhere (MacBurnie, 1989: 193; see also Ruddick, 1990). Nevertheless, the City also subsidized market feasibility studies for less conventional projects and fostered infill development on small, awkwardly positioned parcels of land, which only small developers would take on, by reducing the risks to which these developers were exposed, for example by allowing delayed payment on the land until the housing units were sold. Firms bidding for some of the sites were also encouraged to produce condominium units within housing forms consistent with Montréal's traditional residential architecture of stacked 'plexes and small apartment buildings (Ville de Montréal, 1989). Additionally, although over half the units built under this programme were sold to owner-occupiers, some 22 per cent were privately rented units and 24 per cent went to social housing, including housing cooperatives and non-profit housing agencies who obtained funding from various federal and provincial programmes in force at the time (Cournoyer, 1998).

As it turned out, over two-thirds of purchasers in *Opération 20 000 logements* developments were first-time buyers, and, moreover, almost two-thirds of these had been renters living in Montréal – precisely the target market the City was courting. The programme's success in this respect in the early 1980s, a period of recession and exceptionally high interest rates, was doubtless partly due to its twinning with a successful provincial government incentive programme to stimulate the construction industry to build housing that first-time buyers could afford (Cournoyer, 1998). However, studies exploring the satisfaction and future plans of *Opération 20 000 logements* housing consumers found that the more centrally located

developments were insufficiently 'suburban' to satisfy young families seeking a child-oriented ambience with an adequate amount of private and
public green space and other facilities at an affordable price, and tended
to be viewed as but a transitory phase in the family's housing career
(Charbonneau and Parenteau, 1991; Morin, Rose and Mongeau, 1988).

In the course of the 1990s the City reactivated the policy of selling land
from its land bank for residential development, this time under conditions
where designs were strictly controlled. Once again, land was made available
at favourable prices and terms, although on the whole the parcels still
available are smaller and more difficult to market. They include buildings
repossessed by the City following abandonment or non-payment of taxes.
To ensure their viability, projects selected now had to be designed to target
specific socio-demographic market segments and sometimes required innovative designs (Gaudreau, 1992; Ville de Montréal, 1995). In particular, the
City has explicitly shifted away from its earlier single-minded preoccupation
with getting families with children to stay in the city in favour of an approach
focusing on professionals employed downtown or working out of their
homes, and targeting a diversity of household types – singles, opposite- and
same-sex couples – and a variety of age groups – both young people
and 'empty nesters' – seeking to practise 'urbane' lifestyles. The *20 000
logements* experience had made it clear that high-density infill housing was
manifestly more attractive to couples without children and to single people.
This is especially true with respect to the downtown, Old Montréal and
adjacent districts where the City has developed ambitious repopulation
plans but where densities and the limited possibilities of bringing in an
adequate range of commercial and community services greatly restrict the
feasibility of attracting families with children.

In true post-modern fashion, architectural forms mimicking the traditional
rows of stacked duplexes and triplexes are thus encouraged, with each unit
being sold as a condominium, usually on one floor, but sometimes on two.
This is done both on small infill sites where the new developments abut on
to the existing streetscape, much of it composed of original old 'plex
buildings (Figures 6.2 and 6.3), and on larger sites amounting to new
neighbourhoods. In the latter, however, including *Opération 20 000 logements* developments, it has proven impossible to reproduce the intimate
ambience of streets with traditional 'plex housing in old neighbourhoods. In
large part this is because present-day building code regulations require
much wider streets and greater setbacks, in part because developers resisted
functional mix (Schoenauer, 1998b; MacBurnie, 1989). It seems ironic that
while in other Canadian and in some American cities some of the new
residential forms characteristic of what has become known as the 'new
urbanism' (see for example McCann, 1995) have been inspired by the living
example of old city neighbourhoods such as those of Montréal with their
'plex housing, narrow streets and street-corner businesses (Figure 6.4), new

FIGURE 6.2 Infill housing: the new 'condoplex' adjoining old duplex housing is so 'authentic' that the new melds into the old. (Damaris Rose)

FIGURE 6.3 Post-modern pastiche in the Plateau Mont-Royal? New condos mimic early twentieth century triplexes. In the background, an old industrial building is undergoing conversion to loft-condos. (Damaris Rose)

FIGURE 6.4 'Intimate' streetscape with corner store, typical of the inner city. In background: Maison Radio-Canada; the fire escapes to the left belong to one of the Nouveau Montréal condominium projects. (Damaris Rose)

developments within Montréal supposedly seeking to reproduce these old forms have – except in the case of the occasional demonstration project – been hidebound by classically modernistic site planning regulations.

Even more stark in this respect is the example of the new neighbourhood of Bois-Franc being developed at the time of writing in the inner-suburban municipality of Ville-St-Laurent, one of Montréal's direct competitors for 'new urban middle-class' residents. In the early 1990s, this municipality entered into a deal with the Bombardier transportation equipment corporation (one of Québec's and Canada's most successful enterprises) for the development of some 8000 housing units destined for urban professionals of various household types and income brackets but mostly first-time buyers, on the site of the former Cartierville airport (Wolfe, 1993). Highly accessible both to downtown and to nearby high-tech, research and office complexes, it was to be relandscaped into a verdant and lacustrine environment (Figure 6.5). None of the housing corresponds to the traditional detached single-family form, yet it is ironic that, although Bois-Franc has been marketed as a model based on the 'new urbanism' in the sense that housing is closer to the street than in typical suburban developments and the development includes some triplex units that mix owner-occupiers and renters on the same street, as in Montréal's traditional neighbourhoods, the City would not allow the emulation of a 'gentrified' inner-city neighbourhood through the integration

FIGURE 6.5 The Bois-Franc medium-density housing development in suburban Ville St-Laurent, on site of former Cartierville airport; target market is professionals. (Damaris Rose)

of small businesses (bakeries, boutiques, galleries and the like) into the residential fabric (Klein and Waaub, 1995).

Within the single-family sector, the City of Montréal has also supported innovative designs developed by Montréal architects working in McGill University's Affordable Homes programme, the goal being to produce scaled down (for example narrow-fronted) units and dwellings adaptable to changing household size or work arrangements, so as to make single-family home-ownership accessible to one-earner households (such as lone parents) or those in precarious employment situations, a common phenomenon in Montréal's labour market. In some new developments on land-banked land in peripheral districts the City has reserved a portion of housing for these types of units.

Back in Montréal's inner city, another trend in the 1990s has been for numerous other small infill developments, also mostly based on the 'condo-plex' form, to be constructed outside of the municipal land-banking programme. The municipality has still played a role, however, in that some of these units have been built under incentive schemes involving significant financial assistance to prepare the land and a construction subsidy of a few thousand dollars per unit under a joint municipal-provincial programme targeting certain neighbourhoods, including some of the city's most disadvantaged districts, and, also for a time, parts of the trendy Plateau Mont-Royal (Duff, 1999).

The City also has a policy of acquiring vacated industrial or commercial buildings with architectural merit, and turning them over to be 'recycled' for residential use, together with old municipal buildings no longer needed. Whereas in the 1980s it was the non-profit housing cooperative movement that pioneered this type of recycling, especially of old school buildings, in the 1990s the virtual elimination of funding for housing co-ops has meant that today almost all recycling projects are carried out for profit and sold as condominiums. The Lachine Canal district has been the main focus of such activity in spite of the opposition of community groups who wanted more of the buildings to be retained for industrial use (as mentioned in Chapter 5), and the conversion of public spaces in working-class neighbourhoods, municipal baths for example, to private market housing unaffordable by local residents is a matter of some controversy (Sijpkes, 1998). Nonetheless, it would be misleading to imply that such recycled units are generally aimed at the luxury market; although this is true in some cases, like the celebrated Belding-Corticelli building referred to in the previous chapter (Figure 5.4), most have targeted middle-income purchasers including those interested in 'loft living' (Podmore, 1994 and 1998), for example, the former Montréal Rolling Mill on the Lachine Canal (Figure 6.6). Provincial and municipal programmes of the late 1990s have included a few new recycling projects for social housing, as in the case of part of the old Sherwin-Williams paint factory complex, but these have become the exception rather than the rule. The appeal of these former industrial spaces to gentrifiers is enhanced by their proximity to sections of the *Réseau Vert* (Green Network); this partially completed MUC network of recreational paths (for cyclists, in-line skaters, joggers, etc.), aptly referred to by Sénécal (1997: 386) as the 'reconquest of marginal spaces' (our translation), runs beside natural shorelines, the Lachine Canal, and the Old Port as well as along both still-used and defunct railway lines that were crucial in opening up sectors of the city for industrial development a century ago.

More visible in the mid- to late-1990s, and perhaps more important as symbols of the City of Montréal's efforts to repopulate the city, have been a set of larger residential projects on the fringes of downtown and Old Montréal grouped together under a programme called *Le Nouveau Montréal*. This is designed to increase the residential population of the area by several thousand residents so as to create a critical mass for an array of ancillary services to be provided and thus to entrench a new vision of these downtown fringe zones as places to live as well as work (Wolfe, 1994). Here, the City's 'comprehensive developer' role has mutated into a formal partnership between the municipality, its paramunicipal development corporations and private development companies, with a concerted advertising and marketing campaign run by the City. This type of strategy is perhaps indicative of a shift, beginning in the later years of the MCM administration, toward a more 'corporate' type of urban regime, in which, in the

FIGURE 6.6 Only a stack reminds us that these condominiums were once a major rolling mills complex on the Lachine Canal. To the right new condos are visible as well as an old grain silo. (Damaris Rose)

interests of promoting revitalization in a stagnant urban economy, the private sector is invited to play a greater role in shaping the vision and the practice of urban development, especially in the downtown (Whelan, 1991; see Mayer, 1995).

Nouveau Montréal was to be 'anchored' by five architecturally innovative developments, four of which are complete or under construction at the time of writing (a fifth did not get off the ground, no doubt due to its location adjacent to the 'red light' district). In the case of the Faubourg Québec, an ambitious 'greyfield' project on former Canadian Pacific Railway land east of Old Montréal, major infrastructure investments by the City have been needed to make the site accessible and viable. Other new residential developments (including recycled buildings) in the downtown are also included under the Nouveau Montréal marketing umbrella. The paramunicipal corporation concerned promotes these developments through 'lifestyle marketing': according to a 1998 brochure, organized around miniature postcard vignettes 'because life is a postcard', these projects are 'two steps away from the Cité du Multimédia', evoke 'a renewal of old-time romanticism', are located in 'a little corner of Paris', and so on (our translations). In spite of their central location, many of these units have been marketed at a price that could be afforded by a couple whose earnings correspond to the average income for Montréal, or in some cases by a young single professional.

A key supporting element in the Nouveau Montréal promotion is an incentive designed to fuel consumer demand for central-city living (Cournoyer, 1998). Like many municipalities, the City of Montréal has had a long-standing programme offering a partial property-tax rebate to purchasers of new homes, for the first few years. These were initially targeted to first-time buyers or families with children and, in an effort to promote affordable home-ownership, limited to dwellings sold at less than $100 000 (which is less than the average cost of a home in the Montréal metropolitan area). On some of the lots sold to private developers under the residential construction programme, the City required that a certain number of units be priced within this ceiling (Ville de Montréal, 1992). In recent years, in line with the refocusing of the City's repopulation strategy, these restrictions have been lifted. Whether or not these tax breaks have made any difference to people's *ability* to purchase a home is highly debatable as regards most parts of the city (Gaudreau, 1992). Nevertheless, in the case of the downtown area the credits have been quite generous (although the programme is self-financing for the City over a 10-year time horizon), and they have become an important element in the marketing strategy for new downtown residences, figuring prominently, for example, in a glossy brochure produced by the City in 1998 entitled *Housing in the city for everybody – My Property, A Dream Come True.*

Increasing home-ownership in the existing housing stock: owner-landlords and conversions of 'plexes

For much of the twentieth century, rental tenure, rather than home-ownership, was the normal way of life for middle-class as well as working-class Montrealers, especially (although not exclusively) among franco-phones, so much so that researchers Choko and Harris (1990) concep-tualized this phenomenon in terms of a 'local culture of property'. Social reformers had tried to promote working-class home-ownership for the sake of improved social stability as well as better living conditions (Séguin, 1989) but the overall impact of this movement was minor. The gradual shift toward the typical North American pattern of lifestyles oriented around domesticity and durable consumer goods, which tends to go hand in hand with home-ownership, only began to take hold in Québec in the 1950s as federal government policies led to the diversification of sources of mort-gage credit. It was consolidated with the early Quiet Revolution of the early 1960s which brought about a general secularization of society and a greater range of investment opportunities for francophones beyond traditional sectors like residential real estate.

In the City of Montréal, however, the historical legacy of a housing stock largely in the stacked 'plex format that dominated the urban morphology (see Chapter 3; 'plexes can be seen in Figures 6.2, 6.7 and 6.21) continued to limit the possibilities of home-ownership. By definition, no more than half of all the duplex units and at most one-third of triplexes could be owner-occupied (Choko and Harris, 1990), since condominium tenure did not become legal in Québec until 1969. In reality, the proportion of resident owners in the 'plex stock was much lower than the theoretical maximum. It is true that in many cases, duplexes and even five-plexes had been built with the owner-landlord model in mind, with the main floor unit often being larger and grander. However, not all prospective home-owners had the inclination or the resources to become landlords, and so a large proportion of 'plex buildings did not, and still do not today, have a resident landlord.

Resident landlordism was, and remains, prevalent among some of Montréal's European immigrant communities, many of whose members embarked on their own renovation projects years before the municipality began to take an interest in promoting these old neighbourhoods as desirable places for the 'new urban middle class'. As in the case of other older Canadian inner cities in the 1960s and early 1970s (Goldberg and Mercer, 1986; Ray and Moore, 1991), numbers of immigrant families from Southern Europe bought up inexpensive duplex and triplex units in neighbourhoods such as Saint-Louis and Mile End, and fixed them up using their own 'sweat equity' and, often, informal sources of financing within their ethnic communities, it being difficult to obtain financing from conventional lending institutions (Krohn et al., 1977; see Murdie, 1986). These strategies made significant contributions to the revitalization of the inner city. The typical pattern in the Montréal case was for the owner-landlord to live at street level and rent the other units out either to extended family or other members of the same ethnic community, or, increasingly in some neighbourhoods, to students, artists and other young people – precursors of gentrification, an issue to which we will return later – drawn to the cosmopolitan atmosphere of the area (Krohn et al., 1977). This type of reinvestment, sometimes called 'incumbent upgrading' (Clay, 1979), not only helped arrest decay of the housing stock but tended to lead to better maintenance of rental units – research in Montréal has found that resident landlords maintain their rental units better than absentee landlords (Dansereau et al., 1991) – and reduced turnover in the local housing market. It also created a landscape of brightly painted balconies, front gardens densely planted with flowers, fruit and vegetables and a high degree of street-level interaction between neighbours which contributed to a sense of security among pedestrians and residents. Variations on this theme also emerged through the efforts of resident landlords in parts of old francophone districts like the Plateau Mont-Royal (Figure 6.7). In fact it was the micro-scale ambience of such Montréal neighbourhoods that led architect Oscar Newman (an expatriate Montrealer) to develop the concept of 'defensible space' now applied to urban design in many parts of the world (*Montreal Gazette*, 4 October 1996).

FIGURE 6.7 Verdant multiplex housing in the Plateau Mont-Royal; some are still rental units, others have been converted to condos. (Damaris Rose)

If the City of Montréal wanted to promote home-ownership in the existing housing stock over and above the owner-landlord phenomenon, it needed to increase tenants' options to become home-owners by allowing the conversion of rental apartments to condominium tenure. As mentioned earlier, condominium tenure was legalized in Québec in 1969 and, much as in the rest of Canada and the United States, enjoyed increasing popularity for reasons of convenience (lower maintenance than single-family homes), accessibility to work, cultural and recreational facilities (in the case of centrally located buildings), and, in some segments of the market, affordability (Preston et al., 1993).

In Montréal, however, conversions of existing rental units to condominiums were prohibited (under most circumstances) from 1975 until 1993 by a provincial moratorium designed to protect sitting tenants and conserve rental housing in neighbourhoods experiencing 'gentrification'. Nevertheless, loopholes in the law enabled thousands of conversions from rental units to *de facto* condominiums – 'undivided' co-ownership in which each co-owner owns a share of the whole building, including a share of each of the units – to take place between the mid-1970s and late 1980s. Once all residents were co-owners, the building could be legally converted into actual condominium tenure (i.e. where each unit is individually owned and registered as a separate municipal lot but the structure and common areas are co-owned). This practice was especially prevalent in the Plateau Mont-Royal district, the older eastern section of the enclave municipality of Outremont abutting on the multiethnic Mile End neighbourhood of Montréal, and the old west-end Montréal suburb of Notre-Dame-de-Grâce, which had larger, lower density 'plex units than elsewhere (Sinical et al., 1991). Many of the *de facto* conversions were done by groups of friends getting together to buy the units they already lived in from their landlord or purchase another triplex that came up for sale. Renovations and maintenance were often done cooperatively; this cheap and 'sociable' form of home-ownership especially appealed to relatively 'marginal' young professionals with little capital and insecure incomes, including, for instance, numbers of single women and female single parents (Choko and Dansereau, 1986; Rose, 1989). Moreover, many of the triplex units were very large, their linear orientation (Figures 3.17 and 3.18) appealing to self-employed people with modest incomes who worked out out of their homes and wanted to maintain a separation of workspace and living quarters (Duff and Cadotte, 1997; Chicoine and Rose, 1998). But property developers also seized on the opportunity to buy up rental 'plexes and resell them, at a substantial profit, as co-ownership units, sometimes after renovating them with the aid of generous municipal grants (Hamel et al., 1988; Ley, 1985: 173). Over 16 000 units received renovation grants between 1976 and 1986, representing about 40 per cent of total units for which renovation permits were obtained (Ville de Montréal, 1989); not all were used to create condominiums, but it is notable that in the first half of the 1980s, more generous grants were available in the Greater Plateau Mont-Royal district than elsewhere, a policy clearly intended to accelerate gentri-fication. The arrival to power of the reformist MCM in 1986 (at a time when the city's economy was booming and the housing market rapidly inflating) would lead to a shift in the focus of renovation subsidies to social housing and to improving quality in the private rented sector.

Unregulated 'underground' conversions to undivided co-ownership frequently led to the displacement of tenants unable to afford to purchase their apartments, and several thousand units of rental housing were lost in Montréal's inner city in consequence (Sénécal et al., 1991). Although quan-titatively not a large-scale phenomenon compared with, for example, the case of 'brownstones' in parts of New York City or 'triple-deckers' in parts of Boston (Smith, 1996), this process removed some of the best-quality 'plex housing from the rental stock in some of the most desirable sectors of the inner city. Property taxes – assessed at current market value – skyrocketed in the 1980s, as did rent levels (even when inflation is adjusted for in the calculation), especially in the Plateau Mont-Royal district (Sénécal et al., 1991: 82–85; Rose, 1996).

By the mid-1980s the City, now under the control of the Montréal Citizens' Movement, was seeking ways to regularize the existing informal types of condominiums that had sprung up and allow legal condo conversions to take place, while at the same time wanting to provide some measure of protection for tenants and for the rental housing stock in areas of high demand (Ville de Montréal, 1989). Consequently – and over the sustained objections of community groups who felt the MCM was abandoning one part of its constituency in favour of another, wealthier, faction, namely young urban professionals who were also strong supporters of this 'reform-ist' party (Collin and Léveillée, 1985; Ley, 1994) – various compromise measures were introduced in both provincial legislation and municipal regulations in the early 1990s to allow for conversions under certain speci-fied conditions (Ville de Montréal, 1992a). Changes to Québec's Civil Code also made ownership of both 'informal' and 'official' condominiums more attractive to purchasers by improving regulations covering co-owners' rights and responsibilities as regards mortgage contracts and maintenance. In the mid- and late 1990s, in the wake of several years of high rental vacancy rates and amidst renewed fears of the City losing its middle class, the rules on conversions were further relaxed because only a few hundred units had been converted under the 1993 regulations. In addition, property tax breaks, previously limited to the purchasers of new housing, were now offered to the purchasers of converted units, as a further incentive to encourage those moving from renting into home-ownership to stay in the city.

Most conversions to condominiums do not alter the horizontal structure of 'plexes. However, one innovative way of adapting this stock is to recreate one of the traditional models of duplexes aimed at homeowners – namely a duplex built on three storeys with a two-storey home above a main floor or basement apartment (see Schoenauer, 1998b) – by converting two of the three floors of buildings built as triplexes, so that two of the units are made into a two-storey home, with the third remaining as an apartment. Such conversions, while relatively rare because of the expense, allow for the possibility of 'family-type' housing in the inner city, although in today's economy they are just as likely to be used by professionals wanting a 'home office' separate from their living quarters.

Support for social and affordable housing

In 1996 there were 691 375 renter households in the City of Montréal paying over 30 per cent of their gross income on rent and thus considered likely to have an affordability problem, amounting to 45.8 per cent of all renters. The affordability situation is slightly worse in the City than for renters in the rest of the metropolitan area (42 per cent) even though the City has a higher share of social housing than the suburbs. However, the Montréal CMA as a whole differs little from Canada's three other large metropolitan areas (Toronto, Vancouver and Ottawa-Hull) as far as affordability is concerned; although tenant households in the Montréal region are poorer than in the other three large CMAs, this is counterbalanced by lower rents (Statistics

Canada, 1998c). In Canada as a whole, renters as a group became considerably poorer between the early 1980s and mid-1990s, with increasing numbers not in the labour force or only employed part-time (Canada Mortgage and Housing Corporation, July 1998).

Affordability statistics such as these must be set within the broader housing policy context. Canada is counted among the nations that have opted to rely on the private market to house the majority of low-income households (Bacher, 1993). Only about 7 per cent of the total housing stock is in the form of social housing – a term generally understood in Canada to refer to rental housing developed or assisted by government bodies and owned or managed by either public agencies or non-profit organizations (Pomeroy, 1995), although it is sometimes extended to include for-profit units subsidized by rent allowances (Wexler, 1996). While definitional ambiguities and (often) the lack of a centralized state agency responsible for housing statistics make accurate estimates and international comparisons difficult, social housing is a numerically marginal part of Canada's total housing stock compared to the situation prevailing in many European countries (Morin et al., 1990; Doling, 1997). Although the City of Montréal has much more social housing than suburban municipalities, the proportion differs little from that in Canada as a whole, amounting to roughly 8 per cent of the housing stock.[1]

Until the early 1970s, almost all social housing took the form of public housing, with joint funding from the federal government and the provinces. In Québec (unlike in the other Canadian provinces), a municipal contribution is also required (10 per cent). Public housing in Canada has generally followed a 'residual' model of social housing (Harloe, 1994; Bacher, 1993), serving low-income people deemed to be in severe and high-priority housing need, who pay a rent geared to their income (usually 25 or 30 per cent). Over time, it has increasingly come to be the housing of 'last resort'; it was a policy shift toward increased targeting of the very poor that led to the increased 'ghettoization' of the Little Burgundy public housing complex referred to in Chapter 3.

About half of the City of Montréal's social rental housing today is in the form of public housing (known locally by the French acronym HLM, which means 'low-rent housing'). A paramunicipal body, the Office municipal d'habitation de Montréal, manages most of the stock of some 17 700 units (as of December 1997; Office municipal d'habitation de Montréal, 1998). After the urban renewal projects of the 1950s and 1960s, some 10 000 units of public housing were built from 1968–1978 (Melamed et al., 1984, cited in Ley, 1985). The rhythm of production subsequently slowed, and the programme has been brought to a virtual halt since the end of federal and provincial support in 1994.

The HLM stock is mostly divided between low-rise units for families and medium-rise units for the over-55 age group. In contrast to the complexes built in the urban renewal period, most HLM units built since the early 1970s are in small to medium-sized buildings, ranging from 8 to 100 units, on infill sites fronting on to the street; they are usually quite integrated into the surrounding neighbourhood in a physical sense (Figures 6.8 and 6.9). The massive scale of social problems characteristic of large and isolated suburban public housing complexes in European or US cities (and even in Toronto to some extent) has largely been avoided in the Montréal case. Nevertheless, residents are becoming increasingly impoverished, due in part to cuts in the welfare benefits upon which most tenants depend (Canada Mortgage and Housing Corporation, July 1998). Additionally, the HLM stock is becoming home to increasing proportions of new immigrants from developing countries (Office municipal d'habitation de Montréal, 1998). While these recent arrivals may lack previous experience of high-density urban living in a cold climate, their francophone neighbours are often not used to cultural diversity, and, as often happens when different social or age groups are involuntarily assigned to live at close quarters, with poor soundproofing and inappropriately designed public spaces, neighbouring can become fraught with social tensions (Dansereau and Séguin, 1995). Marginalized youth is also a growing element in public housing. Increasingly, to address these types of needs and foster the development of life skills and social integration, HLM management is working with local community groups to set up support services within HLM buildings – including intercultural services, child care, youth programmes and collective cooking programmes – though they are also accessible to other neighbourhood residents.

Social housing options for Canadians were greatly expanded in the 1970s and 1980s with the introduction of a federal programme to promote rental housing cooperatives, which offered an alternative to individual home-ownership for modest-income households and an alternative to public housing for low-income households. Co-ops are fully non-profit, and democratically managed by their residents. Residents have no equity and cannot make a capital gain. Housing units built as or converted into co-ops under the federal programme were permanently removed from the private market, and rents were set at low-end-of-market levels but with a proportion of units in each co-op being reserved for low-income people who would receive a rent-geared-to-income subsidy. The goal was to move away from the targeting of social housing to the very poor and, instead, foster social mix as well as encouraging tenants to take charge of their living conditions (Hulchanski, 1993). Co-ops received start-up grants, loan guarantees and operating subsidies to reduce their mortgage interest rates, and in the Québec case, they obtained additional support from the provincial government. In Montréal, after the reformist MCM came to power, they received considerable assistance in the form of cession or leasing of land and buildings at nominal cost, as well as provincial–municipal renovation

FIGURE 6.8 Public housing for the elderly (built 1983), integrated into an early twentieth century streetscape, Mile End. (Damaris Rose)

FIGURE 6.9 Former industrial site in Mile End, redeveloped for (left) public housing for low-income families (built 1994), and (right) small condominiums (built 1999). (Damaris Rose)

grants which topped up federal renovation assistance, or substituted for it; the land cession programme enabled construction of close to 1200 new units for co-op and other non-profit housing between 1989 and 1984 (Ville de Montréal, 1995). Although popular across the country (including some 20 000 units in the province of Québec) and internationally acclaimed, the co-op programme was scrapped in 1992, 'social mix' now being deemed a dispensable luxury in the era of cutbacks of the 1990s. Various provincial programmes have enabled some new co-op housing since this time but the rate of addition to the co-op stock is very low compared to the 1980s (Wolfe, 1998).

In Montréal, a larger proportion of co-ops have been produced through renovation, whereas elsewere in Canada new construction has predominated. These include the Milton-Parc cooperatives established out of the celebrated urban renewal versus conservation struggle discussed in Chapter 3. Most inner-city co-ops are in small-to-medium sized buildings integrated into the existing streetscape, including numerous old school buildings, where co-ops in fact pioneered the 'recycling' concept that has since become so popular for condominiums.

As well as housing cooperatives, other kinds of non-profit rental housing have proliferated since the early 1970s. This large and diverse sector – amounting by 1996 to about half of Canada's 600 000-odd social housing units, compared to one-third for public housing and one-sixth for co-ops, according to a recent estimate (Wolfe, 1998) – is funded by a patchwork of sources including all three tiers of government, paragovernmental corporations and private charities. It is more likely to target groups who need supportive services in addition to shelter and who may not be in a position to manage their own housing, such as recent survivors of domestic violence, people who have been living on the streets and marginalized young adults lacking in life skills. As in the case of co-ops, the non-profit sector in Montréal has benefited from municipal renovation grant assistance since the mid-1980s (Ville de Montréal, 1995).

The Canadian experience of cooperative housing has shown that obtaining secure, stable housing and developing skills in managing and maintaining it can help economically marginalized people, women in particular, reintegrate into the labour market (Wekerle, 1993). Moreover, where non-profit housing is combined with support services, such as those for elderly people with some loss of autonomy, who form an increasing share of the population, jobs can be created for other local residents, helping to reduce unemployment. Consequently, these types of housing figure in new experimental programmes for revitalization of some of Montréal's poorest neighbourhoods involving public–private partnerships in what is known as the 'social economy'. A recent provincial initiative with a municipal contribution, the Québec Community Housing Fund, is to fund a few hundred units per year to support projects that correspond to these objectives; the impetus for this programme came from community organizations in impoverished parts of the city (Parent, 1997–1998; Ville de Montréal, 1997).

Most low-income Montrealers do not have access to social housing and live in the privately rented sector. Moreover, the increasing appeal of home-ownership and even of renting in the suburbs has drawn young middle-income households away from renting in the City of Montréal in recent years, leading to increased concerns about 'residualization' of the privately rented housing stock (Serge, 1998; see Pomeroy, 1998). Consequently, municipal interventionism has not been limited to promoting home-ownership and supporting social housing, but has also included measures to encourage private landlords to renovate their stock. After a federally funded renovation programme for landlords was abolished in 1990, the City pressed successfully for a joint provincial–municipal programme to replace it, for which both private landlords and social housing providers were eligible. By 'topping up' the provincial programme for the private sector, the City was, moreover, able to limit rent increases after renovation, thus minimizing displacement of tenants (Gaudreau, 1992: 161); the most recent renovation programme has continued in this vein. Joint provincial–municipal programmes have also helped renovate several thousand rooms in rooming houses for low-income single people, in the private as well as non-profit sectors, helping to replace some of the stock lost to downtown fringe redevelopment or condominium conversion (Ville de Montréal, 1989, 1995).

A different kind of intervention in the private rental market was launched in the late 1980s as part of the MCM's housing policy. A paramunicipal corporation, the Société d'habitation et de développement de Montréal (SHDM), embarked on a programme aimed at acquiring run-down apartment buildings and rooming houses, renovating them with the aid of a provincial–municipal subsidy programme and then ceding them or entrusting them to long-term management by co-ops or non-profit organizations (Ville de Montréal, 1995). Some 3500 dwellings were renovated in this way before the programme, epitomizing the 'comprehensive developer' model of municipal intervention, was terminated shortly after the defeat of the MCM in 1994. Although not without management problems, the programme was very popular among its beneficiaries. The new, less interventionist, Vision Montréal administration, although not abandoning support for social housing entirely, had embarked on a programme of privatizing the assets of its paramunicipal real estate corporations and was unhappy with funds being tied up in low-rental properties over the lengthy time frame before sales to the co-ops or non-profit organizations could take place (Bennett, 1997).

Although rental units were acquired in all nine of the City's arrondissements, the most important element in the SHDM's programme was the focus on concentrated interventions in a small area within a neighbourhood. This

FIGURE 6.10   'Walk-up' apartments in multiethnic Côte-des-Neiges district, renovated by the Société d'habitation et du développement de Montréal. (Damaris Rose)

strategy was employed to its fullest extent in one small but strategic section of the multiethnic Côte-des-Neiges neighbourhood dominated by low-rise post-Second World War apartment buildings of inferior quality and deteriorating rapidly in the face of chronic undermaintenance and, often, a high density of occupation (Blanc, 1995). Here, the programme enabled the renovation of over 400 housing units (Figure 6.10). The hope was that the programme would be exemplary, in that the physical rehabilitation and a reduced turnover of tenants would have positive externalities in the surrounding area: the buildings would be less likely to be sites of crime and their increased attractiveness would stimulate private landlords of adjacent buildings to embark on renovations of their own (*Montreal Gazette*, 6 February 1995). The programme seems to have met with considerable success in both these respects (Bernèche et al., 1997). It improved the quality of life and fostered skills in self-management of housing among immigrant households. It also increased the stock of inner-city housing units, discreetly integrated into existing streetscapes, for single people at risk of homelessness. Subsequent to its abolition, the individuals responsible for this programme have set up a private sector limited-dividend venture capital fund in order to pursue this method of creating social housing, as well as affordable owner-occupied housing, in some of the poorest neighbourhoods.

Overall, the City's commitment to renovation of dwellings needing major upgrading, both in the private sector (owned and rented) and in the social housing stock, has been maintained for two decades. From 1976 to 1990, close to 20 000 units were renovated with the aid of grants. A 1991 survey found that some 50 000 dwellings still needed major renovation. Between 1991 and 1994 a further 10 000 housing units were renovated, with the City's contribution to the grant exceeding that of the province in the case of social housing (Ville de Montréal, 1995: 74). In the 1996–1999 period, about 7000 grant applications have been approved, covering various types of renovation for dwellings in need of major repair as well as fire safety improvements (Ville de Montréal, Service de l'habitation, provisional unpublished data). On the whole, and in part due to the various renovation programmes, the quality of the city's rental stock today is quite good considering its age (one-third built before 1946, one-third between 1946 and 1960). However, the situation remains problematic in certain neighbourhoods.

Renewing the city of villages: revitalizing neighbourhoods

The acquisition–renovation programme of the SHDM was more than just a municipal *housing* programme. In a sense it epitomizes the neighbourhood-oriented vision of urban revitalization which has predominated since the late 1970s. It is to this vision and its practical applications that we now turn, since the neighbourhood forms the crucial context for the housing policy measures we have discussed so far.

Actively promoting the revitalization and beautification not only of housing but of the residential and commercial streetscapes of Montréal neighbourhoods has been a continuous feature of municipal policy since the late 1970s. The first such Montréal initiatives date back even further, to the mid-1960s, and in fact helped inspire the Canadian federal government to ditch its demolition–redevelopment oriented urban renewal programme in 1973 in favour of subsidies for 'neighbourhood improvement' and grants to residential property owners to rehabilitate their dwellings (Morin, 1985; Filion, 1988). In the mid-1970s the City of Montréal used a combination of federal, provincial and its own funding programmes to target parts of the working-class districts of Centre-sud and St-Henri for such 'improvement'. Street infrastructure was improved, parks developed, public housing was built on infill sites and home-owners and small landlords were offered grants to cover part of the costs of renovation. Much of the municipal expenditure would, of course, be recouped in increased property taxes. While this programme did create new housing units for low-income families, an underlying goal was to make these neighbourhoods more attractive to middle-class home-owners, in other words to foster gentrification. Moreover, grants to property-owners were conditional on their undertaking, within a short space of time, all the renovations required by inspectors to bring the property up to housing code standards; this was often not an affordable proposition and consequently many owners simply waited to be bought out by wealthier purchasers who could take advantage of the grants (Morin, 1985).

A slew of further conservation-oriented neighbourhood revitalization programmes were embarked on by the City from 1980 onwards. The *Programme d'Intervention dans les Quartiers Anciens* (PIQA) targeted for streetscape embellishment 11 delimited sectors in the Plateau Mont-Royal and other districts, where the housing stock was of clear architectural merit, with the intent of stimulating gentrification. As we have already seen, with the arrival of the reformist MCM, low-income rental districts with severely deteriorated housing became the focus of revitalization efforts. Other programmes subsidized the beautification of laneways and the demolition of tens of thousands of obsolete coal sheds attached to the back of 'plexes, which were often fire hazards in addition to being unsightly.

At times, when resources were not as scarce, housing renovation grant programmes have been available city-wide, but by the mid-1990s there was once again increased targeting of particular neighbourhoods. A joint provincial–municipal programme initiated in 1995 at the City of Montréal's instigation included subsidies for new construction, renovation grants to homeowners and for social and private rental housing for units in need of major upgrading to meet current housing code standards, as well as infra-structural improvements – but most of the resources have been focused on five selected 'intervention sectors'. These include the Hochelaga-Maison-neuve neighbourhood, one of the most run-down districts, which has significant concentrations of badly deteriorated housing and high vacancy rates (Figure 6.11), but also a very active network of community groups keen to help revitalize the area. At the same time, parts of the Mile End and St-Louis districts, where the housing stock is also old but where some gentrification has already taken place, are also included in the programme. The most generous renovation subsidies were offered for buildings with resident landlords, as an incentive to revive this traditional type of tenure relation. One does not have to read far between the lines of the pro-gramme's statements of objectives and interim achievements to infer that a compromise was being sought between the goals of improving conditions for low-income residents and of stabilizing the tax base by encouraging middle-class and wealthier families to remain in or move into the targeted areas (Ville de Montréal, Service de l'habitation, 1998).

More generally, the housing policy adopted under the MCM administration made explicit reference to the link between housing objectives and improvements to habitat in the wider sense, meaning neighbourhood life and facilities. The City Plan adopted in 1992 pursues this theme, stressing the

FIGURE 6.11   Run-down row housing in need of renovation, Hochelaga district in the east end. (Damaris Rose)

importance of tailoring planning policies to the specific characteristics of different neighbourhoods (Ville de Montréal, 1992). Mayor Jean Doré promoted Montréal as a 'federation of villages', evoking an image nostalgic for the daily life of the traditional *paroisse* yet resonant with the persistent tendency of many Montrealers to identify, at least at the level of discourse, with a territorially bounded community (Sénécal, 1992a). Even the downtown area is constructed as a 'neighbourhood' in this discourse. Enhancing and vaunting neighbourhoods' distinct qualities is seen as a strategy to counter the outflow to the suburbs. Thus, for example, zoning policies would support the mix of functions integral to the character of the heterogeneous and young-adult oriented Plateau Mont-Royal (Gaudreau, 1992) while in neighbourhoods such as Notre-Dame-de-Grâce, still popular among families with children, the emphasis was to be placed on improving green space, traffic management, and child-oriented community facilities. Severe financial restraint in the 1990s is, however, making it difficult for the City to live up to the neighbourhood 'liveability' image as regards family-oriented services. For example, the province of Québec has historically not had a tradition of investing in public libraries (compared with Canada's anglophone provinces); Montréal has tried to improve this situation by developing neighbourhood libraries but these have not escaped budget cutbacks.

The shift to a 'localist' neighbourhood-oriented vision of urban revitalization also extended to commercial streets. The municipal administration,

FIGURE 6.12 Prince-Arthur, a pedestrianized street in St-Louis district just off Boulevard St-Laurent, abuzz with summertime strollers. (Damaris Rose)

first in the later years of Civic Party rule and then under the MCM, developed various programmes to help revitalize neighbourhood commercial arteries. Mayor Drapeau had always resisted the development of inner-city shopping centres so as to protect small business, and the commercial revitalization policy was consistent with this orientation. The provincial government eventually also came to contribute to such programmes. As in the case of residential streets, civic beautification and heritage conservation initiatives were involved, but the lynchpin is assistance in the form of grants and loans channelled through local merchants' associations. Known as SIDACs (Société d'initiatives et de développement des artères commerciales), these have been set up with the help of municipal seed money, and have input from local residents. Although funded under economic development initiatives, these programmes clearly recognized the symbiotic relationship of local commercial and residential reinvestment and revitalization (Deschatelets, 1995). Some of the early efforts entailed pedestrianization, as in the case of Prince-Arthur, a street located just off Boulevard St-Laurent, which has become a highly sucessful tourist attraction (and no longer affordable to the traditional types of neighbourhood businesses once located there) (Figure 6.12) but in most cases it was decided that these revamped neighbourhood commercial streets should remain open to

FIGURE 6.13 Avenue Mont-Royal, a neighbourhood commercial street that has benefited from a revitalization programme. On the left is the local Maison de la Culture. (Damaris Rose)

vehicular traffic in order to maximize their economic viability, with various 'traffic-calming' measures instituted.

Although the original, somewhat romanticized idea was for the revitalized street to help recreate something of the old 'parish' atmosphere (Léveillée, 1988), the 1992 City Plan places such initiatives within a revamped and post-modernist conception of 'villages within the city' (Ville de Montréal, 1992). In practice elements of both notions can be seen on streets that have been involved in commercial revitalization initiatives. For example, rue Masson in the old working-class district of Rosemont still has a traditional ambience, its lack of trendy neighbourhood bakeries and bistros appreciated by some, bemoaned by others who see these as essential to attracting more young middle-class residents (*La Presse*, 4 October 1998). A few kilometres to the west, the character of avenue Mont-Royal in the heart of the Plateau Mont-Royal district has been largely transformed: its highly eclectic mix of stores still serving a socially diverse clientele but including a large number of pâtisseries, cafés and communications-service businesses (Figure 6.13) (*Hour*, 1996). These reflect the partial gentrification of the surrounding neighbourhood by highly educated but not necessarily wealthy professionals, and cater in particular to the large number of self-employed professionals who work out of their own homes on adjacent streets. In contrast, in the case of a section of the 'Upper Main' (the upper part of Boulevard St-Laurent) where commercial revitalization was left entirely to an unfettered market, most of the new businesses catered to 'yuppies' from outside the area, leading the street exposed to boom–bust cycles following economic trends and without the stabilizing effect of stores catering to the everyday needs of the local population of the Mile End district.

Although the City maintains tight zoning regulations as regards the types and spatial concentrations of retail stores and services permitted on different kinds of commercial arteries, it has moved away somewhat from the modernist policy of promoting a strict separation of residential and commercial functions that had prevailed under the Drapeau/Lamarre administration. Whereas residential tenants had been evicted when they lived on streets zoned for commercial use and the landlord wanted to replace them with a commercial tenant, the MCM administration ended this practice with a return to the older tradition of allowing housing above retail units on neighbourhood commercial streets. Conversely, there were moves to 'legalize' retail businesses long-established on residential streets. This policy recognizes that the success of promoting the 'urban village' model as an attraction of living in an inner-city Montréal neighbourhood depends on intense pedestrian activity both by day and in the evenings with local businesses serving as important sites of social interchange, these local 'main streets' being, as the City Plan put it, 'the places where people meet and interact, ensuring a large part of the neighbourhood's vitality' (Ville de Montréal, 1992: 31).

More ambitious neighbourhood commercial revitalization initiatives have been undertaken by the City in the case of its public fruit-and-vegetable markets. Once numbering about 30, a few survived retail suburbanization and urban renewal. These City-owned buildings – parts of which have significant heritage value – were renovated in the mid-1990s with federal and provincial grants and their management was turned over to a non-profit corporation. The Jean-Talon market in 'Little Italy' in north-central Montréal has a multiethnic customer base while the proximity of the Atwater market, and recent improvements to it, are contributing to the dynamic of gentrification in the Lachine Canal district in the late 1990s. Most recently, the imposing Maisonneuve market, in the heart of the depressed east end district that was once a prosperous industrial suburb and is today also the target of major residential renovation efforts, has been reopened in the hope of contributing to the area's reinvigoration (Figure 6.14) (David Rose, 1995; Sénécal, 1995).

The new urban village concept also embraces cultural institutions. In the Victorian and modernist eras, it was buildings of monumental proportions located in the downtown core, typified respectively by the Musée des Beaux-Arts and Place des Arts, that gave Montréal its cultural signature

FIGURE 6.14   Marché Maisonneuve, typical of the City Beautiful movement in an
early twentieth century suburb. Reproduced by permission from
Marc-Aurèle Marsan

(Latouche, 1994a). In the 1980s and 1990s the City of Montréal (both under
Drapeau and the MCM) made a sustained attempt to promote and improve
the facilities for major cultural institutions that made the city a major
regional cultural centre, such as the Montréal Symphony Orchestra, L'Opéra
de Montréal and Les Grands Ballets Canadiens, as well as supporting the
arts and artists in general; part of the funding for such initiatives came from
the Arts Council of the Montréal Urban Community. Yet the centre of
gravity was at this time shifting to some extent to the neighbourhoods.
Beginning in the later years of the Drapeau regime, the City of Montréal
developed a network of about a dozen Maisons de la Culture (neighbourhood cultural centres) administered by the City and used for local art
exhibits, concerts and theatre (Ville de Montréal, Commission permanente
de la culture et du développment communautaire, 1993). This concept was
first developed in France by André Malraux, a government minister who
was also a major writer and who had a major impact on the cultural
planning policy, included at the municipal level. This idea was imported
into Montréal at the district level. It has no equivalent in anglophone North
America or even in the rest of Québec – where one finds instead community centres that include space reserved for local cultural activities,
exhibits and the like. The Maisons de la Culture have in fact rapidly evolved
towards a more community-oriented model while nevertheless remaining

FIGURE 6.15 Many of Montréal's theatres are now located in the neighbourhoods: 'Espace Go' is on the 'Upper Main' section of Boulevard St-Laurent. Reproduced by permission from Marc-Aurèle Marsan

municipal institutions. The Maisons de la Culture are typically housed in recycled institutional buildings on neighbourhood commercial streets (see Figure 6.13).

Additionally, there has been a proliferation of small theatre companies operating in renovated spaces, often also located on neighbourhood commercial arteries or on the downtown fringes, such that attendees of the various thematic theatre festivals that come to Montréal will find themselves visiting a variety of city neighbourhoods as they wend their way through their festival programmes (Figure 6.15).

As regards museums and similar institutions, the recent trend has been towards developing more specialized facilities and collections. Numerous others are located in renovated facilities in the downtown area: to name but a few, the Canadian Centre for Architecture, the Montréal Museum of Archaeology and History (see Chapter 3), the International Museum of Humour and a museum (under development at the time of writing) devoted to Dance – long one of the City's strengths in terms of artistic creation. Some specialized collections have also been set up in historic buildings in more residential neighbourhoods, such as the Firefighters' Museum in the former town hall of the defunct City of St Louis. Funding sources for these facilities vary greatly but usually involve contributions by more than one level of government and increasingly frequently entail public–private partnerships.

These types of small- and medium-sized cultural facilities have proliferated, survived and in some cases prospered in spite of the lack of a coherently articulated cultural policy on the part of the City of Montréal and in spite of the tendency for governments to reduce culture to its contributions to the urban economy (Laperrière and Latouche, 1996; Lafortune, 1990). This is perhaps testament not only to the strength of the cultural sectors in Montréal and the vibrancy of local pools of talent but also, more broadly, to the emergence of new relationships between 'city' and 'culture' (Friedberg, 1987; Latouche, 1991; Zukin, 1995). The fragmentation of the cultural consumer base as well as the growing commercialization of culture – inextricably linked to its growing role in tourism development strategies, as we saw in Chapter 5 – have largely modified the way new cultural facilities are conceived as well as where they are located (Laperrière, 1995).

Not only has this effervescence of cultural institutions greatly contributed to the expansion of various branches of artistic activity (and ancillary employment), but certain of these activities have also contributed to revitalization of local neighbourhoods (Laperrière and Latouche, 1993). An interesting case is that of the new Mega-Library (a provincially directed project under construction at the time of writing); when various locations were touted for this project, a network of community organizations from the impoverished Centre-sud district lobbied (successfully, as it turned out) for a site on the boundary between downtown's northeastern fringe and their neighbourhood in the belief that it would have positive spin-offs for local residents in terms of job creation and the quality of the local infrastructure. Cultural and artistic facilities and activities are also deeply imbricated in the dynamics of gentrification (Ley, 1996; Smith, 1996). For instance, mindful of the contribution of artists to the life of the city, and to their importance in stimulating the revival of interest in run-down neighbourhoods, the City has also modified its zoning bylaws so as to legalize and facilitate artists' combining living space and studio space in the same rental unit, in lofts, for example (Lessard, 1997). If culture has today become a major element in the marketing of cities as tourist destinations (as we saw in Chapter 5; see also Ley, 1996: 329–330), it is also the case that active cultural institutions in attractive venues in or adjacent to downtown, as well as retail art galleries showcasing local talent (Smith, 1996), are key elements in retaining or attracting the new middle class to the inner city – especially the older generation of 'empty nesters' grown dissatisfied with suburban living now that they have more time to themselves and more disposable income.

In the decade and a half of proactive housing and neighbourhood policies outlined above, and in view of the tertiarization of employment structures in the downtown and inner city discussed in the previous chapter, how have the inner-city population and social structure evolved? This is the question we explore in the remainder of the chapter.

THE SOCIAL PROFILE OF THE INNER CITY IN THE LATE 1990S: TRANSFORMATIONS AND CONTINUITIES

Population, household structure and housing tenure

In spite of the panoply of policies and programmes discussed above, the population continued to decline in the City of Montréal between 1981 and 1996, both in absolute terms and relative to the metropolitan area as a whole (Figure 6.1).[2] Had it not been for new housing construction in the suburban districts of Rivière-des-Prairies and Pointe-aux-Trembles, the overall decline would have been much greater, as can be seen from Figure 6.16, which also shows an increase in population in the downtown area as well as in the Ahuntsic/Cartierville arrondissement where a number of *Opération 20 000* developments were built. In this arrondissement, as well as in Côte-des-Neiges/NDG, the population increase is also due to an influx of young recent immigrant families.

In the most recent intercensal period (1991–1996) the rate of population decline in the City of Montréal as a whole has slowed to a negligible 0.1 per cent; whether this is really a testament to the success of municipal policies, or more an effect of economic recession (which generally tends to slow the rate of household formation and moves to the suburbs) remains to be seen, although it is striking that the City of Montréal 'captured' 16 per cent of the Montréal region's new housing starts in 1998, up from 9.5 per cent in 1993. The steepest decline from 1991 to 1996 was in the Hochelaga-Maisonneuve arrondissement (part of which was subsequently targeted by the City's most recent renovation programme). In contrast, population numbers have virtually stabilized in the Plateau Mont-Royal/Centre-Sud arrondissement, parts of which have seen considerable infill housing construction, and show a marked increase (almost 6 per cent) in the Ville-Marie (downtown) arrondissement, the latter undoubtedly a consequence of municipal repopulation initiatives in the central core.

Regarding age structure (Figure 6.17; Figure 4.7), that of the City differs from that of the rest of the metropolitan area in several respects: not surprisingly, there are proportionately fewer children and more elderly people. Compared to the province as a whole, young adults comprise a greater share of the City's population, reflecting its regional importance as a place to study or obtain a footing in the labour market (Mongeau, 1994: 7–8). Striking differences exist within the city. For example, while the Plateau Mont-Royal/Centre-Sud arrondissement attracts a disproportionately high share of the 15–44 age group, few of these have children. In contrast, the large recent immigrant population of neighbourhoods such as Côte-des-Neiges and

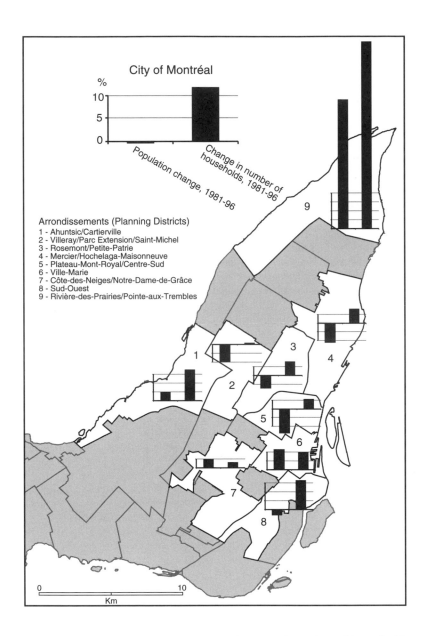

FIGURE 6.16 Percentage change in population and number of households in
the nine arrondissements (major planning districts) of the City of
Montréal, 1981–1996

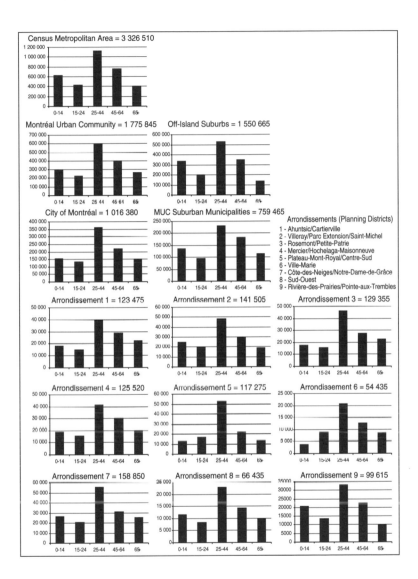

FIGURE 6.17 Age structure: Montréal Census Metropolitan Area, Off-island suburbs, Montréal Urban Community, MUC suburban municipalities, the City of Montréal, and its nine arrondissements, 1996

TABLE 6.3 Selected household characteristics, arrondissements of the City of
Montréal, 1991

		% of households comprising couples with children	% of households comprising persons living alone	Average number of persons per household
1	Ahuntsic/Cartierville	25.6	35.5	2.2
2	Villeray/St-Michel/Parc-Extension	27.2	32.4	2.4
3	Rosemont/Petite-Patrie	17.7	42.2	2.0
4	Mercier/Hochelaga-Maisonneuve	22.6	34.6	2.2
5	Plateau Mont-Royal/Centre-sud	13.0	46.6	1.9
6	Ville-Marie	7.8	60.9	1.6
7	Côte-des-Neiges/Notre-Dame-de-Grâce	20.2	40.6	2.1
8	Sud-ouest	22.4	35.0	2.2
9	Rivière-des-Prairies/Pointe-aux-Trembles	44.5	16.7	2.8
	City of Montréal	21.8	38.5	2.1

Source: Ville de Montréal, 1995: 41 (from census data)

St-Michel (see Chapter 7) is contributing to a more youthful age structure in their respective arrondissements whereas the highest proportion of elderly is to be found in the Rosemont/Petite-Patrie arrondissement, mostly comprising traditional francophone neighbourhoods that have seen little immigration. Only in the Rivière-des-Prairies/Pointe-aux-Trembles arrondissement, the main target of the City's new housing construction promotions for families, does the age structure correspond to the typical profile of a growing, family-oriented suburb.

The number of *households* in the City has continued to grow even in those districts where population has declined (Figures 6.1b and 6.16); this is indicative of decreasing household size and in particular, the increasing concentration of non-family households (meaning households not including an opposite-sex couple or a single parent) in inner-city neighbourhoods. In 1991, whereas family households comprised two-thirds of all households in the metropolitan area as a whole, and over 80 per cent in part of the outer suburban fringe, in the City of Montréal the corresponding figure was only 53 per cent (Mongeau, 1994, Table 1.18). The 'non-traditional' character of some inner-city districts can be seen from Table 6.3, which provides certain demographic indicators for 1991. The 1996 data were not fully available at the time of writing but preliminary figures indicate that the concentration of one-person households has become even more pronounced in the Plateau/Centre-Sud and Ville-Marie arrondissements.

As to housing tenure, while 'a city of tenants' remains an appropriate epithet for Montréal compared to most of its suburbs (Figure 6.18), the

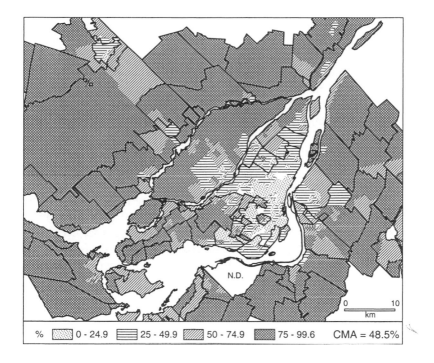

% ▦ 0 - 24.9 ≡ 25 - 49.9 ▨ 50 - 74.9 ▦ 75 - 99.6 CMA = 48.5%

FIGURE 6.18 Percentage of households who own their own home, by census tract, Montréal Census Metropolitan Area, 1996

increase in home-ownership rates during the 1980s and early 1990s (Table 6.2), though modest, was significant especially when contrasted with the trend in the rest of urban Canada, and was undoubtedly related to the municipal policies we have discussed above as well as, within certain neighbourhoods, to the growth of the condominium tenure form within the existing housing stock.

The inner-city resident labour force: 'social upgrading' and gentrification in a marginal metropolis

We saw in the previous chapter that the Montréal metropolitan region's economy today has not only a strong 'advanced tertiary' sector but also important concentrations of both labour-intensive and high-technology manufacturing production, and that the restructuring which produced this situation was clearly reflected in the changing occupational composition of the workforce between 1971 and 1991 (Table 5.4 in Chapter 5). We also noted that its central core has been relatively successful in drawing or maintaining employment in 'knowledge-based' sectors, and that labour-intensive industries were concentrated in the north-central and north-east parts of the island whereas capital-intensive sectors had largely suburban-ized. These tendencies are to some extent mirrored in the *residential* location of the workforce in different economic sectors (Statistics Canada, Census of 1991, unpublished special tabulations for D. Rose). North Shore and some South Shore suburbs have disproportionately drawn workers employed in the capital-intensive manufacturing that has decentralized to these areas. Workers in labour-intensive manufacturing (of whom a high percentage are recent immigrants) are over-represented residentially in north-central and north-east zones where such industries are located. Some West Island and South Shore suburbs have a high relative concentration of workers in public administration and finance; most of these are probably downtown commuters. In some parts of downtown, in adjacent zones of new upper-middle-class housing and in traditional elite inner suburbs, there are high relative concentrations of financial and business services workers. Education, health and social services workers are over-represented in tra-ditional elite and middle-class neighbourhoods, while workers in cultural, communications and personal services are over-represented in the Plateau Mont-Royal and other more working-class neighbourhoods.

Although these data cover workers in all types of occupations within each economic sectoral group, they hint strongly at a link between the concentration of advanced tertiary jobs in the downtown core and a strong residential presence of 'knowledge workers' in the surrounding residential neighbourhoods. The extensive literature on 'gentrification' has shown that a downtown concentration of advanced tertiary jobs is a necessary but not a sufficient condition for new middle-class settlement in inner city neigh-bourhoods (see e.g. Ley, 1996; Rose, 1989; Smith, 1996). The City of Montréal's housing and neighbourhood policies have clearly been oriented to encourage many of these 'knowledge workers' to take up or maintain *residence* in the inner city, especially those 'new urban professionals' who live in the kinds of households and hold the kinds of values most compatible with the physical and social landscape of Montréal neighbour-hoods. While the impact of public policies on the extent of 'social upgrading' that has taken place in inner-city Montréal since the early 1970s is not itself measurable, the portrait revealed by research on this phenom-enon is certainly suggestive in this respect.

Research by David Ley has tracked the occupational structure of the resident labour force of six major Canadian metropolitan areas over three intercensal periods: 1971–1981, 1981–1986 and 1986–1991 (Ley, 1996). In all cases, the inner city considerably increased its share of 'quaternary' or 'senior white collar workers' (those in professional, managerial, administra-tive and technical occupations) relative to the rest of the CMA such that by 1991 a higher percentage of inner-city workers held such jobs than did outer-city residents. These changes were due not only to absolute increases in professionals and managers in the inner city but also, in most cases, to

TABLE 6.4 Presence of professionals in Canada's four largest CMAs, 1981, 1986 and 1991

a) Professionals as a percentage of the total resident labour force, inner city and outer city

	Inner city			Outer city		
CMA	1981	1986	1991	1981	1986	1991
Toronto	16.1	18.8	22.3	14.1	14.3	16.4
Montréal	*15.1*	*17.7*	*20.9*	*13.4*	*13.8*	*14.4*
Vancouver	15.5	17.6	19.5	12.5	13.1	13.3
Ottawa-Hull	20.1	21.5	22.9	19.3	19.5	20.6

b) Inner city's share of metropolitan area professionals (per cent)

	1981	1986	1991
Toronto	20.6	20.6	19.3
Montréal	*28.7*	*29.2*	*27.1*
Vancouver	28.1	28.5	28.0
Ottawa-Hull	18.8	18.1	15.7

Source: Census of Population, special tabulations for D. Rose. CMA boundaries are those of 1981.

marked absolute decreases in 'non-quaternary' occupations due to a combination of deindustrialization and suburbanization, and nowhere was this truer than in the case of Montréal (Ley, 1996: 83–87). Similar research by Rose but using a narrower definition of 'professionals' (more tightly focused on those in occupations with control over knowledge and information; see Rose, 1996, note 2) and, in the case of Montréal, a more inclusive definition of the 'inner city', yields comparable results but the case of Canada's four largest CMAs shows a slight slippage in the inner city's share of metropolitan area professionals in the latter half of the 1980s, presumably due to the growth of suburban high technology clusters (Table 6.4).

Ley also documented social status change at the census tract level for the inner cities in his study, using an aggregate index measuring the percentage of the labour force in professional, managerial, administrative and technical jobs and the percentage of the population with some university education (Ley, 1988; Ley, 1992; Ley, 1996). His Montréal maps are reproduced (by permission) in Figure 6.19. For the 1971–1981 period, the greatest increases in social status – indicative of gentrification taking place – occur in tracts adjacent to existing upper- and middle-class districts (Westmount, Outremont, parts of Notre-Dame-de-Grâce) (Figure 6.20) and close to environmental amenities (Mount Royal, Lafontaine Park). The earliest gentrification in the city (prior to the introduction of municipal renovation programmes) involved large, formerly bourgeois Victorian townhouses on the downtown fringes with exceptional architecture that had deteriorated and were

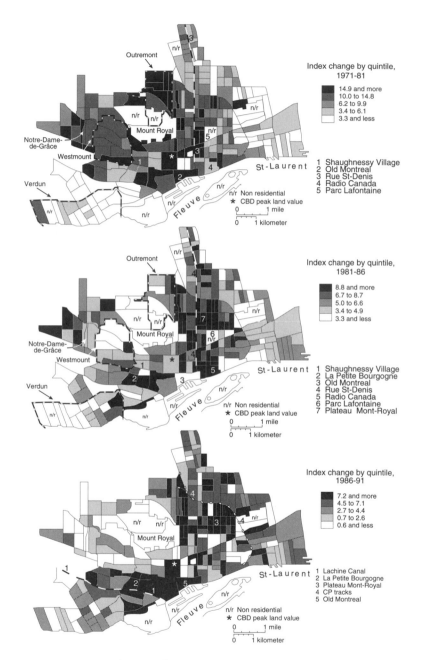

FIGURE 6.19   Social status change in inner-city Montréal: (a) 1971–1981,
(b) 1981–1986, (c) 1986–1991. Sources: Ley, 1988; Ley, 1992; Ley,
1996. Used by permission of David Ley

FIGURE 6.20   Middle-class housing in Outremont, an 'enclave' municipality, with skaters in a neighbourhood park. (Damaris Rose)

'reclaimed' in the 1970s by professionals. This was the case for Shaugnessy Village, adjacent to the west end of downtown (Corral, 1986), and for the St-Louis Square district, just off rue St-Denis and close to the Université du Québec à Montréal, to francophone cultural institutions and the public sector employment complex in the east end of downtown (Dansereau and Beaudry, 1986), both of which also show up on Ley's map, as does a sector of Centre-sud close to the Maison Radio-Canada. For the 1981 to 1986 period, when the City's renovation-stimulation programmes were in full swing, especially in the Plateau Mont-Royal, Ley's map shows a spread of 'social upgrading' from the Lafontaine Park sector of the Plateau into more working-class parts of this district. The effect of new construction and recycling of industrial buildings into housing in the Lachine Canal district, discussed earlier, is also striking. Finally, between 1986 and 1991, infill housing and to a lesser extent tenure conversions reveal themselves in new signs of social upgrading in a number of 'pockets' within working-class districts to the north and east of the Plateau, while the prior trend along the Lachine Canal is consolidated (Ley, 1996: 89–102).

   To replace the inner city in its wider metropolitan context, mapping the percentage of adults holding a university degree (a stricter criterion than that used in Ley's index) points to two major zones of highly educated potential or actual 'knowledge workers' (Figure 6.22). First, there is a large cluster of exceptionally highly educated residents (census tracts where over 40 per

FIGURE 6.21   Neighbours digging out. Some of this turn of the twentieth century housing in a gentrifying sector of the Mile End neighbourhood has more than tripled in value since the mid-1980s. (Damaris Rose)

cent of the population aged 15 and over is a university degree holder) in the central part of the island (shown in the zoomed inset), not only in the traditional elite and middle-class neighbourhoods but also in the Plateau Mont-Royal district, Old Montréal and Île des Soeurs (Nun's Island) – the latter is an island in the St Lawrence in the municipality of Verdun but only a few minutes' drive from downtown, which has been developed for new condominiums and is home to a large concentration of wealthy dual-earner professional couples (Rose and Villeneuve, 1998). The second cluster comprises some of the West Island suburbs, traditionally middle-class anglophone bastions but now increasingly mixed in ethno-linguistic terms and increasingly home to high tech industries (as we saw in Chapter 5). Lesser clusters are seen in some of the South Shore suburbs. Unpublished census-based research by Rose on the characteristics of professionals shows a spatial patterning for 1991 almost identical to that of the university-educated (map not shown here). Moreover, there are clear links between the employment clusters we discussed in the previous chapter and residential location: notably, professionals living on the West Island are more likely to be in science- and technology-based occupations and employed in the specialized manufacturing sector than their counterparts in gentrifying districts of the inner city, who are more likely to be in social science-based

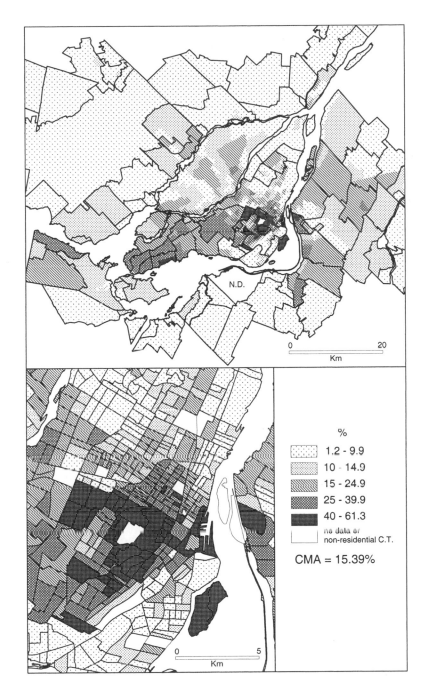

FIGURE 6.22 Percentage of Census Metropolitan Area residents aged 15 years and over with a university degree, by census tract, 1996

occupations and employed in the communications and cultural or education, health and welfare sectors (Dansereau and Beaudry, 1986; Rose, 1989; Rose, unpublished findings from census data).

While 'urban professionals' now represent a significant component of inner city residents of Montréal, this general label masks their considerable internal diversity. Data for 1990 show that while professionals aged over 45 have greater annual earnings than their suburban counterparts, younger inner-city professionals' earnings are lower than those of suburbanites. The relatively marginal situation of Montréal's young urban professionals is intimately linked to the nature of its advanced tertiary sector and the restructuring this has undergone, discussed in the previous chapter. 'Precarious' work – contractual, self-employed or part-time – is rampant in the parapublic, cultural, artistic and communications sectors in which young urban professionals are concentrated. Language and associated cultural factors, attachment to the 'Montréal way of life' and the low cost of living all tend to deter 'economically rational' migration to cities offering more secure employment opportunities (Chicoine and Rose, 1998). Many of the Montréal region's young professionals do nonetheless have stable employment, but those who are part of a family household with children tend to gravitate to the suburbs, given the high cost of single-family housing in the inner city, the scarcity of neighbourhood green spaces, much valued by those with young children, and the relative ease of commuting to a downtown job (Rose, 1996). Female professionals who are single parents constitute an important exception, greatly valuing the accessibility to jobs and services offered by inner-city neighbourhoods, provided that housing is affordable (Rose and Le Bourdais, 1986). An examination of professionals by family status thus reveals a polarization between affluent dual professional couples without children living in traditional elite areas or in redeveloped infill sectors, and large numbers in one-person households (the majority of whom are women, who earn less than men) living in fairly modest circumstances.

A brief comparison of professionals in the three Montréal districts that 'professionalized' the most between 1981 and 1991 and by 1991 had a much higher proportion of professionals than in the metropolitan area as a whole helps highlight some of these differences in 'social upgraders' and in the forms taken by upgrading (Rose, 1996). In the central Plateau Mont-Royal and the contiguous and traditionally multiethnic St Louis and Mile End neighbourhoods, professionals' incomes (both individual employment incomes and family incomes of dual professional couples) were among the lowest in the metropolitan area, whereas in the Little Burgundy/ Griffintown/St Anne sector – embracing parts of the Lachine Canal district and some sectors of infill construction under *Opération 20 000 logements* – incomes were close to the metropolitan average. Professionals in the latter district were much more likely to work in business services and much less likely to be in the communications or culture fields. Women comprised a slight majority of professionals in the St Louis/Mile End district but less than one-third in the Little Burgundy/Griffintown/St Anne district. Among households whose principal maintainer was a professional, 65 per cent were home-owners in the latter district, compared with 30 per cent in the central Plateau and only 24 per cent in St Louis/Mile End (Rose, 1996).

Overall, while about 60 per cent of the increase in *numbers* of urban professionals took place in low-to-modest income districts where 'social upgrading' mainly took the form of renovation, most of the increase in aggregate *earnings* of inner-city professionals took place either in existing elite and middle-class areas or in zones of extensive new condominium activity (Rose, 1996). Consequently, and given that the housing stock strongly favours small households, the quantitative importance of the gentrification phenomenon in Montréal up until the mid-1990s should not be overestimated, in that the numbers alone do not necessarily translate into vast increases in consumer purchasing power. Nevertheless, as we have mentioned earlier with regard to neighbourhood commercial arteries and condomium conversions, they do considerably modify styles of consumption of services and housing.

Social diversity and the patterning of poverty

Socio-economic diversity remains an enduring feature of all three of the 'upgrading' districts referred to above. In both St Louis/Mile End and the central Plateau in 1991, low-skilled workers and people not in the labour force still comprised about half of all principal household maintainers, although their numbers did drop over the decade of the 1980s in absolute and relative terms. The diversity of residential form at a micro-scale so typical of the city-building process in Montréal neighbourhoods, with lower-quality units as well as infill pockets of social housing mixed in with the more desirable, more 'gentrifiable' stock, has reduced – although not eliminated – the extent of direct and indirect displacement of low-income people out of these neighbourhoods. To a large extent neighbourhood commercial streets are patronized both by 'traditional' and 'new' residents – an indication that cultural appropriation by the new middle-class is far from complete. Moreover, Montréal has a tradition of young professionals being involved in neighbourhood-based community activism with low-income residents, working on a precarious, contractual basis in organizations that survive on government grants (Sénécal, 1992b; Favreau, 1989); this may help to reduce the social distance between 'old' and 'new' residents (Séguin, 1998), although in the case of the extensive network of cooperative child daycare centres that now exists in these neighbourhoods as a result of community activism there are indications of an orientation toward a primarily middle-class clientèle (Rose, 1990; Rose, 1993). Ethnic hetero-geneity also figures in the persistence of social class mix in St Louis/Mile End, this being the part of Montréal's 'traditional' immigrant corridor where much of the city's garment and textile industry is located and where the 'incumbent upgrading' by working-class immigrants from Southern Europe, mentioned earlier, took place in the 1970s, and where substantial numbers of low-income recent immigrants from diverse countries still live (although, as we shall see in Chapter 7, to a much lesser extent than in the past).

Whereas social and ethnocultural mix in a 'village' ambience are much-vaunted and valued attributes in the discourses that urban professionals in the Plateau and Mile End construct about their neighbourhoods, and seem to go beyond 'flâneurism' or pseudo-cosmopolitanism (Rose, 1995; Chicoine and Rose, 1998; see Caulfield, 1994: 185), the situation in Little Burgundy, the traditional heart of Montréal's oldest-established black com-munity (see Chapter 7) and now increasingly multiethnic, is very different. Here, two out of five principal household maintainers are not in the work-force, reflecting the high concentrations of public housing in this district, which we referred to earlier. The urban fabric of this area is highly frag-mented, streetscapes lack a sense of intimacy and there is no neigh-bourhood commercial artery where people from different social and ethnic or racial groups can cross paths and become familiar with the 'other'. Whereas in Mile End and the Plateau there is a long tradition of community organizing in which young, well-educated residents have been highly involved, the new urban professionals of Little Burgundy do not identify with the neighbourhood, seeing themselves more as downtown commuters, and have not become involved in campaigns to improve local community services (Germain, 1998). The huge 'urban renaissance' project (funded by the federal and municipal governments as well as the private sector) that will, by the middle of the first decade of the twenty-first century, transform all 14 kilometres of the Lachine Canal into an 'urban waterway heritage park' and restore it as a navigable waterway for pleasure craft – inspired by a similar initiative in Birmingham, England – is likely to reinforce the local contrasts between the new middle class and the poor as underused land in several working-class neighbourhoods along the length of the Canal is targeted for condominium development. This project fits within a post-modern conception of urban planning in which the entire city becomes, in a sense, a park (Sénécal, 1997). But whether this can embrace a socially inclusive vision is an open question.

These examples point to the fineness of the line between social mix and social polarization, an issue which community activists and planners will continue to face as the City of Montréal pursues its repopulation initiatives. 'Engineered' social mix in new developments and infill sites has met with varied degrees of success. In Montréal, as in other Canadian cities, well-intentioned attempts at mixing public housing, cooperatives and condominiums at a micro-scale in new residential developments facing away from the street have generated social tensions in cases where the design fails to provide buffer zones or distinct public areas for young and old (Dansereau, Germain and Éveillard, 1997). In contrast, the redevelopment of a large section of the former Angus railway shops and yard in the east-end Rosemont district for close to 2600 housing units has been a much greater success in this respect. The fruit of various political compromises and land acquisition by the provincial rather than municipal government in the dying days of the Drapeau administration, in the wake of opposition to an exclusively middle-income project proposed by the real estate arm of Canadian Pacific, this development, mostly in townhouses, 'plexes and other low-rise multifamily buildings, is made up of owner-occupied housing (45 per cent), private-rental (15 per cent) and a very high 40 per cent in cooperative, municipal (public) and other forms of non-profit housing. Although ensuring a mix of housing tenures, and thus of income groups, was a major thrust of the project, in practice the public open spaces maintain spatial and social distance between the different types of buildings, so that a peaceful *modus vivendi* rather than significant interactions between the various social and ethnic groups is the order of the day; nevertheless, the project is generally viewed as a successful example of a socially mixed development and its residents have some shared representations as to the identity of the neighbourhood (Dansereau, Germain and Éveillard, 1997).

Negotiating both socio-economic diversity and the compatibility of different 'urban ways of life' has been a particular challenge for the residents of Montréal's 'Gay Village'. Located in the heart of Centre-Sud, one of the city's poorest and most deindustrialized neighbourhoods, partially razed by urban renewal and the construction of the Maison Radio-Canada complex in the 1960s and 1970s (Morin, 1987), the 'Village' has developed rapidly since the 1970s, with the section of St Catherine Street that runs through it becoming the commercial heart of the gay and lesbian community for the Greater Montréal region (and indeed for much of the province of Québec and northern New England) and the surrounding city blocks a major residential area for gay men (Remiggi, 1998). Unlike the trajectory of many of North America's gay neighbourhoods (Knopp, 1992), gentrification has been quite limited so that there is considerable income mix within the local gay male community and relatively little perceived threat of displacement of 'traditional' residents. Lesbians, however, being poorer on the whole than gay men, as well as more likely to have children, find both financial and 'lifestyle' barriers to full participation in the commercial and cultural life of the Village (Ray and Rose, 2000). As to relations between the gay community and the 'traditional' residents of the surrounding neighbourhood, ongoing key issues are to ensure that peaceful

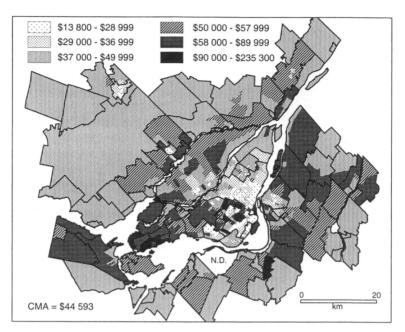

$13 800 - $28 999		$50 000 - $57 999	
$29 000 - $36 999		$58 000 - $89 999	
$37 000 - $49 999		$90 000 - $235 300	

N.D.

0   20
km

CMA = $44 593

FIGURE 6.23 Mean household income in 1995, Montréal Census Metropolitan Area, by census tract 1996

coexistence is maintained and to lobby around common objectives such as improving the infrastructure on the commercial strip and rectifying urban design components that reduced public safety (Remiggi, 1998; *Montreal Gazette*, 16 June 1997, 1 Aug. 1998).

The overall pattern of socio-economic diversity between census tracts in the Montréal region is summarized in Figure 6.23. The close spatial proximity of elite districts and some of the city's poorest neighbourhoods, a remarkable feature of Montréal's social geography since the nineteenth century, as we saw earlier in this book, has persisted through to the 1990s. Gentrification has begun to affect parts of the traditional 'city below the hill' but a new 'city below the hill' has developed on the other side (north-west) of Mount Royal in the post-war suburb of Côte-des-Neiges, parts of which have become a major immigrant reception area (see Chapter 7).

That the metaphor of the City of Montréal as being the 'hole in the doughnut' as regards incomes is not without considerable resonance can be seen from this map. Nevertheless, though highly localized and modest, the impacts of inner-city social upgrading on average incomes are discernible in a few zones. It can be seen that poverty is not restricted to the City's territory: there are pockets of low-income households in a number of the region's inner-suburban municipalities. It is to the patterning of poverty that we now turn to conclude this chapter.

'Poverty' as understood in the Canadian context is a relative term referring to deprivation compared to a norm rather than an absolute notion of dire need. The census and official statistical surveys use a threshold of 'low-income cut-offs', which identify the point at which households of different sizes have to devote much more of their pre-tax income to the essential needs of housing, food and clothing than the norm for the size of city they live in. Nevertheless, the terms 'low-income' and 'poverty' tend to be used interchangeably in both popular and most scientific parlance, a practice we will follow here.

The 1991 census showed that the Montréal metropolitan region had the highest percentage of low-income persons (22 per cent) of any metropolitan area in Canada. In spite of improvements to public pension and income support to the elderly, it is the over-70s who have the highest rates of poverty (37 per cent), but rates are also high among households with children under 6 (Mongeau, 1994). The City of Montréal has more than its 'fair share' of metropolitan area low-income residents: one-third of its residents were in poverty in 1991, and, although comprising just under a third of the metropolitan population, the City was home to close to half of its poor (Séguin, 1998).

As regards spatial distributions and concentrations of households or individuals in poverty, it is widely accepted in the literature that zones where rates of low income amount to 40 per cent and over can be considered zones of 'concentrated poverty' (Ley and Smith, 1997). In the case of the Montréal region in 1990–1991, there were 130 census tracts where 40 per cent or more individuals had incomes below the low-income cut-offs, amounting to 18 per cent of all census tracts; the majority of them were located within the City of Montréal although some older working-class suburbs such as Longueuil on the South Shore also have some high concentrations of poverty (Séguin, 1998) (Figure 6.24). There are also pockets of poverty in some suburban neighbourhoods that are of higher average income, generally corresponding to sectors of low-quality walk-up apartments that draw female-headed lone-parent families or recent immigrants (Mayer-Renaud and Renaud, 1989). However, this type of situation arises much less in the Montreal case than in the Toronto metropolitan area, where there are many more suburban zones with high rates of poverty (Ley and Smith, 1997), due in part to the very widespread gentrification of Toronto's inner city, in part to the policy of locating low-income social housing in the suburbs and in part to the *déclassement* of certain suburban high-rise developments, a rarity in Montréal. The largest contiguous concentrations of very poor census tracts are to be found in the heavily deindustrialized east end districts of Centre-Sud and Hochelaga-Maisonneuve, and in south-west Montréal, beginning in the historically poor 'city below the hill' and moving out through deindustrialized Pointe St-Charles to the oldest part of the inner suburban municipality of Verdun.

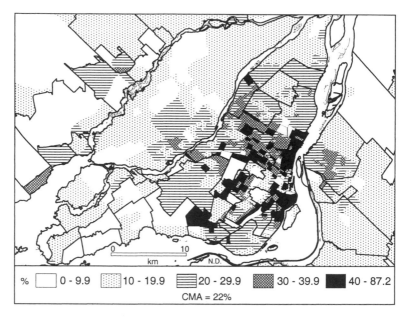

FIGURE 6.24   Percentage of individuals with personal incomes below the 'low income cut-offs' in 1990, Montréal Census Metropolitan Area, by census tract, 1991

An extensive debate about the 'urban underclass' has permeated much of the urban studies literature and policy milieux in North America and Europe in the past decade or so. This has prompted Canadian researchers to ask whether the significant number of zones of intense poverty in major cities, revealed by recent censuses, might not in fact signify the presence of a population experiencing what is termed 'multiple deprivation', in short an emergent underclass at risk of long-term social exclusion perpetuated over the generations (Ley and Smith, 1997; Séguin, 1998). Only longitudinal studies tracking individuals and the families they live in can really answer this question, but Canadian data sources following individuals' movements in and out of poverty (the National Child Development Survey and the Survey of Labour and Income Dynamics) have only recently been established, and cannot be used for analyses at the urban scale. Nevertheless, examination of the aggregate socio-economic characteristics of census tracts with high concentrations of poverty can provide some clues.

Séguin (1998) examined the prevalence of a number of factors generally regarded as putting people at risk of poverty or economic deprivation for each group of census tracts identified on the 1991 map of rates of low income in Montréal-region census tracts (Figure 6.24), as well as for the metropolitan area as a whole. She found that, at first glance, census tracts with high rates of poverty are associated with some of the 'classic' indicators of deprivation. These include higher than average incidence of unemployment, of persons with less than nine years of schooling, of one-person households (these typically having higher subsistence costs relative to their incomes), and of recent immigrants (who are often on the lowest rungs of the labour market). However, she points out that a more detailed examination of the data shows that even in the tracts with highest rates of poverty, a (small) majority of males hold down full-time jobs and a (slightly larger) majority of people have 13 or more years of schooling. The 'working poor' have in fact been a growing phenomenon across North America since the early 1980s as the burgeoning consumer services sector generates mainly low-waged jobs; in Canada, minimum wages (which are provincially determined) have not kept up with inflation, so by the late 1980s a single person working full-time for minimum wage in a large metropolitan area had annual earnings below the low-income cut-off point (Gunderson, Muszynski and Keck, 1990).

Séguin also points out that the contribution of new immigrants to high concentrations of poverty should not be exaggerated since recent immigrants comprise overall only one out of seven residents of the poorest census tracts. Nevertheless, there are a few census tracts where poverty and recent immigration are strongly associated (Ley and Smith, 1997). As we shall see in Chapter 7, low-income recent immigrants today tend to settle in certain neighbourhoods to the west, north-west and north-east of the old inner city. This – along with the widespread impacts of deindustrialization on working-class neighbourhoods – is one of the reasons why the inverted-T-shaped spatial pattern of socio-economic deprivation first identified by Montréal researchers in the 1960s (embracing 'the city below the hill', the inner east end and the traditional immigrant corridor along St Lawrence Boulevard) has evolved into more of an inverted-S shape (Mayer-Renaud and Renaud, 1989), whose outline can be discerned on the map of low-income tracts we have discussed. Evidence to date, however, indicates that with the passage of time, long hours of employment and the progressive overcoming of linguistic and other access barriers, immigrants to Canadian cities generally move out of the low-income 'reception' areas as they achieve a measure of upward social mobility (Beaujot and Rappak, 1990; Renaud, Desrosiers and Carpentier, 1993); persistent poverty over time among the *same* individuals is thus not a major feature of these neighbourhoods.

In general, in Montréal as in other Canadian cities, a diversity of factors contributes to poverty, and even within any particular zone of concentrated poverty there are likely to be a variety of causes for people having low incomes. Neither Séguin nor Ley and Smith find compelling evidence for the emergence of an urban 'underclass'. Moreover, as Séguin stresses, an infrastructure of support services in the community and in schools, largely underwritten by the state, has mitigated the effects of low incomes, compared to societies with a weaker welfare state system. Nevertheless, there are indications of elements of a 'culture of poverty', perpetuated over more than one generation, in some of the most deindustrialized traditional francophone neighbourhoods. There are also signs of an economic marginalization of visible minority youth from low-income neighbourhoods like Little Burgundy or parts of north-east Montréal.

In the late 1990s the disproportionate concentration of poverty in the core city of the metropolitan area is generating concerns as to whether the current policy of 'downloading' an increasing share of the costs of community services and facilities from the provincial to the municipal level may not be increasing the risk that zones of persistent poverty and long-term social exclusion, so far largely avoided in Montréal, will in fact proliferate in the coming years (Séguin, 1998). Such concerns are reinforced by the trend toward increasing 'entrepreneuralism' on the part of the municipal government, seemingly at the expense of social concerns, as Montréal, like other municipalities, promotes itself so as to better compete for investment on a global scale (Lustiger-Thaler and Shragge, 1998). In this context it is becoming increasingly difficult for community groups in low-income neighbourhoods to sustain their opposition to municipal policies whose goal is to regenerate the tax base by anchoring more middle-class residents to the city; it was, for example, by invoking the 'hole in the doughnut' metaphor that the City overcame opposition to a condominium project that had raised the hackles of community groups in Little Burgundy (*Montréal Mirror*, 1992). Although theorists of middle-class 'reconquest' of the inner city have tended to view social mix at the everyday scale of the neighbourhood as a transitory phenomenon (Rose, 1996), it seems clear that the management of social diversity will remain a cogent economic as well as social issue in Montréal's inner city for years to come. In the next chapter we pursue this theme of the challenges posed by diversity in the metropolis that Montréal strives to be, but we shift the focus to language, immigration and the debate around cultural pluralism.

ENDNOTES

[1] Estimated by D. Rose from data in Ville de Montréal, 1989 and 1995; Office municipal d'habitation de Montréal, 1997 and Statistics Canada, Census of Population, 1996.

[2] Population figures for 1991 and later are not strictly comparable with those for earlier years since non-permanent residents of Canada are now included. If non-permanent residents had not been counted in 1991 the population of the City of Montréal would have shown a decrease of 2.4% since 1986 (Ville de Montréal, 1995: 37).

LANGUAGE, ETHNIC GROUPS AND THE SHAPING OF SOCIAL SPACE

BEYOND THE THESIS OF THE 'TWO SOLITUDES'

Much of our knowledge of how cities came to be what they are is gained from the reinterpretation of previous works and most of all, of previous images inspiring scholars as well as the media and public debates (Deslauriers, 1994). One of those images has proved particularly enduring as a metaphor for the relationship between Canada's two dominant linguistic communities and its inscription in Montréal's social space. *Two Solitudes* was the title of a novel written by Hugh MacLennan in 1945 (MacLennan, 1945). The story was located at Saint-Marc-des-Érables, an imaginary parish in the Québec countryside; but this 'fairly simple tale of people living together in a region where religious traditions made it impossible for them to know one another' (MacLennan, 1978: 292–293) was really about Canada, according to the author. 'Les Anglais' and the 'French Canadians' made up two cultural worlds, were taught two different versions of history, and coexisted in mutual imperviousness. From the time of publication of this novel at least until the Quiet Revolution, the image of two solitudes was frequently used to describe the perpetual puzzle of the relationship of francophone Québec to English speaking Canada.

The two solitudes metaphor also shaped dominant perceptions of Montréal's social geography. When the young MacLennan arrived in Montréal from rural Québec in 1935 in search of work as a school-teacher, the Montréal he first encountered was visibly spatially divided between what was commonly described as 'the British Empire' to the west and the 'French fact' to the east:

> [it] had, so far as I knew, no counterpart anywhere on earth. . . . Here, the two cultures of Canada, without even planning it, had evidently decided that the best way to coexist was to ignore the existence of one another. . . . [Yet] Montréal was perhaps the politest city in the world then. . . . (MacLennan, 1945: 295–296).

Other observers of Montréal's social space, notably including Chicago-school sociologist Everett Hughes (1943), reinforced the popular image of a city whose social fabric was above all shaped by a spatial divide, roughly corresponding to St Lawrence Boulevard, between two distinct communities, each internally cohesive and ignorant of the other. However, as we shall see in this chapter, the major transformations wrought by immigration waves in the socio-cultural space of Montréal since the 1960s are leading to the substitution of the two solitudes image by a new one, that of the multicultural city (McNicoll, 1993), which takes on a uniquely controversial connotation in the prevailing linguistic climate of contemporary Québec. Moreover, the Quiet Revolution, the renewal of Québécois nationalism and the effects of Bill 101 have irrevocably altered the relative socio-economic positioning and cultural geographies of Montréal's francophone and anglophone communities.

In fact, in the light of historical research by a new wave of social scientists, both anglophone and francophone, working in the climate of post-Quiet Revolution Québec, these images look more and more to be at best partial ones and at worst misleading stereotypes regarding the present as well as the past configuration of Montréal's social landscape. Literary works, too, have reflected this shift in perspective. For example, novelist and playwright Michel Tremblay, writing in the 1980s, has underlined how class divisions within the French-Canadian community became entrenched in space by the 1940s, with Park Avenue (a few streets west of St Lawrence Boulevard) forming the boundary between the rich of Outremont and the 'ordinary people' of the Plateau Mont-Royal (Deslauriers, 1994) − a boundary still highly visible in socio-economic maps of the city (Figure 6.23). All in all, in the social life and spatial patterning of the city, language, social class, religion and ethnicity did not overlap to the same extent as received accounts of Montréal's history and geography had implied. (See Figures 4.2 and 7.3 for the location of districts and municipalities referred to in this chapter.)

In particular, 'English Montréal' has never been homogeneous in socio-economic, ethnic and religious terms (Ames, 1972 [1897]; Copp, 1974; Reynolds, 1935; Rudin, 1988). In the mid- and late nineteenth century, alongside the Anglo-Protestant elite could be found an anglophone working-class including Irish Catholic labourers but also skilled workers recruited from England and Protestant Ulster. At the other end of the social scale, Scots were among the most successful entrepreneurs, but a Protestant Irish family, the Molsons, would also join the ranks of the business elite. Working-class and predominantly English-speaking districts like Pointe St-Charles and Verdun in south-west Montréal were quite diverse, with British, French and Irish workers living close by, while numbers of British skilled workers also settled in the mainly francophone suburbs of Maisonneuve and Rosemont, close to their workplaces in the shipbuilding and rolling stock industries. Moreover, during the twentieth century, people claiming to be of British Isles ethnic stock formed an ever-declining percentage of Montréal anglophones. For the province as a whole this percentage dropped from 95 per cent in 1931 to 60 per cent in 1981 (Rudin, 1988), most of the decline being due to the increasing ethnic diversity of 'English' Montréal. If in 1931, persons of British Isles origin still represented 26 per cent of the population on the Island of Montréal, this proportion had dropped to 7 per cent by 1991.

Also, the renewed focus on studying minority groups in their own right has brought into light the existence of groups present in Montréal as early as the mid-nineteenth century and their role in the city-building process. Even if in 1881, 97.5 per cent of the population of the city was of British or French origin, various other ethnic groups were pivotal to the development of certain neighbourhoods. Previous accounts of the city's socio-linguistic space had in various ways effectively marginalized the social geographies of ethnocultural minorities. This was done by assimilating them to the 'British' or 'English' ethnic categories (Lacoste, 1958), by ignoring their presence in significant numbers in parts of the supposedly homogeneous francophone east end, or, most commonly, by lumping all whose mother tongue was neither English nor French to an undifferentiated residual category. These 'others' were seen as forming a third bloc in the residential social geography of Montréal, a wedge in between the French and English blocs, running through the centre of the island from south-east to north-west along the St Lawrence Boulevard axis. In these influential narratives of Montréal's social geography (notably Blanchard, 1947, 1953), this 'immigrant' or 'ethnic corridor' was seen as a world apart, a buffer zone between the French and the English, thus consolidating the two solitudes; and this space, unlike the supposedly homogeneous English and French blocs, was recognized as a cosmopolitan milieu.

Recent studies carried out at a micro-scale, however, have not only uncovered the internal diversity of immigrant districts but have shown that the broad anglophone–francophone spatial divide has long been intersected and underlain by social and ethnocultural mix at a fine scale (Langlois, 1985; Linteau, 1982; Marois, 1989). The spatial patterning has, moreover, never been static, and with the decline of Montréal's anglophone population and the diversification of immigration, forces are at work which, on the whole, point in the direction of increased ethnocultural heterogeneity throughout most of the Island of Montréal and in some of the off-island suburbs.

The persistence of the perception of two homogeneous blocs occupying separate territories on the Island of Montréal stems in part from the conflation of linguistic affiliation and ethnic and cultural identification in academic as well as popular discourse. But today French is no longer spoken only by French Canadians or by immigrants from French colonial countries such as Haiti and Vietnam; it is increasingly becoming the everyday language of immigrants ranging from Latin-Americans to Croatians to Sri Lankans, just as in the days before Québec's language laws earlier waves of immigrants tended to gravitate towards English even if they did not come from English-speaking countries. The outside observer might wonder how, in this context, it is still possible to confuse language and culture. However, while the importance of multiethnicity in Montréal has rendered outdated the 'two solitudes' paradigm, it would be wrong to presume that a multi-cultural model has become a widely accepted substitute. In fact, as we shall see, Montréal's social space is structured by two competing visions, one based on language and the other on culture.

This chapter first sketches out the formation of the city's ethnocultural mosaic up to the mid-1970s. We then discuss the 'new immigration' flows, which have led to an even greater diversity in the cosmopolitan landscape of Montréal, lived out in different ways in different kinds of neighbour-hoods. We situate these trends within the broader context of Québec's immigration and linguistic policies which, in trying to bolster the French language and ensure the survival of a French society, are paradoxically irrevocably changing the culture that the language expresses. Finally, we review the changing situation of Anglo-Montrealers in the multicultural, bilingual city that is officially neither of those things.

THE FORMATION AND RESHAPING OF A MOSAIC

Under the French Regime, Montréal was a somewhat small city of some 5000 inhabitants receiving minimal immigrant flows, amounting to less than 70 persons per year on average for the whole of New France (Henripin, 1968). The mother country sent even fewer people to Acadia, the other French settlement in Canada. This historical fact helps explain why even today French Canadians tend not to perceive their country as a land of immigration, in contrast to most of the rest of North America.

Yet, contrary to widespread assumptions about the homogeneity of Montréal in the seventeenth and eighteenth centuries, this small city was already experiencing some cultural diversity in its daily life. Amerindians were part of the landscape because of the fur trade, and slavery of Amerindians as well as Blacks (some 1400 of them) was introduced into New France in 1628. The slaves worked as domestic servants in cities and the application of the *Code Noir* in 1685 protected owners from slave violence and escape (Williams, 1997). The Black population was not numerous before the British Conquest but this began to change 15 years later when the American War of Independence brought significant numbers of Loyalists to the British Empire in Lower and Upper Canada.

This being said, during its first century, Montréal was clearly a French city and it had to count on natural growth to ensure its development, especially after the British Conquest in 1760. The birth rate of French Canadians in the province of Québec remained high even as other groups were reducing their birth rates. Between 1870 and 1930, their population growth was largely due to an exceptionally high average fertility rate, popularly known as the 'revenge of the cradle' because it was encouraged by Church and State in order to compensate for the declining political weight of Québec within Canada (Henripin and Perron, 1973).

The nineteenth century: a shifting ethnocultural balance

The British Conquest, however, had opened the door to British Isles immigration. In 1831, the French–Canadians became a minority in Montréal and would remain so for the next 35 years. Between 1815 and 1850, Irish immigrants, Protestants as well as Catholics, came in great numbers, including a large wave caused by the potato famine of the 1840s. At the time of the 1871 census, they outnumbered the immigrants from England and Scotland and represented almost 24 per cent of the population of the city. Their arrival in Montréal coincided with intensive construction of public works in the context of the take-off of industrialization: the Lachine Canal and the Victoria Bridge, for example, were built mainly by an Irish labour force. A monument, the Black Rock – at the head of the bridge – recalls today how high was the price of their exodus, since some 6000 died from typhoid or other fevers during the journey or in the quarantine shacks into which they were herded on arrival (Rudin, 1988).

Seeking proximity to work, the Irish settled in southwestern districts such as Griffintown and Pointe St-Charles where they mingled with French–Canadian workers. Religion and social condition, that is poverty, often brought these groups closer together. Even epidemics were opportunities for solidarity: some French Canadians adopted Irish orphans after cholera and typhoid epidemics during the 1830s and the 1840s (Charbonneau and Sévigny, 1997). They were often allowed to keep their last names, which, along with the more important factor of intermarriage, explains why so many of today's francophone Québécois have Irish surnames.

The Catholic Irish did not only find work as day labourers but also occupied niches in other important sectors of the economy, for instance in the shoe and leather industry before its mechanization which led to their replacement by French–Canadian workers (Olson, 1991), whereas the Protestant Irish, as well as Protestants from other parts of the British Isles, were clustered in the skilled metal-working trades. Part of the Irish community also established itself in the east-end industrial suburb of Maisonneuve where they founded the parish of St Aloysius. While Irish Catholics and French Canadians quite often shared the same segment of the employment market (not without some associated rivalry, notably in the construction industry), there was a tendency for the various immigrant groups to carve out specific niches in the Montréal economy and their arrival was frequently associated with boom periods of city-building (Olson and Kobayashi, 1993).

From the late nineteenth century onwards the relative importance of the Irish declined with the arrival of new waves of immigrants from England and Scotland (Bradbury, 1993: 40), and today, it is difficult to locate those of Irish ancestry, especially since small-area census data has not distinguished within the 'British Isles' origin category since 1951. But their importance in the city is not denied; their emblem, the shamrock, is one of the four on the city flag. The St Patrick's Day parade is still the largest street parade in Montréal, attracting people of many different ethnocultural origins, and their Basilica is perhaps one of the best restored churches in the downtown area.

If Irish immigration changed the linguistic demography of Montréal in the early to mid-nineteenth century, rural–urban migration of French Canadians between 1850 and the end of the century was instrumental in re-establishing a French majority in the city by 1871 (Robert, 1982). The Québec rural economy was undergoing major restructuring and the increasing proletarianization of subsistence farmers combined with population growth meant that many French Canadians had to leave their farms in search of work. While around 600 000 of them went to the United States between 1840 and 1900, many to the textile mills of New England (Lavoie, 1973; Ramirez, 1991), Montréal also attracted great numbers. They settled mainly in the east end where light industry was proliferating under the control of francophone as well as anglophone industrialists. French Canadians were over-represented in consumer-goods industries, while anglophones were over-represented in heavy industries (Rennie, 1953). Given that workers still tended to cluster relatively near to their workplaces, this labour market segmentation contributed to what Bradbury (1993: 41) describes as the 'hardening' of Montréal's linguistic geography in the latter part of the nineteenth century.

Another element within English-speaking Montréal – and which was to become of great importance in the twentieth century – was the Jewish community, whose first immigrants were officers in the British army, after the 1760 Conquest. They were followed by British-born merchants. Jewish Montrealers had to wait until 1832 to have their religion legally recognized. This small and prosperous community, well-integrated into the Anglo-Scottish elite, would be greatly disturbed when major waves of immigration bringing in poor Yiddish-speaking Ashkenazi Jews from Eastern Europe escaping anti-Semitism began in the 1880s and were amplified in the early twentieth century.

At the turn of the twentieth century then, Montréal had a French majority but it was still very much a Victorian city in appearance and outlook. In 1901, 60.9 per cent of the inhabitants were of French origin, with 33.7 per cent declaring a British Isles origin. The city's population was thus far less cosmopolitan than that of many American cities at the time (Linteau, 1982: 45). This situation would change significantly over the next few decades. By

1981 (the last year for which a broadly comparable question on ethnic origin was asked in the census) the proportion of the City's residents declaring themselves to be of French origin had changed little (62.3 per cent), whereas those of British origin amounted to only 8.9 per cent, while the number reporting 'other' ethnic origins had climbed to 28.8 per cent.

The makings of a cosmopolitan yet segmented city: immigrant flows and residential patterns, c. 1900 – mid-1970s

Over the first three decades of the twentieth century Montréal experienced further massive in-migration from the French-Canadian countryside. But this was also a time of international immigration to Canada on an unprecedented scale, especially prior to the First World War, as can be seen in Figure 7.1. Montréal shared in this trend, with the largest influx being from the British Isles, but the latter migration was not and would never again be sufficient to overturn the francophone demographic majority in the City of Montréal. Most of the anglophone immigrants were from England although they also included Scots as well as Ulster Protestants displaced from their jobs in the Belfast linen trade. Many were skilled artisans admitted under special recruitment programmes in order to boost the skilled labour force in fields such as marine engineering and trades associated with the railways (Porter, 1965; Reynolds, 1935). British Isles women were also brought in to work as domestic servants for the Westmount bourgeoisie (Westley, 1990).

While many of the new waves of English-speakers continued the traditional pattern of gravitating to the mixed neighbourhoods in the south-west part of the city – including Protestant Irish who settled in the same districts as the Catholic Irish – some settled close to their workplaces in the francophone east-end districts of Rosemont and Maisonneuve. White-collar workers, including descendants of the earlier Irish immigrants, set up house in some of the early 'streetcar suburbs' like Mile End or Verdun, which, also being industrial communities, attracted residents from a range of ethnic groups and social classes. Further upward social mobility, however, brought increased spatial separation from the francophone majority from the 1920s on as middle-class anglophones moved to newer middle-class suburbs like Notre-Dame-de-Grâce in the west end – continuing a westward drift that had begun in the late nineteenth century (Sweeny, 1982), as well as to Park Extension to the north-west and, later, to predominantly anglophone suburbs on the West Island and to the South Shore communities of St Lambert and Greenfield Park (Reynolds, 1935; Rudin, 1988; van Nus, 1984). An exception to this pattern is the modest-income south shore suburb of Chateauguay, to which both English- and French-speakers migrated from south-west Montréal, and which is adjacent to the Mohawk Indian reserve of Kahnawake.

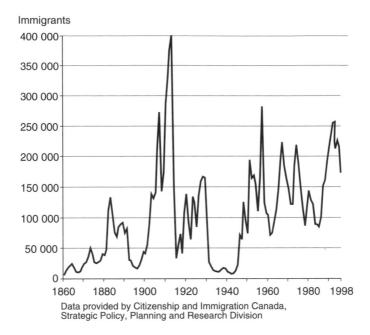

Immigrants

Data provided by Citizenship and Immigration Canada,
Strategic Policy, Planning and Research Division

FIGURE 7.1 Annual international migration flows to Canada, 1860–1998.

Although in 1901 only 6 per cent of Montrealers claimed an ethnic origin other than French or British, this had already risen to 11.2 per cent a decade later. In fact, however, the seeds of a cosmopolitan city had been germinating well before the end of the nineteenth century. Some ethnic groups had already created the nucleus of a community that would sooner or later serve as a cultural hearth for later waves of immigrants. For instance, the city's long-standing though tiny English-speaking Black community began to consolidate in the St Antoine district (now called Little Burgundy) in the later nineteenth century as new migrants arrived from other parts of Canada and from the United States, including numerous escapees from slavery smuggled through the important Hudson Valley/Lake Champlain route of the 'underground railroad'. Migration from the West Indies subsequently reinforced this community. This came about partly as a result of a government programme to recruit female domestic workers for wealthy families; this was the first in a long line of such programmes, which also targeted girls from Britain and Finland (Barber, 1986; Lindstrom-Best, 1986). Black women were in fact from the very beginning at the forefront of a successful and enduring movement to create strong community associations in this neighbourhood, most of them still active today. An even more important catalyst for the growth of the Black community in the early twentieth century was the development of Montréal as a major railway centre. In line with the labour and customer relations policies of the American Pullman Car company, Blacks were first taken on as sleeping car attendants, then as porters (Red Caps) to service the white travelling public (Williams, 1997).

For decades, racism and discrimination severely limited the movement of Black Montrealers into the professions regardless of their qualifications. Moreover, the community could not grow fast because of restrictive immigration policies. In the 1950s, another domestic worker scheme allowed more West Indian women, often well educated, to immigrate. But it was only in 1962 that the racial quotas were removed and that West Indian immigration could occur on a larger scale. Little Burgundy remained the major Black district, but West Indian immigrants also moved to other neighbourhoods, mostly in the west-central part of the island of Montréal, including Côte-des-Neiges, the lower part of Notre-Dame-de-Grâce, LaSalle and Ville St Laurent. In time, economic and social mobility led some to move out to middle-class anglophone suburbs on the West Island and, later, to multiethnic Brossard on the South Shore. In addition to these anglophone Blacks, a small group of French-speaking Haitians immigrated to Montréal in the 1960s, presaging a much larger migration which was to begin in the 1970s. This little group of professionals (doctors, teachers, etc.) gravitated immediately to francophone neighbourhoods (Ledoyen, 1992).

The development of the railway system and the historical orientation of Canadian immigration policies to serve specific and sometimes temporary workforce needs (Hawkins, 1988; Simmons and Keohane, 1992) were also responsible for the emergence of the small Chinese community that developed in Montréal in the late nineteenth century, and for its discontinuous pattern of development. Chinese labourers were recruited to western Canada to work in the forests or the mines, and especially on the construction of the trans-Canada railway line; many migrated to eastern cities after its completion in 1885. After facing difficult conditions and racism on the job, they had to pay a 'Head Tax' to settle in Canada; this was levied on the Chinese so as to discourage the immigration of whole families, whereas European immigrants were exempted from it and were granted inexpensive rural land (Li, 1988). Most of the original community (about 1000 in 1901) consisted of men. They worked as domestics and operated service businesses, including corner stores, restaurants and a large number of hand laundries that serviced the needs of downtown workers (Helly, 1987). The first shop opened on Craig Street in the lower downtown and a small community was established at the south end of St Lawrence Boulevard, which remains today the traditional commercial centre of Montréal's Chinese community and houses a small, low-income resident population. The head tax was eventually replaced by restrictive legislation on bringing family members to Canada, which resulted in half of the Cantonese who had arrived between 1890 and 1921 going back to China. It was not until the 1960s that a new wave of Chinese immigration would begin, primarily from Hong-Kong.

Nevertheless, prior to the 1970s, it was Europeans who dominated immigrant waves to Montréal, as was the case for Canada in general. The first wave, from about 1880 to 1930, comprised Jews, Germans, Polish, Hungarians and Ukrainians and, beginning just after 1900, Italians. The period after the Second World War saw a further wave of immigration (Figure 7.1), this time largely from Central, Eastern and Southern Europe, again including Italy but also Greece and Portugal.

Not all groups followed the same socio-spatial trajectory. For example, whereas the mainly middle-class Germans sought to establish themselves in the same areas as the most successful British immigrants, many of the Ukrainians settled in south-west Montréal or in Hochelaga in the east end close to industrial districts where both men and women could get labouring jobs, or in the Mile End and Park Extension districts close to the Canadian Pacific Railway yards. The latter districts offered greater prospects for the single-family housing much sought after by this cultural group. The then linguistically mixed suburb of Rosemont became a favourite target of the more middle-class second generation of Eastern Europeans (Mamchur, 1934). Although some integrated into the francophone community, a much more common trend in the following generation was to move to anglophone areas in the West End and West Island.

On the whole, however, St Lawrence Boulevard (today officially called Boulevard Saint-Laurent), was the main conduit for European immigration, taking newcomers from the port to their first settlement neighbourhoods in the east and just north of the city core – where as early as 1901, one in six residents was of neither French nor English mother tongue (Sweeny, 1982) – and moving them northwards over time to gain access to more middle-class sectors of what social scientists came to label the 'immigrant corridor'. From there, they or their children would branch out, usually westwards but sometimes north or north-east, to suburban districts. English-speaking Montrealers have long referred to this street as 'The Main', precisely because it served as the city's 'Main Street' for so many of the ethnic groups that now make up Montréal's anglophone population.

This was the classic path of the Jewish community, whose establishment was especially significant for the building of Montréal's ethnic mosaic, and who remain of major importance today among its ethnic minorities, with close to 90 000 residents of the CMA claiming a Jewish ethnic origin in 1996. The different groups of Jewish immigrants to Montréal, coming mainly from Lithuania and Romania, and secondarily from Ukraine and White Russia, formed diversified but mainly working-class communities which remained essentially structured around the tradition of the *shtetl* until the 1940s (Anctil, 1992). Dating back to the Middle Ages, this system of socio-spatial organization produced little towns of artisans and tradespeople with housing, shops, religious and cultural institutions in close proximity, often indeed superimposed in the same building. Social life in these Yiddish-speaking neighbourhoods was intense, with few distinctions between private and public spaces. Concentrated initially in the 'Lower Main' below Sherbrooke Street, within walking distance from the port and the main railway terminus, the Jewish 'enclave' gradually moved up St Lawrence Boulevard into the St Louis district in the early twentieth century. As in many other cities (London, New York, Toronto) it was clustered around small factories and workshops, mainly in the garment trade, which afforded virtually the sole employment opportunities at the time. The Jewish communities effectively made this linear zone into a place immigrants could call their own, paving the way for other groups such as southern Europeans who began to open businesses on The Main in the late 1930s (Weintraub, 1996).

By the outbreak of the Second World War a measure of socio-economic mobility drew the community a little further north, past the 'Mountain', into its first suburb, the Mile End district of Montréal and the first couple of streets of the adjacent municipality of Outremont – this was the 'Jewish quarter' made internationally famous by novelist Mordecai Richler (*St Urbain's Horsemen*, *The Apprenticeship of Duddy Kravitz* . . .; see Deslauriers, 1994). For a time, three-quarters of Montréal's Jewish community was concentrated in this neighbourhood, mostly between Park Avenue and The Main, and several of the census tracts in this area, vacated by earlier migrants from Britain and Ireland as well as by French-Canadians on the move to more distant suburbs, were almost entirely occupied by Jews (Légaré, 1965). This neighbourhood was itself characterized by a fine scale of social stratification from west to east, its wealthier residents living at the fringes of what had become by the 1930s the wealthy francophone suburb of Outremont, its poorest on the streets just east of The Main melding into the working-class francophone Plateau Mont-Royal district. Also located in Mile End was the city's largest synagogue, built in 1945 – today it is a French private school – and the neighbourhood was the hub of Jewish cultural, political and intellectual life, not only for Montréal but for the whole of Canada (Weintraub, 1996). Yiddish was still spoken but the community was rapidly anglicizing as the children received most of their education in English-language public schools. As for many other working-class immigrant groups, public education was seen as crucial to the movement out of the 'ghetto' and into the Canadian middle-class.

Beginning in the 1940s and accelerating in the following decade, Jewish families rapidly vacated this neighbourhood as they attained middle-class status and, following in the footsteps of their Anglo-Scottish predecessors, sought out single-family housing in lower-density suburbs along the north-western flanks of Mount Royal (the Côte-des-Neiges district) and beyond, to Snowdon, Côte-St-Luc, Hampstead, Ville-St-Laurent and eventually to Chomedey on the island of Laval. Seemingly reluctant to move to outer suburbs, however, the Jewish community remains an urban one, deeply involved in the artistic and cultural life of the city. Meanwhile a new wave of low-income Jews settled in the Mile End/Lower Outremont district after the Second World War, including displaced persons from Eastern Europe and ultra-orthodox Yiddish-speaking Hasidim. The latter still live there today, forming a community of several thousand, the second-largest in North America after that of New York, with which there are close social ties maintained by a twice-weekly chartered bus service.

The residential trajectory of Montréal's Jewish community does not fit the theoretical model of dispersion/assimilation developed by the Chicago school of urban sociology: spatial concentrations remain high in a number of neighbourhoods despite economic success. In their settlement patterns, the Jewish community, and to a lesser extent other groups of European immigrants, reproduced the model that governed the coexistence of the francophone and anglophone communities, which might be termed 'integration by segmentation' (Germain, 1998). The strong residential segmentation of the Jewish community, like that of other ethnocultural communities for whom spatial proximity to their own religious and socio-cultural institutions is primordial, can be explained partly by a desire to maintain what the Canadian ethnic studies literature calls 'institutional completeness' (Balakrishnan and Kralt, 1987; Breton, 1964). However, rejection by the dominant culture(s) has also historically played a role. In the Montréal case, the Jewish community was historically not welcome in the neighbourhoods of the Anglo-Scottish elite nor in French neighbourhoods and, crucially, French schools. In the early twentieth century, the cultural identity of French Canadians was still embedded in rurality and a very traditional Catholicism as well as the French language. The sudden and massive arrival of a strongly urbanized group of immigrants rooted in quite another spiritual tradition, and speaking Yiddish in factories and on the streets, provoked a profound shock. As mandated by constitutional legislation in force at the time of Canadian Confederation, the public education system was organized on a religious basis: schools were either Catholic or Protestant. Catholic schools were mostly French but there were also numbers of schools catering for English-speaking Catholics; almost all Protestant schools were English. Concern to protect one of the fundamentals of French-Canadian identity led the Montréal Catholic School Commission to exclude non-Catholics until the 1970s, whereas as early as 1888, the Protestant Committee of the Public School Board had decided to consider all non-Christians Protestants for the purposes of providing them with educational services . . . and collecting their school taxes (Anctil, 1988). This was enshrined in legislation in 1903 with specific reference to Jews, although they were denied decision-making powers in the School Board. This combination of fiscal pragmatism, the liberalism characteristic of the British imperial tradition and the drawing power of English as the language of socio-economic mobility led to most

Jewish and, later, Greek and East European Orthodox families sending their children to English Protestant schools. This played a significant role in the gravitation of non-Catholic immigrants to the more anglophone parts of the city, at least until the language legislation of the 1970s made French the required language of instruction for the children of immigrants (McNicoll, 1993). Among Jewish Montrealers, this pattern began to change in the 1970s with the increasing arrival of French-speaking Sephardic Jews from countries on the Mediterranean fringe.

The first immigrants from Italy arrived also in Montréal in the 1870s–1880s, although the major wave was to take place between about 1910 and 1930, with a renewed influx in the 1950s and 1960s. Italians in fact would become the largest ethnic minority group in Montréal with almost 221 000 residents of the CMA declaring their ethnic origin as Italian in 1996, and Italian immigrants remain today by far the most populous of all the city's immigrant groups (11.2 per cent, that is 72 320 persons), especially among those who settled before 1961 among whom they comprise close to one-third (Statistics Canada, 1998b). On arrival, many found economic niches in the construction industry, or, in the case of women, in the garment trade. Poor farmers left rural regions such as Sicily, Napoli and Calabria, and later also migrated from northern regions, often recruited by Italian agents called *padrones* to work on the Canadian Pacific Railway. The CPR in fact played a major role in the development, and residential location, of some of the city's immigrant communities: between about 1900 and 1930 almost half its workforce were immigrants, including several thousand Italians (Ramirez, 1991: 88–91). Unlike the Chinese, however, the Italian men were encouraged to send for their families so as to form a stable community. The first settlements were located in poor neighbourhoods just east and west of downtown, close to the port and the main east–west railway tracks, a focal point being the Mount Carmel parish just east of the Lower Main. Rather than moving up the 'immigrant corridor' all the way from downtown, however, Italian settlement followed a leapfrog pattern. One major hub was Rosemont, close to the Angus Shops – where many soon integrated into the local francophone community. In 1951, two out of five Italian-born Montrealers were married to French-Canadians (McNicoll, 1993). Many other Italians, like the previously mentioned but far less numerous Ukrainians, gravitated to the northern part of the Mile End district, close to the Outremont rail yards, where they founded their own Catholic parish following friction with the local French parish. In the early decades of the century this was the urban fringe where they could maintain their traditions of grazing domestic animals, growing vegetable gardens and grapes for wine, and in some cases building small single-family houses (Boissevain, 1970; Ramirez, 1981; Ramirez and Del Balso, 1980).

Although the community in Mile End and just to the north, in what became known as Little Italy around the Jean-Talon fruit and vegetable market,

FIGURE 7.2 The 'Little Italy' section of Boulevard St-Laurent in the city's north
end, the traditional focal point of Montréal's Italian community.
(Annick Germain)

continued to consolidate its residential and institutional base until the 1960s
(Figure 7.2), suburbanization became the dominant trend among the Italians
just as for other groups, once the community became more established, and
particularly after the Second World War, when it was reinforced by the arrival
of more middle-class Italian immigrants. By 1961 almost no part of the Island
was without its share of Montrealers of Italian origin (Boissevain, 1970);
nevertheless, the tradition of clustering was reproduced to a considerable
extent in the suburbs. Although not as homogeneous as were the Jewish
neighbourhoods of the 1940s, the Italian neighbourhoods of the mid-to-late
twentieth century Montréal retained much of their 'village' quality with great
emphasis on face-to-face contacts with relatives and friends from the same
community, and Montrealers of Italian origin remain much more likely to
declare Italian as their mother tongue than their compatriots in Toronto,
which also has a very large Italian community. To a considerable extent,
families originating from the same region of Italy grouped together in
the same neighbourhoods (Boissevain, 1970; Painchaud and Poulin, 1988);
this feature is reflected on neighbourhood streets every summer with a

variety of Italian festivals venerating saints associated with the different regions of origin.

Several major suburban flows can be identified for Italian Montrealers. One stream went south-westwards, from the inner city to Ville-Émard and lower NDG through to Lasalle and Lachine. Other streams went north-west to Ville-St-Laurent, and later, off the island to Laval, and from Mile End and Rosemont north-eastwards to the industrial suburbs of St-Michel and Montréal-Nord and, later, on to Rivière-des-Prairies. Most favoured of all, however, was the post-war suburban municipality of St-Léonard, where in 1996 44 per cent of residents claimed Italian ethnic origin. Here, placing great value both on home-ownership and living close to the extended family, the Italians produced their own variant of the typically Montréal duplex. This community would also be the scene of Montréal's most well-known conflict over language in the late 1960s and early 1970s when a riot developed over Catholic school officials' removal of the right to bilingual education; as in the case of many other ethnic groups, the Italians, while one of the most bilingual groups in Montréal, saw mastery of English as an essential conduit to socio-economic and, if need be, geographic mobility (Levine, 1990).

These waves of European immigrants were enriched by the arrival of other ethnic groups from southern Europe, mainly in the 1950s and the 1960s. The first Greek immigrants arrived, in small numbers, at the turn of the century, concentrating in the Lower Main. Knowing only their mother tongue, they worked mainly in businesses run by their compatriots and by 1921 operated over a third of the 150 restaurants owned by 'ethnics'[1] (Lazar and Douglas, 1992: 166). The Greek community's niche in the restaurant industry, as well as their tendency to own small service businesses, has persisted to the present day. After the civil war in Greece in the 1940s, large numbers of unskilled workers immigrated to Montréal, concentrating in Mile End as it was being vacated by the Jewish community, and just to the north, in Park Extension, which would become the city's major Greek neighbourhood. Many obtained work in the garment industry, which has remained a major source of female employment (Labelle et al., 1987). In the 1970s, they would be followed by more urban and skilled immigrants, including professionals. For this community, social mobility generally led to a move to western suburbs, first Côte-des-Neiges, then the West Island and more recently to Chomedey in Laval and to Brossard on the South Shore. As in the case of the Jewish community, the Greeks gravitated strongly towards English-speaking neighbourhoods, most being educated in the Protestant school system (Lazar and Douglas, 1992). Today there are 54 500 Montrealers of Greek ethnic origin.

The Greek wave of immigration was followed shortly after by a stream of Portuguese migration, mostly from poor rural regions in the Azores. Other Canadian cities, most notably Toronto, received a similar influx, which lasted until the mid-1970s. In 1996, 39 300 Montrealers reported their ethnic origin as Portuguese. The labour market profile of the Portuguese was similar to the Greeks although with the men being more likely to work as construction labourers. They settled mainly in the St Louis district around the middle section of The Main and, to a lesser extent, in Mile End, opening retail food establishments, fish-markets in particular, that drew Montrealers from all over town. As noted in Chapter 6, the Portuguese, along with the Greeks, invested their limited capital and a great deal of their labour in restoring dilapidated duplexes and triplexes into the colourful and verdant properties that now characterize these neighbourhoods (Lavigne, 1987). Unlike the Italians and the Greeks, there has been much less suburbanization of the Portuguese away from the initial settlement area, in part because this group has remained relatively low-income, although this is beginning to change. The Portuguese tendency of creating an ethnic housing sub-market has, moreover, affected the suburbanization patterns of this group, with Portuguese real-estate agents helping to channel purchasers to particular neighbourhoods in Laval or on the South Shore (Lavigne and Teixeira, 1990). In terms of language, Portuguese immigrants, who were mostly Catholics, gravitated to French and English in about equal numbers (Jedwab, 1996: 71).

All in all, this European immigration had a tremendous impact on the landscape of the city – from the tradition of front- as well as backyard intensive gardening of both food crops and flowers, to the upgrading of neglected residential architecture, some of it of heritage quality, to the proliferation of 'ethnic' grocery stores and restaurants which would become an integral part of the 'conviviality' that has become so central to the reputation of Montréal. The ethnic 'difference' as well as the humanization of the streetscape helps people of diverse origins feel at home in their neighbourhoods. Nevertheless, close social ties between those from different ethnocultural communities rarely develop in the multiethnic and socially mixed neighbourhoods in the inner city that are the legacy of the European immigration (Germain, 1999; Rose, 1995), while 'ethnic' and more homogeneous neighbourhoods seem to coexist in mutual indifference (Médam, 1989).

While many of these immigrants, skilled or not, were selected for the needs of the local economy, others arrived as 'dependent' relatives of those already here. Regardless, their labour market integration was rapid, frequently assisted by their inclusion in an existing ethnic enclave economy, a residential and workplace clustering which supported 'ethnic' commerce, offered conduits to employment, and, frequently, cheap housing. With the help of connections, successive immigration waves managed to penetrate the various sectors of the economy that were growing at the time they arrived, ranging from transportation and construction to the garment industry and domestic, personal and consumer services, creating particular, although not impermeable, ethnic niches (Olson, 1991). Although many of the European immigrants arrived in Montréal in a state of poverty just as dire as many of the francophones and Irish with whom they first rubbed shoulders in the lower inner city, immigrant trajectories tended to involve greater social mobility over time. The high value placed on education and the long hours worked by many families so as to build up small businesses had much to do with this (McNicoll, 1993). Overall, immigrants to Canada have higher rates of home-ownership than non-immigrants (Lapointe, 1996); in the Montréal case southern Europeans had by far the highest rates of home-ownership compared to other immigrants and non-immigrants, according to 1986 data (Mongeau and Séguin, 1993). Immigrants living in Montréal in 1976 had a higher socio-economic status than the native-born in terms of labour force participation, educational level, occupation and income (Gagné, 1989). As elsewhere in North America, the economic success of an immigration that was largely European was incontestable.

THE 'NEW IMMIGRATION', 1970S–PRESENT

The changing policy context and its implications for immigration and the multicultural experience

The late 1970s and the 1980s saw three fundamental changes to the broader context in which immigration to Montréal took place. These would have major implications for the immigrant settlement process and, as we shall see, would raise a new set of questions about the linguistic character and cultural identity of the city.

First, the provincial government, both under the Parti Québécois and the Liberals, set out to increase the rate of immigration to Québec. Like its federal counterpart (Simmons, 1990), the provincial government sees immigration both as an aid to economic growth and as a means of rejuvenating an ageing population structure. Canada has perhaps the world's most 'liberal' immigration policy, if the ratio of annual immigrant flows to total population is taken as an indicator: on this measure, Canada as a whole in the late 1990s scores 0.7 per cent, compared to 0.4 for Australia and slightly lower for the United States.

However, Québec has never attracted a share of Canadian immigrants commensurate with its population; in 1996 only about 9 per cent of Quebecers were born outside Canada, about half the Canadian average. Moreover, due to out-migration of both native-born Quebecers and immigrants, the province has long had a migratory deficit. For much of the twentieth century, Montréal's port and central railway station were but staging posts on a migratory journey that would lead many international migrants to other Canadian provinces or to the United States; between 1946 and 1971, for example, the rate of loss was about 40 per cent. Under agreements concluded with the federal government in 1978 and 1991, the Québec government gained control over the selection of independent immigrants – that is, those selected according to their educational level, professional qualifications, age, language abilities and suitability *vis-à-vis* labour market needs, as well as entrepreneurs willing to invest in Canada – and partial control over the selection of refugees. Between 1982 and 1996 Québec admitted about 440 000 immigrants, the peak years being the early 1990s (when a large backlog of refugee claims was finally processed). Numerically speaking, the goal of attracting and retaining more immigrants has not been an unmitigated success. In 1991, the province's share of Canadian immigrants (22.4 per cent) did briefly come close to its share of the total population, but the absolute and relative numbers subsequently dropped off, so that in 1996, for example, only 13 per cent of new immigrants settled in Québec compared to 53 per cent who settled in Ontario and 23 per cent in British Columbia (Canada, Citizenship and Immigration, 1998), while the rate of out-migration of immigrants stood at around 23 per cent.

In Québec, the issue of demographic renewal has a particular resonance. This is not only because Québec's birth-rate (about 1.5 in the late 1990s, which is well below replacement level) is even lower than that of Canada as a whole and its age structure older than that of Canada as a whole (Ledent, 1993; Québec, MRCI, 1997; see Figure 4.4), but also because francophones (both within and outside Québec) now constitute less than a quarter of Canada's total population, whereas at the time of Confederation half the population was French-Canadian. Québec's share of the total Canadian population had also shrunk below a quarter by the mid-1990s and provincial government projections suggest that this relative decline will continue into the twenty-first century. These demographic and linguistic shifts have significant implications for the relative power of the two 'founding nations'. This situation has created a need for post-Quiet Revolution Québec to reconcile a growing dependence on immigration with the preservation and affirmation of its French-Canadian – now redefined as Québécois – identity (Anctil, 1996).

Consequently, in order for immigration to be a means of helping to ensure the long-term survival of a French-speaking society and 'public culture' in North America (Bonin, 1976; Québec, 1990), measures had to be taken to curtail the anglicization of immigrants and, instead, encourage their integration into francophone Québec culture. The primary means of 'francisizing' these new Quebecers was to be through the language of instruction of their children. Since the adoption of 'Bill 101' in 1977 (which we referred to in Chapter 5 with regard to the imposition of French as the language of work), all children living in Québec have had to attend French primary and secondary schools, with the exception of children whose parents were educated in English in the province or elsewhere in Canada and the siblings of children already attending English schools. This was the second major shift in the policy environment of immigrant settlement to Montréal, and it represented a sea-change from the previous situation in which, as we have seen, most immigrant children attended English-language schools (Levine, 1990). Its effect was dramatic: by 1991, some 70 per cent of Montréal Island children whose mother tongue was neither English or French were attending French schools, up from only 11 per cent 20 years earlier (Conseil scolaire de l'île de Montréal, 1991).

These important policy shifts in Québec took place precisely at a time when a third, broader-scale change was occurring. This concerned the nature of migration streams on a world-wide scale, and it has had major implications for the types of immigrants available to Canada including Québec. During the 1950s for example, over 80 per cent of immigrants arriving in Canada each year came from European countries; this figure had dropped to 17 per cent by 1994 (Canada, Citizenship and Immigration, 1996). Economic upheavals and wars generated increased flows of non-European immigrants, including both economic migrants and Geneva Convention refugees (Nash, 1989; Simmons, 1990). Meanwhile, interest in emigration to Canada from traditional European source countries diminished due to their increased prosperity and (in the case of certain countries) the re-establishment of democratic regimes. Reforms to federal immigration law in 1962, 1967 and 1976 eliminated racist distinctions in eligibility, abolished privileges given to European immigrants as regards sponsoring relatives and, by opening immigration offices in many parts of the world, made it easier to apply to immigrate (Hawkins, 1989; see Hiebert, 1994 and Nash, 1994 for overviews of federal policy). The effect of these changes on the composition of the Montréal region's immigrant population can be clearly seen in Figure 7.3, which, based on the total immigrant population in 1996, shows the regional origins of the cohorts that arrived in the 1950s or earlier, in the 1960s, 1970s, 1980s and in the first half of the 1990s. A similar trend was observable in other countries with relatively liberal immigration policies (compared to Europe), such as Australia and, to a lesser extent, the USA. This shift in immigrant origins has been deemed so significant by policy makers, organizations involved in assisting the immigrant settlement process and by researchers that it has generated new expressions, 'new wave' immigrants and 'the new immigration' (see e.g. Simmons, 1990). Some see this term as a euphemism, a code-word for groups whose ethnic, 'racial' or cultural backgrounds are uncomfortably different from the dominant profile of the receiving society, but it has passed into such common use that we shall employ it here. The people who make up the new immigration are nevertheless highly diversified in terms of milieu of origin (urban, rural, etc.), educational levels and the socio-economic status they had in their countries of origin.

From the early 1980s to the mid-1990s, the relative importance of various countries of origin among immigrants admitted to Québec has altered

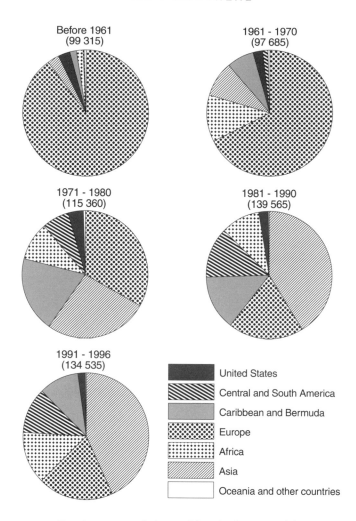

Before 1961
(99 315)

1961 - 1970
(97 685)

1971 - 1980
(115 360)

1981 - 1990
(139 565)

1991 - 1996
(134 535)

United States

Central and South America

Caribbean and Bermuda

Europe

Africa

Asia

Oceania and other countries

FIGURE 7.3 Immigrant population resident in the Montréal Census Metropolitan Area in 1996, by period of immigration, showing region of origin

somewhat from one quinquennial period to the next (Table 7.1), and the portrait differs considerably from that of Canada as a whole (where the United States and United Kingdom still figure among the top 10 source countries). This is in large measure because the government has used the control it gained over immigrant selection to develop a policy of favouring immigration from francophone countries (hence the continued importance of France) from those with a French colonial past (notably Vietnam, Haiti, Lebanon and North African countries) and from those thought to be easily assimilable into francophone society by virtue of their 'Latin' culture (e.g. Central and South Americans) or by their having a Romance language as

TABLE 7.1 Top 15 countries of birth of immigrant arrivals to Québec by five-year period, 1982 to 1996, showing country rank and number admitted

Country of Birth	1982–1986		1987–1991		1992–1996	
	Rank	Number	Rank	Number	Rank	Number
France	3	4697	3	7975	1	12 807
Hong Kong	13	1948	4	6704	2	11 215
Haiti	1	10 414	2	10 617	3	10 832
China	12	2016	6	6056	4	9346
Lebanon	4	3566	1	24 026	5	9195
Romania	–	–	–	–	6	6434
India	8	2524	14	4106	7	5823
Former USSR	–	–	–	–	8	5483
Sri Lanka	–	–	12	4706	9	5424
Former Yugoslavia	–	–	–	–	10	5349
Philippines	–	–	–	–	11	5004
Algeria	–	–	–	–	12	4484
Morocco	11	2201	8	5060	13	4013
Vietnam	2	6558	5	6518	14	3787
Taiwan	–	–	–	–	15	3751
El Salvador	5	3401	7	5355	–	–
Syria	–	–	9	4962	–	–
Portugal	14	1652	10	4859	–	–
Poland	6	3059	11	4699	–	–
Iran	10	2244	13	4621	–	–
Egypt	–	–	15	4039	–	–
United States	7	2908	–	–	–	–
Cambodia	9	2352	–	–	–	–
United Kingdom	15	1781	–	–	–	–
Total, 15 Principal Countries		51 321		104 303		102 947
Total, All Countries		86 689		180 986		176 498

Source: Data supplied by the ministère des Relations avec les citoyens et de l'Immigration du Québec, Direction de la planification stratégique.

mother tongue (e.g. Spanish, Romanian). In the first half of the 1990s, East Asian immigration to Québec also became important – although not nearly to the same extent as in British Columbia and Ontario – due to the impending return of Hong Kong to China, and to the increased priority given in recent Canadian and Québec immigration policies to 'investor' and 'entrepreneur' immigrants (Nash, 1994) and more generally to an increase in independent immigrants. From 1992 to 1996, independent immigrants represented 45 per cent of all immigrants admitted in Québec, refugees counted for 21 per cent, the rest being sponsored by family members already living in Canada under family reunification measures (Québec, MRCI, 1997).

Under the terms of a 1991 agreement, the Québec immigration ministry took control over the design and administration of immigrant and refugee

TABLE 7.2 Immigrants admitted to Québec, 1993–
1997: Language abilities at time of arrival

	Number	Per cent
French only	36 286	23.0
French and English	18 554	11.8
English only	34 114	22.3
Neither French nor English	67 671	42.9
Total	157 620	100

Source: Québec, Institut de la statistique du Québec (1999b).

settlement assistance and integration programmes from the federal government. In turn, the province turns many of the programmes over to other agencies (such as school boards) or 'subcontracts' them to local community organizations capable of servicing immigrants in their own languages. Most of the resources are directed to immigrants' needs during their first three years of settlement. At the time of writing similar agreements are being or have recently been negotiated with other Canadian provinces but in the Québec case one of the distinctive goals has been to direct much of these resources to the priority of francization of newcomers through French-language training programmes for immigrants and their children. As can be seen from Table 7.2, knowledge of the French language upon arrival is still barely more prevalent than knowledge of English and more than two out of five new immigrants know neither language. Present government policy is to increase the proportion of immigrants with knowledge of French prior to arrival.

The socio-economic situations of new immigrants are highly diversified. As we have mentioned, some come in as economic migrants, most with prearranged jobs, others are assisted through sponsorship agreements with family members already settled in Canada, still others are refugees arriving with few material resources. On average, new immigrants are better educated than the non-immigrant population (Gagné, 1995); for example, among 1996 arrivals destined for Montréal, almost 23 per cent had a bachelor's degree or higher (Canada, Citizenship and Immigration, 1998), compared to only 15.4 per cent of all CMA residents aged 15 or over. However, many well-qualified immigrants experience great difficulties in obtaining appropriate employment due to non-recognition of educational and training credentials obtained in their countries of origin and to higher entry barriers to certain professions (Pendakur, 1996; Pendakur and Pendakur, 1998). Immigrants trying to gain employment in the provincial civil service confront the reality of this being a quasi-exclusive domain of Québec-born francophones, a persistent legacy of the Quiet Revolution (Québec, Commission des droits de la personne, 1999), and the situation in the Montréal municipal sector is only fractionally better since employment cutbacks have compromised an equal access hiring programme (Ville de Montréal, 1996). Since 1980 the earnings of 'allophones'[2] declaring themselves to be bilingual (including both immigrants and Canadian-born) have been below those of unilingual francophones of equivalent education and work experience (Stelcner and Shapiro, 1997) – although this finding should be interpreted with some caution since non-francophones have been shown to over-estimate their level of bilingualism in census responses.

Several recent studies concur that the earnings gap between recent immigrants and longer-established immigrants is widening across Canada (Benson and Dupuis, 1998). Lower-skilled immigrants who arrived around the time of the economic recession of the early 1990s have faced considerable difficulty in entering the labour market, particularly given the retrenchment in traditional manufacturing to which we referred in Chapter 5, recent arrivals being especially reliant on low-skilled manufacturing jobs (Gagné, 1995). For example, Montréal's Haitian community is strongly bifurcated in economic terms between the families of professionals who arrived in the 1960s and 1970s and more recent arrivals of refugees with low levels of formal education, who number among the city's poorest residents (*Globe and Mail*, 1999). Moreover, whereas in the past as we have seen, many immigrant groups achieved a measure of economic stability after a few years by obtaining work through ethnic niches or 'enclaves' (Olson, 1991), many of today's immigrants, refugees in particular, do not have a cluster of members of their own ethnic community to which they can gravitate for social and material support during the early stages of the settlement process. Overall, as is the case for the Canadian labour force in general, the socio economic status of new immigrants has become more internally bipolarized in recent years (Helly, 1997).

Nevertheless, even if it seems that many recent immigrants may need more time to get a foothold on the socio-economic ladder than their predecessors who arrived at a time of economic boom, there are also grounds for optimism. The most recent longitudinal research available for Montréal, covering a fairly typical sample of immigrants who arrived in 1989, paints a relatively successful image of immigrants' economic establishment in the first three years – for example, almost one-fifth had become home-owners (Renaud et al., 1993). Furthermore, in recognition of the essential contribution of immigrant women to a family's settlement process and economic well-being, their language-training opportunities, previously very restricted in the case of those admitted to Canada as 'dependants' of a designated wage-earner, have been improved (Boyd, 1997; Lamotte, 1992). In addition, the settlement assistance services mentioned above are highly developed compared to many of North America's and the world's other cities with major concentrations of recent immigrants. Funding to such services has nevertheless been cut back significantly in recent years, particularly to those organizations targeting the needs of a single ethnic group, on the grounds that this practice reflects a 'multiculturalist' philosophy which the Québec government explicitly rejects.

In this context, it is important to underline that in Québec, as in Canada as a whole, the state selects its immigrants with a view to them becoming future citizens and that the selection process is normally completed before arrival. Once admitted as permanent residents immigrants have virtually the same entitlements and responsibilities as Canadian citizens, and they are usually eligible for citizenship after three years. This is very different from the situation in many European nations where immigrants are often not permanent residents, let alone citizens, and may only be eligible for selection as such after many years, if at all. It is for this reason that the state invests heavily in immigrant settlement support services and for this reason that socio-economic marginalization of immigrants, while certainly an issue for certain groups, has not become a structural problem in Québec or in Canada as a whole.

The new immigrant and linguistic geographies of Montréal

As we have mentioned, recent immigrant settlement, like the previous waves, has been disproportionately concentrated in the Montréal region, and especially on the Island of Montréal. This phenomenon of concentration is more pronounced than in the other major Canadian cities relative to their provinces. Government measures to promote the 'regionalization' of immigrant settlement have met with very little success, there being a tendency over time to gravitate to Montréal, where there is a greater concentration of settlement assistance organizations and socio-cultural institutions developed by the various immigrant communities (Séguin and Termote, 1993). This social division of space is yet another element in the contrast between the Montréal region and the rest of the province to which we have alluded at various points in this book and to which we shall return below with regard to the language question.

Within the Montréal area, the ethnic diversity of the new immigration has not simply added new ethnic neighbourhoods to the pre-existing mosaic. In fact, multiethnic neighbourhoods are now mushrooming in many parts of the Montréal region, some of them being new reception areas, others the product of a major reconfiguration of the local ethnocultural profile (Germain et al., 1995; Renaud et al., 1997). We now take a look at the new spatial distribution of immigration in the Montréal region and go on to discuss its socio-political implications in the context of the omnipresent language question.

The diversity of districts where new immigrants settle is testimony to the diversity of socio-economic situations they find themselves in on arrival. Figure 7.4 shows the census tracts where at least 25 per cent of the 1996

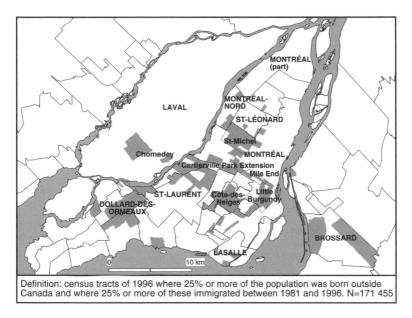

Definition: census tracts of 1996 where 25% or more of the population was born outside Canada and where 25% or more of these immigrated between 1981 and 1996. N=171 455

FIGURE 7.4 Zones of concentration of recent immigrants, Montréal Census Metropolitan Area, 1996

population was born outside Canada and at least 25 per cent of this sub-group arrived between the 1981 and 1996 censuses, amounting to a total of 171 455 persons. The traditional 'immigrant corridor' along St Lawrence Boulevard (where much of the housing is now gentrified) has largely been replaced by newer 'reception areas' where rents are lower, most of which are multiethnic neighbourhoods in the inner suburban ring. These include, most importantly, the post-war low-rise apartment sector in the northern part of Côte-des-Neiges, adjacent to the sector to which Jewish Montrealers migrated in the 1950s – whose major commercial strip on Victoria Avenue has been dubbed the 'New Main' by some commentators (Figure 7.5). Several census tracts in this district are among the very few in Montréal where over 25 per cent of the entire 1996 population had arrived in Canada in the preceding five years. Also of great importance for recent immigrant settlement are the formerly anglophone and more recently Greek neigh-bourhood of Park Extension as well as the St-Michel and Cartierville districts in the north-east and north-west of the City of Montréal, all of which are low-income areas. In some cases, for example Côte-des-Neiges and the Norgate sector of Ville-St-Laurent, their role as immigrant reception areas was fostered by arrangements between the government, resettlement agen-cies for refugees and private landlords (Blanc, 1986; Charbonneau, 1995). The West Island suburb of Dollard-des-Ormeaux, parts of the Chomedey district of Laval, and Brossard on the South Shore, also attract significant

FIGURE 7.5 Victoria Avenue in inner-suburban Côte-des-Neiges, once a Jewish neighbourhood, now the new 'Main Street' for recent immigrants. (Annick Germain)

concentrations of new immigrants; these are middle-class suburbs much like any others in Canada, with a mix of single-family housing, rental apartments and a commercial landscape characterized by shopping malls.

Moving now to the overall picture of where Montrealers not born in Canada are living, regardless of period of immigration, Figure 7.6 indicates the relative concentrations of the Montréal region's 586 465 immigrants in different parts of the CMA, using the location quotient, a measure expressing the percentage of immigrants in a census tract relative to the percentage (which is 17.8 per cent) in the metropolitan area as a whole. The previously mentioned immigrant reception areas seen in Figure 7.4 remain predominant on this map, but in addition to the suburbs popular with low-income new immigrants we now also see the effects of the suburbanization of long-established upwardly mobile immigrants from the earlier waves of European immigration, to communities such as St-Léonard, Montréal-Nord and Rivière-des-Prairies in the north-east (especially favoured by Italians) as well as to west end and southwestern districts such as Lasalle. The significant presence of immigrants in the traditionally anglophone West Island reflects the historical patterns of attraction discussed earlier, but we also see

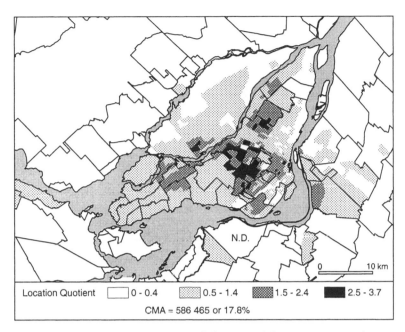

FIGURE 7.6 Immigrant population of the Montréal Census Metropolitan Area, relative concentrations by census tract, 1996

a growing immigrant presence in the traditionally francophone districts in east and north-east Montréal. Detailed mapping by birthplace using 1996 census data (not presented here) shows that Haitian, and to a lesser extent Vietnamese and Latin American immigrants are behind this latter trend; this spatial pattern is consistent with the Québec government's belief that these groups would gravitate toward francophone Montréal, and qualitative research with Haitian immigrant women reveals a strong preference to live among francophones (Ray, 1999). Nevertheless, this map shows quite strikingly that immigrants remain virtually absent from the *outlying* parts of the metropolitan area. Suburbanization of immigrants, though a growing trend, is still of markedly limited spatial extent, with a tendency towards clustering in established multiethnic suburbs rather than dispersing into newer sectors characterized by suburban sprawl and mainly inhabited by francophones (Paillé, 1996).

The combination of immigrant concentration on the Island and in a few off-Island suburbs with the marked suburbanization of francophones to which we have referred earlier has wrought profound changes to the linguistic geography of the Montréal region, especially to that of the Island of Montréal (Termote, 1992), and raised new questions about the mechanisms through which immigrants are integrated in regard to language and culture. Census data for the mother tongue of residents of the Montréal Urban

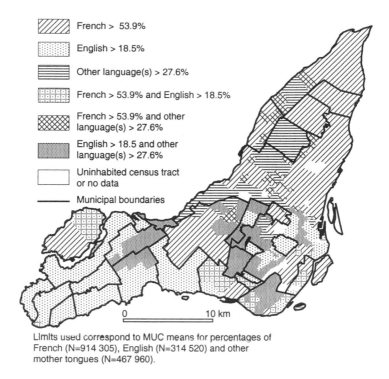

French > 53.9%

English > 18.5%

Other language(s) > 27.6%

French > 53.9% and English > 18.5%

French > 53.9% and other language(s) > 27.6%

English > 18.5 and other language(s) > 27.6%

Uninhabited census tract or no data

Municipal boundaries

0   10 km

Limits used correspond to MUC means for percentages of French (N=914 305), English (N=314 520) and other mother tongues (N=467 960).

FIGURE 7.7 Percentages of resident population with French, English or other mother tongues, Island of Montréal, by census tract, 1996

Community for 1996 show the overall predominance of French (53.9 per cent or 914 305 persons). This represents a slight drop from 1971 (61 per cent), as is the case with English mother tongue (down from 24 per cent to 18.5 per cent or 314 520 persons), while the representation of languages other than English and French increased markedly from 15 per cent to 27 per cent (467 960 persons). Figure 7.7 indicates the census tracts in the MUC where one and/or another mother tongue was more prevalent than the average for the MUC in 1996. Were we to compare this map with a similar map for 1971 (not shown for reasons of space) we would not, despite the increase in immigration, see any increase in the number of tracts where *only* allophones were present in proportions above the MUC average. What we would see, consistent with the changing spatial patterns of immigrant settlement noted earlier, is that the main zones where 'other' mother tongues predominate have shifted to the north-west and north-east of the traditional 'immigrant corridor' while the latter has become more franco-phone and, to a lesser extent, more anglophone, in part due to gentri-fication. It can be seen from Figure 7.7 that there are now a significant number of zones in the traditionally francophone eastern part of the island where not only francophones but also allophones are now present in above average numbers; this indicates that many of Montréal's allophones are now living in neighbourhoods where French is the mother tongue of the majority. There are also a number of zones, in the West Island and west end of the city, with above average presence of both allophones and anglophones. For in spite of their children being required to attend French schools, many recent middle-class immigrants are still drawn to districts with a strong anglophone presence. Their choices may in part be motivated by the wish for their children to become fluent in English – seen as essential to socio-economic mobility and the possibility of geographic mobility beyond the bounds of Québec – through everyday contacts in the neighbourhood (Renaud et al., 1993; Rose and Ray, 1997; Ray and Chmielewska, 1997).

The strategic importance of Montréal to the language question in Québec, and the overall linguistic situation in the Montréal region in the 1990s are perhaps best grasped by looking at the language people generally speak at home (regardless of mother tongue), since over time many allophone immigrants do adopt French or English as their home language, as do their children to a much greater extent. Historically, such 'language transfers' have been less prevalent among allophones in Montréal than in other major Canadian cities; however, recent research indicates that this situation has been reversed as regards recent allophone immigrants (Fournier, 1994). As can be seen from Table 7.3, the language question in Québec is essentially a Montréal issue, since it is in Montréal that most of Québec's anglophones live (59.3 per cent of them live in the MUC and 78.2 per cent in the CMA), it is in Montréal that bilingualism in the workplace is most needed as a job skill (especially, as we saw in Chapter 5, in the most dynamic sectors of the 'new' economy) and it is in Montréal that most of the immigrants settle.

The Québec government, in its immigration and integration policies, aims to foster the use of French among non-native French speakers as the language of 'public life' and commerce, not only in the school, workplace and government as legislated in Bill 101, but also as the everyday means of communication with neighbours, shopkeepers, and so on (Gagné, 1995; Québec, 1996a; Québec, 1996b). Overall, research indicates that its 'francization' policies have been quite successful in that immigrants who arrived since the early 1980s are much more likely than their predecessors to use French in various walks of life than their predecessors (Monnier, 1993; Québec, Conseil de la langue française, 1993; Veltman and Paré, 1993; Renaud et al., 1993; Québec, 1996a); among immigrants who arrived in 1981 or later, almost 70 per cent of those who dropped their mother tongue as the home language adopted French rather than English. More recent immigrants are also more likely to live in neighbourhoods where French is the main home language (Gagné, 1995). Nevertheless, adoption of French

TABLE 7.3 Language spoken at home within the province of Québec, and in Canada, 1996

	Total (single responses only)	Distribution in %		
		French	English	Non-official languages
City of Montréal	948 685	63.9%	16.1%	20.0%
Montréal Urban Community suburban municipalities	713 545	47.1%	37.6%	15.3%
Montréal Urban Community	1 662 230	56.7%	25.3%	18.0%
CMA fringe	1 504 755	86.9%	8.9%	4.1%
Montréal CMA	3 166 985	71.0%	17.5%	11.4%
Rest of Québec province	3 725 915	94.5%	4.2%	1.3%
Québec province	6 892 900	83.7%	10.3%	6.0%
Canada	27 947 670	22.8%	68.1%	9.1%

Source: Statistics Canada, Census of Population, 1996, Data Liberation Initiative files. Note: excluded from this table are those declaring more than one home language, who account for 5.1% of the CMA total but as many as 10% in the MUC suburbs.

as the *lingua franca* remains far from automatic, notably in retail businesses in multiethnic neighbourhoods (Monnier, 1996). Moreover, the neighbourhood of residence still exerts an influence over the language that allophones adopt at home once they drop their mother tongue; for example, when those of Spanish mother tongue adopt one of Canada's official languages at home, it is likely to be English in 90 per cent of cases if they live in the West Island suburb of Kirkland but likely to be French in 90 per cent of cases if they live in Montréal-Nord in the north-east of the Island (*Montreal Gazette*, 29 May 1999a).

The linguistic contrasts between most of the Island of Montréal and the suburban fringe show up strikingly when one maps the use of French as home language (Figure 7.8). This pattern is the result of three main trends: the settlement of most new immigrants on the Island of Montréal and the much greater tendency of the francophone population to move to the suburban fringe, compared to their anglophone counterparts. Bearing in mind the main settlement areas of new immigrants we discussed earlier, it can be inferred from Figures 7.4 and 7.8 that most of the recent immigrant population lives in neighbourhoods where those speaking French as home language are in the minority. For some observers, particularly those espousing strong versions of Québec nationalism, the continued attraction that the more anglophone parts of Montréal have for significant numbers of immigrants is disquieting, especially when coupled with the fact that more than half of all allophone immigrants, including those who arrived after 1976, reported knowing English as well as French (according to their 1991 census declaration; Gagné, 1995). What for the latter is seen a valuable asset is thus for the former a potential cultural threat. Equally controversial, in the context

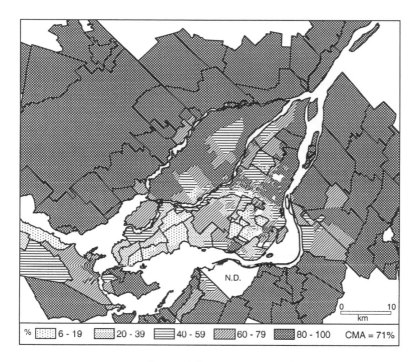

FIGURE 7.8 Percentage of Montréal Census Metropolitan Area population declaring French as their home language, 1996

of the debate about how new immigrants become 'francisized' and how cultural contacts are developed between so-called 'old-stock' Québécois and the new arrivals, are the implications of the growing numbers of immigrants living in 'allophone' neighbourhoods (Conseil scolaire de l'île de Montréal, 1991); in fact, by the mid-1990s, less than half the children in French schools on Montréal Island were mother tongue francophones (McAndrew and Ledoux, 1995). However, since 'allophones' do not constitute a monolithic language bloc, French may well in fact be the most prevalent language in the schoolyard or on the street in multiethnic areas (Jedwab, 1996). Moreover, immigrant parents seemingly feel more at ease in getting involved with their children's schooling in the case of multiethnic schools where no group (francophone, anglophone or other ethnocultural community) is numerically dominant (McAndrew, 1988). Those speaking French at home now number only 45 per cent of residents of on-Island suburbs (a drop of four percentage points since 1991), although they remain a majority in the City of Montréal (Table 7.3). Yet whether or not this can be construed as a threat to the French language in Québec, as some analysts argue, is a matter of interpretation: is the Island or the whole metropolitan region the relevant social and cultural unit; and can French be considered as being in the minority when it is the language used by far and away the largest number of Island residents?

If we take a broader geo-territorial perspective, both Table 7.3 and Figure 7.8 highlight a fundamental socio-spatial division between 'cosmopolitan' versus 'homogeneous' parts of the province, a division that nurtures a host of misunderstandings and reflects some profound differences of outlook. In the 1990s, these have been increasingly mirrored in the voting behaviour of the Montréal Island electorate (opposed to Québec independence) *vis-à-vis* most other regions of Québec including Montréal's outer suburban fringe (in favour of Québec sovereignty). Linguistic geography is in this context a delicate issue and residents of 'cosmopolitan' parts of Montréal find themselves the objects of highly charged debates which may have little resonance in their daily lives.

Living with diversity: social integration issues in a multiethnic city

As we can see then, if the question of the social integration of new immigrants to Montréal has come to occupy a very high profile in policy and academic debate in Québec since the late 1980s, as well as in the media, this is as much because of its ties to the linguistic issue as because of the magnitude of the immigration phenomenon. At least by Canadian standards: the Montréal region has, after all, proportionately far fewer immigrants (18 per cent of the 1996 population) than Toronto (42 per cent) or Vancouver (35 per cent). Moreover, compared to the situation in, say, France, by no stretch of the imagination can even the city's lowest-income and highest immigrant-density neighbourhoods be deemed places of ghettoization or social exclusion, with the partial exception of a few public housing projects which are very small scale by international standards. As mentioned in Chapter 6, maintaining an appropriate balance of proximity and social distance between groups with different daily living practices, as well as delivering appropriate support services to immigrants in public housing, is a recognized issue which government and non-profit agencies are working on. Today's immigrant reception areas, like those of the past, are typically places from which new immigrants move on after a few years, to be replaced by others. Moreover, the excellent transit system makes it quite easy for immigrants in most parts of Montréal Island to travel considerable distances to work or seek out social support from other members or institutions of their ethnic community located in other parts of town (Rose and Ray, 1997).

Nevertheless, like most other cities, Montréal has its share of racist and discriminatory practices in the housing market, of which low-income immigrants from visible minorities bear the brunt, especially if they are single mothers, and this may well have contributed to the concentration of immigrants in poor quality apartment districts considered undesirable by those with greater options in the housing market (Bernèche, 1990; Garon, 1988; McAndrew and Potvin, 1996). As we saw in Chapter 6, the City of Montréal made major efforts in the early 1990s to improve housing conditions in some of these neighbourhoods although much remains to be done, and cutbacks to funding for rental renovation and housing cooperatives have restricted low-income immigrants' housing options. There is no evidence, however, that the experience of racism, either in the labour market or in housing, is in any way associated with living in a highly 'ethnic' neighbourhood (Gagné, 1995; Joly, 1996).

We have referred at several junctures to the growing phenomenon of multiethnic neighbourhoods. These today are found in diverse socio-economic milieux, including both low-income reception areas for new immigrants and suburbs now housing a diversity of longer-established and new immigrants and Canadian-born members of ethnic groups not identified with either of the 'founding nations', as well as those traditionally forming part of the francophone or anglophone communities. Leaving aside the strategic role of these milieux for the 'national question', how do social relations play out in daily life in these kinds of neighbourhoods? One recent study examined the ways public space is used in variety of multiethnic neighbourhoods (Germain, 1999; Germain et al., 1995). Public space is potentially an important place for intercultural contacts, all the more so in Montréal in view of the City's attempt to revive the concept of the 'city of neighbourhoods' anchored on local commercial streets (discussed in Chapter 6), in view of the renaissance of recreational public space in the city centre (the Old Port, Old Montréal, the Mountain . . .) (discussed in Chapter 3) and the increasing importance of the summer 'festival culture' (mentioned in Chapter 5). The research on multiethnic neighbourhoods found that on the whole social relations between members of different ethnocultural groups are characterized by a peaceful but fairly distant coexistence. Difference was accepted as a fact of life, the level of comfort with difference increasing with the frequency of casual daily contacts, such as 'nodding relationships' with neighbours or conversations with local shopkeepers. Feeling that no single group formed a majority in the neighbourhood, as in the case of the study on schools mentioned earlier (McAndrew, 1988), made residents belonging to one or another ethnocultural minority feel more comfortable. In fact, in one area with a tradition of racial and linguistic tension, the arrival of immigrants from diverse continents seemed to facilitate inter-group relations.

At the same time, however, a pronounced ethnic segmentation (reinforced by gender and generational divisions) was evident in social interactions. For example, public parks, while popular with members of virtually all ethno-cultural groups, were rarely places where new contacts were made outside of one's own group, except in the case of young children when not under the inhibiting influence of their parents. On the whole, in settings such as parks,

FIGURE 7.9 A neighbourhood park in a north-end multiethnic district: 'peaceful but distant' coexistence. (Damaris Rose)

or suburban shopping centres, cultural codes had evolved to govern the negotiation of civilized ways to share space while maintaining a certain distance (Figure 7.9). Even in high-density residential environments where disinvestment had reduced the individual and collective resources available to plan and create conditions for living side-by-side harmoniously, community groups helped ensure that social peace was maintained in the micro-spaces of public life. If the social mix of these multiethnic neighbourhoods rarely translated into more than superficial social interactions, this should not be interpreted as a symptom of a social malaise but more as a way of protecting one's privacy and a sense of identity, which, as sociologists such as Simmel argued long ago, are preconditions for the eventual emergence of a genuine openness toward the 'other' in a dense urban setting (Germain, 1999).

All in all, the historical Montréal model of the mosaic was still very much in evidence in the case study neighbourhoods, and in some of them it could, in a sense, be said to have a unifying effect, through the construction of a 'shared image' of the neighbourhood. In one of the case study neighbourhoods, the gentrifying Mile End sector (discussed in Chapter 6), the coexistence of gentrifiers and an ethnically and socio-economically diverse body of older-established residents has created a shared discourse on, and pride in, the neighbourhood's 'cosmopolitanism'. The authenticity or otherwise of this cosmopolitanism is in a sense irrelevant, for its significance lies in the maintenance of a shared image which has in fact enabled diverse local groups to work together for improved community facilities. In contrast, in one of our other case study areas, Little Burgundy, opposing and divergent images of the neighbourhood, and contrasting visions of whether it should be claimed by one 'foundational group' or belong to a mosaic of communities (see Remy, 1990), have caused significant tensions that have at times interfered with the working relationship between community organizations.

Two decades after the first cohort of children of Bill 101 started primary school, riders of the most multiethnic bus and metro lines running north-west and north from downtown will commonly hear teenagers conversing with each other in two or three languages. One will speak French, the other English; or, they will pepper a sentence in one language with words or phrases from one or two other languages, selecting (according to studies done by sociolinguists on this phenomenon) the language they feel most at ease in for the expression of a particular thought or image. Although perhaps distressing to some, to others such linguistic patterns – which are reinforced by a surge in marriages across linguistic lines revealed by the 1996 census – could be an authentic sign of the emergence of a hybrid cosmopolitan identity. Bill 101 seems to have succeeded, at least in part, in assimilating the children of recent immigrants to the French language, but rather than assimilating immigrant cultures into the pre-existing dominant franco-Québec culture, the ultimate effect of the language laws and the 'new immigration' has been to initiate irrevocable transformations in that culture, at least in the social space of Montréal.

THE SOCIAL SPACES – AND PLACES – OF ANGLOPHONE MONTRÉAL

This chapter would not be complete without a brief discussion of how Montréal's English-speaking population is positioned today within the social and geographic space of the city. The Montréal CMA's anglophone population declined by 17 per cent or 13 per cent from 1971 to 1991, depending on whether the mother tongue or home language census variable is used. Enrolment in English schools on the Island of Montréal fell by 64 per cent from 1970 to 1990, while that in French schools declined by 45 per cent (Chambers Task Force on English Education, 1992, cited in Jedwab, 1996: 86). Whereas in the latter case the decline was largely due to the increasing tendency of young families to leave the Island, in the case of the English schools the major factors were migration to other provinces and the requirement that immigrant children attend French schools. Never-theless, in 1996, the Montréal region's anglophone community was still larger in population than most of Canada's census metropolitan areas, a fact which seems to have been increasingly forgotten by the rest of Canada! The actual size of Montréal's anglophone community, like that of other linguistic groups, is a matter of some debate, depending on which of several possible census indicators are used. Those of English mother tongue (single responses only) numbered 426 600 in 1996, but according to the home language indicator (leaving out multiple responses), there were 555 755 anglophones in the Montréal region, whereas their number leaps to 660 185 if we count all those whose first official language spoken was English (because the latter indicator picks up allophones whose second language is English).

It is often the case that when a minority group suffers population losses, we see an increase in the relative spatial concentration of those who remain, as they strive to ensure continued access to their community's specialized services and institutions, many of which are delivered by municipalities (Gilbert and Marshall, 1995). This is what happened in the Montréal case in the 1970s and 1980s, at least in the more suburban areas. Not surprisingly, the anglophone population declined greatly in the north-east part of the Island while remaining quite stable in the West Island where anglophones are still in the majority (in terms of home language), albeit a shrinking one, in most of its municipalities. As shown in Table 7.3, the percentage of English-speakers is much higher in the MUC suburbs than in the City of Montréal; a partial exception is the traditionally anglophone district of Notre-Dame-de-Grâce in the city's west end which, although now also very popular with francophones, remains a major pole of attraction for English-speaking families with children. Nevertheless, as can be seen in the map of mother tongue distribution (Figure 7.7), the old spatial boundaries are becoming more permeable in the western part of the island; in many of the West Island municipalities francophones now form a large minority while the upper-middle class historically anglophone enclave of Town of Mount Royal now has a small majority of francophones.

Elsewhere, however, trends in the 1990s are turning out to be somewhat different. The number of English-speakers has started to increase again in several areas that had experienced a decline, and most especially in what at first sight seems an unlikely part of the Island of Montréal – suburbs in the north-east end of the island such as St-Léonard and Rivière-des-Prairies, as well as in parts of Laval. Here we are seeing the formation of 'new anglo' communities, comprising the children of old-established European immigrants (Italians in particular) who are eschewing the West End and West Island neighbourhoods traditionally associated with English-speakers of British Isles or Jewish stock (*Montreal Gazette*, 29 May, 1 June and 6 June, 1999).

Substantial numbers of English-speakers also live in the downtown area and adjacent neighbourhoods. Anglophone involvement in gentrification is quite significant – perhaps not surprising given the extremely high education levels of Montréal's present-day anglophone community. This phenomenon is also contributing to the permeability of the linguistic divide: while some anglophone gentrifiers have a predilection for the Mile End and St Louis districts (Montréal's traditional immigrant corridor, where some of their parents grew up), others have opted for the Plateau Mont-Royal or the Gay Village, leading to a recent increase in the absolute numbers and percentages of English-speakers in parts of the traditional 'heartland', east of Boulevard St-Laurent.

As regards language abilities, it is interesting to note that bilingualism was historically the rule among the Anglo-Scottish mercantile elite of early eighteenth century Montréal, who needed to function in French in their dealings with the French members of the fur-trading community and other merchants in order to further their business interests (MacKay, 1987: 17). This changed with industrialization, mass immigration from the British Isles and rural–urban migration of poor francophones. Most industrialists were English-speaking and did not have to communicate directly with their French-Canadian workers. As we have seen, anglophone and francophone residential spaces became more segmented over time, beginning in this period. Moreover, the anglophone elite took care of its poor through English-language institutions which played a major role in community building (Copp, 1974; Sweeny, 1982) whereas francophones were mainly serviced by the church and associated organizations. These factors contributed to a high degree of unilingualism among anglophones which endured until the 1970s.

This situation changed dramatically beginning in the 1960s with the Quiet Revolution, and especially in the wake of Bill 101, the language legislation, adopted in 1977. Educated unilingual anglophones in the business field had always had access to jobs oriented towards export markets beyond Québec, but these types of jobs shrank in the 1970s as a consequence of the gravitational shift to Toronto discussed in Chapter 5. Net migration of people of English mother tongue from Québec to other Canadian provinces increased in the 1960s with the onset of the Quiet Revolution (Kaplan, 1994b) and amounted to around 222 000 between 1971 and 1991, almost half of this occurring between 1976 and 1991 (Harrison, 1996; cited in Jebwab, 1996), many of these being individuals who did not want to or could not adapt to a more French environment or who were following their employers to southern Ontario (Levine, 1990; Lo and Teixeira, 1998). 'Old-stock', that is British Isles origin, anglophones were much more likely to leave for other provinces than those of other ethnic backgrounds (southern European, for instance). Out-migrants were also mainly young, much more likely to be unilingual and not as well-educated compared to non-migrants (Locher, 1988; *Montreal Gazette,* 30 May 1999).

Among the anglophones who stayed, and those who settled in Montréal from elsewhere (mainly professionals drawn to the burgeoning high-technology sectors), rates of bilingualism soared, from 37 per cent in 1971 to 60 per cent in 1991 (according to the self-reported census variable; Québec, Conseil de la langue française, 1992). French immersion programmes now attract about half of the children in anglophone families; and they are now, moreover, taught standard Canadian French – until the 1970s, they were taught 'international' i.e. Parisian French, which sounds and 'feels' very different – and this makes them more functional in Québec society than their predecessors. The most recent census data (1996) show that 83 per cent of Quebecers of English mother tongue and aged between 15 and 24 are now bilingual, compared to 56.5 per cent of their francophone counterparts (Jedwab, as yet unpublished census tabulations). However, the majority of adults whose mother tongue is English still mainly use English at work.

In this context, perhaps the most telling expression of the 'power shift' wrought by the Quiet Revolution and the language legislation (and discussed earlier in this book) can be seen in the relative incomes of anglophones and francophones. Census data show that whereas in 1970 the median individual incomes of those of English home language were 27.7 per cent higher than those of their francophone counterparts, in 1995 francophones have a slight (1.2 per cent) advantage (*Montreal Gazette*, 5 June 1999). Even unilingual francophones have slightly higher average salaries than bilingual anglophones, controlling for other pertinent factors such as education. Granted that anglophones may over-report their levels of bilingualism, this is still a stunning reversal of the situation that prevailed in the 1960s. Bilingualism nonetheless carries a premium for both francophones and anglophones while unlingualism puts anglophones at a major disadvantage, especially the youth (Stelcner and Shapiro, 1997) of whom many of the unilingual ones are, what is more, members of 'racialized' visible minorities (Mathews, 1996).

Yet in spite of their greatly increased rates of bilingualism, anglophone teenagers – mostly attending English schools which those of French mother tongue are not allowed to attend, under Bill 101 – have few social contacts with their francophone counterparts during their school and junior college years, and their leisure activities take place mainly in English (Locher, 1994). They feel very unsure of their future prospects in the province, more so than their francophone counterparts, and many still feel that their chances of economic mobility are better elsewhere. They are also uncertain as to whether francophone society sees them as belonging in Québec, although there are no available data to indicate whether or not such feelings are grounded. Within segments of anglophone Montréal, notably in the Jewish community, organizations have been set up to counter this pessimism and assist young people in finding satisfying employment in Montréal after they finish their education.

Nevertheless, anglophone Montrealers who have opted to remain in their home city as adults have adopted a much more positive outlook. There has been a major increase in intermarriage between English- and French-speakers, such that among Québec's English-speakers who are married almost half now have francophone spouses (*Montreal Gazette*, 31 May 1999). Philosopher Charles Taylor, reflecting on anglophone–francophone relations in the mid-twentieth century, comments that 'when I was a kid, people lived in completely watertight compartments' but that this is much less true today (*Montreal Gazette*, 29 May 1999). While social-scientific studies are lacking, anecdotal evidence and the musings, at once humorous and serious, of writers and journalists point to a number of factors that make the anglo-Montrealers of the 1990s intensely loyal to their city, genuinely appreciative of its French character, and, if not always enjoying its paradoxes, at least willing to flow with them. Notably, the Toronto–Montréal rivalry lives on in the mindset of anglo-Montrealers. Toronto, probably now the world's most ethnically diverse city, is still perceived as a staid society controlled by an Upper Canadian elite. It is seen as having a dominant, anonymizing corporate culture in which the work ethic rules all. In contrast, the European, but above all French quality of Montréal, the city of villages and front balconies, is seen as generating greater diversity and as militating against conformism. Nevertheless, beneath this constructed discourse, both anglophones and francophones active in the Montréal cultural scene are sceptical about whether 'biculturalism' really exists in practice.

This helps explain why, against the reality of better career prospects, greater financial rewards, or the larger critical mass in the English-language artistic and cultural sector to be found in Toronto for example, many well-educated but precariously employed anglophones have nonetheless opted to take advantage of the high quality of life Montréal can offer relative to the cost of living. Moreover, since the mid-1990s there have been signs of a renaissance of the Montréal English-language cultural scene – notably a revival of theatre, an effervescence in the literary scene, and the expansion of the *Just for Laughs* comedy festival.

Both the visceral sense of distinctiveness that Montréal anglophones feel from Toronto and the rest of English-speaking Canada, and their feeling that they comprise a minority culture in Québec, despite sharing a majority language and certain important socio-cultural referents with most of the rest of North America, are sentiments that francophone Quebecers find extremely difficult to understand. Unlike most contemporary francophone Montrealers, most anglo-Montrealers have a dual sense of territorial belonging – both to Québec and to Canada; these different senses of territorial identity are fundamental to the never-ending paradox of Canada–Québec relations (Kaplan, 1994a; Lo and Teixeira, 1998; Taylor, 1994). When anglo-Montrealers visit Ontario they feel like Quebecers; when they return home they know they are also Canadians. Some feel they belong to Montréal first and foremost: when the government issued the bill proclaiming the 1995 sovereignty referendum, including a highly romanticized and patriotic

FIGURE 7.10   'Referendum finally over': Neighbouring relations rapidly return to normal in Montréal's inner city after the 1995 referendum on Québec sovereignty. Reproduced by kind permission of Aislin (Terry Mosher)

preamble appealing to the Québec people's sense of 'rootedness in the soil', a prominent local satirist headed his weekly column 'We're rooted not so much in the soil as on the balcony' (Freed, 1995)!

Fundamentally, most anglo-Montrealers cannot accept the singular cultural-territorial identity that is taken for granted by Québec's francophone intelligentsia nor the singular notion of citizenship that is espoused in strong versions of Québec nationalism and is a *sine qua non* of the Québec sovereignty project. However, this is a dilemma that can be avoided in most aspects of daily life even – or perhaps especially? – in the linguistically mixed inner city. The cartoon reproduced as Figure 7.10 was published by the *Montreal Gazette*'s celebrated cartoonist 'Aislin' a couple of days after the 1995 sovereignty referendum, whose extremely close 'No' result followed on a highly charged and divisive campaign. This sketch seems to convey perfectly how the civility that is so typical of life in the city's neighbourhoods tends to supersede, in the world of the everyday, the vested interests that seek to transform difference into polarization.

A CONCLUDING REFLECTION

How then does contemporary Montréal measure up as a 'cosmopolitan city', given that the meaning of this term goes far beyond the demographic? Bonnie Kahn's (1987) humanist, and perhaps utopian, reading of cosmopolitanism sees it as urban culture shared through tolerance, and requiring five conditions to be met: diversity of origins of inhabitants and the valuing of this diversity, genuine opportunities for socio-economic success, an active public life and accessible public spaces, and a sense of 'mission' or a collective 'federating vision'. Montréal appears to be close to meeting the first four conditions, but the fifth appears far more elusive; from this perspective, in the absence of a sense of *affinity* with the 'other' the peaceful coexistence of the Montréal mosaic should perhaps not be taken for granted. Australian planner Leonie Sandercock is less concerned than Kahn about the need for a 'federating vision'. For her, citizenship can be multiple, and her 'cosmopolis' is a 'carnival' where 'citizens wrest from space new possibilities, and immerse themselves in their cultures while respecting those of their neighbours, and collectively forging new hybrid cultures and spaces' (Sandercock, 1998: 218–219). She sees a role for the local and national states, as well as community organizations, in this process. In Québec, however, the notions of multiple citizenship and cultural hybridity seem by definition anathema to the 'national project', at least in its current version (Taylor, 1994). In this context, the distinction between 'urban' and 'national' citizenship seems pertinent (however 'national' is defined . . .), the *de facto* cultural pluralism in Montrealers' everyday lives being not necessarily incompatible with the quest for a common vision of what is meant by integration into civil society at a wider scale.

ENDNOTES

[1] The term 'ethnics', although probably stemming from the tendency of 'old-stock' francophone Québécois to label as *les ethnies* those groups not identified with either of Canada's two founding nations, has been very widely adopted by Montrealers not of French or British ethnic origins as a term of self-identification. It does not have any derogatory connotations.

[2] 'Allophone' is the official term used in Québec to describe a person whose mother tongue is a language other than French or English.

EPILOGUE

At the dawn of the twentieth century, Montréal's status as a major metropolis was an incontestable one and in many ways a defining mark of the city's identity and self-image. Although Canada's largest city it was not so much Canada's metropolis – since Canada was still a satellite possession of Great Britain until 1932 – as imperial Britain's metropolitan foothold in North America. Its Anglo-Protestant elites, though conspicuous in their display of wealth, were but junior partners to London's corporate interests. They were also conservative in outlook, as were the Catholic clergy and the French - Canadian political elites who held sway at the time, and the local civil society these groups forged was less individualist and more 'communitarian' than in major cities south of the American border. As compared to its near neighbour, New York – the primary city of an independent country – Montréal's strategic continental role as a mercantile, industrial and corporate command centre in the nineteenth and early twentieth centuries was thus a somewhat discreet, but nevertheless an important one, as we have shown in these pages.

By the time Montréal's popular image as an international city and Canadian showcase peaked in the 1960s with mega-projects such as the 1967 World's Fair, its strategic economic functions had long been eclipsed, first by New York as regards international trade, and later by Toronto as regards financial activities and corporate headquarters at the Canadian scale. As the twentieth century unfolded it retained an important position in the North American urban system, especially in regards to trade and communications; however, it had become but one metropolitan centre among many. Today, Montréal is certainly no longer Canada's metropolis, but it is far from clear that it has an assured position as the metropolis for a nationalist Québec either. Both scholars and political actors at various levels are divided as to whether the future of Montréal should be as an integrated city-region within a world system of city-regions networked into a 'space of flows' or whether the traditional 'metropolis-hinterland' model still has some resonance. As we have suggested here, the truth will doubtless lie somewhere in between. But as we have also indicated in this book, these are not just academic arguments or political bickering but in fact reflect very different visions of Montréal's identity and its future, differences that are highly interwoven with visions of Québec's future in relation to Canada. Is Montréal a French city in North America – an image that is one of the *leitmotifs* of the Québec independence movement – or a bilingual meeting place between the European *francophonie* and a mainly English-speaking North American continent?

Differing perspectives on the language question still impede the collaboration of local interests with the Québec state in pursuit of the objective of 'reinternationalizing' Montréal. All three of Montréal's mayors over the past two decades, as well as its major business organizations, have taken the position that Montréal, while mainly a French city, should vaunt its intrinsically bilingual character and bicultural identity as major economic and cultural assets so as to attract private and public investments from the rest of Canada and internationally. This issue has grown in importance as Montréal rebuilds its economy around internationally mobile 'knowledge workers'. Recognizing bilingualism is, however, anathema to strong versions of the Québec nationalist project, for which the long-term survival of the French language and francophone culture requires that no other languages be recognized as an official part of 'public culture'. This paradox has led to some absurd situations: for example, a 1996 brochure put out by the Québec government's International Affairs Ministry and destined for international investors described Montréal as a 'bilingual, cosmopolitan city where business, industry, culture and academia are thriving', but when this was reported in the local press, embarrassed ministers rushed to explain that just because Montréal has a lot of bilingual people, that didn't make it a bilingual city! Nevertheless, Montréal is, as satirical columnist Josh Freed puts it, 'the only place in Canada where bilingualism works in practice if it doesn't work in theory'.

Voters on the Island of Montréal consistently come out, in elections and referendums, strongly opposed to the sovereignist project for Québec, in contrast to most of the rest of the province. This situation constantly makes Montréal centre stage for Canada's unceasing constitutional debate. It also, in a sense, holds it hostage: notably, one of the main reasons why the region's metropolitan governance and poverty problems are both so hard to resolve is that the national question polarizes positions between recognizing the specificity of Montréal or simply treating it as one of Québec's many regions, with the latter position usually winning out. Similarly divergent positions are generated around the question of international immigration, an essentially Montréal phenomenon but one of strategic importance for Québec's demographic future. One position underlines the unique cosmopolitanism of Montréal and defends pluralistic politics for immigrant settlement and integration recognizing the specific problems immigrants may face over access to jobs and services; the other position puts the emphasis on the rapid promotion of a sense of 'Québec citizenship' by minimizing 'special' programmes for immigrants and encouraging their dispersal to the regions.

Ultimately, if Montréal is to transcend such squabbles and create a new sense of mission for itself as a metropolis it will probably have to embrace

Jean Rémy's (1998) insightful idea that individuals, social groups, or, for that matter, cities, can legitimately have plural identities constituted over territories that are only partially overlapping. It is still not clear how one might reconcile, on the one hand, the multiple and overlapping cultural and territorial identities claimed by many Montrealers – and which correspond to the intrinsic character of the modern/post-modern metropolis as the place where difference is encountered and incorporated into wider social identities (Christopherson, 1994: 424) – with, on the other hand, the singular cultural identity of a group whose cohesiveness has traditionally been based on cultural homogeneity and identification with a *singular* territory. Regardless, Montréal has no choice but to include a cosmopolitan character and transcultural outlook in its envisioning of its role in the twenty-first century. It will be a fascinating laboratory where conflicting positions as to the nature of 'integration' and 'transcultural hybridizing' will be worked out in practice, and to a large extent at the micro-scale of daily life, irrespective of formal political ideologies.

Despite the litany of divergent visions linked to the constitutional question, most of Montréal's economic and political actors, and its ordinary citizens, vaunt their city's 'liveability'. Up until now, it has managed to avoid most of the problems normally associated with large and mid-size metropolitan areas, such as high rates of crimes against the person, systematic social exclusion of marginalized groups, severe traffic congestion and air pollution, housing unaffordable for the middle and the working class, and so on. These assets – and the way they are marketed – are far from negligible in a globalized economy where businesses rank 'liveability' high on their list of location factors. Nevertheless, as the Montréal region enters a new century there are shadows on the horizon that could menace some aspects of Montréal's liveability and conviviality. Importantly, as the economy of much of the Island recovers from its long depression, while urban sprawl continues unabated, Montréal's traffic problems have worsened considerably – the bridges to the Island are operating beyond capacity, the Champlain Bridge linking downtown to the South Shore being the busiest in Canada – but these problems can only be regulated satisfactorily within a comprehensive regional transportation plan, which in turn requires a resolution of the long-standing impasse over metropolitan governance.

As we go to press (February 2000), Montréal's unemployment rate has finally dropped below the Canadian average and in fact to its lowest level since 1976. Nevertheless, another major challenge is posed by the persistence of high rates of poverty and the concentration of low-income residents in the core city. We have shown that the Montréal economy and labour force are increasingly polarized with a serious mismatch between the skills demanded by the 'new economy' and the low education levels of substantial fractions of the population who can no longer count on employment in the city's traditional industries, their employment levels gutted by deindustrialization or economic globalization. Neither the (mostly low-wage) service jobs generated by the 'festival tourism' that Montréal is increasingly embracing nor the localized efforts to create community-based employment in hard-hit neighbourhoods amount to more than a drop in the bucket. This too, is a problem requiring intervention at a regional, rather than a municipal scale, and greater recognition by the provincial government of the specificity of Montréal's dilemma.

The changing urban demography also raises uncertainties about the future form of the metropolis. The Montréal region has an ageing population structure, which creates challenges not only for social service agencies but for municipal officials, concerning the accessibility of public and commercial services, the need for adapted transportation, the growing mismatch between much of the suburban housing stock (largely comprising three-bedroom bungalows) and the size and composition of households, and so on. Many other metropolitan areas of eastern and central North America face similar challenges, but the rate of population ageing is faster than in other Canadian cities owing to Montréal's lower rates of international immigration. At the other end of the population pyramid, housing demand may be affected by the renewed tendency for young adults to remain in the family home until their mid- or late twenties, which is due to the prevalence of 'precarious employment' as well as the tendency of young people to pro-long their studies in order to improve their labour market opportunities (Rose, Mongeau and Chicoine, 1999). Another uncertainty is the extent to which young families' predilection for suburban living will continue unabated, especially if the costs of urban sprawl are eventually billed to its consumers.

Montréal is in a sense relatively well placed to deal with such unknowns since its residential morphology is diverse, even in many of its suburbs, and quite adaptable to accommodating a variety of 'lifestyles' at a fine spatial scale. Nevertheless, such socio-demographic changes also require imaginative urban and social planning, and in Québec, Montréal included, these qualities are quite thin on the ground, for the province and its elected municipal officials have never really embraced the 'urban professions', which consequently are lacking both in vision and moral authority. In one area of housing planning, however, the City of Montréal has achieved undeniable success, namely the programmes to repopulate the inner city, especially the downtown fringes, with particular socio-demographic segments of the middle class drawn to the distinctive 'quality of life' features that Montréal can offer. In this context it is not necessary to be an apologist for 'gentrification' to recall that the quirky history of municipal development in the central part of Montréal Island has long deprived the core city of thousands of middle and upper-middle class potential taxpayers (those living in the enclaves of Outremont, Westmount and Ville-Mont-Royal). Yet the very success of these programmes poses with renewed acuity the problem of the greatly inadequate resources available for social housing for the city's poor, a situation which will not change significantly in the absence of major policy changes at higher levels of government.

A great deal of central Montréal's appeal, both to residents and to tourists, lies in the imbrication of its cultural fabric and its built forms in an 'intimate' spatial mesh. In spite of the damage inflicted in some areas by the urban renewal frenzies of the 1960s and early 1970s, the legacy and the re-energizing of 'neighbourhood cultures' has helped to preserve and renew much of this fabric, even on downtown commercial arteries like St Catherine Street which has survived and prospered in spite of – or because of? – the development of the 'underground city'. Heated debates over the proliferation of 'big box' superstores show that these qualities of the city cannot be taken for granted. However, if the agglomeration continues to grow at only a slow or a moderate pace, 'reasonable accommodation' of such developments may be possible without fundamentally changing the character of city neighbourhoods. Although Montréal's quest to reinvent itself as a metropolis remains an elusive one, it has certainly held on to its place in the hearts of its inhabitants!

BIBLIOGRAPHY

Agence métropolitaine de transport (1999). *Évaluation de l'application de la loi sur l'Agence métropolitaine de transport: rapport du Conseil d'administration.* Montréal: Agence métropolitaine de transport.

Ames, H.B. (1972) [1897]. *The City Below the Hill: A Sociological Study of a Portion of the City of Montréal, Canada.* Toronto: University of Toronto Press.

Amirahmadi, H. and Saff, G. (1993). Science parks: a critical assessment. *Journal of Planning Literature,* **8** (2): 107–123.

Anctil, P. (1988). *Le rendez-vous manqué: les Juifs à Montréal face au Québec de l'entre-deux-guerres.* Montréal: Institut québécois de recherche sur la culture.

Anctil, P. (1992). Un *shtetl* dans la ville: la zone de résidence juive à Montréal avant 1945, pp. 419–436 in F. Remiggi and G. Sénécal (eds), *Montréal: Tableau d'un espace en transformation.* Montréal: Association canadienne-française pour l'avancement des sciences. (*Cahiers scientifiques* 76).

Anctil, P. (1996). La trajectoire interculturelle du Québec: la société distincte vue à travers le prisme de l'immigration, pp. 133–154 in A. Lapierre, P. Smart and P. Savard, *Language, Culture and Values in Canada at the Dawn of the 21st Century/Langues, cultures et valeurs au Canada à l'aube du XXIe siècle.* Ottawa: Carleton University Press.

Anderson, J.D. (1972). Non partisan urban politics in Canadian cities, pp. 5–21 in J.K. Masson and J.D. Anderson, *Emerging Party Politics in Urban Canada.* Toronto: McClelland and Stewart.

André, P., Deslisle, C. and Fortin, É. (1998). La gestion de la neige à Montréal, pp. 30–34 in C. Manzagol and C. Bryant (eds), *Montréal 2001: Visages et défis d'une métropole.* Montréal: Les Presses de l'Université de Montréal.

Archambault, J. and Godbout, J. (1988). Le rural en ville: Laval. *Recherches sociographiques,* **29** (2–3): 445 454.

Archambault, M., Arsenault, P. and Paradis, S. (1996). *Étude de positionnement touristique des quatre grands festivals d'été de Montréal: Jazz, Juste pour rire/Just for Laughs, Francopholies, Films du monde: Rapport final.* Montréal: Université du Québec à Montréal, École des sciences de la gestion, Chaire du Tourisme.

Aubin, H. (1995). Montreal's 'doughnut effect' remains a pressing problem. *Montreal Gazette,* 17 January, B3.

Auf der Maur, N. (1976). *The Billion-Dollar Games: Jean Drapeau and the 1976 Olympics.* Toronto: James Lorimer.

Bacher, J.C. (1993). *Keeping to the Marketplace: The Evolution of Canadian Housing Policy.* Montréal and Kingston: McGill-Queen's University Press.

Balakrishnan, T.R. and Kralt, J. (1987). Segregation of visible minorities in Montreal, Toronto and Vancouver, pp. 138–157 in L. Driedger (ed.), *Ethnic Canada: Identities and Inequalities.* Toronto: Copp Clark Pitman.

Banfield, E.C. and Wilson, J.Q. (1963). *City Politics,* Cambridge. MA: Harvard University Press.

Barber, M. (1986). Sunny Ontario for British Girls, pp. 55–73 in J. Burnet (ed.),

Looking into My Sister's Eyes: An Exploration in Women's History. Toronto: Multicultural History Society of Ontario.

Barlow, M. and Slack, B. (1985). International cities: Some geographical considerations and a case study of Montreal. *Geoforum*, **16** (3): 333–345.

Barratt Brown, M. (1974). *The Economics of Imperialism.* Harmondsworth: Penguin Books.

Bataïni, S.-H. and Coffey, W. (1998). The location of high knowledge content activities in the Canadian Urban System, 1971–1991. *Cahiers de géographie du Québec*, **42** (115): 7–34.

Bataïni, S.-H., Martineau, Y. and Trépanier, M. (1997). *Le secteur biopharmaceutique québécois et les investissements directs étrangers: dynamique et impacts des activités de R-D.* Québec, Qc: Gouvernement du Québec, Conseil de la science et de la technologie.

Beaudet, G. (1998). Laval, entre anarchie et utopie, pp. 272–276 in C. Manzagol and C.R. Bryant (eds), *Montréal 2001. Visages et défis d'une métropole.* Montréal: Presses de l'Université de Montréal.

Beaudet, G., Beauregard, L. and Wolfe, J.M. (1998). Anciennes et nouvelles banlieues, pp. 259–282 in C. Manzagol and C.R. Bryant (eds), *Montréal 2001. Visages et défis d'une métropole.* Montréal: Presses de l'Université de Montréal.

Beaudin, A. (1987). Le chômage des jeunes: une réalité mouvante. *Le marché du travail* (December), 78–82.

Beaudoin, C. and Collin, J.-P. (1997). Partage de la croissance de l'assiette fiscale municipale et dynamique d'agglomération, pp. 143–157 in Tellier, L.-N. (ed.), *Les défis et les options de relance de Montréal.* Montréal: Les Presses de l'Université du Québec.

Beaujot, R. and Rappak, J.P. (1990). The evolution of immigrant cohorts, pp. 111–140 in S.S. Halli, F. Trovato and L. Driedger (eds), *Ethnic Demography: Canadian Immigrant, Racial and Cultural Variations.* Ottawa: Carleton University Press.

Beauregard, L. (1998). Outremont, haut lieu de l'élite francophone, pp. 260–272 in C. Manzagol and C.R. Bryant (eds), *Montréal 2001. Visages et défis d'une métropole.* Montréal: Presses de l'Université de Montréal.

Beauregard, R. (1989). Between modernity and postmodernity: the ambiguous position of US planning. *Environment and Planning D: Society and Space*, **7** (3): 381–396.

Beauregard, R.A. (1994). *Voices of Decline: The Postwar Fate of US Cities.* Cambridge, MA and Oxford: Blackwell

Bélanger, Y. and Léveillée, J. (1996). Le développement de la région de Montréal, où est l'obstacle? *Policy Options Politiques*, **17** (7): 49–52.

Bellavance, M. (1993). Montréal au XIXe siècle: conformité et originalité par rapport au modèle occidental de croissance urbaine. *Recherches sociographiques*, **34** (3): 395–415.

Bennett, A. (1997). A short anecdotal and partial history of the fight for housing in Montreal, pp. 1–16 in A. Bennett (ed.), *Shelter, Housing and Homes: A Social Right.* Montreal: Black Rose.

Benoît, M. and Gratton, R. (1991). *Pignon sur rue: les quartiers de Montréal.* Montréal: Guérin.

Benson, A. and Dupuis, D. (1998). *Patterns of Canadian Immigrants' Employment Earnings.* Victoria, BC: Government of British Columbia, Ministry Responsible for Multiculturalism, Human Rights and Immigration, Immigration Policy Division.

Bernèche, F. (1990). *Problématique de l'habitation pour les ménages formant la nouvelle immigration à Montréal: éléments d'information et d'intervention.*

Rapport produit pour le Service de l'habitation et du développement urbain. Montréal: Ville de Montréal.

Bernèche, F., Shaw, M. and Luba S., for the Société d'habitation et de développement de Montréal (1997). *Interventions publiques en habitation: leur rôle dans l'amélioration de la sécurité et la prévention de la criminalité. L'exemple de quartiers montréalais.* Ottawa: Canada Mortgage and Housing Corporation.

Bernier, L. and Bédard, G. (1999). *Americanité et pratiques culturelles des Québecois.* Report submitted to the Ministère de la Culture et des Communications Montréal and Québec, Qc: Institut national de la recherche scientifique, INRS-Culture et Société and Groupe interdisciplinaire de recherche sur les Amériques.

Besner, J. (1991). Perspectives historiques. *Actualité immobilière* (Fall, Cahier spécial sur la ville souterraine): 4–11.

Blake, P. (1966). Downtown in 3-D. *The Architectural Forum*, **125** (2): 29–37.

Blanc, B. (1986). Problématique de la localisation des nouveaux immigrants à Montréal. *Canadian Ethnic Studies/Études ethniques au Canada*, **17** (1): 89–108.

Blanc, B. (1995). Côte-des-Neiges (Nord): quartier de transition et d'enracinement, une vocation multi-ethnique bien assumée et en croissance, pp. 141–168 in A. Germain and D. Rose (eds), *Montréal – A Quest for a Metropolis.* Chichester: Wiley.

Blanc, B. (1995). Urbanisme et communautés culturelles. Une expérience de planification interculturelle à Montréal, pp. 477–487 in F. Ouellet (ed.), *Les institutions face aux défis du pluralisme ethnoculturel.* Montréal: Institut québécois de recherche sur la culture.

Blanchard, R. (1947). *Montréal, esquisse de géographie urbaine.* Grenoble: Imprimerie Allier.

Blanchard, R. (1953). *L'Ouest du Canada français. Montréal et sa région.* Montréal: Beauchemin.

Blumenfeld, H. (1967). *The Modern Metropolis: Its Origins, Growth, Characteristics, and Planning,* in P.D. Spreiregen (ed.), *Selected Essays.* Cambridge: MIT Press.

Boissevain, J. (1970). *The Italians of Montréal: Social Adjustment in a Plural Society.* Ottawa: Information Canada, Studies of the Royal Commission of Bilingualism and Biculturalism, no. 7.

Boisvert, F. (1992). L'industrie manufacturière de haute technologie dans la région de Montréal: tendances spatiales et facteurs de localisation, pp. 127–140 in F. Remiggi and G. Sénécal (eds), *Montréal. Tableaux d'un espace en transformation.* Montréal: Association canadienne-française pour l'avancement de sciences (*Cahiers scientifiques* 76).

Bonin, B. (1976). L'immigration étrangère au Québec, pp. 269–276 in R. Tremblay (ed.), *L'économie québécoise.* Montréal: Les Presses de l'Université du Québec.

Bouchard, M.J. and Chagnon, L. (1998). Le développement des communautés locales à la croisée des partenariats. *Économie et solidarité*, **29** (2): 42–50.

Bowlby, G., Lévesque, J.-M. and Sunter, D. (1997). Youths and the Labour Market. *Labour Force Update* (Statistics Canada, cat. 71–005–XPB), **1** (1).

Boyd, M. (1997). Migration policy, female dependency, and family membership: Canada and Germany, pp. 142–169 in P.M. Evans and G.R. Wekerle (eds), *Women and the Canadian Welfare State: Challenges and Changes.* Toronto: University of Toronto Press.

Bradbury, B. (1993). *Working Families: Age, Gender, and Daily Survival in Industrializing Montréal.* Toronto: McClelland and Stewart.

Breton, R. (1964). Institutional completeness of ethnic communities and the personal relations of immigrants. *American Journal of Sociology*, **70** (1): 193–205.

Brouillette, B. (1943). Le port et les transports, pp. 115–182 in E. Minville (ed.), *Montréal économique*. Montréal: Éditions Fides and École des Hautes Études commerciales.

Brown, D. (1990). La ville intérieure: des débuts organiques à la croissance contrôlée. *Trames*, **3** (1): 54–60.

Brown, D. (1992). La ville intérieure. *Continuité*, **53** (Spring): 27–30.

Bruchési, J. (1943). Histoire économique, pp. 13–35 in E. Minville (ed.), *Montréal économique*. Montréal: Éditions Fides and École des Hautes Études commerciales.

Bussière, Y. (1989). L'automobile et l'expansion des banlieues: le cas de Montréal. *Revue d'histoire urbaine/Urban History Review*, **18** (2): 159–165.

Bussière, Y. and Dallaire, Y. (1994a). Tendances socio-démographiques et demande de transport dans quatre régions métropolitaines canadiennes. Éléments de prospective. *Plan Canada* (May): 9–16.

Bussière, Y. and Dallaire, Y. (1994b). Étalement urbain et motorisation: où se situe Montréal par rapport à d'autres agglomérations. *Cahiers de géographie du Québec*, **38** (105): 327–344.

Bussière, Y., Thouez, J.-P. and Laroche, P. (1993). Vieillissement et demande de transport des personnes à mobilité réduite. Un modèle de prospective appliqué au cas montréalais, 1986–2011. *Routes et Transports*, **23** (3): 34–44.

Bussière, Y., Bernard, A. and Thouez, J.-P. (1998). Les mouvements quotidiens, pp. 189–205 in C. Manzagol and C.R. Bryant (eds), *Montréal 2001. Visages et défis d'une métropole*. Montréal: Presses de l'Université de Montréal.

Caldeira, T. (1996). Fortified enclaves: the new urban segregation. *Public Culture*, **8**: 303–328.

Callow, A.B. (ed.) (1976). *The City Boss in America: An Interpretative Reader*. New York and Toronto: Oxford University Press.

Canada [Government of], Citizenship and Immigration Canada (1996). *Profiles: Total Immigrant Population: Highlights*. Immigration Research Series. cat. C&I-62–2/14–1996. Ottawa: Supply and Services Canada.

Canada [Government of] (1985). *Commission of Inquiry on the Pharmaceutical Industry*. Report. Ottawa: Supply and Services Canada.

Canada [Government of], Citizenship and Immigration Canada (1998). *Facts and Figures 1997. Immigration Overview*. cat. C&I-291–08–98E. Ottawa: Public Works and Government Services Canada.

Canada [Government of], Environment Canada (1987). *The Climate of Montréal*. Climatological Studies No. 39, The Climate of Canadian Cities, No. 4. Ottawa: Supply and Services Canada, cat. En57–7/39E.

Canada [Government of], Industry Canada (1998). Strategis Internet data base, http://strategis.ic.gc.ca, consulted 1998/07/14.

Canada Mortgage and Housing Corporation (1998). Changing working conditions and renter core housing need in 1996. *Research & Development Highlights, Socio-economic Series* (39). Ottawa.

Cannon, J. (1996). Restructuring in mature manufacturing industries: the case of Canadian clothing, pp. 215–219 in J. Britton (ed.), *Canada and the Global Economy: The Geography of Structural and Technological Change*. Montréal and Kingston: McGill-Queen's University Press.

Careless, M. (1954). Frontierism, metropolitanism and Canadian history. *Canadian Historical Review*, **35**, 1–21.

Careless, M. (1979). Metropolis and region: the interplay between city and region in Canadian history before 1914. *Revue d'histoire urbaine/Urban History Review*, **3**: 99–118.

Careless, M. (1989). *Frontier and Metropolis: Regions, Cities and Identities in Canada before 1914.* Toronto: University of Toronto Press.

Carr, S., Francis, M., Rivlin, L.G. and Stone, A.M. (1992). *Public Space.* Cambridge (UK) and New York: Press Syndicate of the University of Cambridge and Cambridge University Press.

Carter, T. and McAfee, A. (1990). The municipal role in housing the homeless and the poor, pp. 226–263 in G. Fallis and A. Murray (eds), *Housing the Homeless and the Poor: New Partnerships among the Private, Public and Third Sectors.* Toronto: University of Toronto Press.

Castells, M. (1989). *The Informational City.* New York and Oxford: Blackwell.

Caulfield, J. (1994). *City Form and Everyday Life: Toronto's Gentrification and Critical Social Practice.* Toronto: University of Toronto Press.

Chambers, G. (1992). *Task Force on English Education: Report to the Minister of Education of Québec.* [Québec, QC]: Task Force.

Charbonneau, J. (1995). Norgate: un quartier atypique de la proche banlieue, pp. 201–224 in A. Germain et al., op cit.

Charbonneau, A. and Sévigny, A. (1997). *1847, Grosse-Île: A Record of Daily Events.* Ottawa: Patrimoine Canada, Parcs Canada.

Charbonneau, F. and Parenteau, R. (1991). Opération 20 000 logements et l'espace social de Montréal. *Recherches sociographiques,* **32** (2): 237–254.

Charbonneau, F., Hamel, P. and Barcelo, M. (1994). Urban sprawl in the Montréal area, pp. 459–495 in F. Frisken (ed.), *The Changing Canadian Metropolis: A Public Policy Perspective,* 2. Berkeley and Toronto: University of California and Canadian Urban Institute.

Charney, M. (1980). The montrealness of Montréal: Formations and formalities in urban architecture. *Architectural Review,* **167** (999): 299–302.

Chevalier, J. (1993). Toronto-Ottawa-Montréal: concentrations majeures canadiennes de l'innovation par la recherche-développement. *Canadian Geographer/Le géographe canadien,* **37** (3), 242–257.

Chicoine, N. and Rose, D. (1989). Restructuration économique, division sexuelle du travail et répartition spatiale de l'emploi dans la Région métropolitaine de Montréal. *Espace, populations, sociétés,* **1989** (1): 53–64.

Chicoine, N. and Rose, D, with Guénette. N. (1998). Usages et représentations de la centralité: le cas de jeunes employés du secteur tertiaire à Montréal, pp. 315–333 in Y. Grafmeyer and F. Dansereau (eds), *Trajectoires familiales et espaces de vie en milieu urbain.* Lyon: Presses Universitaires de Lyon.

Choko, M.H. (1989). *Une cité-jardin à Montréal. La Cité-jardin du tricentenaire.* Montréal: Éditions du Méridien.

Choko, M.H. (1994). Le boom des immeubles d'appartements à Montréal de 1921 a 1951. *Revue d'histoire urbaine/Urban History Review,* **23** (1): 3–18.

Choko, M. and Dansereau, F. (1986). *Restauration résidentielle et copropriété au centre-ville de Montréal.* Montréal: INRS-Urbanisation, Études et documents no 53.

Choko, M.H. and Harris, R. (1989). *L'évolution du mode d'occupation des logements à Montréal et à Toronto depuis le milieu du XIXe siècle.* Montréal: INRS-Urbanisation.

Choko, M. and Harris, R. (1990). The local culture of property: a comparative history of housing tenure in Montreal and Toronto. *Annals of the Association of American Geographers,* **80** (1): 73–95.

Choko, M.H., Collin, J.-P. and Germain, A. (1987). Le logement et les enjeux de la transformation de l'espace urbain: Montréal 1940–1960. *Revue d'histoire urbaine/ Urban History Review,* **15** (2): 127–136 and **15** (3): 243–253.

Chorney, H. (1990). Urban economics: the challenge of full employment, pp. 90–98 in J.-H. Roy and B. Weston (eds), *Montréal: A Citizen's Guide to Politics*. Black Rose Books: Montréal.

Christopherson, S. (1994). The fortress city: privatized spaces, consumer citizenship, pp. 409–427 in A. Amin (ed.), *Post-Fordism. A Reader*. Oxford, UK and Cambridge, MA: Blackwell.

Christozov, D. (1995). Underground Urban Planning in Montréal: A Tool for a Sustainable Metropolitan Development. Paper presented at the sixth international conference 'Espaces et Urbanisme Souterrains', Paris (September).

Clark, G. (1982). *Montreal: The New Cité*. Toronto: McClelland & Stewart.

Clay, P.L. (1979). *Neighborhood Renewal*. Lexington, MA: Lexington Books.

Coffey, W. (1994). *The Evolution of Canada's Metropolitan Economies*. Montréal: Institute for Research on Public Policy.

Coffey, W. (1998). La géographie des services, pp. 135–148 in C. Mangazol and C.R. Bryant (eds), *Montréal 2001. Visages et défis d'une métropole*. Montréal: Presses de l'Université de Montréal.

Coffey, W. and Drolet, R. (1994). La décentralisation intramétropolitaine des activités économiques dans la région de Montréal, 1981–1991. *Cahiers de géographie du Québec*, **38** (105): 371–394.

Coffey, W. and Polèse, M. (1993). Le déclin de l'empire montréalais: regards sur l'économie d'une métropole en mutation. *Recherches sociographiques*, **34** (3): 417–437.

Coffey, W., Drolet, R. and Polèse, M. (1996). The intrametropolitan location of high-order services: patterns, factors and mobility in Montreal. *Papers in Regional Science*, **75**: 293–323.

Cohen, M. (1991). Exports, unemployment and regional inequality: economic policy and trade theory, pp. 83–102 in D. Drache and M.S. Gertler (eds), *The New Era of Global Competition: State Policy and Market Power*. Montréal and Kingston: McGill-Queen's University Press.

Colgan, F. (1985). 'The Regional Impact of Restructuring in the Canadian Manufacturing Sector, 1960–1982: The Case of the Quebec Textile and Clothing Industries'. MA thesis, Department of Geography, McGill University.

Collin, J.-P. (1984). La cité sur mesure: spécialisation sociale de l'espace et auto-nomie municipale dans la banlieue montréalaise, 1875–1920. *Revue d'histoire urbaine/Urban History Review*, **13** (1): 19–34.

Collin, J.-P. (1997). City management and the emerging welfare state: evolution of city budgets and civic responsibilities in Montréal, 1931–1951. *Journal of Policy History*, **9** (3): 338–357.

Collin, J.-P. (1998a). A housing model for lower and middle-class wage earners in a Montréal suburb. *Journal of Urban History*, **24** (4): 468–490.

Collin, J.-P. (1998b). La dynamique intramétropolitaine dans l'agglomération montréalaise, pp. 63–82 in H. Capel and P.-A. Linteau (eds), *Barcelona–Montréal. Développement urbain comparé*, Barcelona: Universidad de Barcelona.

Collin, J.-P. and Beaudoin, C. (1993). *Une proposition de partage régional de la croissance de l'assiette fiscale (tax base sharing) pour Montréal et sa région*. Montréal: Ville de Montréal, Groupe de travail sur la décentralisation gouvernementale et fiscale.

Collin, J.-P. and Germain, A. (1986). Les transformations du pouvoir local à Montréal: retour historique sur quelques expériences d'aménagement, pp. 19–28 in J.-L. Klein, C. Andrew, P.W. Boudreault and R. Morin (eds), *Aménagement et développement. Vers de nouvelles pratiques?* Montréal: Association canadienne-française pour l'avancement de sciences (*Cahiers scientifiques* 38).

Collin, J.-P. and Léveillée, J. (1985). Le pragmatisme des nouvelles classes moyennes. *Revue internationale d'action communautaire*, **13** (53): 95–102.

Collin, J.-P. and Mongeau, J. (1992). Quelques aspects démographiques de l'étalement urbain à Montréal de 1971 à 1991 et leurs implications pour la gestion de l'agglomération. *Cahiers québécois de démographie*, **21** (2): 5–29.

Collin, J.-P., Gaudreau, M. and Pineault, S. (1996). *La gestion métropolitaine au Canada et aux États-Unis. Typologie des modèles et quelques études de cas.* Montréal: INRS-Urbanisation. Groupe d'étude régionalisation, décentralisation et gestion locale (RÉDÉGEL), 68 pp. (Études et documents 68).

Collin, J.-P., Champagne, É., Hamel, P.J. and Poitras, C. (1998). *La Rive-Sud de Montréal. Dynamique intermunicipale et intégration métropolitaine.* Montréal: INRS-Urbanisation.

Comité pour la relance de l'économie et de l'emploi de l'Est de Montréal (CREEEM) (1987). *L'Est de Montréal: se prendre en main. Rapport final.* Montréal.

Comité pour la relance de l'économie et de l'emploi de l'Est de Montréal (CREEEM) (1986). *Est de Montréal: portait socioéconomique, 1986.* Montréal: Office de planification et de développement du Québec, Direction régionale de Montréal.

Comité pour la relance de l'économie et de l'emploi du Sud-Ouest de Montréal (CREESOM) (1989a). *Sud-Ouest: diagnostic.* Montréal (April).

Comité pour la relance de l'économie et de l'emploi du Sud-Ouest de Montréal (CREESOM) (1989b). *South-West Montréal: Building Our Future Together. Final Report.* Montréal (Nov.).

Communauté urbaine de Montréal (1995). *Montréal, Quality of Life.* Montréal: Economic Development Office.

Conseil des Affaires sociales du Québec (1989). *Deux Québec dans un. Rapport sur le développement social et démographique.* Montréal: Gaëtan Morin.

Conseil scolaire de l'île de Montréal (1991). *Mémoire sur l'Énoncé de politique en matière d'immigration et d'intégration.* Montréal.

Cooper, J.I. (1942). *Montréal, the Story of Three Hundred Years,* Montréal: Imprimerie de Lamirande.

Copp, T. (1974). *The Anatomy of Poverty: The Condition of the Working Class in Montréal 1897–1929.* Toronto: McClelland and Stewart. (The Canadian Social History Series).

Corral, I. (1986). 'Inner-City Gentrification: The Case of Shaughnessy Village, Montreal'. Supervised research project, Master's in Urban Planning, McGill University.

Cossette, A. (1982). *La tertiarisation de l'économie québécoise.* Chicoutimi: Gaëtan Morin.

Côté, M. (1996). Nos vieux démons nous hantent. Pourquoi Montréal demeure-t-elle enlisée au dernier rang des grandes villes nord-américaines? *La Presse*, Opinions, 21 Nov., B3.

Cournoyer, F. (1998). Accéder à la propriété dans la ville centre ou dans sa banlieue, pp. 221–233 in Y. Grafmeyer and F. Dansereau (eds), *Trajectoires familiales et espaces de vie en milieu urbain.* Lyon: Presses Universitaires de Lyon.

Culver, D. (1996). Montreal has exciting future. *Montreal Gazette*, Board of Business Contributors, 12 Sept., D2.

Dansereau, F. and Beaudry, M. (1986). Les mutations de l'espace habité montréalais: 1971–1981, pp. 283–308 in S. Langlois and F. Trudel (eds), *La morphologie sociale en mutation au Québec.* Montréal: Association canadienne-française pour l'avancement de sciences (*Cahiers scientifiques* 41).

Dansereau, F. and Foggin, P. (1976). *Quelques aspects du développement spatial de l'agglomération montréalaise.* Montréal: INRS-Urbanisation.

Dansereau, F. and Germain, A. (1995). Les vertus de l'espace public: faut-il y croire? *Interface* (Nov.-Dec.): 17–25.

Dansereau, F. and Lacroix, B. (1988). *Habiter au centre: tendances et perspectives socio-économiques de l'habitation dans l'arrondissement Centre.* Montréal: Ville de Montréal and INRS-Urbanisation, Dossier Montréal 3.

Dansereau, F. and Séguin, A.-M. (1995). *La cohabitation interethnique dans l'habitat social au Québec.* Montréal: Société d'habitation du Québec.

Dansereau, F., Beaudoin, C., Charbonneau, F., Choko, M. and Séguin, A.-M. (1991). *L'état du parc résidentiel locatif de Montréal.* Montréal: INRS-Urbanisation.

Dansereau, F., Germain, A. and Éveillard, C. (1997). Social mix: old utopias, contemporary experiences and challenges. *Canadian Journal of Urban Research*, **6** (1): 1–21.

de Laplante, J. (1990). *Les parcs de Montréal des origines à nos jours*, Montréal: Éditions du Méridien.

Dear, M. (1986). Postmodernism and planning. *Environment and Planning D: Society and Space*, **4** (3): 367–384.

Décarie, G. (1996). Montreal: the grain of mustard seed. *New City Magazine*, **17** (special issue): 42–45.

Delage, J. (1943). L'industrie manufacturière, pp. 183–281 in Esdras Minville (ed.), *Montréal économique.* Montréal: Éditions Fides and École des Hautes Études commerciales.

Demchinsky, B. (1999). Book review of Witold Rybczyski, *A Clearing in the Distance: Frederick Law Olmsted and North America in the Nineteenth Century* (New York: HarperCollins). *Montreal Gazette*, 4 July, I1.

Deschatelets, G. (1995). L'avenue du Mont-Royal ou comment sauver sa rue principale. *Continuité* **66**: 32–34.

Deschênes, G. (1988). *L'année des Anglais: la Côte-du-sud à l'heure de la conquête.* Sillery: Editions du Pélican/Septentrion.

Deslauriers, P. (1994). Very different Montreals: pathways through the city and ethnicity in novels by authors of different origins, pp. 109–123 in P. Preston and P. Simpson-Housley (eds) *Writing the City: Eden, Babylon and the New Jerusalem.* London and New York: Routledge.

Divay, G.and Gaudreau, M. (1984). *La formation des espaces résidentiels: le système de production de l'habitat urbain dans les années soixante-dix au Québec.* Montréal and Québec: INRS-Urbanisation and Les Presses de l'Université du Québec, (Questions urbaines et régionales 1).

Doling, J. (1997). *Comparative Housing Policy: Government and Housing in Advanced Industrialized Countries.* Basingstoke: MacMillan.

Ducas, S. (1987). 'La Communauté urbaine de Montréal, 1970–1986: structure métropolitaine et interventions en aménagement'. MA thesis, Faculté de l'aménagement, Université de Montréal.

Ducas, S. and Trépanier, M.-O. (1998). Une commission métropolitaine à Montréal: les difficultés d'un consensus régional. *Plan Canada*, **38** (3): 24–28.

Duff, J. (1999). *Densification résidentielle en quartier central.* Research report, External Grants Programme. Ottawa: Canada Mortgage and Housing Corporation.

Duff, J. and Cadotte, F. (1997). *Travail à domicile et ajustements résidentiels.* Report prepared for the Centre for Future Studies in Housing and Living Environment, CMHC, Ottawa.

Dufresne, Dumas, Mizoguchi associés (1999). *Vieux-Montréal, sondage clientèles et statistiques d'achalandage.* Report prepared for the ministère de la Culture et des Communications du Québec and the Ville de Montréal. http://www.vieux.montreal.qc.ca, accessed 18 June 1999.

Esser, J. and Hirsch, J. (1994). The crisis of Fordism and the dimensions of a 'post-Fordist' regional and urban structure, pp. 71–97 in A. Amin (ed.), *Post-Fordism: A Reader*. Oxford, UK and Cambridge, USA: Blackwell.

Evenden, L. and Walker, G.E. (1993). From periphery to centre: the changing geography of the suburbs, pp. 234–251 in L.S. Bourne and D. Ley (eds), *The Changing Social Geography of Canadian Cities*. Montréal and Kingston: McGill-Queen's University Press.

Fauteux, M. (1986). *Bilan socio-economique, Montréal*. Québec, QC: Office de la panification et du developpment du Québec.

Favreau, L. (1989). *Mouvement populaire et intervention communautaire de 1960 à nos jours. Continuités et ruptures*. Montréal: Centre de formation populaire and Éditions du fleuve.

Favreau, L. and Charbonneau, R. (1943). La finance, pp. 273–326 in E. Minville (ed.), *Montréal économique*. Montréal: Éditions Fides and École des Hautes Études commerciales.

Ferretti, L. (1990). 'La société paroissale en milieu urbain: Saint-Pierre-Apôtre de Montréal, 1848–1930', PhD thesis, Département d'histoire, Université du Québec à Montréal.

Filion, P. (1988). The neighbourhood improvement program in Montréal and Toronto: two approaches to publicly-sponsored upgrading, pp. 87–101 in T.E. Bunting and P. Filion (eds), *The Changing Canadian Inner City*. Waterloo, Ont.: University of Waterloo, Department of Geography Publication Series no. 31.

Financial Post (1998). *Financial Post FP 500: An investors' handbook*. Toronto.

Fournier, É. (1994). Allophone immigrants: language choices in the home. Statistics Canada, cat. 11–008E. *Canadian Social Trends* **35**: 23–25.

Frank, J. (1996). *After High School: The First Years. First report of the School Leavers Follow-up Survey, 1995*. Ottawa: Human Resources Development Canada, cat. MP78–4/12–1996.

Freed, J. (1995). We're rooted not so much in the soil as on the balcony. *Montreal Gazette*, 9 September, A2.

Frégault, G. (1969). *La civilisation de la Nouvelle-France: 1713–1744*. Montréal: Éditions Fides.

Friedberg, U. (1987). *La municipalisation de la culture*. Paris: Ministère de la Culture et de la Communication, Direction de l'administration générale et de l'environnement culturel, Département des études prospectives.

Friedmann, J. (1995). Where we stand: a decade of world city research, pp. 21–27 in P. Knox and P.J. Taylor (eds), *World Cities in a World-system*. Cambridge, UK: Cambridge University Press.

Frisken, F. (1994). Provincial transit policymaking for the Toronto, Montréal, and Vancouver regions, pp. 497–540 in F. Frisken (ed.), *The Changing Canadian Metropolis: A Public Policy Perspective*. Berkeley and Toronto: University of California and Canadian Urban Institute, Vol. 2.

Gagné, M. (1989). L'insertion de la population immigrée sur le marché du travail au Québec. Éléments d'analyse des données de recensement. *Revue internationale d'action communautaire*, **21** (61): 153–163.

Gagné, M. (1995). L'intégration des immigrants au Québec: choix et illustration de quelques indicateurs. Paper presented at the Huitièmes Entretiens du Centre Jacques Cartier conference, colloquium on 'Anciennes et nouvelles minorités', Lyon, 5–8 December.

Gagnon, L. (1999a). Montréal's enduring problem. *The Globe and Mail*, 5 June, D3.

Gagnon, L. (1999b). Why the suburbs resist merging with Montréal?. *The Globe and Mail*, 12 June, D3.

Gappert, G. (ed.) (1987). *The Future of Winter Cities*. Newbury Park, CA: Sage.

Garon, M. (1988). *Une expérience de testing de la discrimination raciale dans le logement à Montréal*. Montréal: Commission des droits de la personne.

Garreau, J. (1991). *Edge City: Life on the New Frontier*. New York: Doubleday and Co.

Gaudreau, M. with Mathews, G. (1992). *Politique municipale et enjeux d'habitation en ville centrale: le cas de Montréal*. Ottawa: Canada Mortgage and Housing Corporation.

Gauvin, M. (1978). The reform and the machine: Montréal civic politics from Raymond Préfontaine to Médéric Martin. *Revue d'études canadiennes/Journal of Canadian Studies*, **13** (2): 16–26.

Germain, A. (1983). L'émergence d'une scène politique: mouvement ouvrier et mouvements de réforme urbaine à Montréal au tournant du siècle – essai d'interprétation. *Revue d'histoire de l'Amérique française*, **37** (2): 185–199.

Germain, A. (1985). *Les mouvements de réforme urbaine à Montréal au tournant du siècle : modes de développement, modes d'urbanisation et transformations de la scène politique*, Montréal: Université de Montréal, Centre d'information et d'aide à la recherche (CIDAR), 415 pp. (*Cahiers du CIDAR* 6).

Germain, A. (1988). Patrimoine et avant-garde. Le cadre bâti: entre le passé et l'avenir. *Cahier de recherche sociologique*, **6** (2): 115–129.

Germain, A. (1990). L'industrie en ville: anachronisme ou avant-gardisme? Enjeux et controverses à Montréal. *Journal of Canadian Studies/Revue d'études canadiennes* **29**: 19–27.

Germain, A. (1995). La Petite-Bourgogne: un quartier tourmenté à la reconquête de son image, pp. 169–200 in A. Germain et al., op cit.

Germain, A. (1997). *Montréal et le retour des métropoles?* Montréal: Institut national de la recherche scientifique. Culture et ville. Groupe de recherche et de prospective sur les nouveaux territoires urbains.

Germain, A. (1998). Le quartier: un 'lieu commun'?, pp. 447–461 in Y. Grafmeyer and F. Dansereau (eds), *Trajectoires familiales et espaces de vie en milieu urbain*. Lyon: Presses Universitaires de Lyon.

Germain, A. (1999). Les quartiers multiethniques montréalais: une lecture urbaine. *Recherches sociographiques*, **40** (1): 9–32.

Germain, A. and Guay, J.-P. (1985). Post-modernisme, urbanisme et patrimoine urbain. *Continuité*, **29**: 24–27.

Germain, A., Archambault, J., Blanc, B., Charbonneau, J., Dansereau, F. and Rose, D. (1995). *Cohabitation interethnique et vie de quartier*. Final report to the ministère des Affaires internationales, de l'Immigration et des Communautés culturelles and to the Ville de Montréal. Gouvernement du Québec, Les Publications du Québec, MAIICCQ, Direction des communications, (collection *Études et recherches*, No 12).

Gilbert, A. and Marshall, J. (1995). Local changes in linguistic balance in the bilingual zone: francophones de l'Ontario et anglophones du Québec. *Canadian Geographer/Géographe canadien*, **39** (3): 194–218.

Glick-Schiller, N., Basch, L. and Szanton-Blanc, C. (1995). From immigrant to transmigrant: theorizing transnational migration. *Anthropological Quarterly*, **68** (1): 48–63.

Globe and Mail [Toronto] (1995). Montreal mounts comeback: Non-traditional job sectors provide backbone for recovery, by B. McKenna. 9 January, B1.

Globe and Mail [Toronto] (1997). CBRS to move base to Toronto, by K. Yakabuski. 8 March, B3.

Globe and Mail [Toronto] (1999). Smart Numbers: Immigration Part II: Many Montreal immigrants unemployed, by M. MacKinnon. 31 May, B1.

Godbout, J. (1995). Le NFB à Toronto. Silence, on détourne. En réalité, c'est la fin de l'ONF-NFB qui vient d'être annoncée, et peut-être même la fin du pays que l'on connait. Idées [collaboration spéciale]. *Le Devoir*, 21 Dec., A7.

Goldberg, M.A. and Mercer, J. (1986). *The Myth of the North American City: Continentalism Challenged*. Vancouver: University of British Columbia Press.

Gordon, D.M. (1978). Capitalist development and the history of Canadian cities, pp. 25–64 in W.K. Tabb and L. Sawers (eds), *Marxism and the Metropolis: New Perspectives in Urban Political Economy*. New York: Oxford University Press.

Grégoire, G. et al. (1999). *Atlas Région de Montréal. Premières explorations*. Montréal: INRS-Urbanisation, Service de cartographie.

Gunderson, M. and Muszynski, L. with Keck, J. (1990). *Women and Labour Market Poverty*. Ottawa: Canadian Advisory Council on the Status of Women.

Hall, P.A. (1984). *The World Cities*, 3rd edn. London: Weidenfeld and Nicholson.

Hall, P.A. (1986). National capitals, world cities and the new division of labour, pp. 135–145 in H.-J. Ewers, J.B. Goddard and H. Matzerath (eds), *The Future of the Metropolis, Berlin, London, New York, Economic Aspects*. New York: Walter de Gruyter.

Hall, P.A. (1988). *Cities of Tomorrow. An Intellectual History of Urban Planning and Design in the Twentieth Century*. Oxford and New York: Basil Blackwell.

Hamel, P. (1989). Le développement urbain dans le contexte montréalais des années quatre-vingts and le mouvement communautaire, pp. 385–395 in C. Gagnon, J.-L. Klein, M. Tremblay and P.-A. Tremblay (eds), *Le local en movements*. Chicoutimi: Université du Québec à Chicoutimi, Groupe de recherche et d'intervention régionales.

Hamel, P. (1995). Mouvements urbains et modernité: l'exemple montréalais. *Recherches sociographiques*, **36** (2): 279–305.

Hamel, P., Choko, M. and Dansereau, F. (1988). *La spéculation foncière*. Montréal: INRS-Urbanisation.

Hanna, D.B. (1980). Creation of an early Victorian suburb in Montréal. *Revue d'histoire urbaine/Urban History Review*, **9** (2): 42–50.

Hanna, D.B. (1992). L'architecture de l'échange, pp. 85–92 in R. Boivin and R. Comeau (eds), *Montréal. L'ousts du Nord*. Paris: Éditions Autrement.

Hanna, D.B. (1998). Les réseaux de transport et leur rôle dans l'étalement urbain de Montréal, pp. 117–132 in H. Capel and P.-A. Linteau (eds), *Barcelona-Montréal. Développement urbain comparé*. Barcelona: Universidad de Barcelona.

Harloe, M. (1994). Social housing – past, present and future. *Housing Studies*, **9** (3): 407–416.

Harris, R. (1996). *Unplanned Suburbs: Toronto's American Tragedy, 1900–1950*. Baltimore and London: Johns Hopkins University Press.

Harrison, B. (1996). *Youth in Official Language Minorities, 1971–1991*. Ottawa: Statistics Canada, Demography Division.

Harvey, D. (1990). *The Condition of Postmodernity: An Enquiry into the Origins of Cultural Change*. Cambridge, MA and Oxford, UK: Blackwell.

Hatton, W. and Halton, B. (1976). *A Feast of Gingerbread from our Victorian Past*. Montréal: Tundra Books of Montréal and Plattsburgh: Tundra Books of Northern New York.

Hawkins, F. (1988). *Canada and Immigration: Public Policy and Public Concern*, 2nd edn. Montréal and Kingston: McGill-Queen's University Press.

Hawkins, F. (1989). *Critical Years in Immigration: Canada and Australia Compared*. Montréal and Kingston: McGill-Queen's University Press.

Hays, S.P. (1974). The changing political structure of the city in industrial America. *Journal of Urban History,* **1** (1): 6–38.

Helly, D. (1987). *Les Chinois à Montréal, 1877–1951.* Québec, QC: Institut québécois de recherche sur la culture.

Helly, D. (1997). *Revue des études ethniques au Québec.* Document préparé pour Politique, planification et recherche stratégiques et le projet Metropolis, Citoyenneté et Immigration Canada.

Helman, C. (1987). *The Milton Park Affair. Canada's Largest Citizen-Developer Confrontation.* Montréal: Véhicule Press.

Henripin, J. (1968). *Tendances et facteurs de la fécondité au Canada. Monographie sur le recensement de 1961.* Ottawa: Federal Bureau of Statistics.

Henripin, J. and Perron, Y. (1973). La transition démographique de la province du Québec, pp. 21–44 in H. Charbonneau (ed.), *La population du Québec: Études rétrospectives.* Études d'histoire du Québec, 4. Montréal: Boréal Express.

Hiebert, D. (1994). Canadian immigration: policy, politics, geography. *Canadian Geographer/Géographe canadien,* **38** (3): 254–258.

Hopkins, J. (1996). Excavating Toronto's underground streets: in search of equitable rights, rules, and revenue, pp. 63–81 in J. Caulfield and L. Peake, *City Lives and City Forms: Critical Research and Canadian Urbanism.* Toronto: University of Toronto Press.

Hoskins, R. (1986). 'A Study of the Point St Charles Shops of the Grand Trunk Railway in Montreal, 1880–1917'. MA thesis, Department of Geography, McGill University.

Hour [Montréal] (1996). Royal renaissance: Mont-Royal Avenue is an urban renewal triumph and a lesson to Mayor Bourque: locals know best, by P. Bailey. 5–11 September, p. 8.

Howard, E. (1946 [1898]). *Tomorrow: A Peaceful Path to Real Reform,* (Reissued as *Garden Cities of Tomorrow,* 1902 reprint). London: Faber & Faber.

Hughes, E. (1943). *French Canada in Transition.* Chicago: University of Chicago Press.

Hulchanski, J.D. (1993). New forms of owning and renting, pp. 64–75 in J.R. Miron (ed.), *House, Home and Community: Progress in Housing Canadians, 1945–1986.* Montréal and Kingston: McGill-Queen's University Press and Ottawa: Canada Mortgage and Housing Corporation.

Hulchanski, J.D., Eberle, M., Lytton, M. and Olds, K. (1990). *The Municipal Role in the Supply and Maintenance of Low Cost Housing: A Review of Canadian Initiatives.* Report prepared for the Centre for Future Studies in Housing and Living Environment, CMHC. Vancouver: University of British Columbia, Centre for Human Settlements.

Jedwab, J. (1996). *English in Montreal: A Layman's Look at the Current Situation.* Montréal: Les Éditions Images.

Joly, J. (1996). *Sondage sur l'opinion publique québécoise à l'égard des relations sociales interculturelles.* Montréal: Gouvernement du Québec, ministère des Relations avec les Citoyens et de l'Immigration (collection *Études et recherches,* No.15).

Kahn, B.M. (1987). *Cosmopolitan Culture: The Gilt-Edged Dream of a Tolerant City.* New York: Atheneum.

Kain, J. (1992). The spatial mismatch hypothesis: three decades later. *Housing Policy Debate,* **5** (3): 271–360.

Kaplan, D.H. (1994a). Population and politics in a plural society: the changing geography of Canada's linguistic groups. *Annals of the Association of American Geographers,* **84** (1): 46–67.

Kaplan, D.H. (1994b). Two nations in search of a state: Canada's ambivalent spatial identities. *Annals of the Association of American Geographers*, **84** (4): 585–606.

Kerr, D.P. (1965). Some aspects of the geography of finance in Canada. *The Canadian Geographer/Le géographe canadien*, **9** (4): 175–192.

Kerr, D.P. (1968). Metropolitan dominance in Canada, pp. 531–555 in J. Warkentin (ed.), *Canada: A Geographical Interpretation*. Toronto: Methuen.

Klein, J.-L. and Waaub, J.-P. (1995). Reconversion économique, développement local et mobilisation sociale: le cas de Montréal. *Recherches sociographiques*, **37** (3): 497–515.

Klein, J.-L., Fontan, J.-M., Tremblay, D.-G. and Tardif, C. (1998). Les quartiers péricentraux: le milieu communautaire dans la reconversion économique, pp. 241–254 in C. Mangazol and C.R. Bryant (eds), *Montréal 2001. Visages et défis d'une métropole*. Montréal: Presses de l'Université de Montréal.

Knopp, L. (1992). Sexuality and the spatial dynamics of capitalism. *Environment and Planning D: Society and Space*, **10**, 651–69.

Kotval, Z., Moriarty, M. and Mullin, J. (1993). The greenfield versus brownfield debate. *Economic Development Commentary*, **17** (2): 18–23.

Krohn, R., Fleming, B. and Manzer, M. (1977). *The Other Economy: The International Logic of Local Rental Housing*. Montréal: Peter Martin Associates.

L'Actualité [Montréal] (1995). Comment sortir Montréal du trou. Cinq défis pour une métropole déchue. 15 May, 50–57.

La Presse (1991). L'Est de Montréal agonise: 10 000 chômeurs de plus qu'en 1986, by A. Noël. 18 September, A3.

La Presse [Montréal] (1998). Rosemont: une 'banlieue' urbaine tranquille de classe moyenne, by É. Trottier. 4 October, A9.

La Presse [Montréal] (1999). De Saint-Bruno à Montréal: le choc, by M. Ouimet. 13 June, A6.

Labelle, M., Turcotte, G., Kempeneers, M. and Meintel, D. (1987). *Histoires d'immigrées. Itinéraires d'ouvrières Colombiennes, Grecques, Haïtiennes et Portugaises de Montréal*. Montréal: Boréal.

Labelle, S., Nepveu, J.-P. and Turbide, B. (1998). Le développement économique communautaire à Montréal. *Économie et solidarité*, **29** (2): 51–58.

Lacoste, N. (1958). *Les caractéristiques sociales de la population du Grand Montréal. Étude de sociologie urbaine*. Montréal: Faculté des sciences sociales, économiques et politiques, Université de Montréal.

Lafortune, B. (1990). Les politiques culturelles à San Francisco, Barcelone, et Montréal: investissement, décentralisation et participation. *Trames*, **3**: 39–55.

Lagacé, L. (1993). Chiffrer l'intangible. *L'Hospitalité*, **17** (3): 20–21.

Lambert, P. and Stewart, A. (eds) (1992). *Montréal, ville fortifiée au XVIIIe siècle*. Montréal: Centre canadien d'architecture.

Lamonde, P. (1990). *Le financement du transport en commun métropolitain: de Montréal à Rabat*. Montréal: INRS-Urbanisation, 80 pp. (Études et documents 64).

Lamonde, P. (1994). *Les secteurs publics fédéral et provincial à Montréal. Évolution, structure et rôle économique*. (Research report prepared for the City of Montréal). Montréal: INRS-Urbanisation (*Rapports de recherche* No. 16).

Lamonde, P. and Martineau, Y. (1992). *Désindustrialisation et restructuration économique. Montréal et les autres grandes métropoles nord-américaines*. (Research report prepared for the City of Montréal). Montréal: INRS-Urbanisation (*Rapports de recherche* No. 14).

Lamonde, P. and Polèse, M. (1984). L'évolution de la structure économique de Montréal 1971–1981: désindustrialisation ou reconversion? *L'actualité économique. Revue d'analyse économique*, **60** (4): 471–494.

Lamonde, P. and Polèse, M. with Johnson, L. (1985). Le déplacement des activités économiques à l'intérieur de la région métropolitaine de Montréal: synthèse des résultats. Paper presented at the Annual Conference of the the Canadian Association for Regional Science, Montréal (29–30 May). Montréal: INRS-Urbanisation.

Lamotte, A. (1992). *Situation socio-économique des femmes immigrées au Québec*. Montréal: Gouvernement du Québec, Ministère des Communautés culturelles et de l'Immigration, Direction des études et de la recherche.

Langlois, A. (1985). Évolution de la répartition spatiale des groupes ethniques dans l'espace résidentiel montréalais, 1931–1971. *Cahiers de géographie du Québec*, **29** (76): 49–66.

Laperrière, H. (1995). 'Sur les traces de la culture, équipements de diffusion et projet urbain à Montréal depuis 1879'. PhD thesis, Faculté de l'Aménagement, Université de Montréal.

Laperrière, H. and Latouche, D. (1993). *Les loisirs et le développement communautaire à Montréal* (3 vols). Montréal: INRS-Urbanisation.

Laperrière, H. and Latouche, D. (1996). *So Far from Culture and So Close to Politics: The New Art Facilities in Montréal*. Montréal: INRS-Urbanisation, Collection Culture et Ville.

Lapointe Consulting Inc. with Murdie, R. (1996). *Immigrants and the Canadian Housing Market: Living Arrangements, Characteristics and Housing Preferences*. Ottawa: Canada Mortgage and Housing Corporation, Policy and Economic and Social Research Division.

Laserre, J.-C. (1972). Le Saint-Laurent à Montréal/The St Lawrence River at Montréal, pp. 55–60 in L. Beauregard (ed.), *Montréal. Guide d'excursions/Field Guide, 22nd International Geographical Congress*. Montréal: Presses de l'Université de Montréal.

Laserre, J.-C. (1980). *Le Saint-Laurent: Grande porte de l'Amérique*. Montréal: Hurtubise.

Latouche, D. (1991). La ville dans ses rapports à la culture et aux arts: le cas des équipements culturels à Montréal, pp. 201–231 in A. Germain (ed.), *L'aménagement urbain. Promesses et défis*. Montréal: Institut québécois de recherche sur la culture.

Latouche, D. (1994a). *Les activités culturelles et artistiques dans la région métropolitaine de Montréal*. Étude réalisée pour le Bureau fédéral de développement régional (Québec). Montréal: INRS-Urbanisation.

Latouche, D. (1994b). *Les organisations internationales dans la région métropolitaine de Montréal*. Étude réalisée pour le Bureau fédéral de développement régional (Québec). Montréal: INRS-Urbanisation.

Lavigne, G. (1987). *Les ethniques et la ville. L'aventure urbaine des immigrants portugais à Montréal*. Montréal: Le Préambule.

Lavigne, G. and Teixeira, C. (1990). Mobilité et ethnicité. *Revue européenne des migrations internationales*, **6** (2): 123–132.

Laville, M. (ed.) (1994). *L'économie solidaire: une perspective internationale*. Paris: Desclée de Brouwer.

Lavoie, Y. (1973). *L'émigration des Canadiens aux États-Unis avant 1930: mesure du phénomène*. Montréal: Presses de l'Université de Montréal.

Lazar, B. and Douglas, T. (1992). *The Guide to Ethnic Montreal*. Montréal: Véhicule.

Leacock, S. (1942). *Montréal: Seaport and City*. Garden City, NY: Doubleday, Doran.

Le Bourdais, C. and Beaudry, M. (1988). The Changing Residential Structure of Montreal, 1971–81. *Canadian Geographer/Le géographe canadien*, **32** (2): 98–113.

Ledent, J. (1993). *L'impact de l'immigration internationale sur l'évolution démographique du Québec*, Québec: Gouvernement du Québec, ministère des

Communautés culturelles et de l'Immigration (collection *Études et recherches*, No. 8).

Ledoyen, A. (1992). *Montréal au pluriel. Huit communautés ethno-culturelles de la région montréalaise*, Québec: Institut québécois de recherche sur la culture (collection *Documents de recherche*, No. 32).

Leduc, M. and Marchand, D. (1992). *Les maisons de Montréal*. Québec: ministère des Affaires Culturelles.

Lee, R. and Schmidt-Marwede, U. (1993). Interurban competition? Financial centres and the geography of financial production. *International Journal of Urban and Regional Research*, **17** (4), 492–515.

Légaré, J. (1965). La population juive de Montréal est-elle victime d'une ségrégation qu'ellese serait elle-même imposée? *Recherches sociographiques*, **6** (3): 311–326.

Legault, R. (1989). Architecture et forme urbaine. L'exemple du triplex à Montréal de 1870 à 1914. *Revue d'histoire urbaine/Urban History Review*, **18** (1): 1–9.

Lemelin, A. and Morin, R. (1991). L'approche locale et communautaire au développement économique des zones défavorisées: le cas de Montréal. *Cahiers de géographie du Québec*, **35** (95): 285–306.

Léonard, J.-F. and Léveillée, J. (1986). *Montréal after Drapeau*. Montréal: Black Rose.

Lessard, M. (1997). Quand la culture devient un atout dans les problématiques de reconversion. *Trames*, **12**: 44–48.

Léveillée, J. (1988). Pouvoir local et politiques publiques à Montréal: renouveau dans les modalités d'exercice du pouvoir urbain. *Cahiers de recherche sociologique*, **11** (2): 37–64.

Léveillée, J. and Whelan, R. (1990). Montreal: The struggle to become a 'world city', pp. 152–170 in D. Judd and M. Parkinson (eds), *Leadership and Urban Regeneration: Cities in North America and Europe*. Newbury Park, CA: Sage (Urban Affairs Annual Reviews, 37).

Levine, M.W. (1990). *The Reconquest of Montréal: Language, Policy and Social Change in a Bilingual City*. Philadelphia: Temple University Press.

Levitt, B. (1996). 'Montréal, métropole nord-américaine: Les dirigeants d'entreprise s'expriment'. Rapport du comité responsable de l'étude auprès de 36 dirigeants d'entreprise. Mimeo.

Lewis, R. (1985). 'The Segregated City: Residential Differentiation, Rent and Income in Montréal, 1861–1901'. MA thesis, Department of Geography, McGill University.

Ley, D. (1985). *Gentrification in Canadian Inner Cities: Patterns, Analysis, Impacts and Policy*. Report submitted to Canada Mortgage and Housing Corporation. Vancouver: University of British Columbia, Department of Geography.

Ley, D. (1988). Social upgrading in six Canadian inner cities. *Canadian Geographer*, **32** (1): 31–45.

Ley, D. (1992). Gentrification in recession: social change in six Canadian inner cities, 1981–1986. *Urban Geography*, **13** (3): 230–256.

Ley, D. (1994). Gentrification and the politics of the new middle class. *Environment and Planning D: Society and Space*, **12** (1): 53–74.

Ley, D. (1996). *The New Middle Class and the Remaking of the Central City*. Oxford Geographical and Environmental Studies. Oxford: Oxford University Press.

Ley, D. and Smith, H. (1997). *Is there an Immigrant 'Underclass' in Canadian Cities?* Vancouver: Vancouver Centre of Excellence, Research on Immigrant and Integration in the Metropolis, Simon Fraser University (Working Paper No. 97–08).

Li, P. (1988). *The Chinese in Canada*. Toronto: Oxford University Press.

Limonchick, A. (1982). The Montréal economy: The Drapeau years, pp. 179–206 in

D. Roussopoulos (ed.), *The City and Radical Social Change*. Montréal: Black Rose Books.

Lindstrom-Best, V. (1986). 'I won't be a slave!' – Finnish domestics in Canada, 1911–30, pp. 33–53 in J. Burnet (ed.), *Looking into My Sister's Eyes: An Exploration in Women's History*. Toronto: Multicultural History Society of Ontario.

Linteau, P.-A. (1982). Le montée du cosmopolitisme montréalais, pp. 23–53 in *Questions de culture 2. Migrations et communautés culturelles*. Québec, QC: Institut québécois de recherche sur la culture.

Linteau, P.-A. (1985). *The Promoters' City: Building the Industrial Town of Maisonneuve, 1883–1918*. Toronto: James Lorimer.

Linteau, P.-A. (1989). *L'économie de Montréal: essai d'interprétation historique*. Montréal: Ville de Montréal, Service de la planification et de la concertation.

Linteau, P.-A. (1992). *Histoire de Montréal depuis la Confédération*. Montréal: Boréal.

Linteau, P.-A., Durocher, R., Robert, J.-C. and Ricard, F. (1991). *Quebec Since 1930*. (Translated by R. Chodos and E. Garmaise). Toronto: James Lorimer.

Lipsig-Mummé, C. (1983). The renaissance of homeworking in developed countries. *Relations industrielles*, **38**: 543–567.

Lo, L. and Teixeira, C. (1998). If Quebec goes . . . The 'exodus' impact? *Professional Geographer*, **50** (4): 481–497.

Locher, U. (1988). *Les anglophones de Montréal: émigration et évolution des attitudes, 1978–1983*. Conseil de la langue française, Dossiers 29. Québec, QC: Les Publications du Québec.

Locher, U. (1994). *Youth and Language: Language Use and Attitudes among Young People Instructed in English (Secondary IV through CEGEP)*. (English version of a study for the Conseil de la langue française du Québec.) Ottawa: Government of Canada, Heritage Canada.

London, M. (1997). The Lachine Canal. Presentation to the School of Urban Planning, McGill University, 31 October.

Lustiger-Thaler, H. and Shragge, E. (1998). The new urban left: parties without actors. *International Journal of Urban and Regional Research*, **22** (2): 233–244.

MacBurnie, I. (1989). Downtown housing: filling in the gaps, pp. 191–196 in B. Demchinsky (ed.), *Grassroots, Greystones and Glass Towers: Montreal Urban Issues and Architecture*. Montréal: Véhicule Press.

MacKay, D. (1987). *The Square Mile: Merchant Princes of Montreal*. Vancouver and Toronto: Douglas & McIntyre.

MacLaran, A. (1993). *Dublin: The Shaping of a Capital*. World Cities Series. London and New York: Belhaven Press.

MacLennan, H. (1945). *Two Solitudes*. Toronto: Macmillan.

MacLennan, H. (1978). Two Solitudes: Thirty-three years later, pp. 288–299 in H. McLennan (Introductions by E. Cameron), *The Other Side of Hugh McLennan*. Toronto: Macmillan.

Macmillan, D.S. (ed.) (1972). *Canadian Business History: Selected Studies, 1949–1971*. Toronto: McClelland and Stewart.

Magnusson, W. and Sancton, A. (eds) (1983). *City Politics in Canada*. Toronto: University of Toronto Press.

Mamchur, S. (1934). 'The Economic and Social Adjustment of Slavic Immigrants in Canada: With Special Reference to the Ukrainians in Montreal'. MA thesis, Department of Sociology, McGill University.

Manzagol, C. (1972). L'industrie manufacturière à Montréal/Manufacturing industry in Montreal, pp. 125–135 in L. Beauregard (ed.), *Montréal. Guide d'excursions/*

Field Guide, 22nd International Geographical Congress. Montréal: Presses de l'Université de Montréal.

Manzagol, C. (1983). L'évolution récente de l'industrie manufacturière à Montréal. *Cahiers de géographie du Québec*, **27** (71): 237–253.

Manzagol, C. (1998). La restructuration de l'industrie, pp. 119–134 in C. Mangazol and C.R. Bryant (eds), *Montréal 2001. Visages et défis d'une métropole*. Montréal: Presses de l'Université de Montréal.

Manzagol, C. and Sénécal, G. (1998). 'Edge city' en pointillé, cité-jardin incertaine. *Relations*, **637**: 9–12.

Marois, C. (1989). Caractéristiques des changements du paysage urbain dans la ville de Montréal. *Annales de géographie*, **548**: 385–402.

Marsan, J.-C. (1981). *Montréal in Evolution: Historical Analysis of the Development of Montréal's Architecture and Urban Environment*, Kingston and Montréal: McGill-Queen's University Press.

Marsan, J.-C. (1990). *Sauver Montréal: chroniques d'architecture et d'urbanisme*. Montréal: Boréal.

Marsan, J.-C. (1991). L'aménagement du Vieux-Port de Montréal: les avatars de l'urbanisme promoteur, pp. 27–60 in A. Germain (ed.), *L'aménagement urbain: promesses et défis*. Québec: Institut québécois de recherche sur la culture.

Marsan, J.-C. (1994). *Montréal en évolution: historique du développement de l'architecture et de l'environnement urbain montréalais*, 3rd edn. Laval, QC: Éditions du Méridien.

Martineau, Y. and Rioux, P. (1994). *L'industrie manufacturière dans la région métropolitaine de Montréal*. Étude réalisée pour le Bureau fédéral de développement régional (Québec). Montréal: INRS-Urbanisation.

Massey, D. and Meegan, R. (1982). *The Anatomy of Job Loss*. London: Methuen.

Mathews, L. (1996). *Étude sur les producteurs des comportements racistes lors de l'insertion à l'emploi des jeunes travailleurs de 15 à 29 ans. Volet 2 – Six groupes ethniques minoritaires visibles*. Research report presented to the ministère des Affaires internationales, de l'Immigration et des Communautés culturelles. Montréal: L'Indice Recherche-Marketing.

Mayer, M. (1995). Urban governance in the post-fordist city, pp 231–249 in P. Healey, S. Cameron, S. Davoudi, S. Graham and A. Madanipour (eds), *Managing Cities: The New Urban Context*. Chichester, UK: Wiley.

Mayer-Renaud, M. and Renaud, J. (1989). *La distribution de la pauvreté et de la richesse dans la région de Montréal en 1989. Une mise à jour*. Montréal: Centre de services sociaux du Montréal métropolitan.

McAndrew, M. (1988). *Les relations école/communauté en milieu pluriethnique montréalais*. Montréal: Conseil scolaire de l'île de Montréal.

McAndrew, M. and Ledoux, M. (1995). La concentration ethnique dans les écoles de langue française de l'île de Montréal: un portrait statistique. *Cahiers québécois de démographie*, **24** (2): 343–368.

McAndrew, M. and Potvin, M. (1996). *Le racisme au Québec: éléments d'un diagnostic*. Montréal: Gouvernement du Québec, ministère des Affaires internationales, de l'Immigration et des Communautés culturelles (collection *Études et recherches*, No. 15).

McCalla, R.J. (1994). *Water Transportation in Canada*. Halifax, NS: Formac Publishing.

McCann, E.J. (1995). Neotraditional developments: the anatomy of a new urban form. *Urban Geography*, **16** (3): 210–233.

McCann, L. and Smith, P. (1991). Canada becomes urban: cities and urbanization in historical perspective, pp. 69–99 in T. Bunting and P. Filion (eds), *Canadian Cities in Transition*. Toronto, New York and Oxford: Oxford University Press.

McMurtry, T. (1993). The loan circle programme as a model of alternative community economics, pp. 60–75 in E. Shragge (ed.), *Community Economic Development: In Search of Empowerment and Alternatives*. Montréal: Black Rose.

McNicoll, C. (1993). *Montréal. Une société multiculturelle*. Paris: Bélin.

McRoberts, K. (1998). *Quebec: Social Change and Political Crisis*, 3rd edn. Toronto: McLelland & Stewart.

Médam, A. (1989). Ethnos et polis. A propos du cosmopolitisme montréalais. *Revue internationale d'action communautaire*, **21** (61): 137–149.

Melamed, A., Schaecter, J. and Emo, M. (1984). The effects of forced relocation in Montreal. *Habitat*, **27** (4): 29–36.

Mendell, M. and Evoy, L. (1993). Democratizing capital: alternative investment strategies, pp. 44–59 in E. Shragge (ed.), *Community Economic Development: In Search of Empowerment and Alternatives*. Montréal: Black Rose.

Mercer, J. (1992). Montréal en Amérique du Nord, pp. 49–68 in F.W. Remiggi with the participation of G. Sénécal (ed.), *Montréal: Tableaux d'un espace en transformation*. Montréal: Association canadienne-française pour l'avancement de sciences (*Cahier scientifique* 76).

Miller, Z.L. (1973). *The Urbanization of Modern America: A Brief History*. New York: Harcourt Brace Jovanovich, 241 pp. (The Harbrace History of the United States).

Milroy, B. (1998). 'Who says Toronto is a good city?' Paper presented at a conference, World Class Cities: Can Canada Play? International Council for Canadian Studies, Ottawa, 28 May.

Molotch, H. (1976). The City as a Growth Machine. *American Journal of Sociology*, **82** (2): 309–332.

Mongeau, J. (1994). *La population, le revenu et la pauvreté dans la région métropolitaine de Montréal*. Study prepared for the Federal Office of Regional Development (Québec). Montréal: INRS-Urbanisation.

Mongeau, J. and Séguin, A.-M. (1993). Les profils résidentiels des ménages immigrés et non immigrés dans la région montréalaise. *Actualité immobilière*, **17** (3): 4–10.

Monnier, D. (1993). *Les choix linguistiques des travailleurs immigrants et allophones*. Report of a survey conducted in 1991. Québec, QC: Conseil de la langue française (*Dossiers*, No. 37).

Monnier, D. (1996). Langue d'accueil et de service dans les commerces. *Bulletin du Conseil de la langue française*, **13** (2): 4.

Montreal Gazette (1992). Can soil cleanup bring the east end back to life? by D. Johnston. 1 November, A1.

Montreal Gazette (1995). First on the block, by M. Lamey. 6 February, F8.

Montreal Gazette (1995). Software so hot: Key personnel at Metrowerks follow clients to Austin, Texas, by J. Ravensbergen. 28 October, F1.

Montreal Gazette (1996). Deadline looms in Point St Charles rail talks, by E. Cherney. 27 January, D3.

Montreal Gazette (1996). Jobs follow people to suburbs: Montreal feeling the 'doughnut' effect, by C. Clark. 28 September, A1.

Montreal Gazette (1996). Montreal native plugs safe, livable communities, by M. Lamey. (House Talk.) 4 October, F3.

Montreal Gazette (1996). Montreal targets rich N.Y. tourists, by S. McGovern. 17 October, D7.

Montreal Gazette (1996). Tango dancing the Net away: Alis's multilingual Web Browser is putting the world onto the World Wide Web, by A. Riga. 28 October, C6–7.

Montreal Gazette (1996). Astra's vote of confidence in Montreal: Swedish firm spending $300 million, by S. McGovern. 7 November, E3.

Montreal Gazette (1997). Thriving Matrox Graphics hedges its bets on Montreal's future, by Jay Bryan. 25 March, D6.

Montreal Gazette (1997). Sunny tourism outlook: City benefits from improvements to attractions, popularity of festivals, by S. McGovern. 7 June, F1.

Montreal Gazette (1997). Gay businesses join forces to turn the area around, by P. Brooks. 16 June, H1.

Montreal Gazette (1997). Canal zone retro: Discreet Logic takes the lead in developing a high-tech industrial park in the Lachine Canal district just west of Old Montreal, by A. Riga. 19 July, C1.

Montreal Gazette (1997). Skilled workers, not subsidies, is the carrot, by J. Bryan. 13 September, E1.

Montreal Gazette (1997). Old Montreal investment: SoftImage chief Daniel Langlois buys heritage Harbour Building, by S. McGovern. 14 November, E1.

Montreal Gazette (1998). Vive la différence. The Gay Village is true to the rainbow symbol of gay pride – home to many, by C. Fidelman. 1 August, W11.

Montreal Gazette (1999). Technodome: Theme park has officials queuing up, by M. Mainville. 15 April, A1.

Montreal Gazette (1999). The new anglo: A new anglo emerges, by A. Norris. 29 May, A1.

Montreal Gazette (1999). The new anglo: English: it's where you live, by A. Norris. 29 May, B1.

Montreal Gazette (1999). The new anglo: Happy to be here/Behind the exodus, by A. Norris. 30 May, A1.

Montreal Gazette (1999). The new anglo: Language labels melt away, by A. Norris. 31 May, A1.

Montreal Gazette (1999). The new anglo: British roots aren't showing, by A. Norris. 1 June, A1.

Montreal Gazette (1999). The new anglo: Language wage gap narrows by A. Norris. 5 June, B1.

Montreal Gazette (1999). The new anglo: English thriving far from bastions, by A. Norris. 6 June, A1.

Montreal Mirror (1992). Condos 1800, people 0. How John Gardiner put down a revolt in Little Burgundy, by A. Roslin. 24 September–1 October, p.7

Morin, R. (1983). Désindustrialisation et mutations des quartiers anciens. *Actualité immobilière*, **8** (3): 8–13.

Morin, R. (1985). La revitalisation des quartiers anciens: enjeux locaux et stratégies municipales, pp. 27–42 in A. Germain and R. Hamel (eds), *Aménagement et pouvoir local*. Montréal: Association canadienne-française pour l'avancement des sciences. (*Cahiers scientifiques* 31).

Morin, R. (1987). *Réanimation urbaine et pouvoir local. Les stratégies des municipalités de Montréal, Sherbrooke et Grenoble en quartiers anciens.* Sillery, QC: Presses de l'Université du Québec and Montréal: INRS-Urbanisation.

Morin, R. (1997). Les corporations de développement économique communautaire et la relance des zones industrielles en déclin, pp. 39–56 in L.N. Tellier (ed.), *Les défis et les options de la relance de Montréal*. Ste-Foy, QC: Presses de l'Université du Québec.

Morin, R., Dansereau, F. and Nadeau, D. (1990). *L'habitation sociale: synthèse de la littérature.* Montréal: INRS-Urbanisation (*Rapports de recherche*, No 13).

Morin, R., Rose, D. and Mongeau, J. (1988). *La formation de ménages chez les jeunes*, Montréal: INRS-Urbanisation (*Études et documents*, 58).

Morisset, G. (1941). *Coup d'oeil sur les arts en Nouvelle-France*, Québec: Charrier et Dugal.

Murdie, R. (1986). Residential mortgage lending in Metropolitan Toronto: a case study of the resale market. *Canadian Geographer/Le géographe canadien*, **30** (2): 88–110.

Myers, G. (1975). *A History of Canadian Wealth*. Toronto: James Lorimer.

Nader, G.A. (1976). *Cities of Canada*, Vol. 2, *Profiles of Fifteen Metropolitan Centres*. Toronto: Macmillan of Canada and McLean-Hunter Press.

Nantel, A.-G. (1910). *La métropole de demain: avenir de Montréal*. Montréal, A. Ménard.

Nash, A. (1989). *International Refugee Pressures and the Canadian Public Policy Response*. Ottawa: Institute for Research on Public Policy. (Studies in Social Policy Discussion Paper 89.B.1).

Nash, A. (1994). Some recent developments in Canadian immigration policy. *Canadian Geographer/Géographe canadien*, **38** (3): 258–261.

Naylor, R.T. (1987). *Canada in the European Age: 1453–1919*. Vancouver: New Star Books.

Niosi, J., with Bergeron, M., Sawchuck, M. and Hade, N. (1995). *Flexible Innovation: Technological Advances in Canadian Industry*. Montréal and Kingston: McGill-Queen's University Press.

Office municipal d'habitation de Montréal (1997). *Low-Rent Housing in Montreal: An Overview. Descriptive Listing of Low-Rent Housing, December 31, 1997*. Montréal.

Office municipal d'habitation de Montréal (1998). *Beyond Concrete and Brick . . . 1997 Annual Report*. Montréal.

O'Keefe, D. (1996). Canada's East Coast container ports, do they compete with or complement one another in the race for the North American container traffic?, pp. 154–169 in *Logistics in a Changing Global Economy. Canadian Transportation Research Forum, Proceedings of the 33rd Annual Conference, Edmonton* (25–28 May). Saskatoon: CTRF/University of Saskatchewan.

Olmsted, F.L. (1987 [1870]). Public parks and the enlargement of towns, pp. 222–261 in N. Glazer and M. Lilla, *The Public Face of Architecture. Civic Culture and Public Spaces*. New York: The Free Press.

Olson, S. (1991). Ethnic strategies in the urban economy. *Canadian Ethnic Studies* **33** (2): 39–64.

Olson, S. and Kobayashi, A. (1993). The emerging ethnocultural mosaic, in L.S. Bourne and D. Ley (eds), *The Changing Social Geography of Canadian Cities*. Montréal and Kingston: McGill's University Press, pp. 138–152.

Pacione, M. (1990). Urban liveability: a review. *Urban Geography*, **11** (1): 1–30.

Paillé, M. (1996). La migration des Montréalais francophones vers la banlieue: les faits. *Bulletin du Conseil de la langue française*, **13** (2): 6–7.

Painchaud, C. and Poulin, R. (1988). *Les Italiens au Québec*. Montréal: Les Éditions Asticou et Les Éditions critiques.

Parazelli, M. (1997). 'Les pratiques de socialisation marginalisée des jeunes de la rue dans le contexte de revitalisation du centre-ville est de Montréal (1985–1995)'. PhD thesis, joint PhD programme in urban studies, Institut national de la recherche scientifique and Université du Québec à Montréal.

Parent, S. (1997–1998). Fonds québécois d'habitation communautaire: un levier pour les municipalités. *Municipalité* (Dec. 1997–Jan. 1998): 13–15.

Podmore, J. (1994). 'Loft Conversions in a Local Context: The Case of Inner City Montreal'. MA thesis, Department of Geography, McGill University.

Podmore, J. (1998). (Re)Reading the 'Loft Living' habitus in Montréal's inner city. *International Journal of Urban and Regional Research*, **22** (2): 283–302.

Polèse, M. (1988). *Les activités de bureau à Montréal: structure, évolution et perspectives d'avenir*. Dossier Montréal I. Montréal: Ville de Montréal and INRS-Urbanisation.

Polèse, M. (1990). La thèse du déclin économique de Montréal, revue et corrigée, *L'actualité économique. Revue d'analyse économique*, **66** (2), 133–146.

Polèse, M. (1996). Montréal: city in search of a country. Learning to live with uncertainty. *Policy Options Politiques*, **17** (7): 31–34.

Pomeroy, S. (1995). A Canadian perspective on housing policy. *Housing Policy Debate*, **6** (3): 619–653.

Pomeroy, S. (1998). *Residualization of Rental Tenure: Attitudes of Private Landlords toward Housing Low Income Households*. Ottawa: Canada Mortgage and Housing Corporation.

Port de Montréal (1997). Tout sur le port de Montréal. http://www.port-montreal. com/french/ features/index.htm, consulted on-line 23 January 1997.

Porter, J. (1965). *The Vertical Mosaic*. Toronto: University of Toronto Press.

Pressman, N. (ed.) (1985). *Reshaping Winter Cities: Concepts, Strategies and Trends*. Waterloo: Livable Winter City Association.

Preston, V., Murdie, R. and Northrup, D. (1993). Condominiums: an investment decision or lifestyle choice? A comparative study of resident and nonresident condominium owners in the City of Toronto. *Netherlands Journal of Housing and the Built Environment*, **8** (3): 281–300.

Puxley, E. (1971). *Poverty in Montreal*. Montréal: Dawson College Press.

Québec [Province], Commission nationale sur les finances et la fiscalité locales and Denis Bédard (Président) (1999). *Pact 2000, Report of the Commission nationale sur les finances et la fiscalité locales*, Québec: Les Publications du Québec.

Québec [Province], Ministère des Affaires Municipales. Groupe de travail sur Montréal et sa région (1993). *Montréal a City-Region: Efficient, Prosperous and Vibrant, International by Vocation, at the Service of its Citizens*. Montréal: Task Force on Greater Montréal.

Québec [Province], Commission des droits de la personne et des droits de la jeunesse (1999). Press release: Les programmes gouvernementaux laissent à désirer, 28 Jan. http://www.newswire.ca/government/quebec/french/releases/ January.

Québec [Province], Conseil de la langue française (1992). *Indicateurs de la situation linguistique au Québec, édition 1992*. Québec: Gouvernement du Québec.

Québec [Province], Conseil de la langue française (1993). *Les choix linguistiques des travailleurs immigrants et allophones*. Québec: Gouvernement du Québec.

Québec [Province], Conseil des relations interculturelles (1997). *La capacité du Québec d'accueillir de nouveaux immigrants en 1998, 1999 et 2000. Avis présenté au ministre des Relations avec les citoyens et de l'Immigration*. Montréal.

Québec [Province], Institut de la statistique du Québec (1999). Données thématiques régionales, tableau 12, Ensemble des industries manufacturières et PME (1995). La communauté urbaine de la région administrative de Montréal (06), http:// www.stat.gouv.qc.ca/donstat/ regions/thematiq/t1295r06.htm, consulted on-line 28 June 1999.

Québec [Province], Ministère de la Culture et des Communications (1996a). *Le français langue commune, enjeu de la société québécoise: bilan de la situation de la langue française au Québec en 1995*. Report of the Interdepartmental Committee on the status of the French language in Québec. Québec, QC.

Québec [Province], Ministère de l'Industrie, du Commerce, de la Science et de la

Technologie (1996b). *Profil économique de la région du Grand Montréal.* Québec, QC: Direction générale de l'analyse économique, Direction de l'analyse des PME et des régions.

Québec [Province], Ministère des Communautés culturelles et de l'immigration (1990). *Au Québec, pour bâtir ensemble.* Énoncé de politique en matière d'immigration et d'intégration. Montréal: MCCIQ, Direction des communications.

Québec [Province], Ministère des Relations avec les citoyens et de l'Immigration (1997). *Le Québec en mouvement. Statistiques sur l'immigration.* Édition 1997. Montréal.

Ramirez, B. (1981). Montreal's Italians and the socio-economy of settlement, 1900–1930: some historical hypotheses. *Urban History Review/Revue d'histoire urbaine,* **10** (1): 38–48.

Ramirez, B. (1991). *On the Move: French-Canadian and Italian Migrants in the North Atlantic Economy, 1860–1914.* Toronto: McClelland & Stewart.

Ramirez, B. and del Balso, M. (1980). *The Italians of Montréal: From Sojourning to Settlement, 1900–1921.* Montréal: Les Éditions du Courant

Ray, B. (1999). 'Negotiating identity and integration: experiences of Haitian immigrant women in René-Goupil'. Paper presented at the Annual Meeting of the Association of American Geographers Annual Meeting, Honolulu, March 25–29; mimeo, Department of Geography, McGill University, Montréal.

Ray, B. and Chmielewska, E. (1997) 'To Dwell Among Friends: The roles played by friends in settlement processes among Polish immigrant women in Montréal'. Paper presented at the 14th biennial conference of the Canadian Ethnic Studies Association. Montréal, 20–23 November.

Ray, B. and Moore, E. (1991). Access to home-ownership among immigrant groups in Canada. *Canadian Review of Sociology and Anthropology,* **28** (1): 1–29.

Ray, B. and Rose, D. (1999). Cities of the everyday: socio-spatial perspectives on gender, difference and diversity, pp. 502–524 in T. Bunting and P. Filion (eds), *Canadian Cities in Transition: The Twentieth Century,* 2nd edn. Toronto: Oxford University Press Canada.

Reid, B. (1991). Primer on the corporate city, pp. 63–78 in K. Gerecke (ed.), *The Canadian City.* Montreal: Black Rose.

Remiggi, F.W. (1998). Le Village gai de Montréal: entre le ghetto et l'espace identitairem, pp. 267–289 in I. Demczuk and F.W. Remiggi (eds), *Sortir de l'Ombre: Histoires des Communautés Lesbienne et Gaie de Montréal.* Montreal: VLB Éditeur.

Rémillard, F. and Merrett, B. (1990). *L'architecture de Montréal: guide des styles et des bâtiments.* Montréal: Éditions du Méridien.

Rémy, J. (1990). La ville cosmopolite et la coexistence interethnique, pp. 85–106 in A. Bastenier and F. Dasseto (eds), *Immigrations et nouveaux pluralismes. Une confrontation des sociétés.* Brussels: Université de Boeck, Éditions universitaires.

Rémy, J. (1998). Les sociabilités urbaines: effets de milieu et trajectoires sociales, pp. 501–521 in Y. Grafmeyer and F. Dansereau (eds), *Trajectoires familiales et espaces de vie en milieu urbain.* Lyon: Presses Universitaires de Lyon.

Renaud, J., Carpentier, A. and Lebeau, R. (1997). *Les grands voisinages ethniques dans la région de Montréal en 1991: une nouvelle approche en écologie factorielle,* Québec: Gouvernement du Québec, Ministère des Relations avec les citoyens et de l'Immigration, Direction de la planification stratégique.

Renaud, J., Desrosiers, S. and Carpentier, A. (1993). *Trois années d'établissement d'immigrants admis au Québec en 1989: Portraits d'un processus.* Montréal: Université de Montréal, Département de sociologie and Institut québécois de recherche sur la culture.

Rennie, D.L.C. (1953). 'The Ethnic Division of Labour in Montreal from 1931 to 1951'. MA thesis, Department of Sociology, McGill University.

Reynolds, L.G. (1935). *The British Immigrant: His Social and Economic Adjustment in Canada*. Toronto: Oxford University Press.

Robert, J.-C. (1982). Urbanisation et population. Le cas de Montréal en 1861. *Revue d'histoire d'Amérique française*, **35** (4): 523–535.

Robert, J.-C. (1994). *Atlas historique de Montréal*. Montréal: Art Global and Libre Expression.

Roberts, L. (1969). *Montreal: From Mission Colony to World City*. Toronto: Macmillan of Canada.

Roby, Y. (1976). *Les Québecois et les investissements américains: 1918–1929*. Sainte-Foy: Les Presses de l'Université Laval.

Rose, D. (1989). A feminist perspective of employment restructuring and gentrification: the case of Montréal, in J. Wolch and M. Dear (eds), *The Power of Geography: How Territory Shapes Social Life*. London and Boston: Allen & Unwin.

Rose, D. (1990). 'Collective consumption' revisited: analysing modes of provision and access to childcare services in Montréal. *Political Geography Quarterly*, **9** (4): 353–380.

Rose, D. (1993). Local childcare strategies in Montréal, Québec: the mediations of state policies, class and ethnicity in the life courses of families with young children, pp. 188–207 in C. Katz and J. Monk (eds), *Full Circles: Geographies of Women over the Life Course*. London and New York: Routledge.

Rose, D. (1995). Le Mile-End: un modèle cosmopolite? pp. 53–95 in A. Germain et al., op cit.

Rose, D. (1996). Economic restructuring and the diversification of gentrification in the 1980s: a view from a marginal metropolis, pp. 131–172 in J. Caulfield and L. Peake (eds), *City Lives and City Forms: Critical Research and Canadian Urbanism*. Toronto: University of Toronto Press.

Rose, D. (1997). *La revitalisation des zones industrielles à proximité des centres des affaires: un aperçu de quelques expériences*. Montréal: INRS-Urbanisation (collection *Culture et ville*, No. 97–95).

Rose, D. and Le Bourdais, C. (1986). The changing conditions of female single parenthood in Montréal's inner city and suburban neighborhoods. *Urban Resources*, **3** (2): 45–52.

Rose, D. and Villeneuve, P. (1993). Work, labour markets and households in transition, pp. 153–174 in L.S. Bourne and D. Ley (eds), *The Changing Social Geography of Canadian Cities*. Montréal and Kingston: McGill-Queen's University Press (Canadian Association of Geographers Series in Canadian Geography).

Rose, D. and Villeneuve, P. (1998). Engendering class in the metropolitan city: occupational pairings and income disparities among two-earner couples. *Urban Geography*, **19** (2), 123–159

Rose, D., Mongeau, J. and Chicoine, N. (1999). *Housing Canada's Youth/Le logement des jeunes au Canada*. Ottawa: Canada Mortgage and Housing Corporation, cat. no. PED310 (English), PF0310 (French).

Rose, D. and Ray, B. with Chicoine, N. and Charbonneau, J. (1997). 'Discovering the city? Mobility patterns in the use of services during immigrant women's settlement process in Montréal'. Paper presented at annual meeting of the Canadian Association of Geographers, St John's, Nfld., 19–23 August.

Rose, D. (1995). Market is being put back into Marché Maisonneuve. Strategy aims to draw people to neighborhood. (Special to The Gazette) *Montreal Gazette*, 18 March, H5.

Rossi, A. (1981). *L'architecture de la ville*. [Translated from Italian by F. Brun.] Paris: L'Équerre.

Roweis, S.T. (1981). Urban planning in early and late capitalist societies: outline of a theoretical perspective, pp. 159–177 in M. Dear and A.J. Scott (eds), *Urbanization and Urban Planning in Capitalist Society*. London and New York: Methuen.

Roweis, S.T. and Scott, A.J. (1978). The urban land question, pp. 38–75 in K.R. Cox (ed.), *Urbanization and Conflict in Market Societies*. Chicago: Maaroufa.

Roy, J. (1984). *Un modèle de planification globale pour le transport routier des marchandises*. Montréal: Université de Montréal, Centre de recherche sur les transports.

Ruddick, S. (1990). The Montreal Citizens' Movement: The Realpolitik of the 1990s?, pp. 287–316 in M. Dabis, S. Hiatt, M. Kennedy, S. Ruddick and M. Sprinker (eds), *Fire in the Hearth: The Radical Politics of Place in America* (The Year Left, Vol. 4). London and New York: Verso.

Ruddick, S. (1996). *Young and Homeless in Hollywood*. London and New York: Routledge.

Rudin, R. (1988). *Banking en français. The French Banks of Québec: 1835–1925*. Toronto: University of Toronto Press, 188 pp. (Social History of Canada 38).

Samson, M. (1994). *L'activité touristique dans la région métropolitaine de Montréal*. Étude réalisée pour le Bureau fédéral de développement régional (Québec). Montréal: INRS-Urbanisation.

Sancton, A. (1983). Montréal, pp. 58–93 in W. Magnusson and A. Sancton (eds), *City Politics in Canada*. Toronto: University of Toronto Press.

Sancton, A. (1985). *Governing the Island of Montréal: Language Differences and Metropolitan Politics*. Berkeley: University of California Press.

Sandercock, L. (1998). *Towards Cosmopolis: Planning for Multicultural Cities*. Chichester: Wiley.

Schecter, S. (1982). Urban politics in capitalist society, pp. 110–128 in D. Roussopoulous (ed.), *The City and Radical Social Change*. Montréal: Black Rose Books.

Schoenauer, N. (1998a). After the Angus Shops. Phase 2 of housing project going up on CPR site. (Special to The Gazette) *Montreal Gazette*, 19 September, I5.

Schoenauer, N. (1998b). For many owners, duplexes do it better. (Special to The Gazette) *Montreal Gazette*, 5 December, J6.

Séguin, A.-M. (1989). Madame Ford et l'espace: lecture féministe de la suburbanisation. *Recherches féministes*, **2** (1), 51–68.

Séguin, A.-M. (1998). Les espaces de pauvreté, pp. 221–236 in C. Manzagol and C. Bryant (eds), *Montréal 2001: Visages et défis d'une métropole*. Montréal: Presses de l'Université de Montréal.

Séguin, A.-M. and Termote, M. (1993). La dimension territoriale de l'immigration internationale au Québec. *Cahiers de géographie du Québec*, **37** (101): 241–262.

Semple, R.K. (1996). Quaternary places in Canada, pp. 352–371 in J. Britton (ed.), *Canada and The Global Economy: The Geography of Structural and Technological Change*. Montréal and Kingston: McGill-Queen's University Press.

Sénécal, G. (1992a). Les villages de la ville, pp. 93–104 in R. Boivin and R. Comeau (eds), *Montréal, L'Oasis du Nord*. Paris: Éditions Autrement.

Sénécal, G. (1992b). Systèmes d'espaces, systèmes d'acteurs: le cas de la Pointe Saint-Charles, pp. 153–170 in F. Remiggi and G. Sénécal (eds), *Montréal: Tableaux d'un espace en transformation*. Montréal: Association canadienne-française pour l'avancement de sciences (*Cahiers scientifiques* 76).

Sénécal, G. (1995). Le quartier Hochelaga-Maisonneuve à Montréal: le réaménagement d'une zone industrielle ancienne face à la nouvelle urbanité post-moderne. *Canadian Geographer/Le géographe canadien*, **39** (4): 353–362.

Sénécal, G. (1997). Les récits du déclin et de la relance de Montréal face aux défis de l'aménagement urbain. *Cahiers de géographie du Québec*, **41** (114): 381–391.

Sénécal, P., Tremblay, C. and Teufel, D. (1991). *Gentrification or Urban Sprawl? Central Montréal and Surrounding Area*. Montréal: Société d'habitation du Québec, Direction générale de la planification et de la recherche, Direction de l'analyse et de la recherche.

Serge, L. (1998). *Le secteur locatif privé et sa nouvelle clientèle*. Research report submitted to Canada Mortgage and Housing Corporation, External Research Grants Programme. Ottawa: Canada Mortgage and Housing Corporation.

Shearmur, R. (1997). La répartition des secteurs high-tech dans le système urbain canadien, 1971–1991. *Revue d'économie régionale et urbaine* **1997** (4): 619–646.

Shearmur, R. (1999). *Les secteurs manufacturiers traditionnels à Montréal. Secteurs du vêtement, du plastique-caoutchouc et du meuble*. Montréal: INRS-Urbanisation.

Sher, E. (1991). Cities: Picture postcards of Montreal. *The Globe & Mail*, 7 June, A16.

Sijpkes, P. (1998). Home is where the baths were in the Point (special to The Gazette). *Montreal Gazette*, 14 November, I5.

Simmons, A.B. (1990). 'New wave' immigrants: origins and characteristics, pp. 141–159 in F. Trovato and L. Driedger (eds), *Ethnic Demography: Canadian Immigrant, Racial and Cultural Variations*. Ottawa: Carleton University Press.

Simmons, A.B. and Keohane, K. (1992). Canadian immigration policy: state strategies and the quest for legitimacy. *Canadian Review of Sociology and Anthropology*, **29** (4): 421–452.

Sitte, C. (1979). *The Art of Building Cities: City Building According to its Artistic Fundamentals*, Westport, CT: Hyperion Press.

Slack, B. (1992). Montréal: un centre de services de transport, pp. 141–152 in F. Remiggi and G. Sénécal (eds), *Montréal: Tableaux d'un espace en transformation*. Montréal: Association canadienne-française pour l'avancement de sciences (*Cahiers scientifiques*, 76).

Slack, B. (1996). Personal e-mail communication to D. Rose about the Port of Montréal, 10 October.

Smith, N. (1996). *The New Urban Frontier: Gentrification and the Revanchist City*. New York and London. Routledge.

Société de Développement Angus (1997), documents posted at http://www.sda-angus.com/projet.html, consulted on-line, 10 July 1998.

Société québécoise de développement de la main d'oeuvre de Montréal (1995). *Le marché du travail et la problématique du chômage pour la région de Montréal*. Montréal: Société québécoise de développement de la main-d'oeuvre.

Sorkin, M. (ed.) (1992). *Variations on a Theme Park. The New American City and the End of Public Space*. New York: Hill and Wang.

Spragge, G.L. (1975). Canadian planners' goals: Deep roots and fuzzy thinking. *Canadian Public Administration*, **18** (2): 214–234.

Stanback, T.M., Jr. (1991). *The New Suburbanization. Challenge to the Central City*. Boulder, CO: Westview Press.

Statistics Canada (1993). Census of 1991, customized unpublished tabulations compiled for D. Rose, INRS-Urbanisation, Montréal.

Statistics Canada (1998a). *Census of 1996: The Nation, electronic product no. 93E 0029XDB96005*. Ottawa.

Statistics Canada (1998b). Census of 1996, Top 10 Places of Birth for Immigrants,

Internet table. http://www.statcan.ca/english/census96/nov4/table15.htm, consulted on-line 15 November 1999.

Statistics Canada (1998c). Households spending 30% or more of income on housing. *The Daily*, 9 June.

Steed, G. (1976a). Locational factors and dynamics of the Montreal garment complex. *Economic Geography*, **52** (3): 193–205.

Steed, G. (1976b). Standardization, scale, incubation and inertia: Montreal and Toronto clothing industries. *Canadian Geographer/Le géographe canadien* **20** (3): 298–309.

Steedman, M. (1986). Skill and gender in the Canadian clothing industry, 1890–1940, pp. 153–176 in C. Heron and R. Storey (eds), *On the Job: Confronting the Labour Process in Canada*. Montréal and Kingston: McGill-Queen's University Press.

Stelcner, M. and Shapiro, D. (1997). Language and earnings in Quebec: trends over twenty years, 1970–1990. *Canadian Public Policy*, **23** (2): 115–140.

Stelter, G. and Artibise, A.F.J. (1977). *The Canadian City: Essays in Urban History*. Toronto: McClelland and Stewart.

Stone, C.N. and Sanders, H.T. (eds) (1987). *The Politics of Urban Development*. Lawrence, KS: University of Kansas Press.

Sufian, A.J.M. (1993). A multivariate analysis of the determinants of urban quality of life in the world's largest metropolitan areas. *Urban Studies*, **30** (8): 1319–1329.

Sutcliffe, A. (1981). *Towards the Planned City: Germany, Britain, the United States, and France 1780–1914*. Oxford: Blackwell.

Sweeny, R. (1982). Esquisse de l'histoire économique du Québec anglophone, pp. 73–92 in G. Caldwell and E. Waddell (eds) *Les Anglophones du Québec: De majoritaires à minoritaires*. Québec, QC: Institut québécois de recherche sur la culture. (collection *Identité et changements culturels* No. 1).

Swift, J. (1995). *Wheel of Fortune: Work and Life in the Age of Falling Expectations*. Toronto: Between the Lines.

Taylor, C. (1994). *Reconciling the Solitudes: Essays on Canadian Federalism and Nationalism*. Montréal and Kingston: McGill-Queen's University Press.

Termote, M. (1992). Le comportment démographique des groupes linguistiques à Montréal. *Cahiers de démographie du Québec*, **21** (2): 77–92.

Trépanier, E. (1987). *Peintres juifs et modernité/Jewish Painters and Modernity, Montréal 1930–1945*. Montréal: Saidye Bronfman Centre.

Trépanier, M.-O. (1993). Metropolitan government in the Montréal area, pp. 53–105 in D.N. Rothblatt and A. Sancton (eds), *Metropolitan Governance: American/Canadian Intergovernmental Perspectives*. Berkeley, CA: University of California Press.

Trépanier, M.-O. (1998). Les défis de l'aménagement et de la gestion d'une grande région métropolitaine, pp. 319–340 in C. Manzagol and C.R. Bryant (eds), *Montréal 2001. Visages et défis d'une métropole*. Montréal: Presses de l'Université de Montréal.

Trépanier, M. and Bataïni, S.-H. (1993). *L'industrie microélectronique*. Sectorial study no. 2110–0126 prepared for the Comité du Bilan de l'activité scientifique et technologique de la région de Montréal. Québec: Gouvernement du Québec, Conseil de la Science et de la Technologie.

Trépanier, M., Godin, B., Mathurin, C. and Lafond, D. (1994). *La haute technologie, la recherche et le développement dans la région métropolitaine de Montréal*. Study prepared for the Federal Office of Regional Development (Québec). Montréal: INRS-Urbanisation.

Trottier, M. (1998). *The Montréal Economy, 2nd and 3rd quarters 1996*. **9** (2–3).

http://www.ville.montreal.qc.ca/devecon/economtl/96t3/es/es6q3.htm, consulted on line 10 December 1998.

Tufts, S. (1998). Community unionism in Canada and labor's (re)organization of space. *Antipode*, **30** (3): 227–250.

Vaillancourt, F. (1993). The economic status of the French language and francophones in Quebec, pp. 407–412 in A.-G. Gagnon (ed.), *Quebec: State and Society*, 2nd edn. Scarborough, ON: Nelson Canada.

van Nus, W. (1984). The role of suburban government in the city-building process: the case of Notre Dame de Grâce, Québec, 1876–1919. *Urban History Review/ Revue d'histoire urbaine*, **13** (2): 91–103.

Veltman, C. and Paré, S. (1993). *L'adaptation linguistique des immigrants de la décennie 80*. Montréal: Gouvernement du Québec, Ministère des Affaires internationales, de l'Immigration et des Communautés culturelles (collection *Études et recherches* No. 7).

Ville de Montréal (1989). *Habiter Montréal. A Policy Statement on Housing: City of Montréal*. Montréal.

Ville de Montréal (1992). L'étalement urbain à Montréal, pp. 75–83 in Ville de Montréal, *Cahier d'information économique et budgétaire 1993*. Montréal: Service de la planification et de la concertation, Module des communications.

Ville de Montréal (1995). L'économie de Montréal face à l'Aléna et à l'Uruguay Round, pp. 89–109 in *Cahier d'information économique et budgétaire*. Montréal.

Ville de Montréal (1996). *Programme d'accès à l'égalité en emploi pour les membres des communautés culturelles. Bilan 1995 et plan d'action 1996*. Montréal: Human Resources Department.

Ville de Montréal, Cabinet du comité exécutif (1997). *Social housing: Montréal earmarks $3-million for the new AccèsLogis program*. Press release, 21 Nov.

Ville de Montréal, Commission permanente de la culture et du développement communautaire (1993). *Consultation publique sur l'énoncé d'orientation concernant les Maisons de la culture*. Montréal.

Ville de Montréal, Service de l'habitation (1995). *L'habitation à Montréal: bilan et perspectives*. Document de réflexion. Dec. 1994 (revised Feb. 1995). Montréal.

Ville de Montréal, Service de l'habitation (1998). *Bilan de la phase I du programe de revitalisation des quartiers centraux*, http://www.ville.montreal.ca/habitation/ habitation.htm, consulted on-line 15 December 1998.

Ville de Montréal, Service de l'habitation et du développement urbain (1992a). *New Housing Choices in Montréal. Draft By-Law concerning Derogations from the Prohibition to Convert Rental Buildings to Divided Co-ownership in Montréal*. Montréal.

Ville de Montréal, Service de l'habitation et du développement urbain, Plan d'urbanisme (1992b). *Orientations and Strategies of the Montréal City Plan: Project*. Montréal.

Ville de Montréal. Service d'urbanisme (1967). *Montréal: horizon 2000*. Montréal: Service d'urbanisme.

Ville de Montréal. Service d'urbanisme (1968). *Urbanisation. Étude de l'expansion urbaine dans la région de Montréal/A Study of Urban Expansion in the Montréal Region*, 2nd edn, Ville de Montréal (*Bulletin technique* 5).

Weintraub, W. (1996). *City Unique: Montreal Days and Nights in the 1940s and 50s*. Toronto: McClelland & Stewart.

Wekerle, G. (1993) Responding to diversity: housing developed by and for women. *Canadian Journal of Urban Research*, **2** (2): 95–113.

Westley, M.W. (1990). *Remembrance of Grandeur: The Anglo-Protestant Elite of Montréal, 1900–1950*. Montréal: Libre Expression.

Wexler, M. (1996). A comparison of Canadian and American housing policies. *Urban Studies*, **33** (10): 1909–1921.

Whelan, R.K. (1991). The politics of urban redevelopment in Montreal: regime change from Drapeau to Doré. *Québec Studies*, **12**: 155–169.

Williams, D.W. (1997) *The Road to Now. A History of Blacks in Montréal*. Montréal: Véhicule Press.

Wilson, P., Poussart, A. and Lelièvre, F. (eds) (1999). *Montréal, by Bridge and Crossing*. Montréal: Éditions Nota bene.

Wolfe, J.M. (1989). Theory, hypothesis, explanation and action: The example of urban planning, pp. 63–77 in A. Kobayashi and S. Mackenzie (eds), *Remaking Human Geography*. Boston: Unwin Hyman.

Wolfe, J.M. (1994). Our common past: An interpretation of Canadian planning history, *Plan Canada* (July): 12–24.

Wolfe, J.M. (1998). Canadian housing policy in the nineties. *Housing Studies*, **13** (1): 121–133.

Wolfe, J.M., Skelton, I. and Drover, G. (1980). Inner-city real estate activitity in Montreal: institutional characteristics of decline. *Canadian Geographer/Le géographe canadien*, **24** (4): 349–367.

Wolfe, J. (1993). St Laurent housing project has some innovative ideas. With room for 25,000, Bois Franc is whole new city. (Urban Planning column) *Montreal Gazette*, 16 October, J2.

Zeekendorf, W. with McCreary, E.A. (1970). *Zeckendorf: The Autobiography of William Zeckendorf*. New York: Holt, Rinehart and Winston.

Zukin, S. (1992). *Landscapes of Power*. Berkeley, CA: University of California Press.

Zukin, S. (1995). *The Culture of Cities*. Cambridge, MA: Blackwell.

LIST OF FIGURES

Cover: McGill College Avenue, looking toward McGill University and the 'Mountain'. (Damaris Rose)

LIST OF TABLES

INDEX

Index compiled by Val Porter